IN NO TIME

Internet Basics

IN NO TIME

Internet Basics

Second Edition

Ingo Lackerbauer

AN IMPRINT OF PEARSON EDUCATION

PEARSON EDUCATION LIMITED

Head Office:
Edinburdh Gate
Harlow CM20 2JE
Tel: +44 (0) 1279 623623
Fax: +44 (0) 1279 431059

Head Office:
128 Long Acre
London WC2E 9AN
Tel: +44 (0) 20 7447 2000
Fax: +44 (0) 20 7240 5771

First published in Great Britain 2000.
© Pearson Education Limited 2000.

First published in 1999 as *Internet: leicht, klar, sofort*
by Markt & Technik Buch- und Software-Verlag GmbH
Martin-Kollar-Straße 10–12
D-81829 Munich
GERMANY

Library of Congress Cataloging in Publication Data
Available from the publisher.

British Library Cataloguing in Publication Data
A CIP catalogue record for this book can be obtained from the British Library.

ISBN 0-13-018322-9

All rights reserved. No part of this publication may be reproduced, stored
in a retrieval system, or transmitted, in any form or by any means, electronic,
mechanical, photocopying, recording or otherwise, without prior
permission, in writing, from the publisher.

10 9 8 7 6 5 4 3 2 1

Translated and typeset by Cybertechnics, Sheffield.
Printed and bound in Great Britain by Henry Ling Ltd at The Dorset Press, Dorchester, Dorset.

The publishers' policy is to use paper manufactured from sustainable forests.

Contents

Dear reader — 1

The keyboard — 2

Typewriter keys 3
Special keys, function keys,
status lights, numeric key pad 4
Navigation keys 5

The mouse — 6

'Click on' 6
'Double-click on' 7
'Drag' 7

1 Get your PC ready for the Internet — 8

Modems & Co. 10
Software is everything! 16
Installing the TCP/IP protocol 24
Accessing the Internet with
Windows 95 29
Accessing the Internet with
Windows 98 and IE5 37
Internet here we come! 45

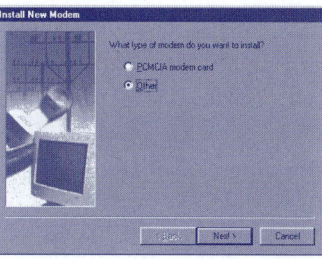

2 Let's go WWW — 48

Installing Internet Explorer 4.x 50
Microsoft Internet Explorer 4 in
detail 58
Updating to Internet Explorer 5 63
Your first steps in the
World Wide Web 67
Creating a bookmark list 72
The Internet Explorer's user
interface 77
The Active Desktop 79
Saving a file to the hard disk 83
Loading saved pages 86
Browsing Web pages 88
Printing Web pages 89

3 On the hunt for Information — 92

How does a search engine work? 94
Using Lycos search engine 98
Primeval Internet: Gopher 104

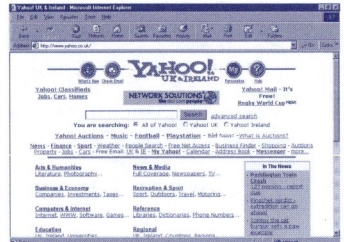

VI

CONTENTS

4 Internet access via an online service — 120

Accessing the Internet with AOL 122
Accessing the Internet with BT Click   141

5 The Netscape Communicator — 164

Installing Netscape
Communicator 4.7 166
Configuring the Netscape
Communicator 172
The Communicator's postman –
the Messenger 177
Newsgroups with the Netscape
Messenger 183

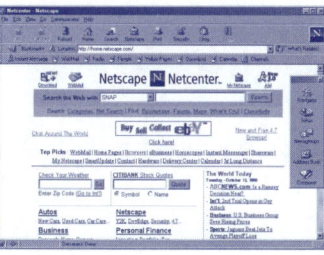

6 Music on the World Wide Web — 190

Rock, pop and classical music on
the Web 192
Internet Explorer and its 'Players' 194
Getting started with RealPlayer 201
RealPlayer in detail 203
CD quality music – MP3 206

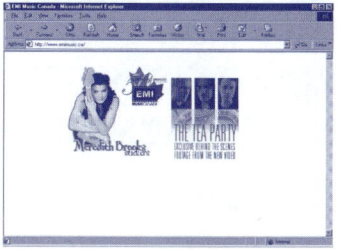

VII

7 A quick look at the day's news — 216

Video on the Internet – how does it work? 218
A look at the day's news 219

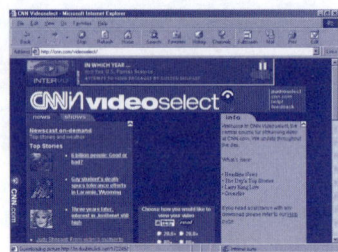

8 Your coffee party on the Web — 222

What is an IRC chat? 224
Installing the Microsoft Chat program 225
Hello, is anyone there? 231
Modifying the program 236

9 Telephoning over the Internet — 240

Using the Internet to telephone – how does it work? 242
Making a call over the Internet 243

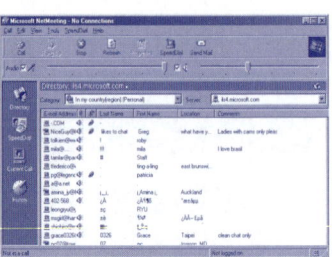

CONTENTS

10 Downloading files from the Internet   248

How does FTP work? 250
Let's find an FTP program 251
Decompressing a file 254
Installing the FTP program 255
Using FTP to download a file
to your computer 258
Adding a new FTP address 262

11 Discussions on the Internet: newsgroups   266

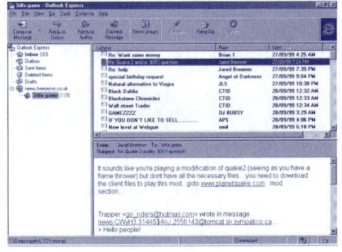

From A to Z – newsgroups have
something for everyone 268
Outlook Express and IE4 270
Configuring the newsgroup reader   276
Reading and subscribing to
newsgroups 280
IE5 and Outlook Express 5 284
Netiquette 293

IX

12 Why not send an e-mail instead   296

What is e-mail? 298
Configuring Microsoft's IE4
e-mail program 300
Sending e-mail 304
Using IE5 and Outlook Express 5
as an e-mail program 309

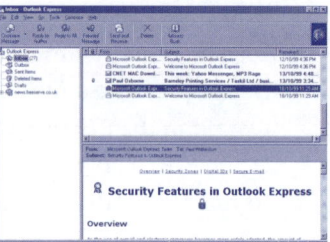

13 Your own home page on the WWW   316

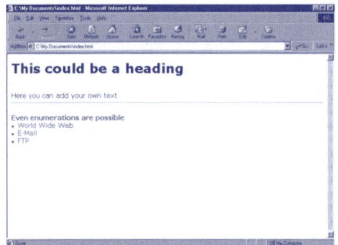

Only a few basic notions are
needed 318
Your own home page 319
Publishing a home page via an
online service 322

14 Finding Internet friends online with ICQ   324

Downloading an ICQ program
from the Internet 326
Using the ICQ program 341

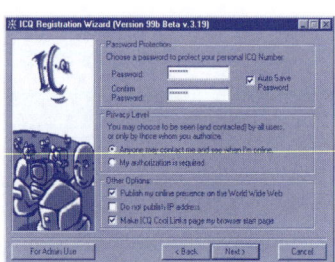

x

First aid for if you're having problems... 344

Glossary 346

Index 351

Dear reader

In the past months and years more and more people have discovered a new hobby – virtual travel through the Internet. Online surfers use their PCs to bridge thousands of kilometres in seconds, without setting foot outside their door. On their travels they discover new areas of knowledge and make new acquaintances. It somehow makes you feel like a true explorer when you are navigating the depths of the Internet, while time runs away and only hours later do you become aware of reality again.

This book is addressed to all those who wish to discover this new world and to learn how to handle modern communication techniques in an easy and entertaining way. It is intended to take the beginner by the hand and guide him or her, step by step, through the new features and possibilities offered by the Internet. This book will teach you the most important elements of dealing with the Internet and its most widely used services. The book's basic approach is to follow those frequently quoted words 'learning by doing' – only in this way is a playful and hands-on entry into the online world possible.

To conclude, I wish you much fun both in rummaging through this book and in online Internet surfing, and I hope that you gain new friends and knowledge on the way.

See you online!

Yours

Ingo Lackerbauer

The keyboard

The following three pages show you how your computer keyboard is structured. Groups of keys are dealt with one by one to make it easier to understand.
Most of the computer keys are operated exactly as keys on a typewriter. However, there are a few additional keys, which are designed for the peculiarities of computer work.
See for yourself.

The keyboard

Typewriter keys

Use these keys exactly as you do on a typewriter.
The Enter key is also used to send commands to your computer.

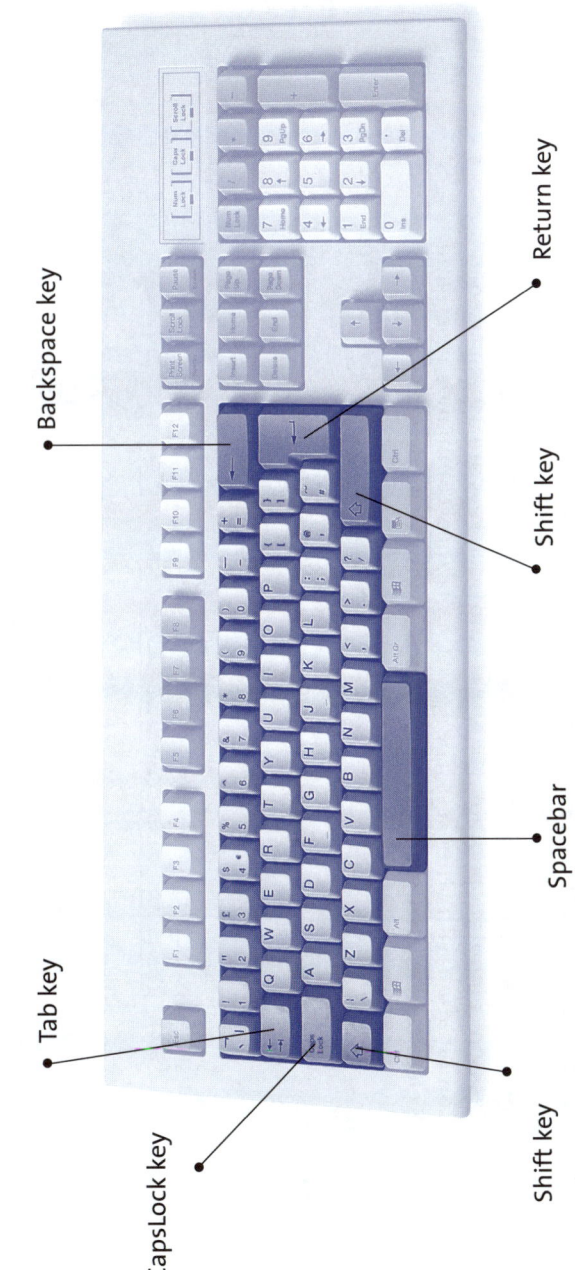

- Tab key
- CapsLock key
- Shift key
- Spacebar
- Backspace key
- Shift key
- Return key

3

Special keys, function keys, status lights, numeric key pad

Special keys and function keys are used for special tasks in computer operation. Ctrl -, Alt - and AltGr keys are usually used in combination with other keys. The Esc key can cancel commands, Insert and Delete can be used, amongst other things, to insert and delete text.

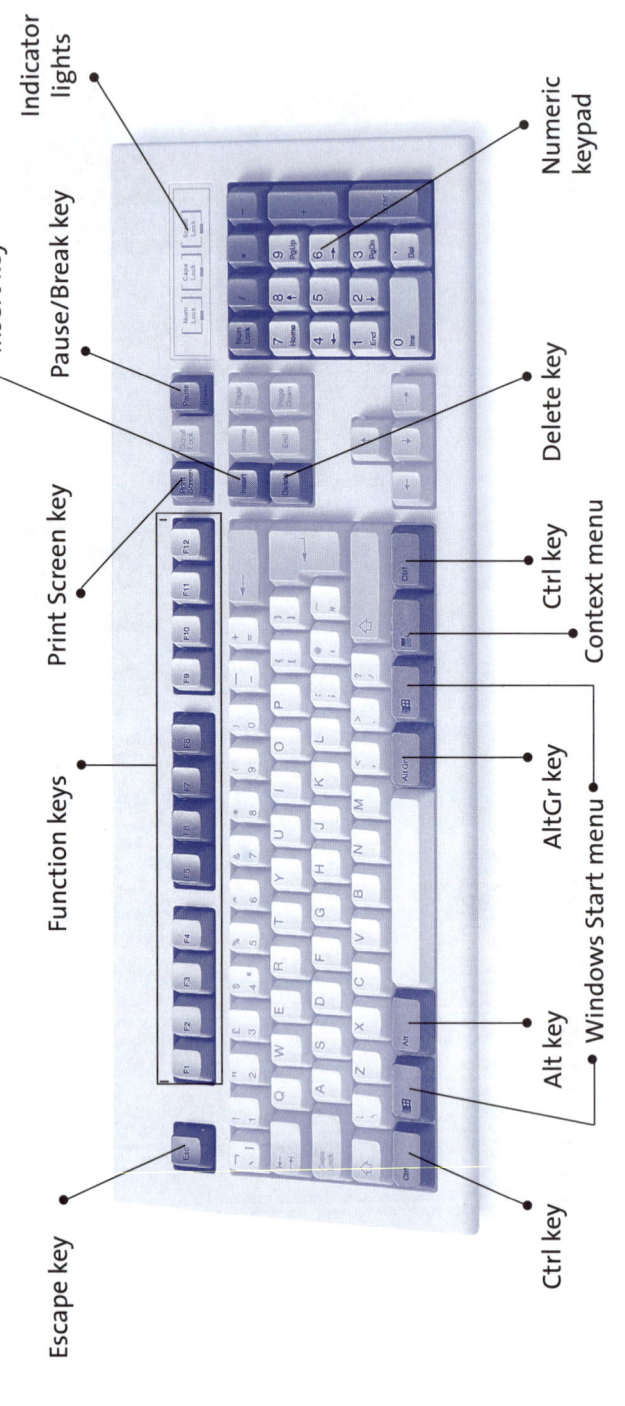

- Escape key
- Ctrl key
- Alt key
- Windows Start menu
- AltGr key
- Context menu
- Ctrl key
- Function keys
- Print Screen key
- Pause/Break key
- Insert key
- Indicator lights
- Numeric keypad
- Delete key

4

The keyboard

Navigation keys

These keys are used to move around the screen.

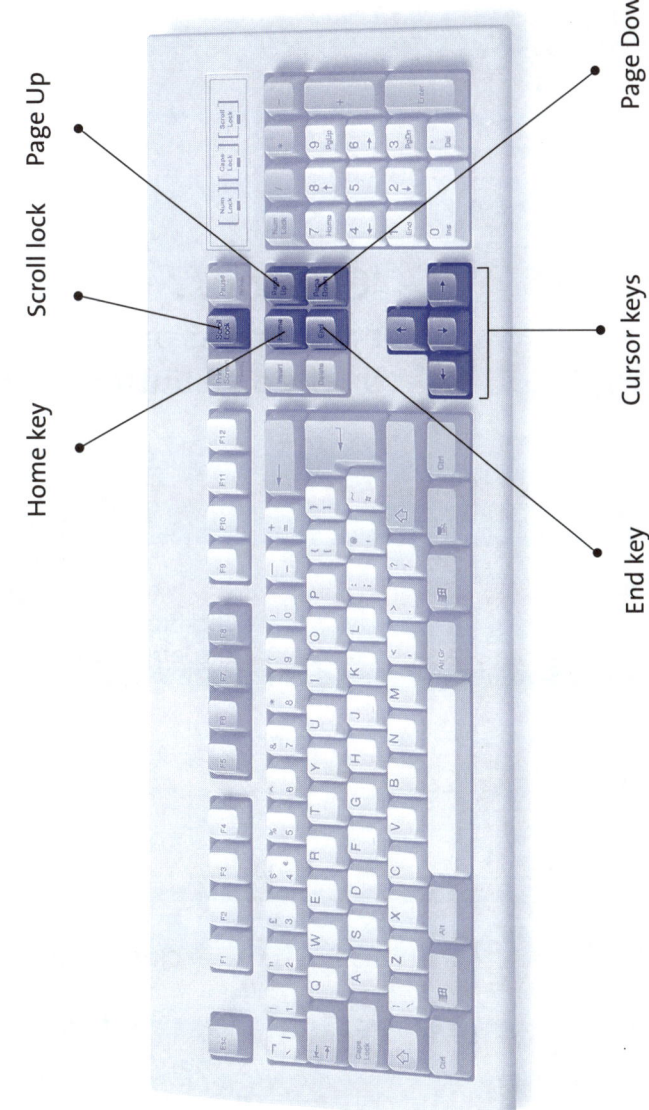

Page Up
Page Down
Scroll lock
Cursor keys
Home key
End key

The mouse

'Click on...'
means press once briefly on a button.

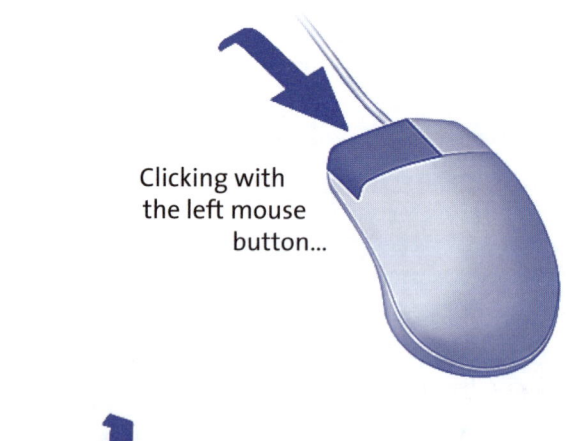

Clicking with the left mouse button...

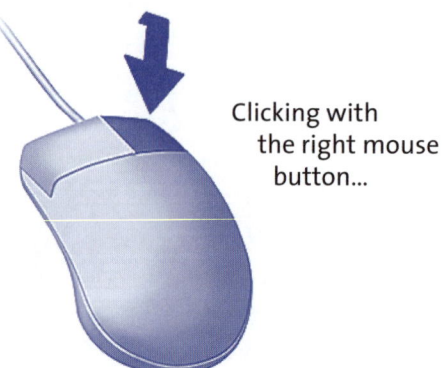

Clicking with the right mouse button...

'Double-click on...'

means press the left button twice briefly in quick succession.

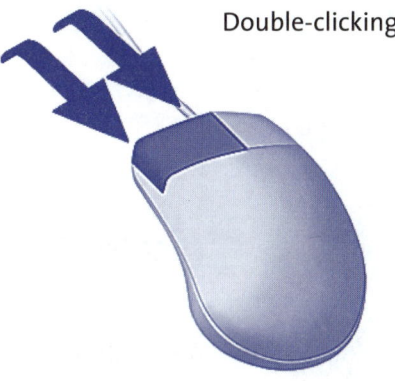
Double-clicking

'Drag...'

means click on an object with the left mouse button, keep the button pressed, move the mouse and thus drag the item to another position.

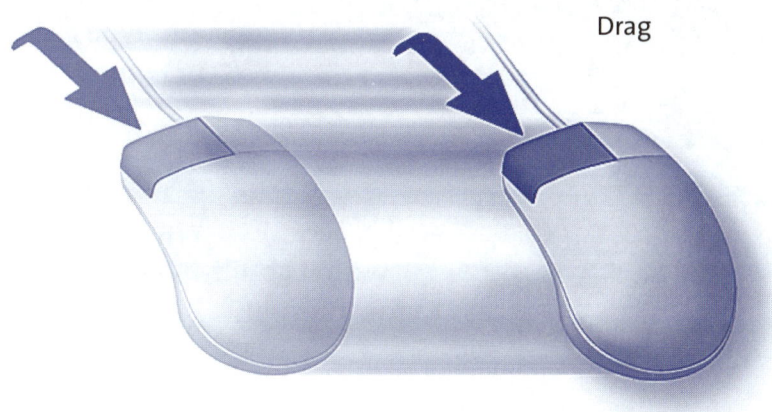
Drag

Get your PC ready for the Internet

What's in this chapter:

The following pages tell you the requirements your computer must meet to participate actively in what's happening on the Internet. You will get to know all about modems and software needed to make your stay on the Internet a pure pleasure. You will be introduced to different types of modem and take a look into Windows 98 with its built-in possibilities of access to the Internet.

Your progress meter

You are going to learn about:

Modems & Co.	10
The importance of software	16
Installing the TCP/IP protocol	24
Accessing the Internet with Windows 95	29
Accessing the Internet with Windows 98 and IE5	37
Establising a connection to the Internet	45

9

Modems & Co.

WHAT'S THIS? The **processor** is the very heart of your computer. It carries out the necessary mathematical operations in fractions of seconds and is the real workhorse of your computer.

To enable a computer to make contact with the Internet you need a couple of technical appliances and some basic knowledge. But don't panic; no 'hardware freaks' or 'software junkies' are needed at this point. Maybe you are thinking of high-cost special equipment, expensive computers with powerful processors and complicated installation procedures – simply forget all these prejudices.

If you had been reading this book, let's say, ten years ago, this one chapter would have been the same length as the whole book. The technical knowledge needed in those days practically required the user to have a degree in computer science. **Computers** used to fill whole rooms and were extremely difficult to operate. But times have changed – a true revolution has taken place. Today, you can buy a PC in any department store, at a more than acceptable price. If you feel that this is still too expensive, you can get used machines at bargain prices through countless sales and small ads. You don't need a computer worth hundreds and hundreds of pounds and loaded with all sorts of special features to travel around on the Internet. You don't need an 'Arab stallion' but a solid 'workhorse'. You just need to make sure that the appropriate operating system, in our case Windows 98, is stable and runs without errors. If this is the case, nothing much can go wrong. The following paragraphs show you which hardware and software requirements need to be met to give you painless access to the Internet.

WHAT'S THIS? The computer's **operating system** works by translating the entries that you input into a series of ones and zeros, so that the processor can understand your commands.

The computer is our number one hardware component. Forget specific brands and manufacturers. The main issue is the **operating system**. The present book refers to Windows 98 because this system is today nearly as widespread as the

computer itself. However, it is obviously possible to conquer the Internet with other operating systems, such as IBM's OS/2, Apple's Mac OS, the Amiga or some other exotic contraption.

POT or HomeHighway

The first thing you need in order to connect your computer to the Internet is a phone line. This can be the 'POT' – the plain old telephone – as is already present in millions of British households, or something more hi-tech, such as BT's latest 'invention' – the HomeHighway. POT is obviously the cheaper alternative, but while you are surfing the Web, none of your family or other household members can use the phone (or fax). On the other hand, while someone is phoning or faxing on your line, you cannot use your computer on the Internet.

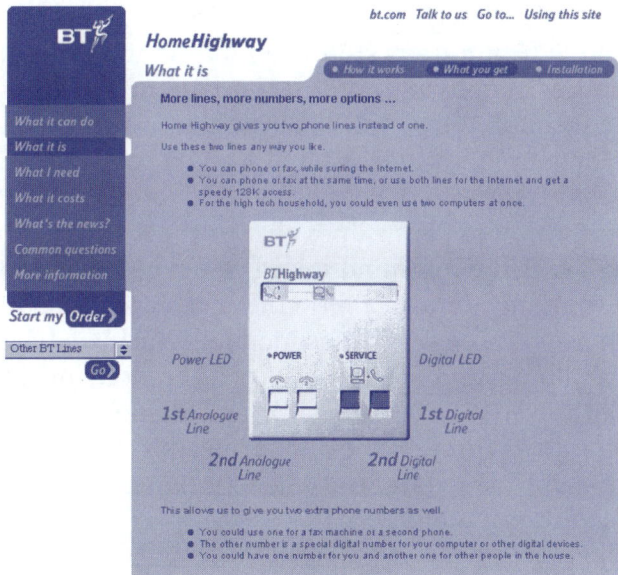

Two analogue and two digital lines on three phone numbers – no more conflicts in the family.

Thus, you need either two POTs (which will obviously be expensive) or something else that allows surfing, phoning and/or faxing at the same time. BT's offer is called HomeHighway (see an excerpt of their Web site above) and it costs only slightly more per day than your normal BT line.

The modem is your door to the world

Fasten your seatbelts – it's about to get technical! You will now be introduced to the first high-tech device you will need to access the Internet – the **modem.** The modem connects your PC to the telephone network. This enables you to transmit programs and texts via the phone line to other computer users, and also to receive such data. One might say that the modem functions as a kind of **interpreter** between the language of the PC and that of the telephone, making sure that those two worlds can communicate with each other.

What do you do when you talk to someone on the phone? Very simple – you transmit sounds that your partner at the other end of the line understands as your contribution to the conversation. What at this point sounds so easy and straightforward, however, is a big problem for our PC. Computers store their information in a digital form, as sequences of ones and zeros. Language, on the other hand, is transmitted through the phone line in analogue form, as electric **oscillations**. For your PC this means that its data sequences must first of all be converted into the corresponding sound signals, before they can be sent through phone lines all over the world. Furthermore, at the receiver's end, the incoming **sounds** must be converted back into the corresponding data, in a form the computer understands. This transformation is the task of the modem, which mediates between the analogue and the digital world. The word 'modem' is a contraction of the two words **'mo**dulator' and **'dem**odulator', because when sending signals through the phone line, the modem changes (modulates) the outgoing data, and when receiving signals, it decodes (demodulates) them.

> **TIP**
> A fast modem will pay off in the end! Thus, when you buy a new modem, you should really get yourself one that has a speed of 56 kbits/second. Today, this is quickly becoming the standard, and even though it may still cost a bit more, it will pay off after a short time because it significantly reduces downloading times from the Internet.

How fast should your modem be?

With the number of modems

Modems & Co.

> **What's this?**
> **Bit:** a bit is the smallest unit of information a computer can process. A bit can have one of two states, one or zero.

available on today's market, you certainly cannot complain about a lack of choice.

The top decision criterion when buying a modem is certainly the speed. It can generally be said that the faster a modem can send and receive data via the phone line, the more fun the user gets when surfing the Internet. The unit of measurement for the speed of a modem is a baud, hence the term 'baud rate'.

In magazines and computer shops you may also have encountered the term 'bps' which stands for 'bits per second'.

A computer needs eight bits to store a character (letter or digit). To find out how many characters a modem transmits in one second, you need to divide its transfer rate (baud rate) by eight. A small example to illustrate this: a 56,600 bps modem sends or receives 7,075 characters per second (56,600/8 = 7,075). Today, modems with a baud rate of 56,600 bps represent the standard and the most up-to-date state of technology. With regard to power, modems with this speed are already getting relatively close to ISDN cards and so make surfing a pleasure. Avoid modems with baud rates lower than 28.800 bps. 28.800 bps represent an absolute minimum and are really only suited for sending and receiving e-mail. Anything else, such as surfing the WWW, becomes quite a nerve-racking exercise and leaves you totally frustrated after a couple of hours. Since modem prices have continued to fall over the past years and months, you can actually buy a modem with a 56,600 bps transfer rate for a reasonable amount of money, without plunging into financial ruin – believe me, it's worth it.

But don't rejoice too early! The transfer rates calculated above are peak values which in practice are hardly ever reached. Quite often the fault lies with 'bad' phone connections with their well-known rustling and crackling. Another reason is that, besides pure data, sender and receiver exchange additional information as to whether all of the data sent has correctly reached the receiver.

What does Hayes compatible mean?

Once you have decided to buy a modem, you should definitely make sure that this modem is 'Hayes compatible'. The American company Hayes belongs to the pioneers of modem development. Hayes developed a set of commands with which a computer and a modem can 'talk' to each other. There are commands which, for example, control transmission speed, or tell the modem how to behave when a line is engaged. Since all of these commands begin with the letters 'AT', the Hayes command set is also called the **AT Standard**.

In the course of time, this command set was adopted as an international standard. When a modem corresponds to this standard, it is described as Hayes compatible. Most of the data transfer programs available on the huge software market rely on the fact that your modem is Hayes compatible. If this is not the case, massive problems will occur in the communication sector, and the corresponding software will be at a complete loss. Today, the majority of modems present on the market are Hayes compatible, so no problems should arise out of this particular issue. However, it certainly won't hurt you to ask your supplier whether your choice of modem is Hayes compatible before you actually buy it.

Does it need to be a fax modem?

Many of the modems on offer today not only have a part that can transmit data, but also a part capable of sending and receiving **faxes**. Such modems include the complete electronics of a fax machine. While even cheap fax machines still cost around 200 pounds, you pay significantly less for a bargain offer 14,400 or 28,800 bps fax modem. A fax modem converts your PC into a fax machine which does not have to fear comparison with traditional fax machines – on the contrary! Thanks to smartly designed fax programs you can send faxes in an easier and more user-friendly way than with a traditional fax machine.

> For the sake of simplicity, integrated data/fax modems are generally just called fax modems. As a rule, pure fax modems are not available at all.

Thus, if you have the chance to buy such a modem, by all means do it! Even though you may not yet need to use such a combined device, the time will come when you will learn to appreciate the advantages of a fax modem.

The voice modem

A new type of modem – the voice modem – has been conquering the market for some time now. These modems are capable of transferring voice information at the same time as a data or fax transmission is taking place in the background. This allows you, for example, to call another user on the telephone, have a chat and, if and when necessary, send him or her a fax or transfer a file, without having to interrupt the conversation.

Speeding things up with ISDN

You will get completely carried away by the speed you can achieve when you have a digital phone connection via the ISDN network of British Telecom or one of the other suppliers. **ISDN** allows you much higher transfer rates than analogue modems. With an ISDN line you can access the Internet at a speed of 64,000 bps (or 128,000 bps with 'channel bundling', see below) – for comparison, the fastest analogue modems only reach a 'mere' 56,000 bps.

But speed has its price: with ISDN, you usually get three phone numbers on two lines, at about the cost of two standard phone lines. Therefore, ISDN only pays off if you (or members of your family) need to phone or fax while you (or members of your family) are surfing the Web, or if you frequently need to download huge amounts of data, using both of the ISDN channels.

Once you have decided on an ISDN connection and have had it installed somewhere near your computer, the time has come to choose an ISDN card for your PC. Here you have the choice between **active** and **passive** cards. Active ISDN cards have their own processor which takes on most of the tasks needed during a data transfer, relieving the computer's CPU from all those chores. The disadvantage is that such cards are much more expensive than their passive 'siblings'.

A much cheaper solution is represented by the passive cards which, because they don't have a processor of their own, just sit there twiddling their thumbs and let the main CPU do all the data transfer work. For very large amounts of data, such as video-conferencing, it is a very good idea to use an active ISDN card.

Installation of an ISDN card is carried out in the same way as a modem card (we will see later how this is done). Usually, ISDN cards are shipped together with an installation program which takes over most of the installation work. When ISDN was first introduced, only Germany had a national digital network which, quite obviously, worked with its own national standard. When more European countries joined the ISDN network, a common standard was established, called **E-DSS1** or **Euro-ISDN**. If you ever plan to connect directly via ISDN to a partner in any of the European countries, make sure that your ISDN card supports the Euro-ISDN standard.

Software is everything!

The basis of our excursions into the Internet is Windows 98. This operating system from Microsoft allows you for the first time to fully exploit the communication capabilities of your PC. Windows 98 is an **operating system** with a **graphical user interface** (also known as a GUI) which can be controlled with the aid of a mouse. Windows 98 is probably the most widespread graphical operating system in the world and has successfully replaced its predecessors, Windows 3.x and Windows 95. The continuous success of **Windows 98** lies in the fact that you can just switch on your computer and start working without needing any previous knowledge of computing.

However, it's not a problem if you are still using Windows 95. The steps described in this book are by and large the same as the ones needed in Windows 95.

Windows 98 and your modem

After making sure that the serial interfaces of your computer work properly, you can then start integrating your modem into the operating system. This step is necessary because you need to tell Windows 98 which modem is connected to your computer. A program called 'Modem Wizard' will help you install a modem in Windows 98 and relieve you of a large part of the installation work.

To install a modem you first need to call the Windows 98 **Control Panel**. Here you can tell Windows 98 all about your computer's hardware and software components.

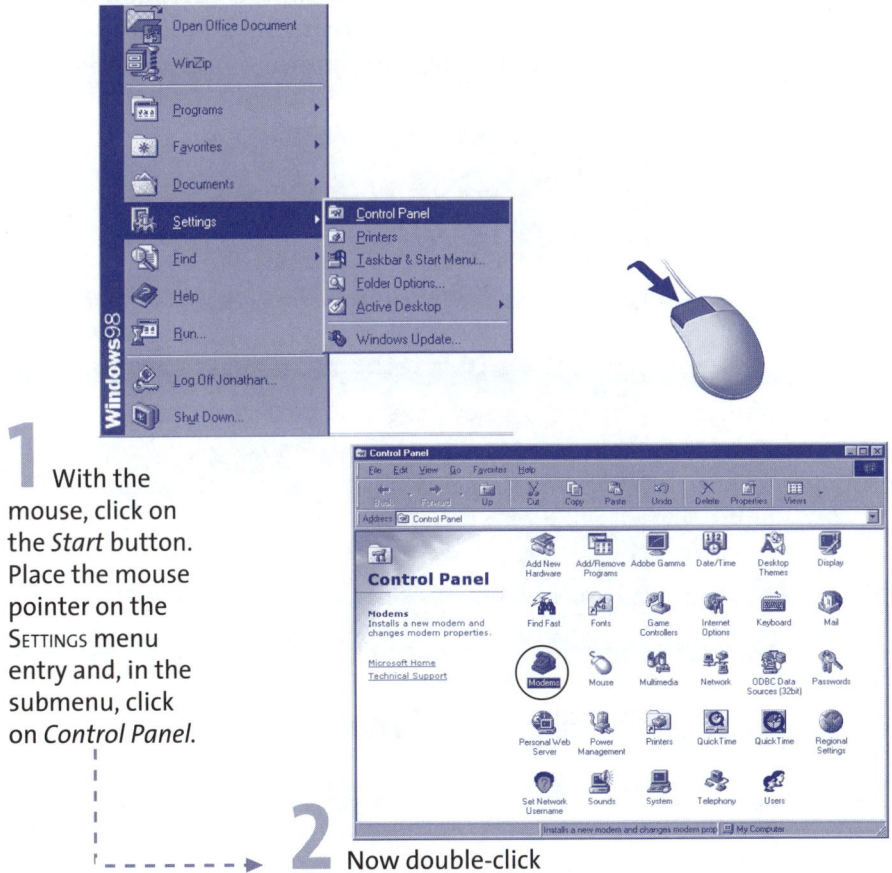

1 With the mouse, click on the *Start* button. Place the mouse pointer on the SETTINGS menu entry and, in the submenu, click on *Control Panel*.

2 Now double-click on the *Modem* icon.

Finally – allow me to introduce myself, I am the **Modem Wizard**. As you can see, nothing appears. This is not surprising, since you have not installed any modem until now. In order to introduce a new modem to the operating system, you need to add it now.

> **WHAT'S THIS?**
>
> **Notebooks** are portable computers which, when folded, are no bigger than an A4 sheet of paper, but which are as powerful as their 'big brothers'.

After clicking on the *Add* button you will see a window appear, in which you need to tell the Modem Wizard what kind of modem you would like to install. You may choose between a PCMCIA modem card for notebooks and *Other*. At this point, you should select *Other*, as it is assumed that you do not wish to install a modem card in a notebook computer.

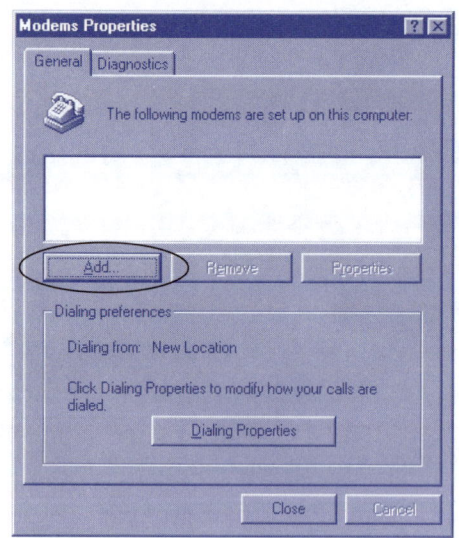

1 Click once on the *Add* button.

18

SOFTWARE IS EVERYTHING!

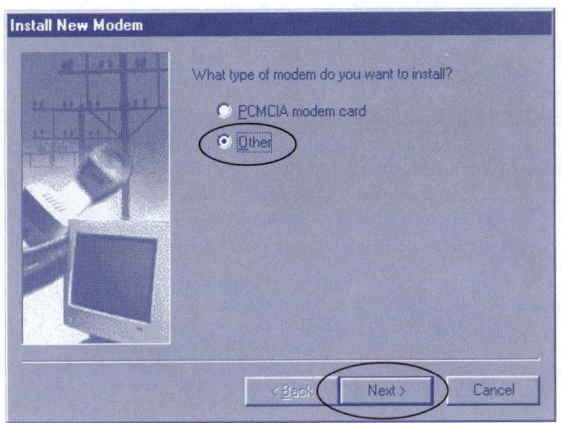

2 Now click on the *Other* option box and then on *Next*.

Now matters are getting serious. If, in the window that is displayed next, you don't select the checkbox *Don't detect my modem, I will select it from a list*, WIndows 98 will attempt to identify the devices connected to the individual interfaces (in this case the modem) automatically. Obviously, your modem needs to be switched on (if it is an external modem). If, on the other hand, you do tick the checkbox, Windows 98 leaves it to you to enter the modem manually. This should, however, only be taken into consideration with more 'exotic' kinds of modems – and when installing certain ISDN cards.

WHAT'S THIS?

Interfaces are used by computers to communicate with external devices, such as printers, modems, scanners or cameras.

Windows 98 now takes the **interfaces** and checks, one after another, whether a modem can be found on any of them. Please be patient at this point, since this process may take several minutes. To make sure that your computer has not crashed halfway through the procedure, you should take a look at the modem itself where, from time to time, some LEDs should flicker. This is a sure sign that your computer is still active.

19

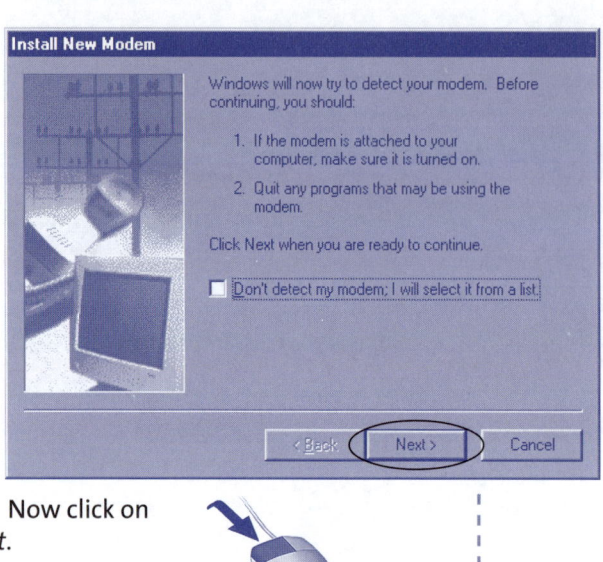

3 Now click on *Next*.

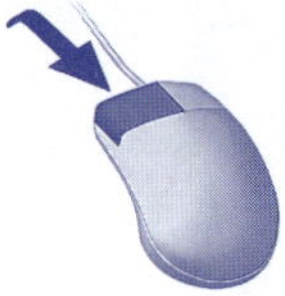

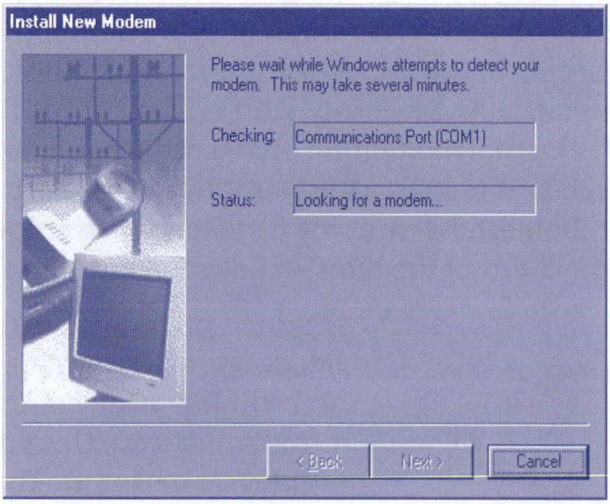

4 The interfaces are checked for the presence of a modem – all you have to do is wait and see.

SOFTWARE IS EVERYTHING!

If the search process was concluded successfully, the window shown below will appear. You can breathe again – the computer and Windows 98 have recognised your modem. If you are using a common modem known to Microsoft, the exact type is shown, and you do not need to worry about further configuration steps. Otherwise, (as in our case) Windows 98 will propose a so-called **standard modem**. This is a kind of setting which all modems can generally cope with. By clicking on the *Change* button, you will be able to select your modem type from a list.

The list box of the window displayed now contains a selection of companies that manufacture modems. As a rule, your **modem manufacturer** should be included in this list. Once you have found it, click on the company name to view a list of modems produced by the corresponding manufacturer in the right-hand list box. If this is not the case, there still remains the possibility of copying the relevant data via the *Have Disk* button. Most modem packages include a diskette with the appropriate **drivers** for Windows 98 – it is now that you will actually need it.

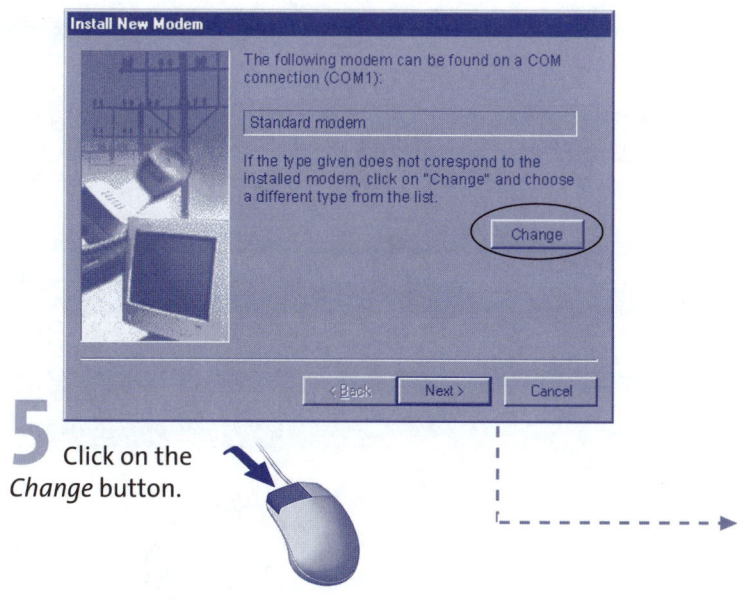

5 Click on the *Change* button.

21

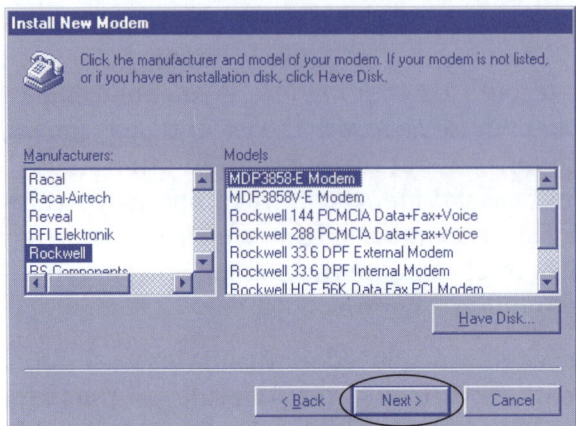

6 To conclude, click on *Next*.

After you have selected your required modem, Windows 98 displays the modem type and the corresponding interface once more. Everything's correct? Then let's go on!

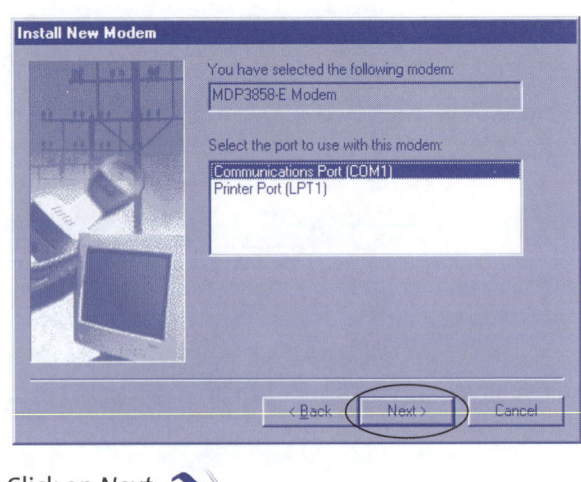

7 Click on *Next*.

Next you are shown a window containing location information. Here you need to enter information regarding the geographical location of the PC to be used with the modem, in particular the country (for example, the United Kingdom) and the area code (for example, 0114 for Sheffield). If your modem is connected to a phone exchange, you need to specify the number to be dialled from the modem's extension to obtain an external line. Another important question is whether you have pulse or tone dial. If you do not know which of the two methods your telephone system uses, you will need to find out by listening. If you hear the old-fashioned clicking, you (still) have pulse dial, while the sounds of 'Mission impossible' coming out of the speaker tell you that you have tone dial.

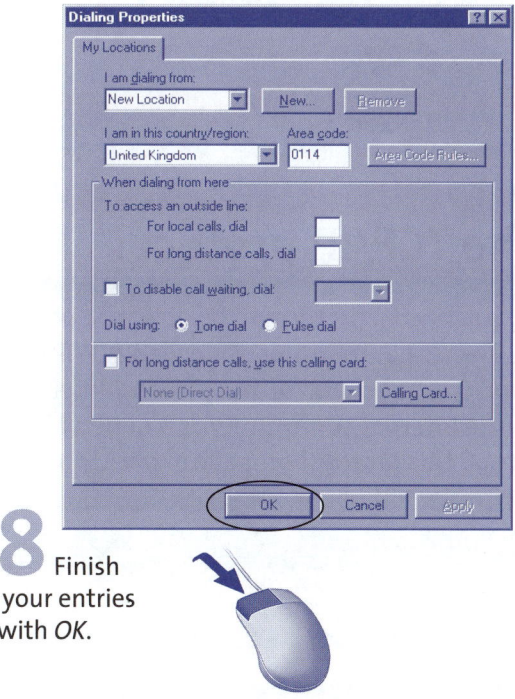

8 Finish your entries with *OK*.

And there you are! Your modem is installed, configured, and ready to be used. Nothing should now hold you back from unrestrained surfing on the World Wide Web!

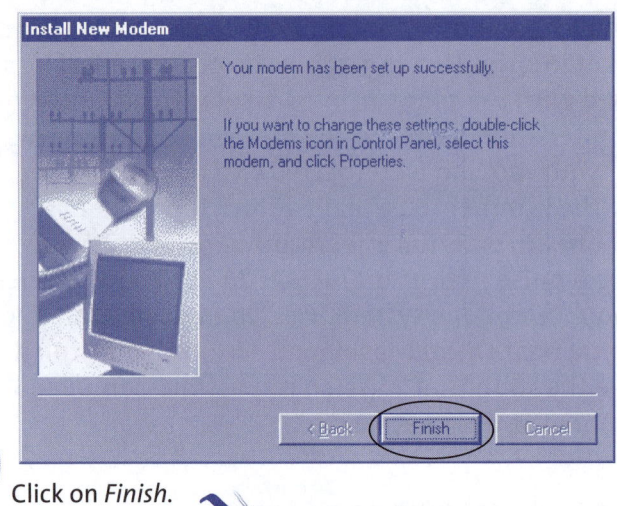

9 Click on *Finish*.

Installing the TCP/IP protocol

As you already know, you need a protocol to be able to send and receive data via the Internet. The standard protocol is called **TCP/IP** (where TCP stands for *Transmission Control Prototcol* and IP for *Internet Protocol*), and is used by the entire Internet community as a general transmission standard. In Windows 98 this protocol must be explicitly installed and configured.

INSTALLING THE TCP/IP PROTOCOL

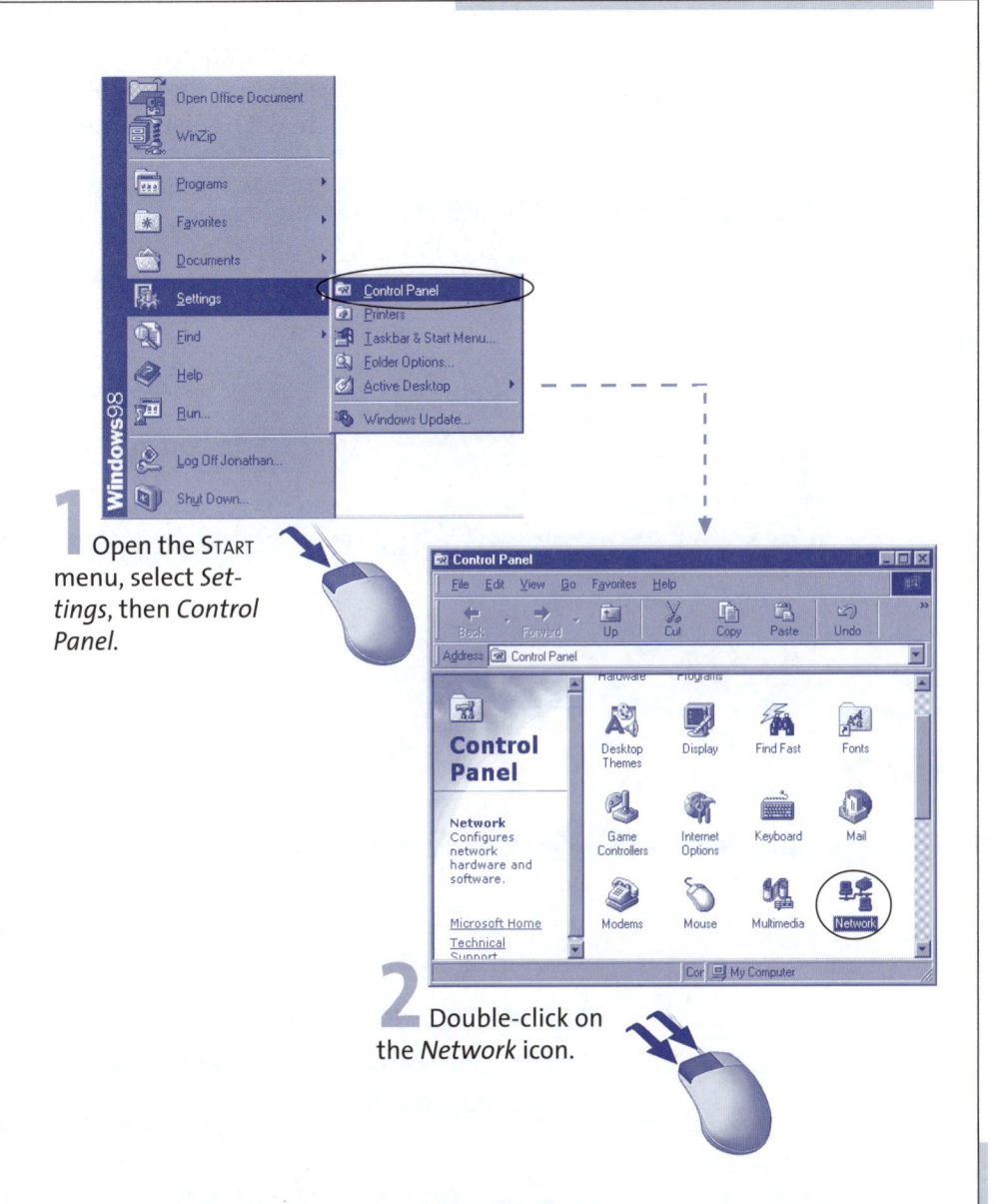

1 Open the START menu, select *Settings*, then *Control Panel*.

2 Double-click on the *Network* icon.

Now, having opened the **Network configuration** window in Windows 98, you may already see some entries, as in our case.
This window displays all **network protocols** and devices needed to connect your computer to a network. Normally, however, your window should be empty.

25

Next you need to set up the Microsoft network adapter and the TCP/IP protocol to enable your computer to communicate with the Internet.

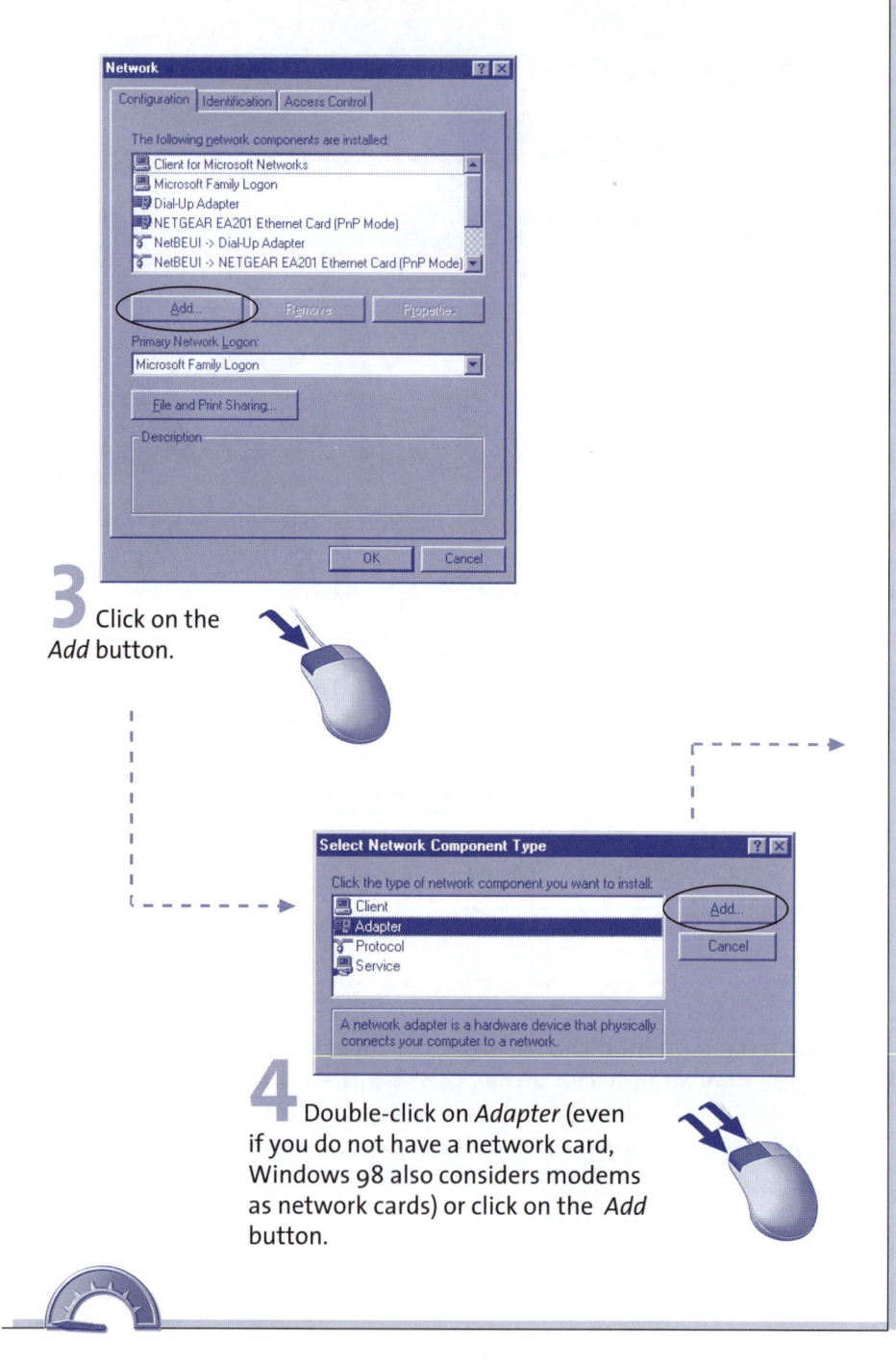

3 Click on the *Add* button.

4 Double-click on *Adapter* (even if you do not have a network card, Windows 98 also considers modems as network cards) or click on the *Add* button.

26

INSTALLING THE TCP/IP PROTOCOL

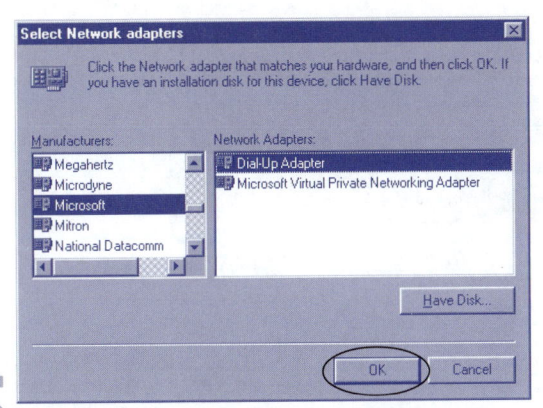

5 Select the *Microsoft* entry and highlight *Dial-Up Adapter*. Confirm your choices by clicking on *OK*.

In the next installation step you need to set up the protocol itself, in our case TCP/IP, by selecting Microsoft's TCP/IP protocol from the Microsoft folder. Subsequently, your Network configuration window should show the two newly installed components (**Dial-Up Adapter** and **TCP/IP**). If this is the case, click on *OK*. Windows 98 will now prompt you to insert the Windows 98 Installation CD, so that the appropriate files can be copied. Once this has finished, you will need to restart your computer for the modifications to become effective.

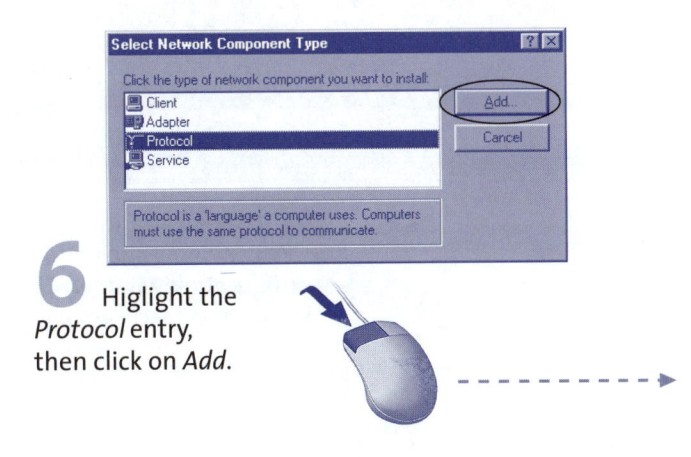

6 Higlight the *Protocol* entry, then click on *Add*.

27

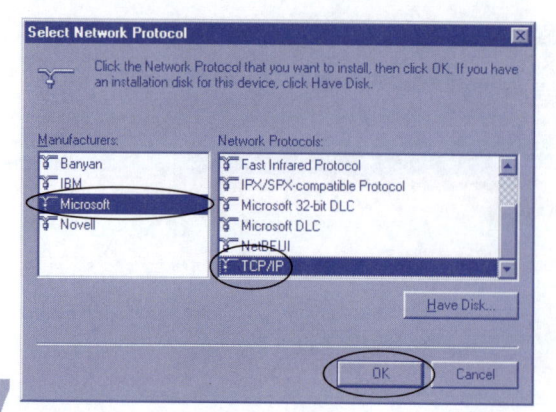

7 Highlight the *Microsoft* entry, then select the *TCP/IP* protocol in the right-hand list box. Confirm your choice by clicking on *OK*.

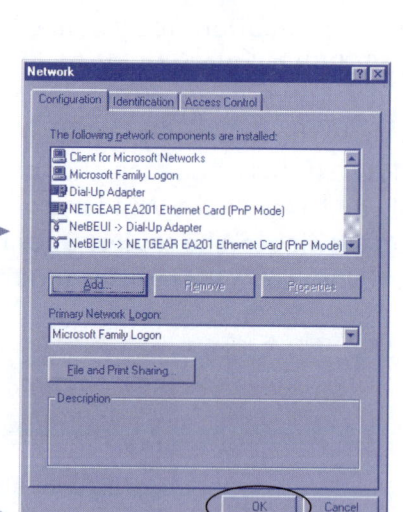

8 Dial-Up Adapter and TCP/IP are now shown in the configuration window. Close the window by clicking on *OK*.

Accessing the Internet with Windows 95

> **Tip:** Protect your **password** against unauthorised access. Whoever knows your password or ID can assume your identity in the Internet and surf at your expense.

After you have installed the modem and TCP/IP, the time has come for establishing contact with the Internet. The Windows **Internet Setup Wizard** helps you create a connection with an Internet Service Provider. The program asks you for all necessary specifications one by one and subsequently puts them into practice.

You should carry out these installation steps only after you have contacted an Internet Service Provider and have all necessary documentation and specifications (phone number, dial-in node, password, etc.) available.

There is, however, a small drawback: the Internet Setup Wizard is not part of the standard distribution of Windows 95. This useful tool is only distributed with the Microsoft Plus! CD, which also contains the Microsoft Internet Explorer.

First of all, you are going to install the Internet Setup Wizard from the Microsoft Plus! CD.

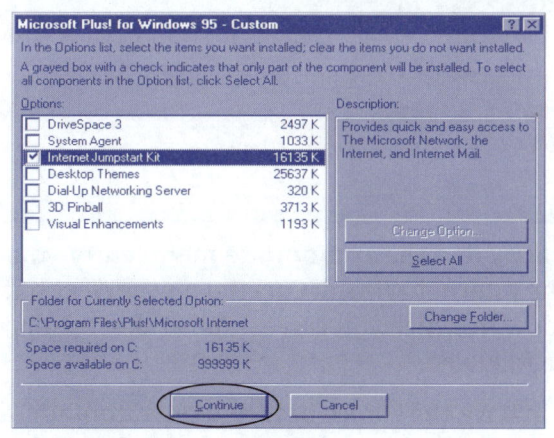

1 Tick the *Internet Jumpstart Kit* checkbox, then click on *Continue*.

After you have clicked on the button, all files of this application will be copied onto your hard disk. Finally, Windows 95 asks you to restart your computer. Once this has been done, you can call up the *Internet Connection* Wizard entry in the PROGRAMS/ACCESSORIES/INTERNET TOOLS folder of the *Start* menu.

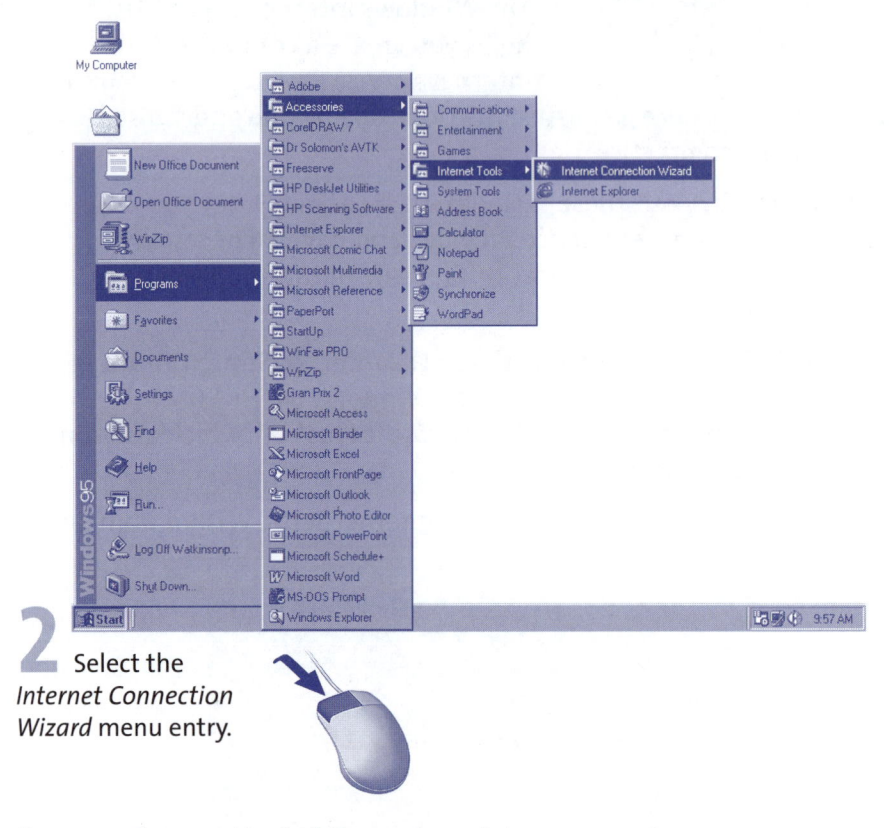

2 Select the *Internet Connection Wizard* menu entry.

Once you have activated the appropriate menu entry, you are welcomed by the Internet Wizard. Clicking on the *Next* button takes you to the window in which you can establish the installation procedure to be followed.

At this point, you have the choice between an automatic, a manual and a current **installation procedure**. Here, you should follow the manual installation procedure because it is the most suitable for giving you a detailed insight into the functioning principles of Windows 95 Internet access.

Accessing the Internet with Windows 95

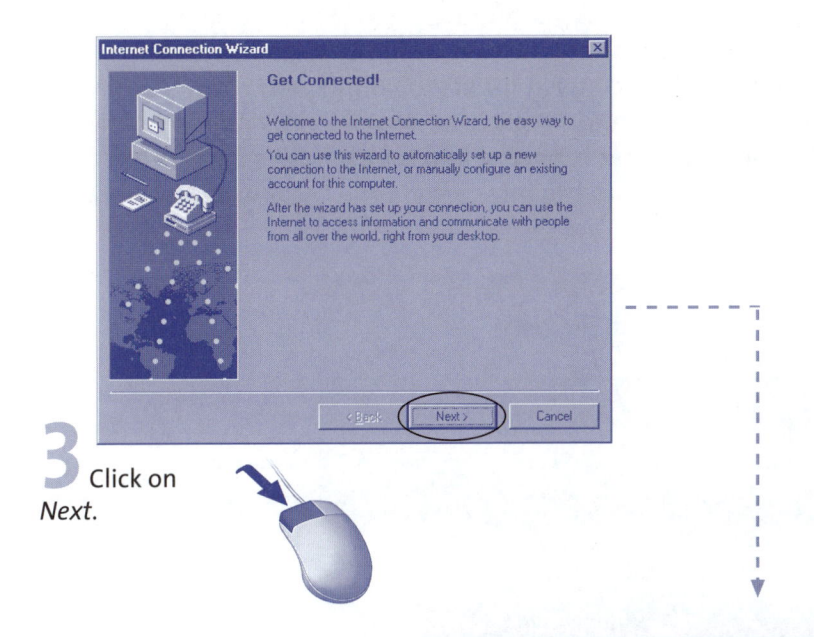

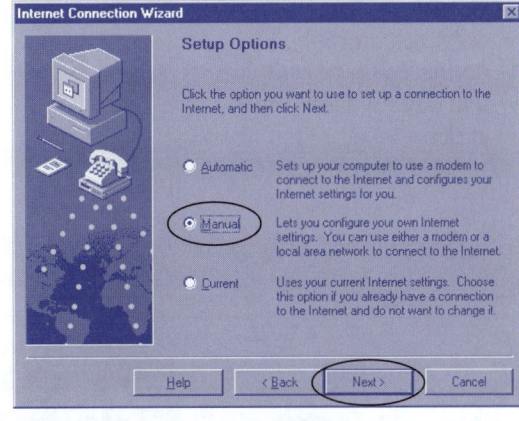

3 Click on *Next*.

4 Select the *Manual* option and confirm your choice with *Next*.

Now we are getting down to business. First, you are officially welcomed by the Internet Wizard. You can leave this window straightaway, to arrive at the point which determines the way you are going to connect with the Internet. Our choice is the *Connect using my phone*

31

line option. This means that you have a single PC and a **modem** and that these are going to be used for establishing your connection with the Internet. The *Connect using my Local Area Network* option is only activated if your computer is part of a network. In this case, the computers will connect to the Internet via the **Local Area Network**.

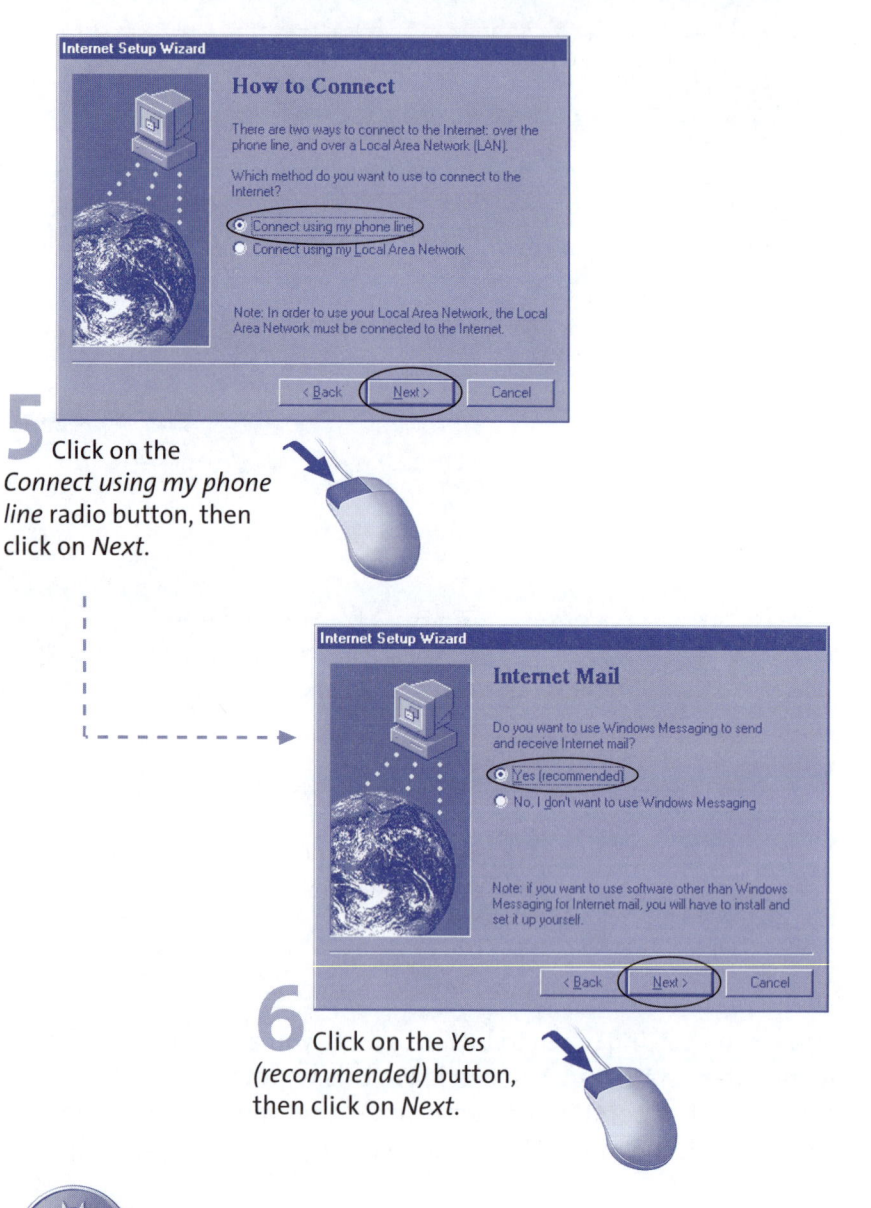

5 Click on the *Connect using my phone line* radio button, then click on *Next*.

6 Click on the *Yes (recommended)* button, then click on *Next*.

ACCESSING THE INTERNET WITH WINDOWS 95

Now, after having specified that you are going to use a modem (which you have already installed) for establishing contact with the Internet, your Internet Service Provider needs to be set up. First of all, you will need to give the connection profile a name. **Profile** is a technical term which denotes all settings (phone number, login name, password, etc.) needed to establish a communication with the Internet Service Provider. Once this is done, you need to enter the phone number you will use to dial into the Internet. This phone number is included in the documentation supplied to you by your Internet Service Provider.

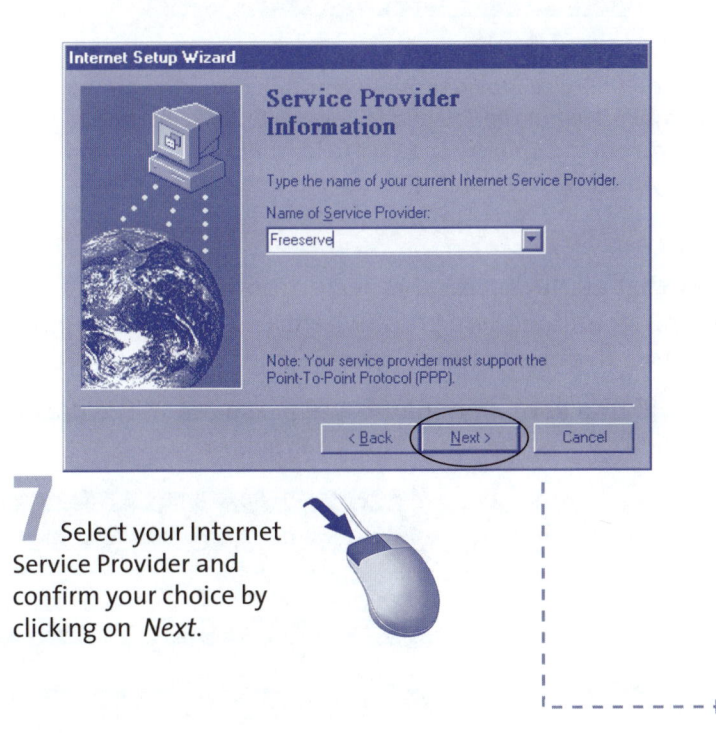

Internet Setup Wizard

Service Provider Information

Type the name of your current Internet Service Provider.

Name of Service Provider:
Freeserve

Note: Your service provider must support the Point-To-Point Protocol (PPP).

< Back | Next > | Cancel

7 Select your Internet Service Provider and confirm your choice by clicking on *Next*.

33

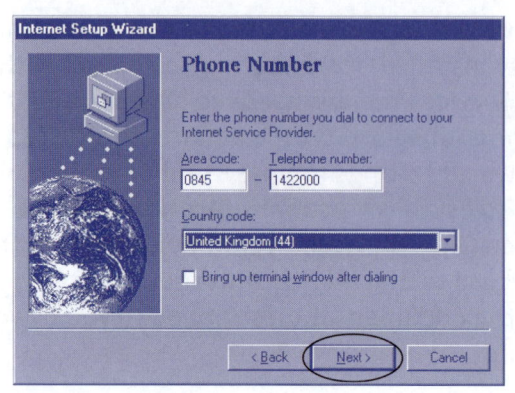

8 In the *Area code* field, enter the area code of your Internet Service Provider's phone number, and the phone number itself in the *Telephone number* field. Select the country in the *Country code* list field, for example United Kingdom (44) or Ireland (353). Confirm your choices by clicking on the *Next* button.

Now that all the necessary specifications have been entered and your computer and modem know where and how to dial into the Internet, it is time to enter your **login name** and your **password**.

You will find your login name and password in the documentation supplied by your Internet Service Provider.

9 In the *User name* field, enter your login name, and your secret password under *Password*. Confirm your entries by clicking on *Next*.

ACCESSING THE INTERNET WITH WINDOWS 95

After you have entered your **user name** and **password**, the Internet Setup Wizard asks you to enter an IP number. As you already know, this is the number which uniquely identifies each individual computer on the Internet. If your Internet Service Provider, for example EUnet, has assigned you a fixed number, you need to use the *Always use the following* option. If, on the other hand, your Service Provider assigns you a dynamic IP, you must select the *My Internet Service Provider automatically assigns me one* option. This is based on the idea that each Internet Service Provider possesses a large pool of IP addresses that can be freely assigned to different users. Thus, when you dial up your Internet Service Provider, you are dynamically assigned one of these addresses. Today this is the most common way of handling IP addresses for dial-up connections.

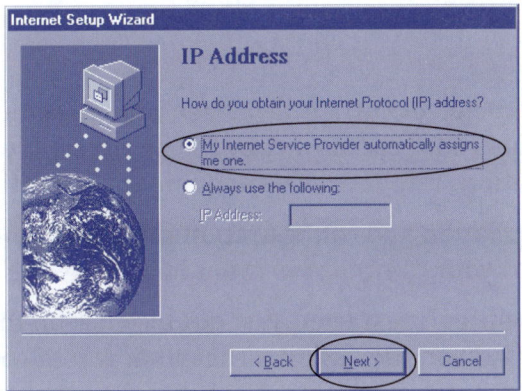

10 Select the *My Internet Service Provider automatically assigns me one* option, then click on *Next*.

Clicking on *Next* takes you to a window which asks you to enter at least the IP address of the DNS server and, where present, also the address of the secondary DNS server in the corresponding entry fields. The address of the EUnet Internet Service Provider, for example, is 192.76.144.66, while the secondary DNS server has the IP address 149.174.211.5.

35

11 Enter the IP address of the DNS server in the appropriate field and – where present – the address of the secondary DNS server as well. Click on the *Next* button.

You're nearly there. All entries have been properly entered, and the Internet Setup Wizard can now copy the necessary files and transfer your specifications into the corresponding configuration files.

Once the installation and configuration process is complete, you will need to restart your computer in order to activate the new settings.

Once the computer is restarted, just double-click on the *My Computer* icon on the desktop. The window that comes up now contains a folder icon (or program group) called **Dial-Up Networking**. This is where you can find your newly created profile which can now be used to connect with your Internet Service Provider.

12 Click on the *Finish* button.

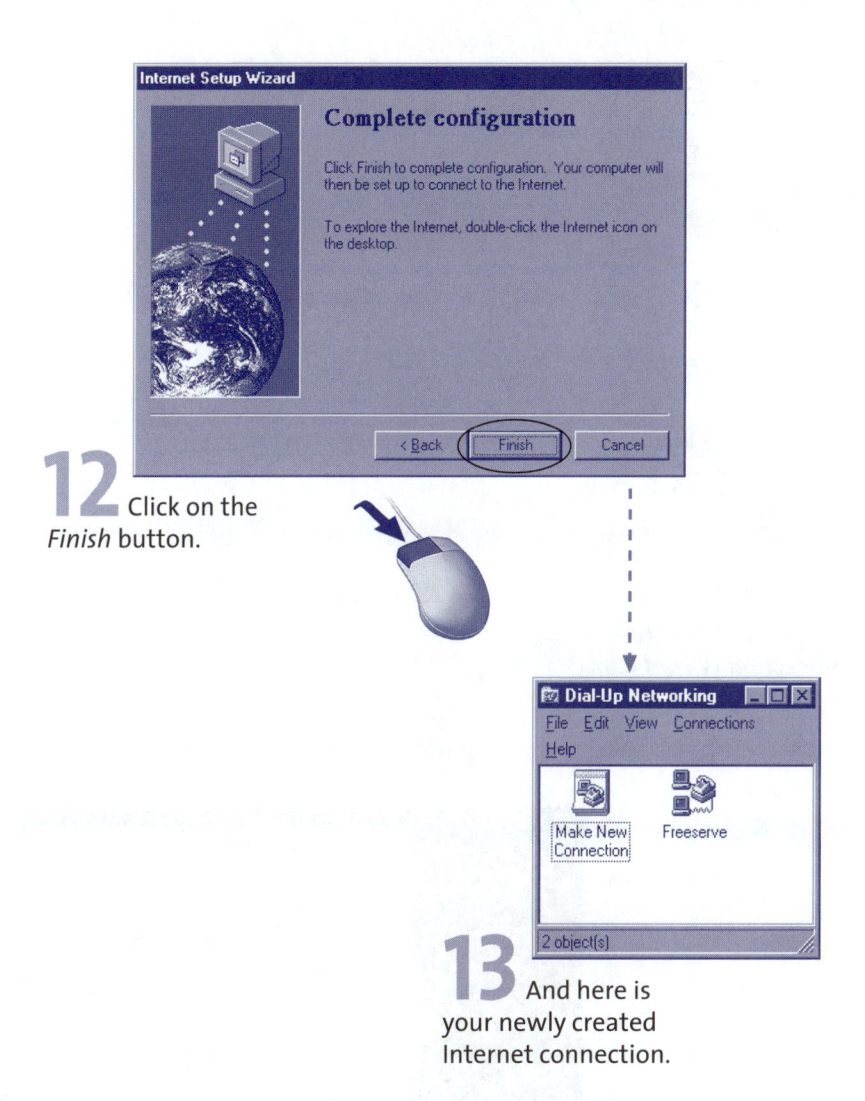

13 And here is your newly created Internet connection.

Accessing the Internet with Windows 98 and IE5

Windows 98, in connection with Internet Explorer 5 (IE5), also provides you with an Internet Connection Wizard to help you establish an Internet connection.

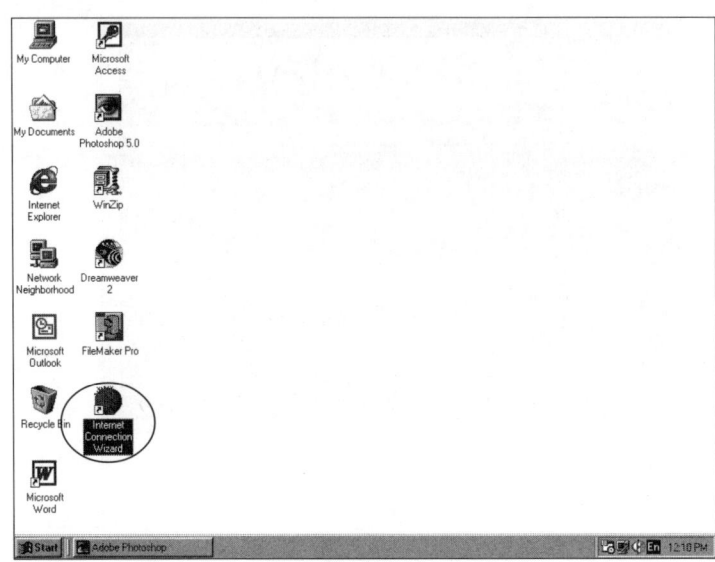

1 Click on the *Internet Connection Wizard* icon.

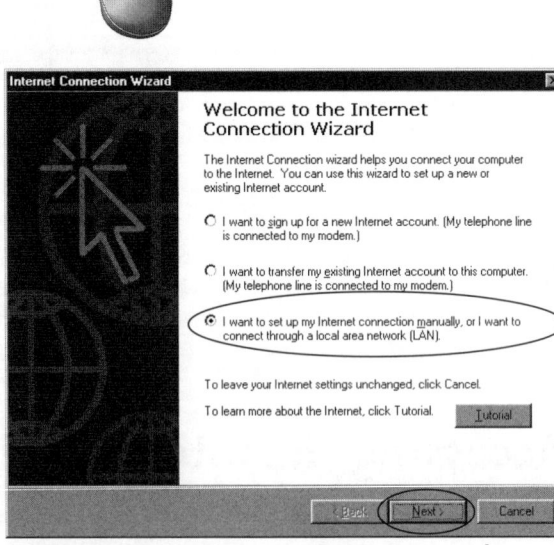

2 Select the third option *I want to set up my Internet connection manually*, then click on *Next*.

38

ACCESSING THE INTERNET WITH WINDOWS 98 AND IE5

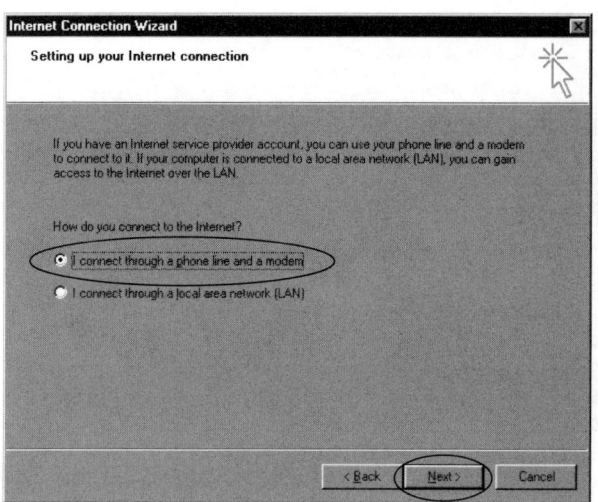

3 Select the option *I connect through a phone line and a modem*. Click on *Next*.

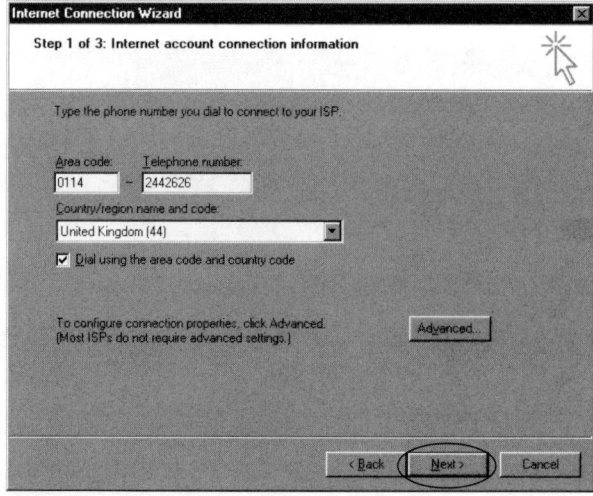

4 Type the phone number you use to connect to your Internet Service Provider, then click on *Next*.

39

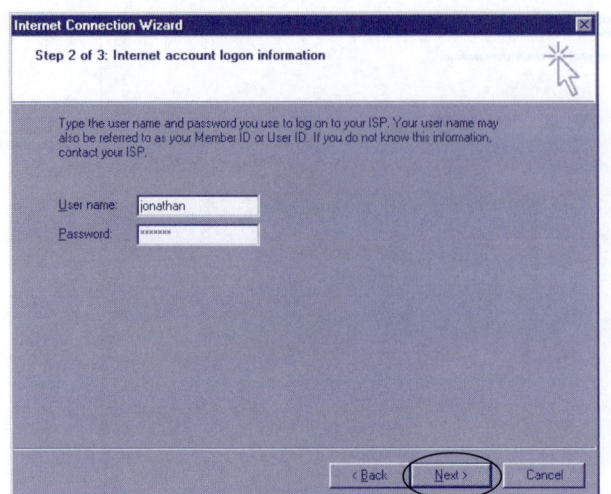

5 Now enter your access data (user name and password) and click on *Next*.

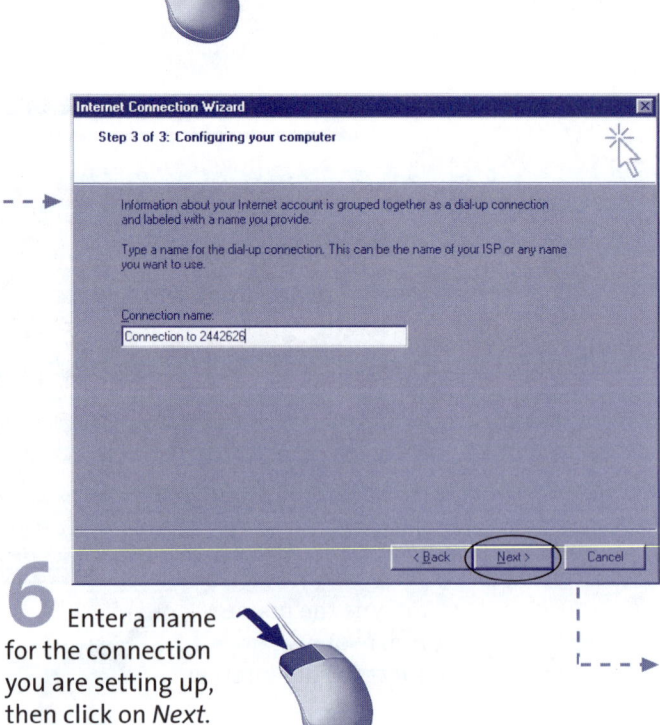

6 Enter a name for the connection you are setting up, then click on *Next*.

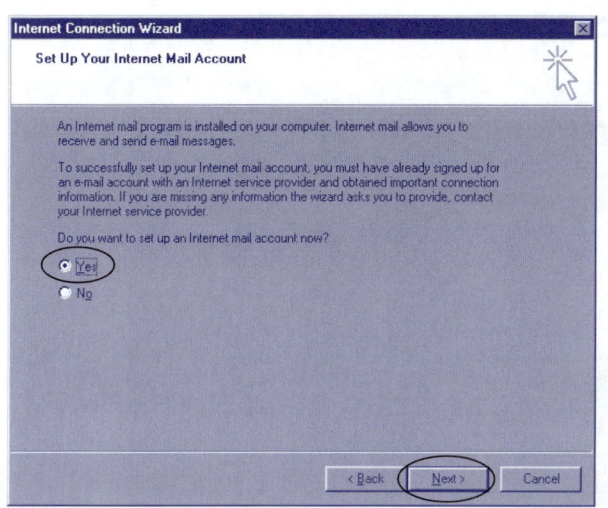

ACCESSING THE INTERNET WITH WINDOWS 98 AND IE5

7 You are now going to create an e-mail account. Select the *Yes* option, then click on *Next*.

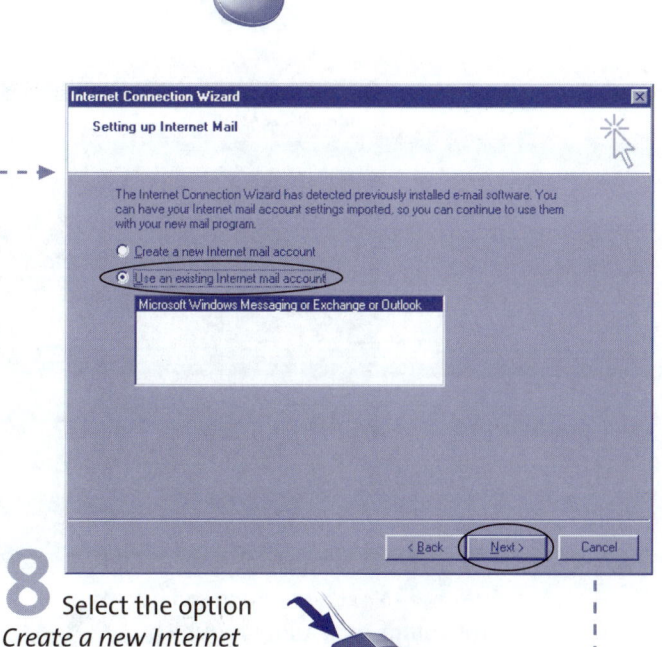

8 Select the option *Create a new Internet mail account*, and once again click on *Next*.

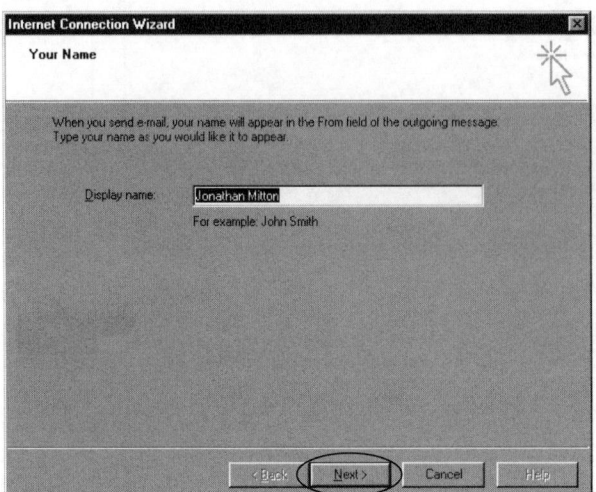

9 Enter your full name and click on *Next*.

10 Next, you are asked for your e-mail address (which is assigned to you by your Internet Service Provider). After typing it in, click on *Next*.

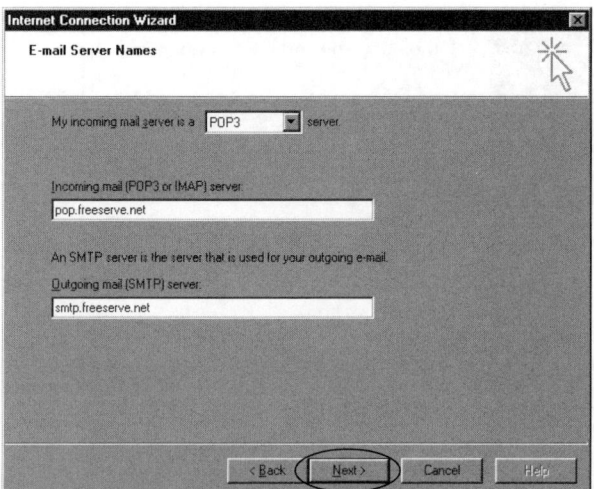

ACCESSING THE INTERNET WITH WINDOWS 98 AND IE5

Internet Connection Wizard
E-mail Server Names

My incoming mail server is a [POP3] server.

Incoming mail (POP3 or IMAP) server:
pop.freeserve.net

An SMTP server is the server that is used for your outgoing e-mail.
Outgoing mail (SMTP) server:
smtp.freeserve.net

< Back **Next >** Cancel Help

11 Now fill in the appropriate entry fields with your Internet Service Provider's mail server names, then click on *Next*.

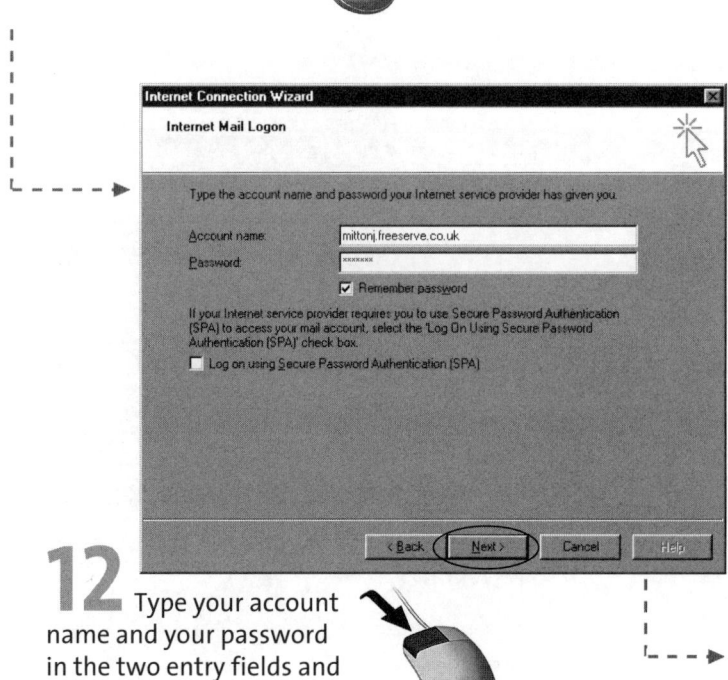

Internet Connection Wizard
Internet Mail Logon

Type the account name and password your Internet service provider has given you.

Account name: miltonj.freeserve.co.uk
Password: *******
☑ Remember password

If your Internet service provider requires you to use Secure Password Authentication (SPA) to access your mail account, select the 'Log On Using Secure Password Authentication (SPA)' check box.

☐ Log on using Secure Password Authentication (SPA)

< Back **Next >** Cancel Help

12 Type your account name and your password in the two entry fields and click on *Next*.

43

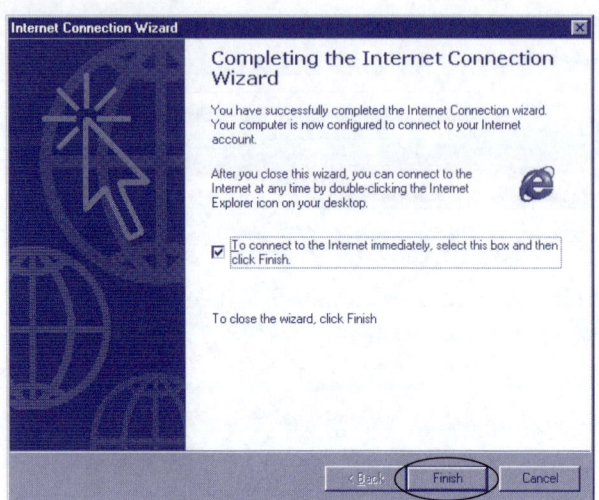

13 All entries are completed. Click on *Finish* to test the newly created connection straight away.

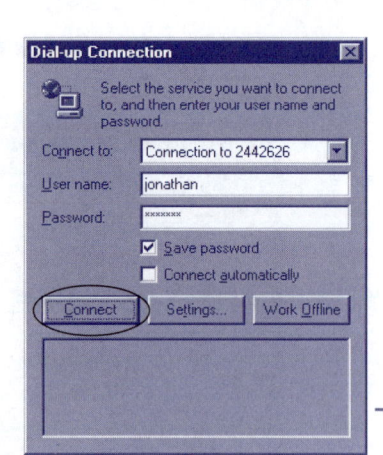

14 Click on *Connect*.

INTERNET, HERE WE COME!

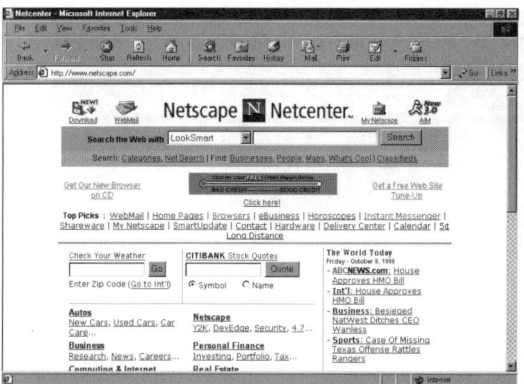

15 On the Internet via the new connection.

Internet, here we come!

On the Windows desktop, first double-click the *My Computer* icon and then the *Dial-Up Networking* folder icon.

This opens a window which displays all modem connections defined for your computer – including our sample connection with the Internet Service Provider EUnet.

1 Double-click the *Dial-Up Networking* icon.

45

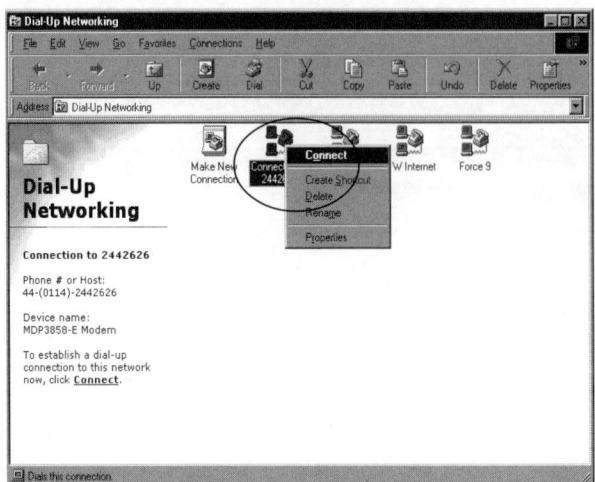

2 Right-click on the newly created connection with the Internet Service Provider.

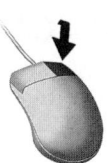

In order to establish a connection to your Internet Service Provider, right-click on the required connection icon. This displays a context menu with several entries. The last one, *Properties*, displays all sorts of details about the connection in question. The first menu entry you are offered, *Connect*, will eventually establish the connection. Click on this entry.

A window opens which summarises the data you have already entered during the setup of your profile, including user name and password which, at this point, you may still modify. When you select the *Save password* checkbox, you will no longer need to enter your password every time you wish to connect.

As soon as you click on *Connect*, your computer and the modem dial up your Internet Service Provider and establish a stable connection. You can terminate this either by clicking on the *Disconnect* button in the Dial-Up Status window or by selecting *Disconnect* in the Dial-Up Networking context menu.

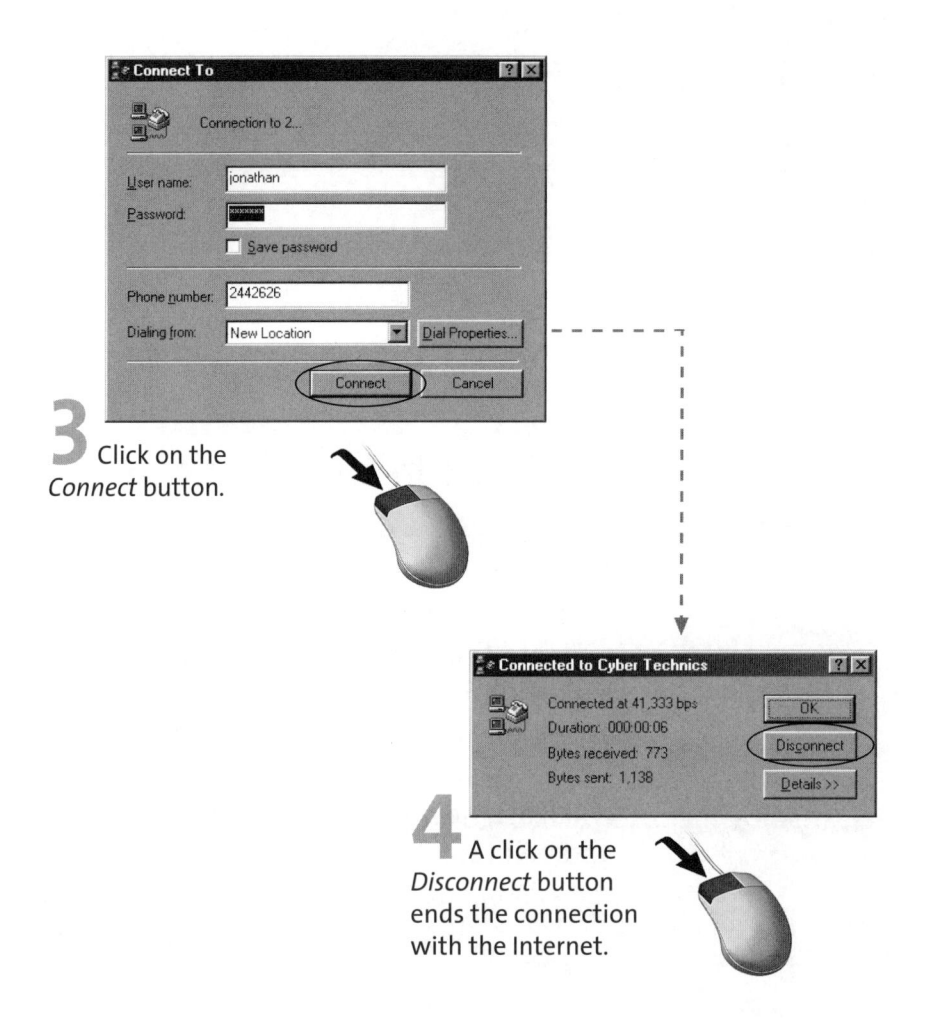

3 Click on the *Connect* button.

4 A click on the *Disconnect* button ends the connection with the Internet.

You have to laugh – the best computer messages

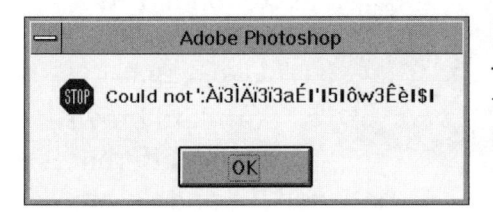

Even computers can get muddled – and for good. Or is this an alien's message transmitted though our PC's silicon brain?

2

Let's go WWW!

What's in this chapter:

After having worked through the previous chapter and done everything necessary to dial into the Internet, you are now ready to install a browser. Doing this will let you access one of the most popular Internet services – surfing the Web! Later on, you will learn how to work the WWW browser and will soon be able to delve deeper into the WWW. You are going to use Microsoft Internet Explorer 4.x as your browser. You will also learn how to update this version to the more recent version 5.x. Later on in this book, IE5 will be used as the standard browser as the differences between IE4 and IE5 are only very slight.

You already know about:

The importance of software	16
Accessing the Internet with Windows 95	29
Accessing the Internet with Windows 98 and IE5	37

You are going to learn about:

Installing Internet Explorer 4.x	50
Microsoft Internet Explorer 4 in detail	58
Updating to Internet Explorer 5	63
Taking your first steps in the World Wide Web	67
Creating a bookmark list	72
The Internet Explorer's user interface	77
Saving a file to the hard disk	83
Loading saved pages	86
Browsing Web pages	88
Printing Web pages	89

Installing Internet Explorer 4.x

WHAT'S THIS?

A **Web browser** is a program you can use to surf around the WWW.

If you already have Windows 98 installed, you can happily ignore this which deals with the installation of IE4. This is because when you install Windows 98, IE4 and all its components are automatically installed as well.

The **Web browser** is the essential tool you will need as you make your way through the mass of information available on the World Wide Web.

In the past, many companies have tried their hand at developing Web browsers. Only two of them, however, have been able to corner the market and gain favour with the Internet community – the American firms Microsoft and Netscape. In the course of this chapter you will install Microsoft's **Internet Explorer 4.0 (IE4)**. You can obtain the most recent Explorer software from many sources: your Internet Service Provider, a software dealer, copied from friends or colleagues (it is legal in this case) or directly off the Internet. Another good source of software is computer magazines, which are often jam-packed with CD-ROMs containing many useful programs.

You will learn more about Netscape Communicator in Chapter 5.

Microsoft basically offers you three different types of installation. You can decide for yourself which one you will use.

The minimal installation simply includes the Explorer with a few multimedia extensions and is only useful for exploring the Web. It does not support e-mail or newsgroups.

The standard installation offers, alongside the Explorer, all the multimedia extensions as well as Outlook Express for sending and receiving e-mail and accessing newsgroups.

The complete installation adds a whole host of Internet software to the standard installation. Included in this extra software are the Internet conferencing program 'NetMeeting', the 'FrontPage Express' progam for creating your own Web pages, Microsoft's Web Publishing Assistant, the 'Netshow' Explorer extension used to transfer live audio and video from the Internet, and Microsoft Chat, a program which allows you to take part in online discussions on the Internet.

Installing the Internet Explorer from Microsoft's Internet Explorer CD-ROM

Many programs that you find either on the Internet or on a CD-ROM will come in a compressed file format. All this means is that the file has been compressed to a fraction of its original size so that it can be transferred more quickly over the Internet. For these files to be decompressed you will need a program that changes the file back to its original size, once it has been successfully **downloaded**. You can find these programs on the Internet and on CD-ROMs supplied with various computer magazines. You will also come across compressed files with the extension *.exe*. These are files that decompress themselves automatically without needing to use a special utility.

You will install Internet Explorer from the original Microsoft Internet Explorer CD-ROM, so you will not need to decompress it. In its compressed form, Internet Explorer 4 contains about 14 Mb of data, so it is not recommended to download it directly from the Internet. Despite this, we will carry out the process just once, to learn how it works. For users with slow modems, the time required for this, and the ensuing online costs, mean that it is not really acceptable.

Your computer will start up the required installation as soon as you insert the Internet Explorer CD into your CD-ROM drive. You will then be confronted with a whole series of installation windows.

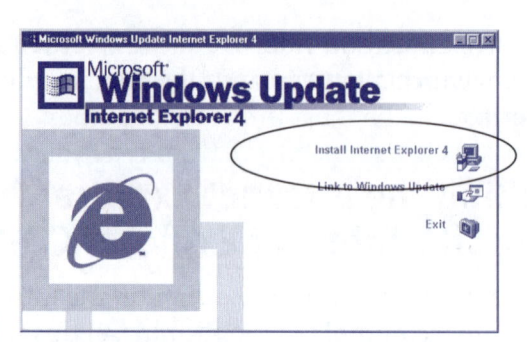

1 Click on the icon to the right of the words *Install Internet Explorer 4*.

2 Click on the *Next* button.

WHAT'S THIS?

The **License Agreement** specifies the legal terms under which you may use the program on your computer and make copies of it.

3 Click on the radio button to the left of the words *I accept the agreement*, then click on the *Next* button.

52

INSTALLING INTERNET EXPLORER 4.x

In the next installation step, Internet Explorer 4 will ask you to decide on an installation type. We find the standard installation most useful here as it copies the most important components onto your hard disk. You can choose the installation type you want by clicking on the drop-down field in the next window. Once you have done this, the installation will ask you if you want to install the Active Desktop. This update of the Windows 95 interface accommodates new Web features as well as new folders and directories.

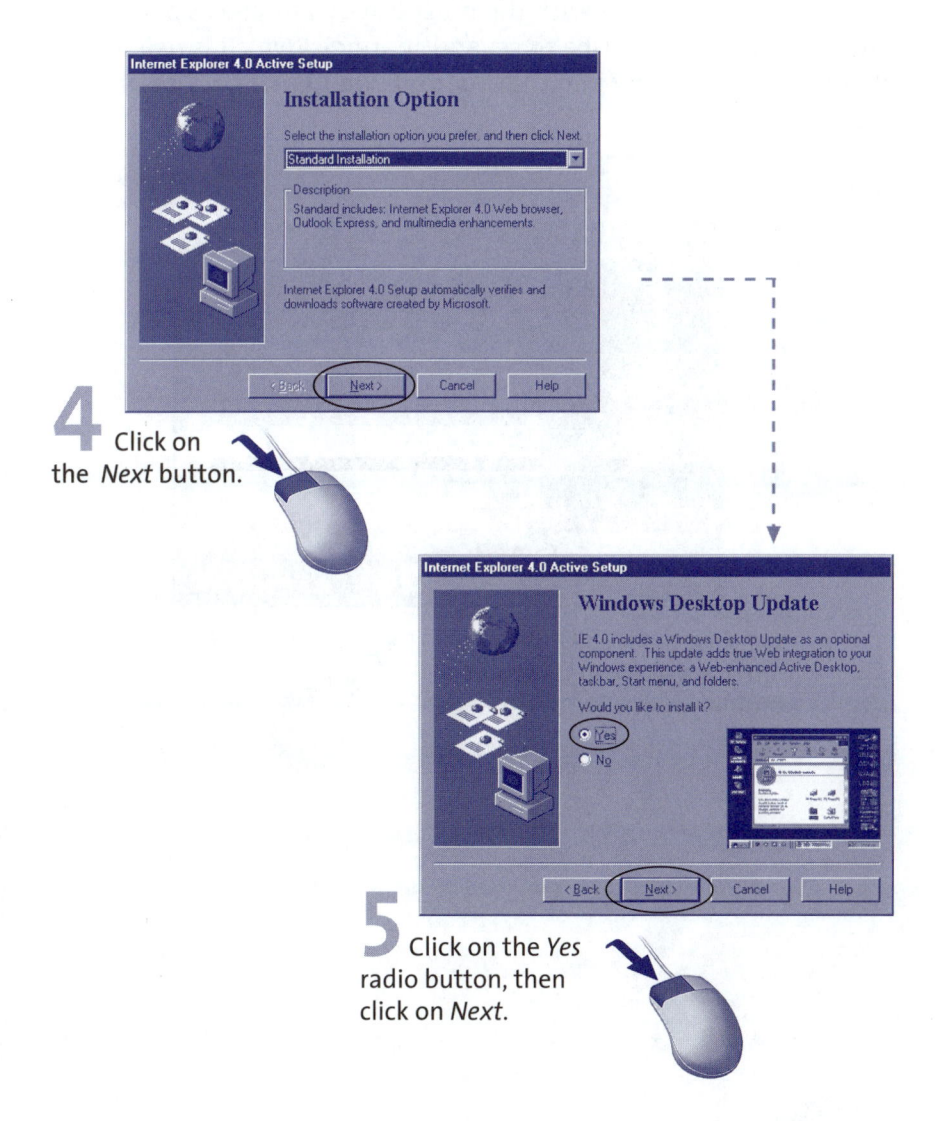

4 Click on the *Next* button.

5 Click on the *Yes* radio button, then click on *Next*.

53

In the next step you will meet the word 'channel' for the first time. A **channel** is really just a normal Web page. The special thing about this Web page, however, is that you can subscribe to it using Internet Explorer 4 and it will then be regularly checked to see if it has been updated. If this is the case, the new page will be downloaded onto your computer. This means that you can look at the page at leisure, without having to pay all the usual online costs. A channel is a particular area in a Web page, which is limited according to subject and only supplies the user with the most important pieces of news and updates. If you subscribe to several channels (which is usually free), you can switch between them as you would using a TV remote control.

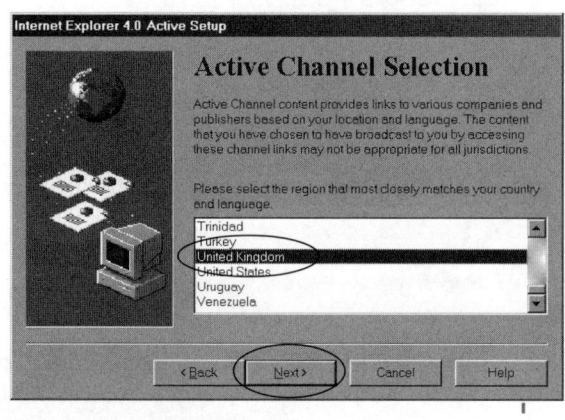

6 Select *United Kingdom* from the list of countries and confirm your choice by clicking on *Next*.

INSTALLING INTERNET EXPLORER 4.x

7 Confirm the installation directory for Internet Explorer 4 by clicking on *Next*.

You can now breathe again – you have completed all the configuration steps and can get down to the real installation process of Internet Explorer 4. All you need to do now is relax and watch the computer go about its business.

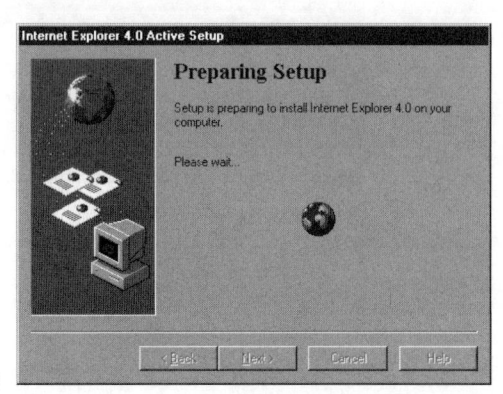

8 You will have to be patient for a while until the computer has copied all the necessary files.

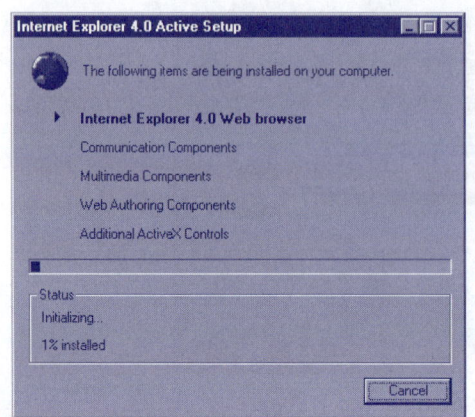

9 All the components of Internet Explorer 4 are now being copied to your hard disk – time for a rest!

When all the files have been transferred to your computer, a message will appear informing you that the installation has been successfully completed.

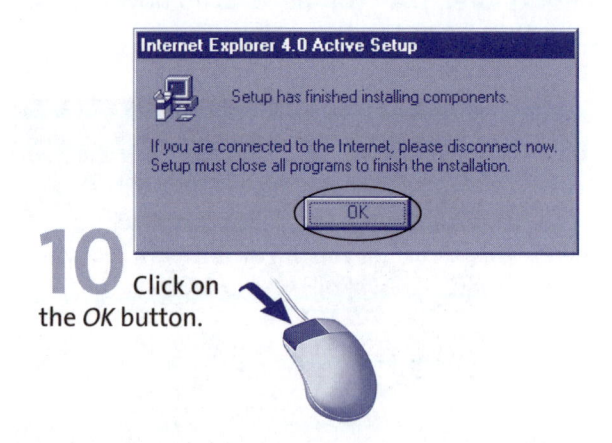

10 Click on the *OK* button.

When you have carried out installation step 10, your computer will restart itself so that the installation can be completed and all the new files activated. A message window will then appear and tell you that the required components have been installed. This process will last a few minutes.

INSTALLING INTERNET EXPLORER 4.X

When your computer has carried out all these tasks, your Windows 95 screen will appear with a brand new look. Don't be worried by this, Microsoft has just given it a few cosmetic improvements. At this point, Microsoft suggests you take a quick tour round your newly installed Internet Explorer. Make the most of it!

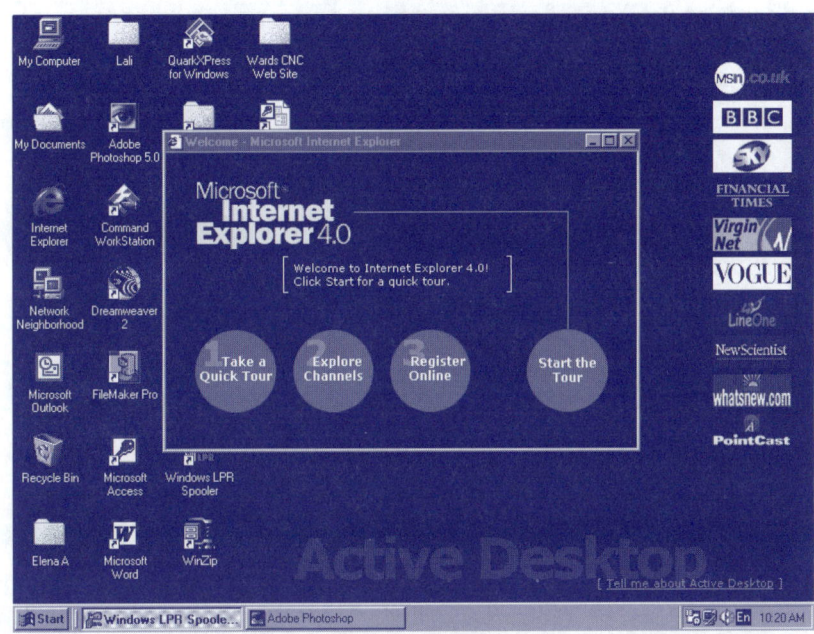

11 And there you are, Internet Explorer 4 has been successfully installed. Clicking on one of the round buttons inside the welcome screen will take you on a tour round the Explorer.

You can start Microsoft Internet Explorer 4 by clicking on the Explorer icon in the Windows 95 main screen or on the taskbar at the bottom of the screen.

57

Microsoft Internet Explorer 4 in detail

You will now need to add a few more basic settings to adapt your Web browser to your specific requirements before you can actually start using Internet Explorer. This includes settings for your e-mail address as well as a definition of the appropriate Internet profile.

1 Start up Internet Explorer by double-clicking the Internet Explorer icon on your Windows desktop.

The Explorer opens with an error message, as the Web browser is trying to access a particular **Web address**. In our case, the Web address is that of Microsoft, as this is the one that is set up by default. First of all, you will need to tell Internet Explorer which profile to use to contact your Internet Service Provider.

MICROSOFT INTERNET EXPLORER 4 IN DETAIL

2 In the VIEW menu open the INTERNET OPTIONS command.

3 Activate the *Connection* tab.

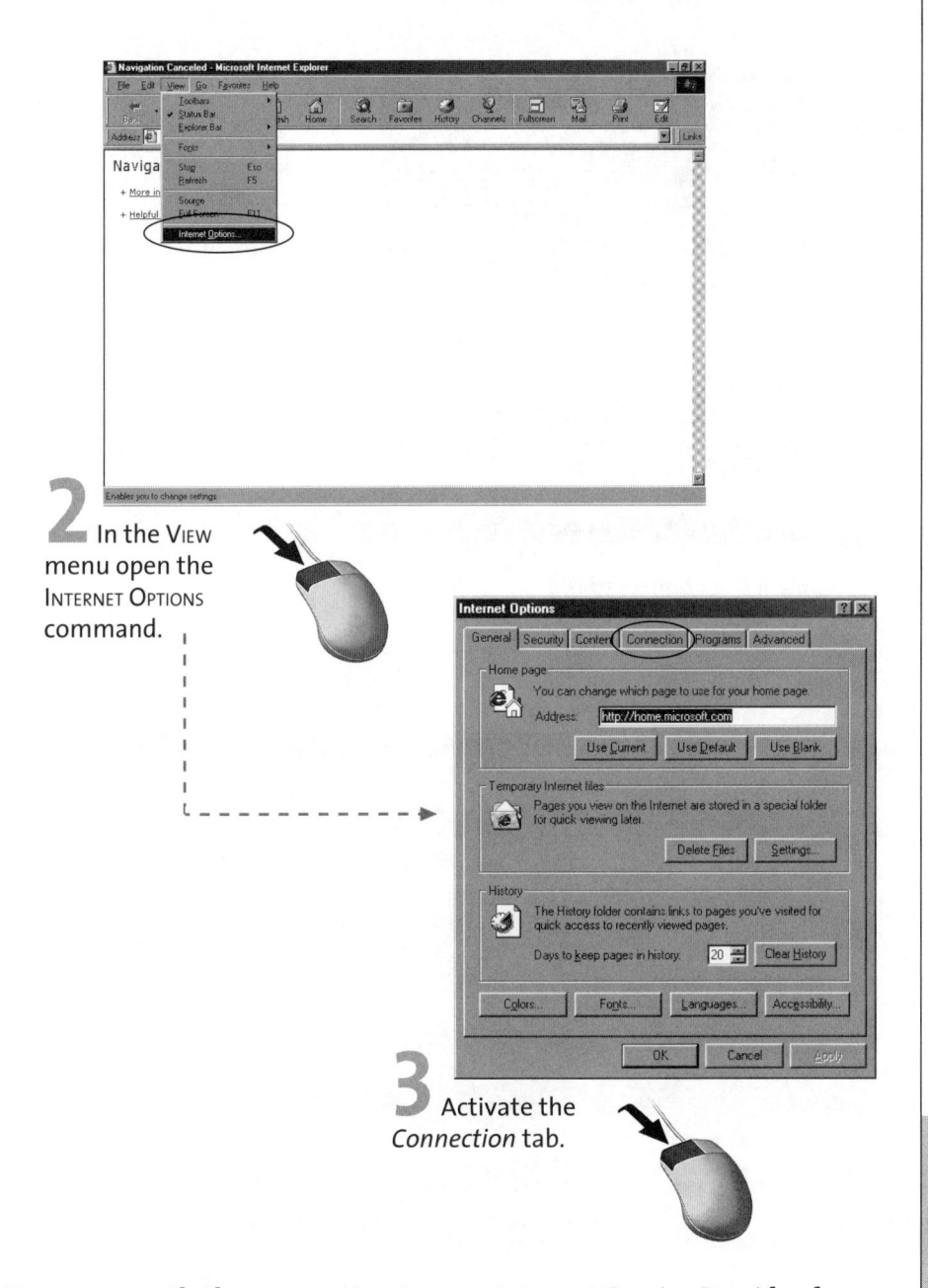

You can specify the connection to your Internet Service Provider from inside the *Connection* tab. This means that as soon as you start up Internet Explorer, the connection profile is automatically called up.

59

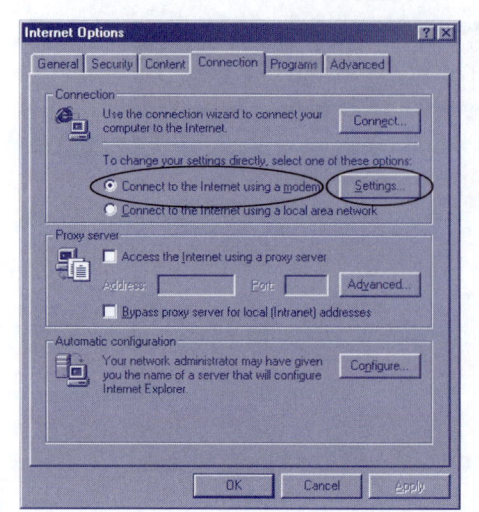

4 Select the *Connect to the Internet using a modem* radio button. Then click on *Settings*.

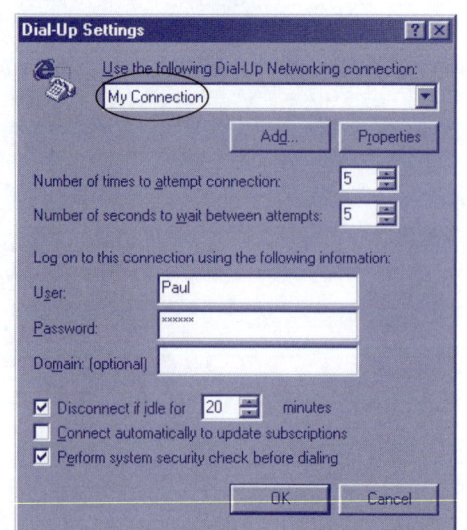

5 Click on the drop-down list at the top of the window and select the appropriate connection profile.

At this point, you can also set your computer to terminate the Internet connection after a given period of inactivity. This will prevent unpleasant surprises when your phone bill arrives. To do this, just mark the checkbox entitled *Disconnect if idle for xx minutes* and then set the required amount of time in the input box. Microsoft's default setting is 20 minutes.

Finally, click on *OK* to confirm your modifications and close the dialog box.

When looking at the *Connection* tab, you may have noticed another option box called *Access the Internet using a proxy server*. What exactly does this mean?

Proxy servers are computers which temporarily save World Wide Web pages locally at an Internet Service Provider's site. If you wish to retrieve these pages again later on, they can be downloaded directly from there. This means that you don't have to waste time downloading them from the Internet. This may drastically speed up access time to frequently used Web pages.

However, there is another side to the coin: when you use a proxy server, your entire communication with the Internet passes through this computer, which allows your surfing to be watched and evaluated – even though it is nobody's business but yours as to which Internet sites you are interested in. Furthermore, proxy servers are not updated very often, so it would be quite possible for you to spend days using an old page from the proxy server, even though the original page on the Internet was updated a long time ago.

It is best to ignore this option therefore, as direct access to the Internet has become so quick that you would only ever be dealing with the negative aspects of proxy servers.

To end this first section of major adaptation work, you will now set up the size of the temporary Internet folder on your hard drive.

Internet Explorer uses this folder to store all the graphics and documents which you viewed most recently when you were online. This temporary store, also known as a **cache**, speeds up your Web

WHAT'S THIS?

The **cache** is a particular storage area in your computer which has the task of keeping frequently used files available for the processor and having them ready when required.

surfing, as the graphics are already partly stored on your local hard disk. This folder must therefore be emptied every now and then so as to avoid cluttering up your hard drive with Internet 'rubbish'. Internet Explorer will do this task for you automatically.

Click on the tab entitled *General* and then go to the section called *Temporary Internet files*.

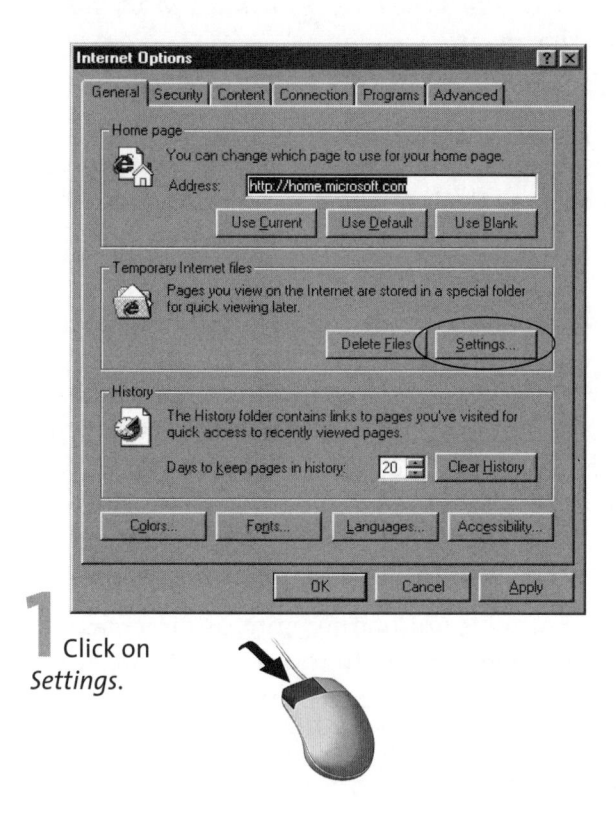

1 Click on *Settings*.

You can change the size of the storage area by clicking on the slide rule and, keeping the mouse button pressed, moving your mouse from side to side. Internet Explorer always uses percentages of the

62

absolute hard disk size. Thus, for example, Internet Explorer will use a folder of 40 Mbytes with a hard disk of 1 Gbyte, whose temporary Internet files size is limited to 4 per cent.

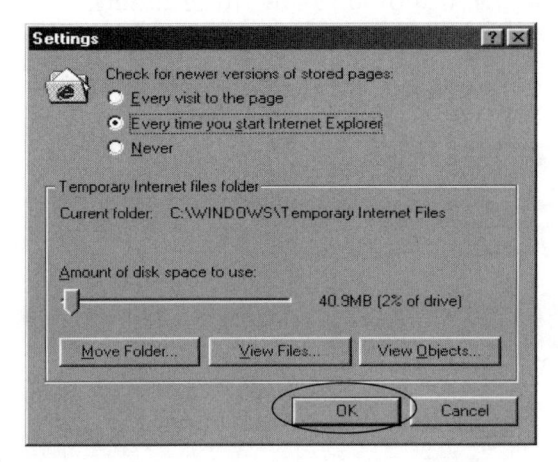

2 Click on *OK* to confirm your selections.

Updating to Internet Explorer 5

Internet Explorer 5 has been available since March 1999. As a user, you can update your current version 4 to the most recent version if you want to. There are few really exciting innovations, as any changes made are mainly cosmetic in nature, so it is not mandatory for you to use this update.

If you are perfectly happy using IE4, then just don't bother with the update. However, this book will adopt the new IE5 because it also gives Outlook Express a 'new look' – more about that later.

Updating to IE5 is very simple: all you need to do is find one of the many CD-ROMs supplied with computer magazines. If you do this you are guaranteed to find a completely free version of the installation. You will find the installation steps explained in the magazine itself, and you should follow these closely.

Insert the appropriate CD-ROM into your CD-ROM drive, select RUN from the START menu, and look for the IE5 installation file.

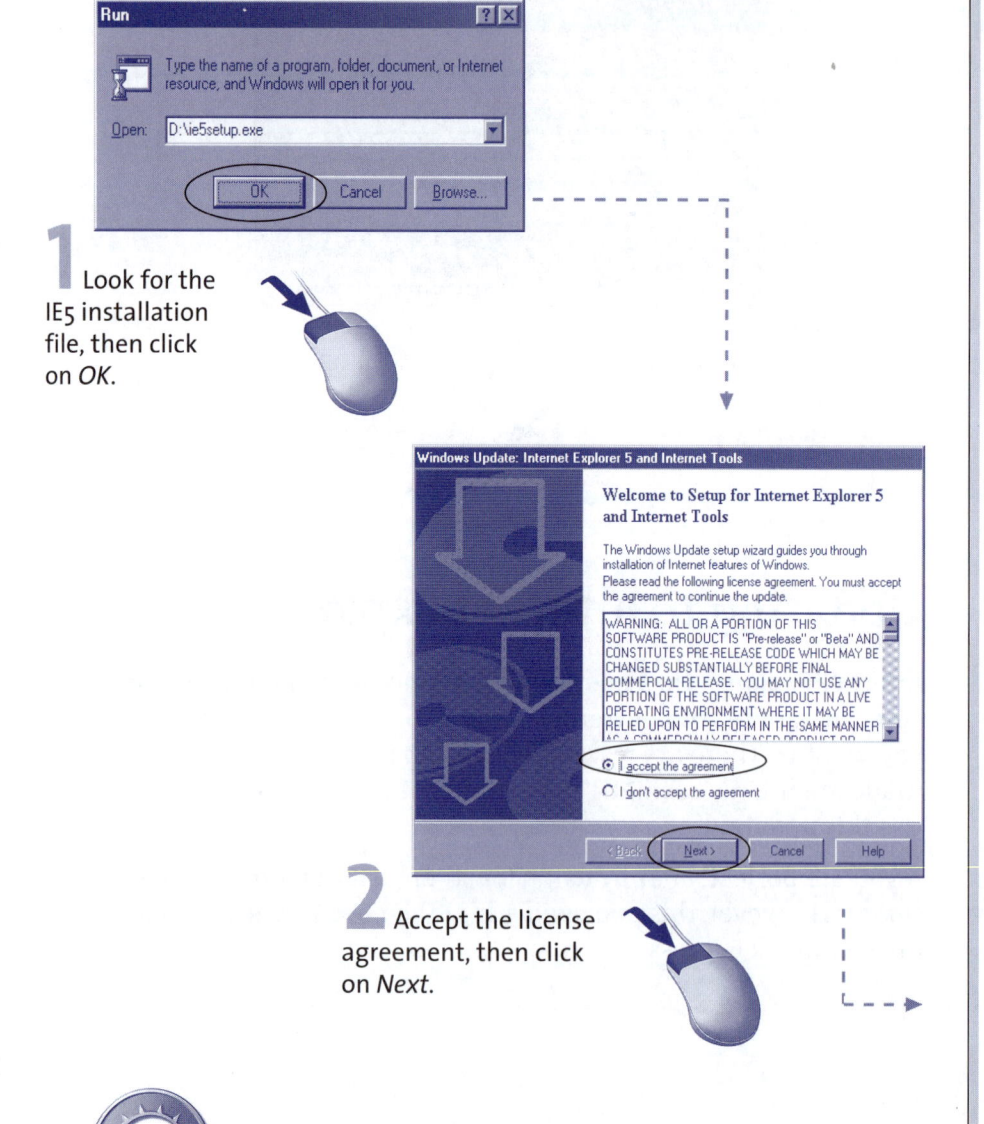

1 Look for the IE5 installation file, then click on *OK*.

2 Accept the license agreement, then click on *Next*.

64

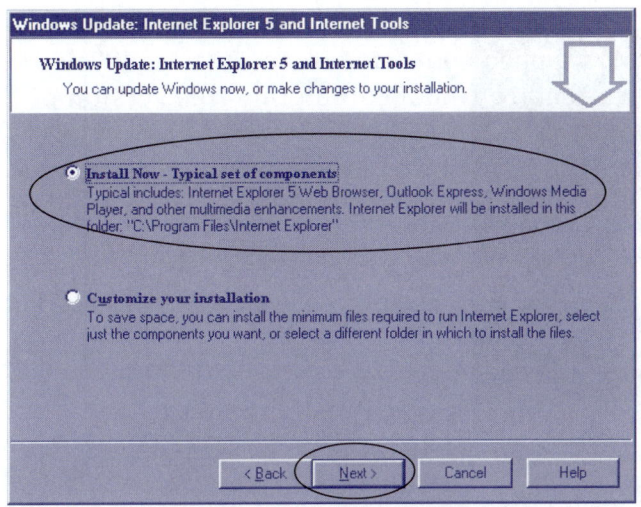

UPDATING TO INTERNET EXPLORER 5

Windows Update: Internet Explorer 5 and Internet Tools

You can update Windows now, or make changes to your installation.

⦿ **Install Now - Typical set of components**
Typical includes: Internet Explorer 5 Web Browser, Outlook Express, Windows Media Player, and other multimedia enhancements. Internet Explorer will be installed in this folder: "C:\Program Files\Internet Explorer"

○ **Customize your installation**
To save space, you can install the minimum files required to run Internet Explorer, select just the components you want, or select a different folder in which to install the files.

[< Back] [Next >] [Cancel] [Help]

3 Click on the *Install now – Typical set of components* radio button, then click on *Next*.

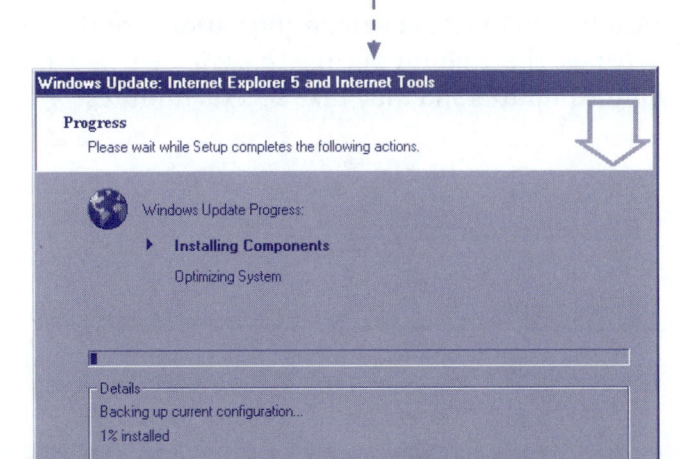

Windows Update: Internet Explorer 5 and Internet Tools

Progress
Please wait while Setup completes the following actions.

Windows Update Progress:
▶ **Installing Components**
  Optimizing System

Details
Backing up current configuration...
1% installed

[< Back] [Next >] [Cancel] [Help]

4 All the IE5 components will now be installed.

65

5 Click on *Finish*.

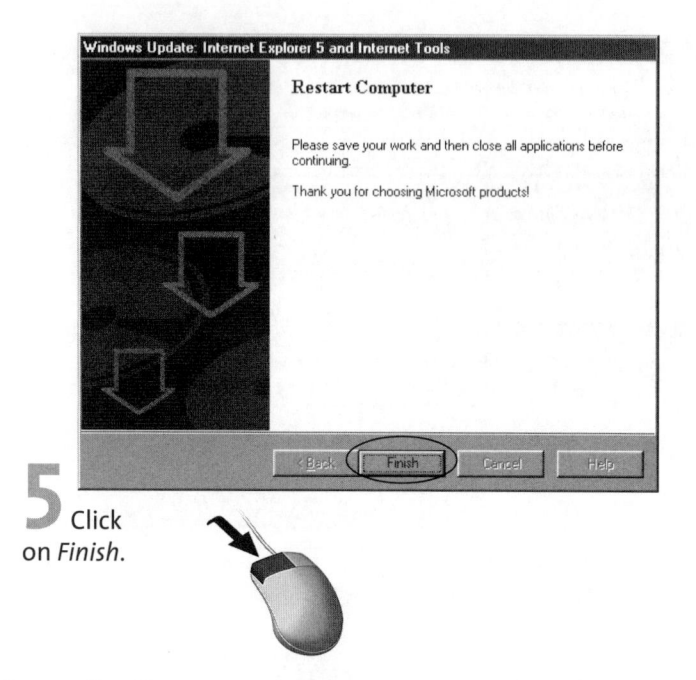

Windows 98 will now restart your computer in order to complete the installation process by updating various configuration and system settings. The amount of time this will take depends on the speed of your computer and may take several minutes.

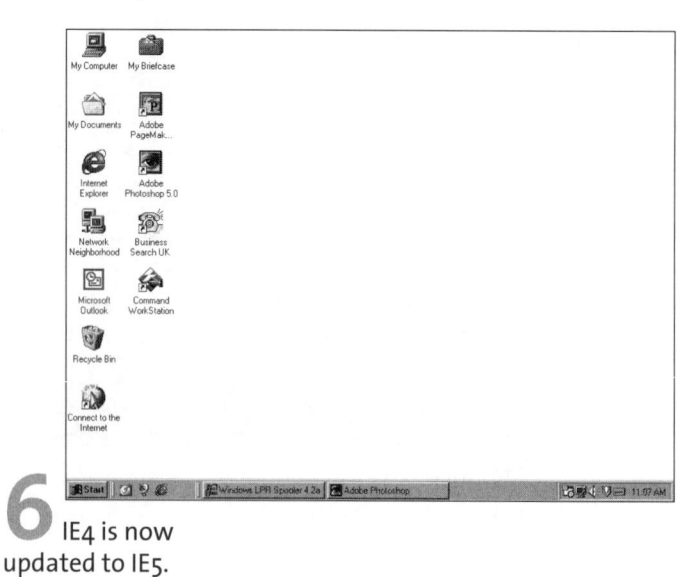

6 IE4 is now updated to IE5.

Your first steps in the World Wide Web

Imagine the World Wide Web as an enormous newsstand that spans the whole world. The many services offered by the Internet are arranged somewhat like newspapers – they are made up of individual pages, which you can leaf through using your Internet Explorer.

The Web browser has to have a target address in order to know where to look for the pages and content you require. The address would look something like this: *http://www.microsoft.co.uk*.

You are bound to have noticed an address like this in many different forms of media, for example in the newspapers, on the radio or television. But what do these symbols actually mean? This collection of full stops, forward slashes and abbreviations is known as a 'Uniform Resource Locator', **URL** for short. A URL is simply the address of a document or Web server on the Internet.

Since there is no directory of every Web page on the Internet, the creators of the system defined the URL as the path to be used (Locator) to reach the target (Resource), in such a way that it would look the same all over the world (Uniform).

The letters 'http://' written at the beginning of the address mean that all the data will be transferred according to the **Hypertext Transfer Protocol**. This refers to a standardised process by which pages from the World Wide Web (that is, the hypertext of a Web page) are transferred onto your computer. You know what a protocol is from the previous chapter but here is a quick refresher: a protocol controls the transport of data over a cable medium (in our case, the Internet) so that all the data arrives at the receiver's end in order, and nothing is lost on the way. Even if some data is lost, the transfer protocol will describe exactly how to deal with it. You will never notice any of this – all the functions of a transfer protocol run in the background, where you can't see them.

Let's break a URL down into its different parts:

http://www.shu.ac.uk/schools/cs/indesign/main.htm

- Microsoft Internet Explorer recognises the *http://* abbreviation and knows that it should use the HTTP transfer method. For us, this means that the required data will be available in the form of a WWW document.

- The next section is *shu.ac*, which means that you are moving to the Web site of Sheffield Hallam University.

- The detail *.uk* tells us that the WWW server is located in the United Kingdom.

- Once you arrive at the University's Web site, you will then be taken further into the section called *schools*, then into *cs* (the department of Computer Science).

- This department has a computer which acts as a Web server and has the required document ready.

- The document you want is stored on the computer in a directory called *indesign*.

- Finally, you access *main.htm*, which is a Web page written in a special language for display as a hypertext document.

Setting up a new home page

Start up Internet Explorer from your Windows 98 desktop by double-clicking on the *Explorer* icon. A window will then appear which will allow you to connect to your Internet Service Provider. Once this connection is successfully established, Internet Explorer will open the Web browser's pre-defined **home page**. The first time you use it, you will be taken to Internet Explorer's introduction page on the Microsoft Web server.

YOUR FIRST STEPS IN THE WORLD WIDE WEB

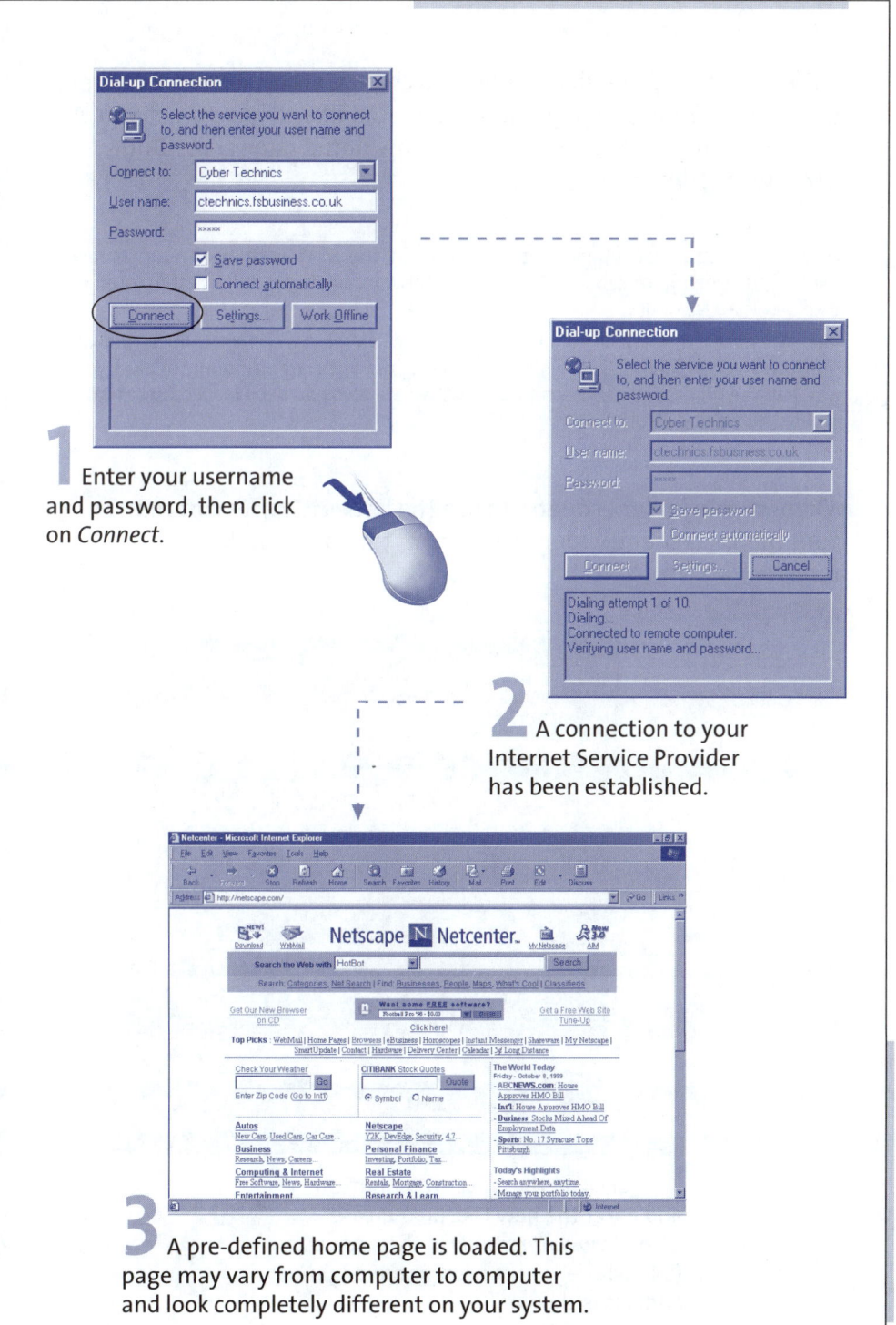

1 Enter your username and password, then click on *Connect*.

2 A connection to your Internet Service Provider has been established.

3 A pre-defined home page is loaded. This page may vary from computer to computer and look completely different on your system.

In the next step you will learn how to change your Internet Explorer's home page. Think of a page that you would like to have greet you. As I am a great movie fan, I decided to set my home page accordingly – *http://www.film.co.uk*.

> The *Explorer* icon in the upper right-hand corner of the window changes its appearance when data is being transferred. This means that you can always tell whether Internet Explorer is active or not.
>
> You also have the possibility of loading just part of a Web page. If you think it is taking too long to download a page, which is often the case with large amounts of data, you can halt the process by clicking on *Stop*. All the data that had been loaded up to that point will then be displayed.

When your browser is open, choose the INTERNET OPTIONS command from the TOOLS menu. Open the *General* tab in the dialog box that appears.

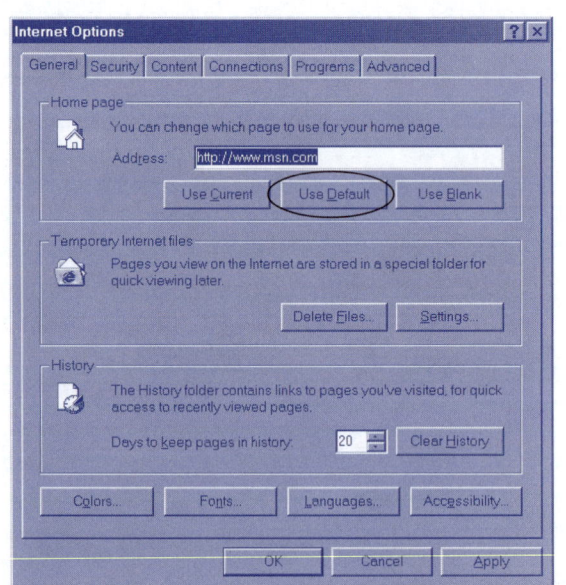

4 Click on the *Use Default* button and enter the new URL (in our case *http://www.film.co.uk*) in the *Address* field where your current home page address is shown.

YOUR FIRST STEPS IN THE WORLD WIDE WEB

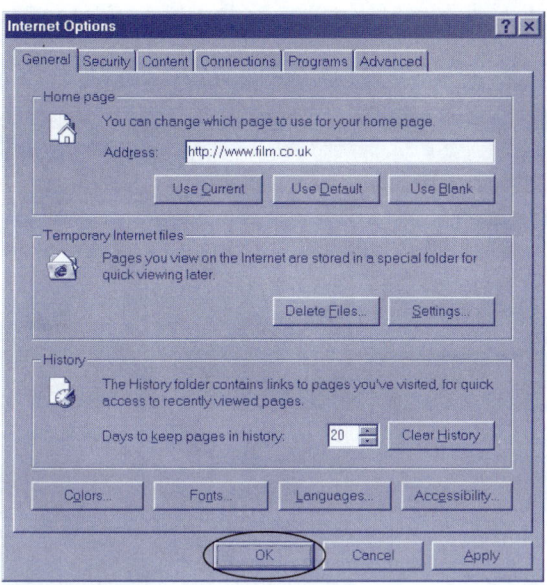

5 Confirm your choices by clicking on *OK* and restart Internet Explorer.

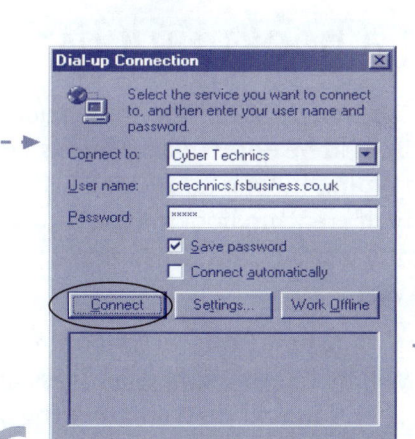

6 Enter your user name and password. Then click on *Connect*.

7 The browser will now open with the home page you just defined.

Creating a bookmark list

While you were setting up your new home page, perhaps you wondered how a new URL could be entered and then saved, so as to avoid having to keep typing in long addresses. Every Web browser offers the opportunity of creating bookmarks. You can use these bookmarks to save frequently visited URLs. This means you can create a list of all your favourite Web pages.

Restart Microsoft Internet Explorer and open an Internet connection. Your first step will be to enter a new address and then add this to your bookmark list. You will then create a themed bookmark group for this entry.

CREATING A BOOKMARK LIST

1 Enter your user name and password. Then click on *Connect*.

2 After deleting the address of your home page, enter a new URL in the *Address* field. Terminate your input by pressing the ⏎ key and the new page will be loaded.

You will now add this page to your bookmark list so that you can access it whenever you want.

73

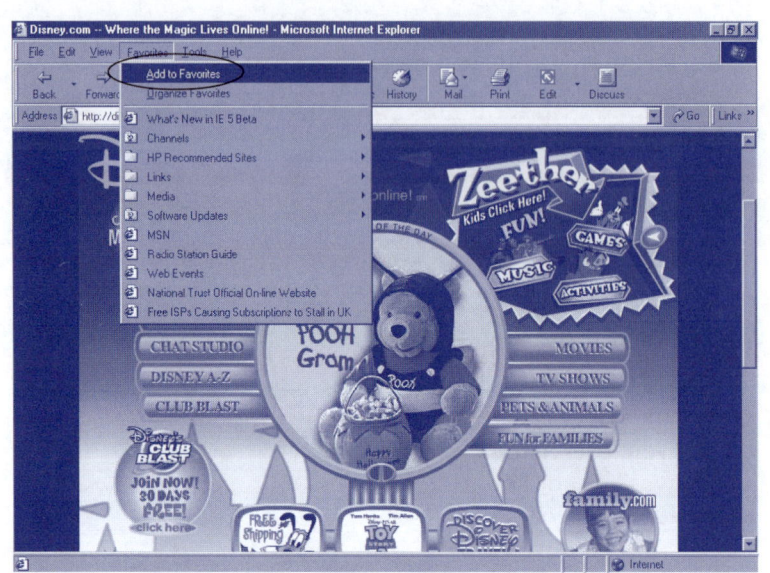

3 Open the Favorites menu and select the Add to Favorites command.

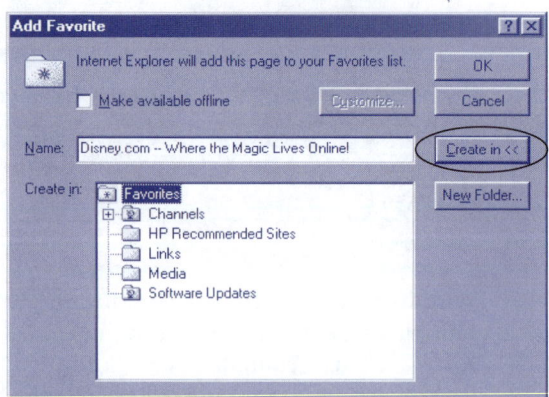

4 Give the Web site a new name, or leave it as it is. Leave the *Make available offline* checkbox unmarked, then click on *Create in*.

CREATING A BOOKMARK LIST

At this point you will be able to create particular folders to contain the URLs you would like to include in the bookmark list. You are now going to create a folder named *Disney*.

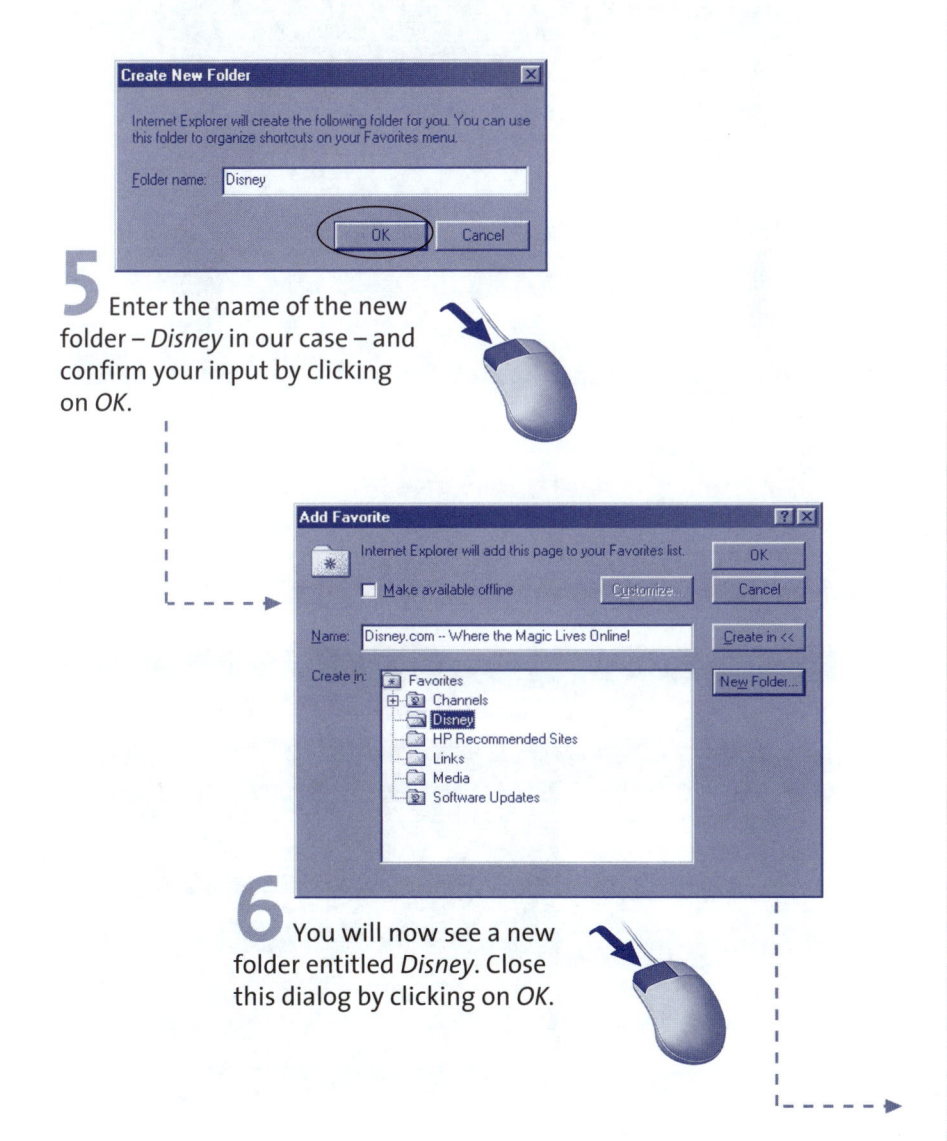

5 Enter the name of the new folder – *Disney* in our case – and confirm your input by clicking on *OK*.

6 You will now see a new folder entitled *Disney*. Close this dialog by clicking on *OK*.

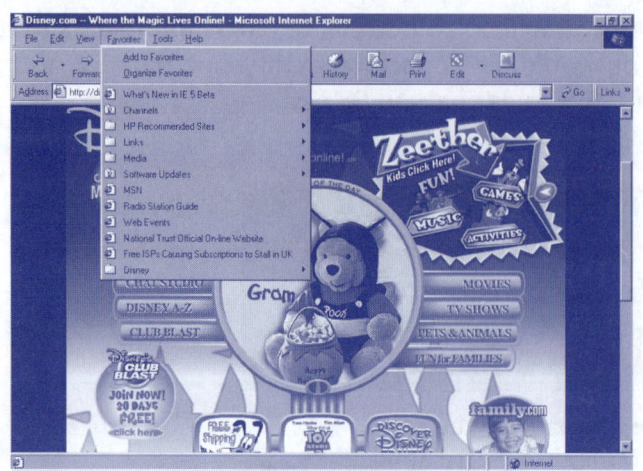

7 In FAVORITES you will now see an entry on the subject of Disney.

You can also open your bookmark list by clicking on the *Favorites* button on the Internet Explorer 5 toolbar.

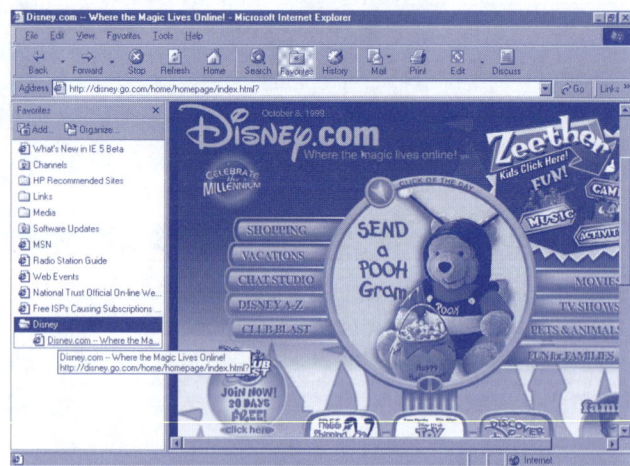

8 Click on the *Favorites* button on the IE5 toolbar. You will now see a different arrangement of your bookmark list.

The Internet Explorer's user interface

You have created the first entry for your bookmark list and are now ready to enter new **Web addresses** yourself. So that you can feel comfortable moving around in a Web page, you will first learn a little about the main Internet Explorer user interface.

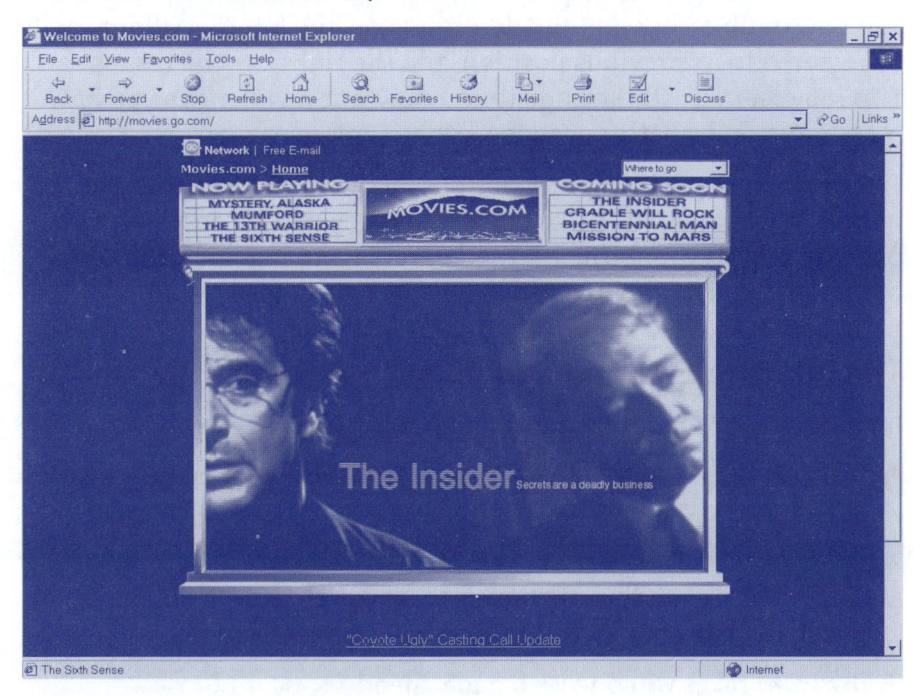

The Internet Explorer screen

The picture above shows you the full Internet Explorer screen. This is divided up into three sections – a menu bar, a toolbar and an address field in which you can enter URLs.

To the right of the menu bar you can see Internet Explorer's status icon. When the Explorer is active, that is when data is being transferred, you will see the globe spinning. The Explorer has another button bar that isn't visible at first. This bar is there to support the first-time Internet user and makes particular Internet applications directly available.

77

You can get to this bar and its additional functions with the aid of the field marked *Links*, underneath the status icon, to the right of the *Go* button.

When you double-click on this button, the address field will disappear and the other buttons will take its place. All the links provided on this bar call up offers from the Microsoft home page. If you now double-click on the *Address* button, the Internet address will be restored to its previous position, and the Links bar will disappear. This may seem a little strange to you now, but it will mean you have more room and a better overview of the Explorer screen.

On the other hand, if you click on the Links field and, keeping the mouse button pressed, drag it down a little, you will see the Links bar open up and stay underneath the Address field. Dragging the Links bar up makes it disappear and shows the Link field as usual.

The Internet Explorer's toolbar

In the Internet Explorer, the most important functions can be accessed by means of buttons on a toolbar.

- *Back* returns you to a previously loaded Web page. If you have not yet loaded any pages, this button will be deactivated.
- *Forward* takes you one Web page ahead.
- *Stop* interrupts the transfer of the Web page currently being loaded from the Internet.
- *Refresh* updates the currently loaded Web page by reloading it.
- *Home* loads the home page you specified in Internet Explorer.
- *Search* takes you to a particular Web page on the Microsoft Web server. Microsoft has incorporated many well-known search engines into this page. Here you can decide on a search engine and tell it to look for a particular topic or term. You will find more information on search engines in the next chapter, 'On the hunt for information – search engines in the WWW'.

- *Favorites* takes you to the entries for bookmark addresses which you archived for later use.
- *History* saves all the Web pages that you have visited in the past few days. You can use this *History* command to open Web pages without needing to know their URL. When you click on the *History* button, a menu with all the necessary information will appear on the left-hand border of the Internet Explorer 5 screen. The folder entitled *Today* contains all the Web pages you have visited that day. If you want to, you can specify the length of time you want visited pages to be saved. Open the TOOLS menu and choose the INTERNET OPTIONS command. In the section called *History* you can enter a value for the number of days after which a page should be removed from the *History* folder.
- *E-mail* starts up the e-mail program that was installed as part of the Internet Explorer 5 standard installation.
- *Print* allows you to print the current Web page.

The Active Desktop

After installing Internet Explorer 5, you will have noticed that your Windows desktop had changed. This is due to the Active Desktop, which considerably modifies the conventional Windows 98 interface. Until now, your desktop's only task was to house various object icons, such as printers, folders and links to all sorts of things. This is now all somewhat different. Move the mouse pointer onto any icon on your desktop. After a moment, information about the highlighted icon will appear (as long as it is a Microsoft application icon and already updated for this kind of use). This modification, however, is just the tip of the iceberg – the real innovations happen much deeper inside the operating system. Microsoft has exchanged the entire, passive Windows 98 desktop for that of the window-less Internet Explorer 5. Internet Explorer 5 is no longer a closed application, but rather a deep-rooted component of your Windows operating system.

You will get a first impression of the new interface when you open any window – for example, that of the control panel. Looking at this screen you will notice the following: the tool and menu bars now look like those of Internet Explorer, and include the standard *Cut* and *Copy* icons. These two frequently used functions are now easily accessible with a click of the mouse, directly from inside the screen of the corresponding window. Furthermore, you can now allocate a different background to each screen – admittedly a fairly unimportant exercise, but fun nonetheless. As you can see, every window has a separate address field. Entering any Web address in this field will immediately open up Internet Explorer 5. You can specify the style in which your window is going to be displayed by clicking on *Folder Options* in the VIEW menu.

Using the so-called Web style will make the content of your window look and work like that of a Web browser. You will be able to open folders or files with a simple mouse click, as you are used to doing

THE ACTIVE DESKTOP

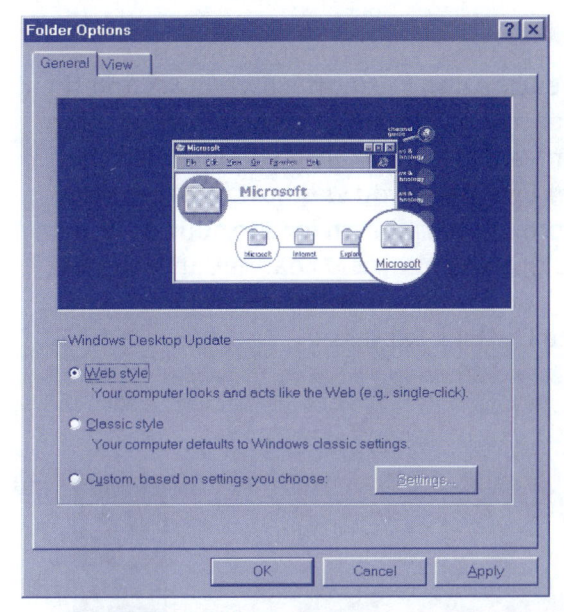

with Web pages. If you decide on this display method, every folder and application on your desktop will be underlined, just like a hyperlink on a Web page.

To set this up, you will need to open a folder and choose the FOLDER OPTIONS command in the VIEW menu. Selecting the *Web style* radio button will activate this type of display.

This display method will save you a mouse click and means you don't have to adapt the way you work when you move from a Web page to the desktop.

81

What's new in the taskbar

The changes made to the desktop don't just affect windows and their external appearance. The central, pivotal point of Windows 98 – the start menu and the taskbar – are also affected. If you installed the standard version of Internet Explorer 5, you will now find four icons in the taskbar. These are, from left to right: an icon to start up the desktop immediately (a desk); an icon to view channels in Internet Explorer 5 (an antenna); an icon to start up Internet Explorer 5 and, finally, an icon for launching Outlook Express.

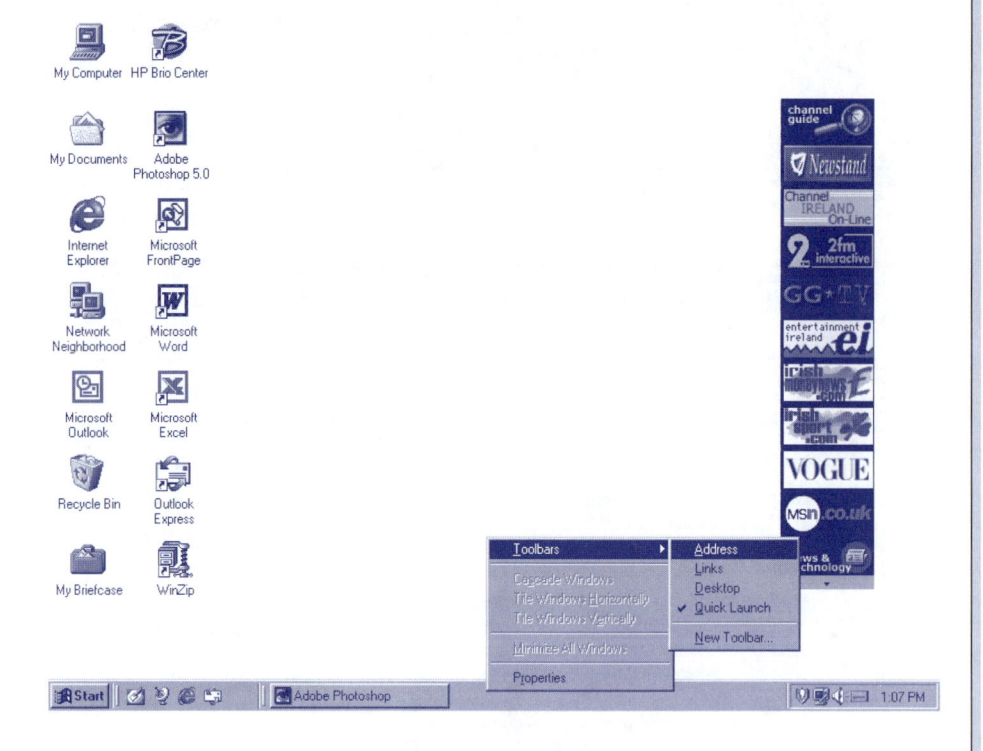

Click with the right-hand mouse button on any empty space in the taskbar. A context menu will appear, which you can use to insert additional icons into the taskbar.

You can add new options to the taskbar by clicking on an entry in the menu.

- ADDRESS – you can use this to access local folders as easily as Internet pages.
- DESKTOP – contains a list of everything currently present on your desktop.
- QUICK LAUNCH – this option is supplied as standard and contains icons for Internet Explorer, Outlook Express, channels and for freeing the desktop.
- NEW TOOLBAR – allows you to arrange your taskbar exactly as you want it.

Saving a file to the hard disk

When you receive data from the Internet, Internet Explorer 5 loads these into your Web browser. This means that the files you need are already located on your computer. This allows you to save important, interesting documents onto your hard disk and to call them up again at some time in the future, without having to open another Internet connection.

This is not all: Internet Explorer can not only display the saved documents in their original layout, it can also include the hyperlinks to other documents and WWW servers.

There are several methods you can use to save your Web files to disk: as complete Web pages (including all of the linked images), as Web archives for e-mailing, as Web pages without images, and as pure text. When pages are saved completely, an additional folder is created for each page, which contains the images. This does not, however, work for video or audio sequences – only 'normal' images can be stored. However, this is not really a serious problem, as most of the important information is usually contained in the text and in still images.

Start up your Web browser as usual, either by double-clicking on the Internet Explorer 5 icon on your desktop or by clicking once on the one in the taskbar.

When you choose the FILE/SAVE AS command, a window will appear, which allows you to save the loaded Web document onto your hard disk.

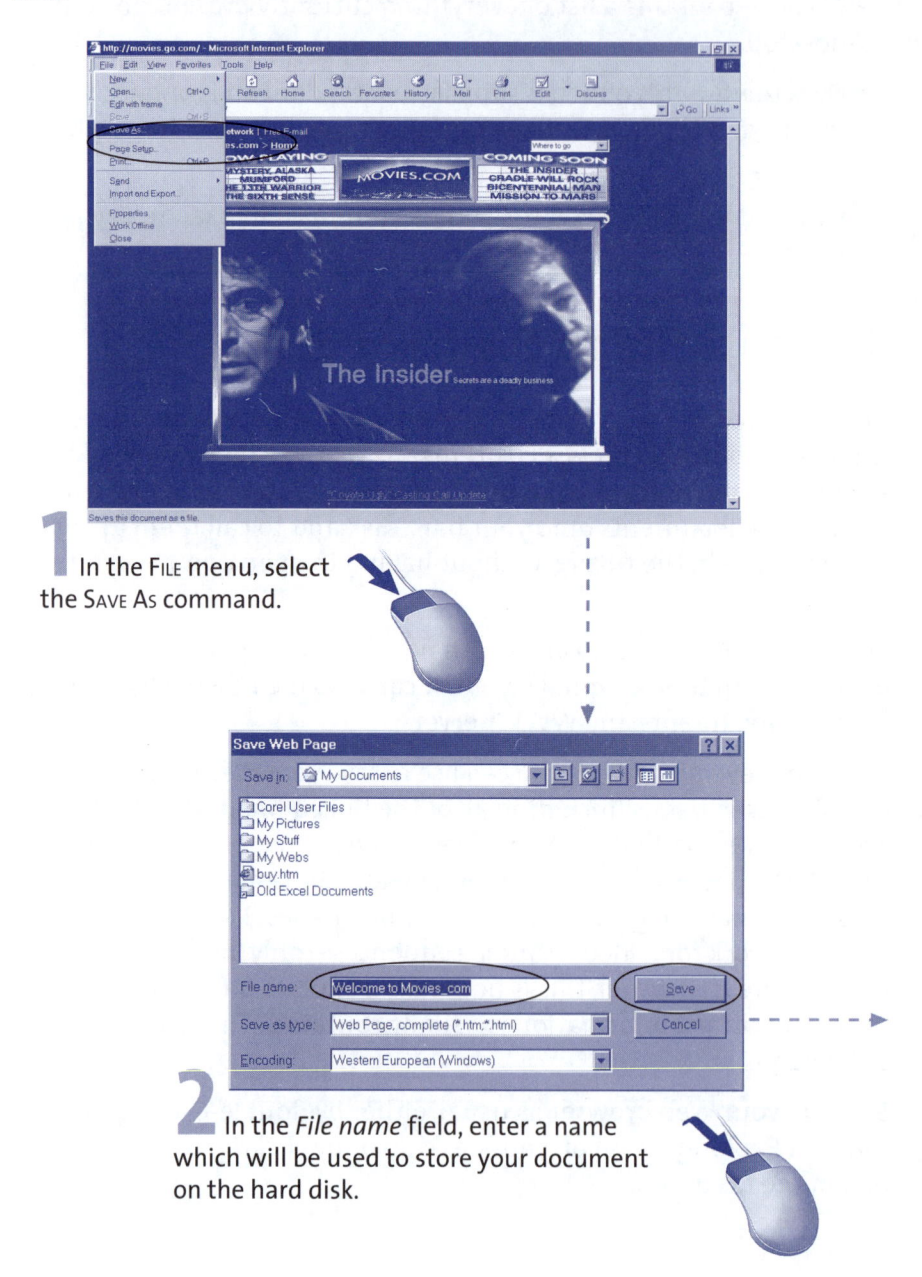

1 In the FILE menu, select the SAVE AS command.

2 In the *File name* field, enter a name which will be used to store your document on the hard disk.

SAVING A FILE TO THE HARD DISK

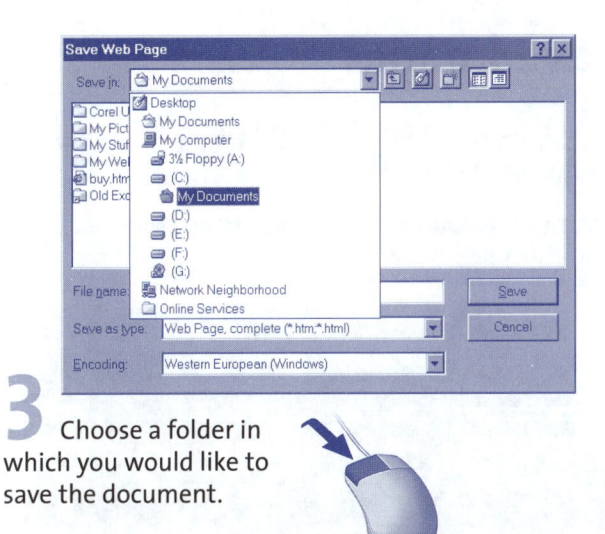

3 Choose a folder in which you would like to save the document.

Make sure that the file you are saving retains the extension *htm* or *html*. This means you can be certain that the file will be saved in **HTML format**, which is the format your Web browser can read.

If you want to, you can also save Web documents as pure text. This means that you can load these Web pages into your text editing program and do further work on them. To do this, you just have to choose the file extension *.txt* in the *Save as type* drop-down list.

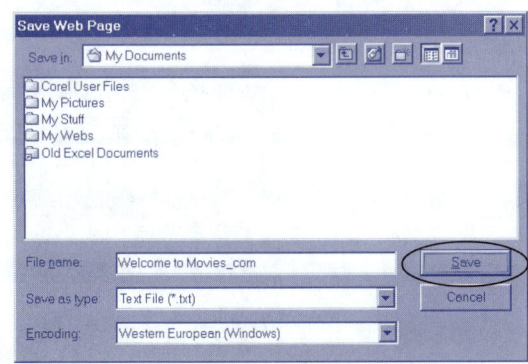

4 In the *Save as type* drop-down list, select the entry *Text File (*.txt)*. Then click on *Save*.

85

Loading saved pages

The reloading of Web pages in the Web browser is as simple as saving them. Just open up your Web browser.

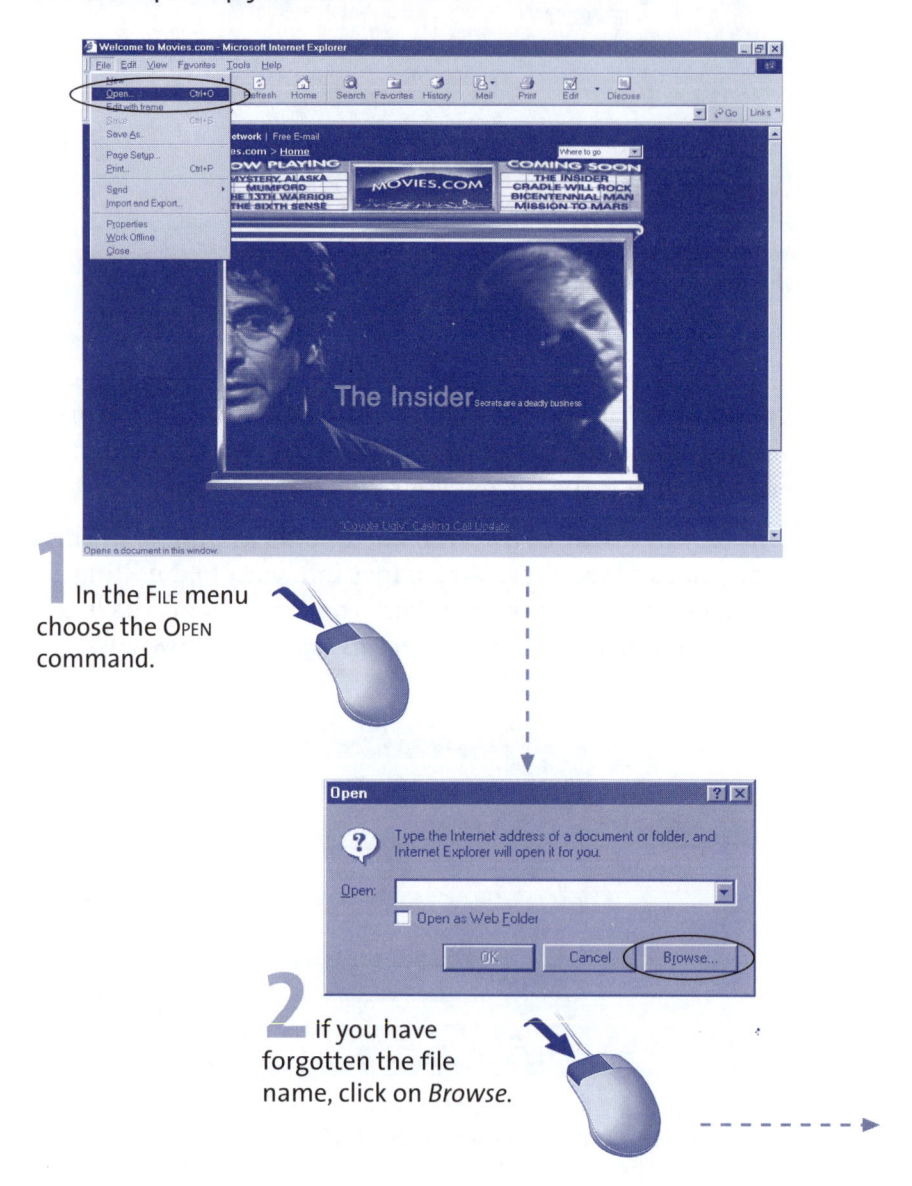

1 In the FILE menu choose the OPEN command.

2 If you have forgotten the file name, click on *Browse*.

LOADING SAVED PAGES

3 Click on the desired file, then click on *Open*.

4 Confirm your choice by clicking on *OK*.

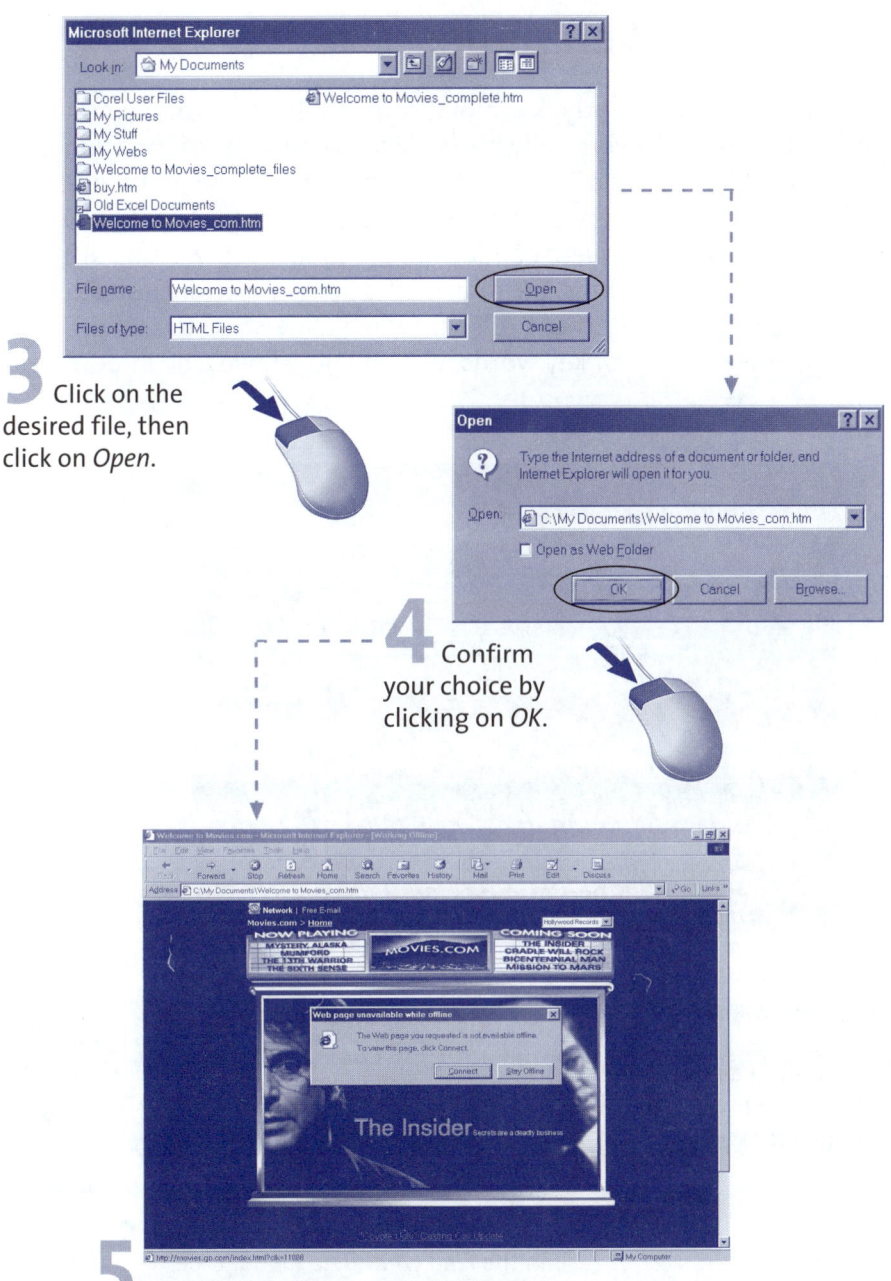

5 The required page is now loaded from your hard disk – sometimes without graphics or with links missing.

87

Browsing Web pages

In time, you will certainly download some Web pages onto your computer. You will eventually build up an **archive** of information on various subjects. As is often the way with archives, you will soon start to lose sight of the overview and will instead start to wonder where you saved a particular piece of information. To save you wasting all your time searching for things, the developers at Microsoft included a **search** function in Internet Explorer, which allows you to search though a Web page for key words. You will now have a go at doing this.

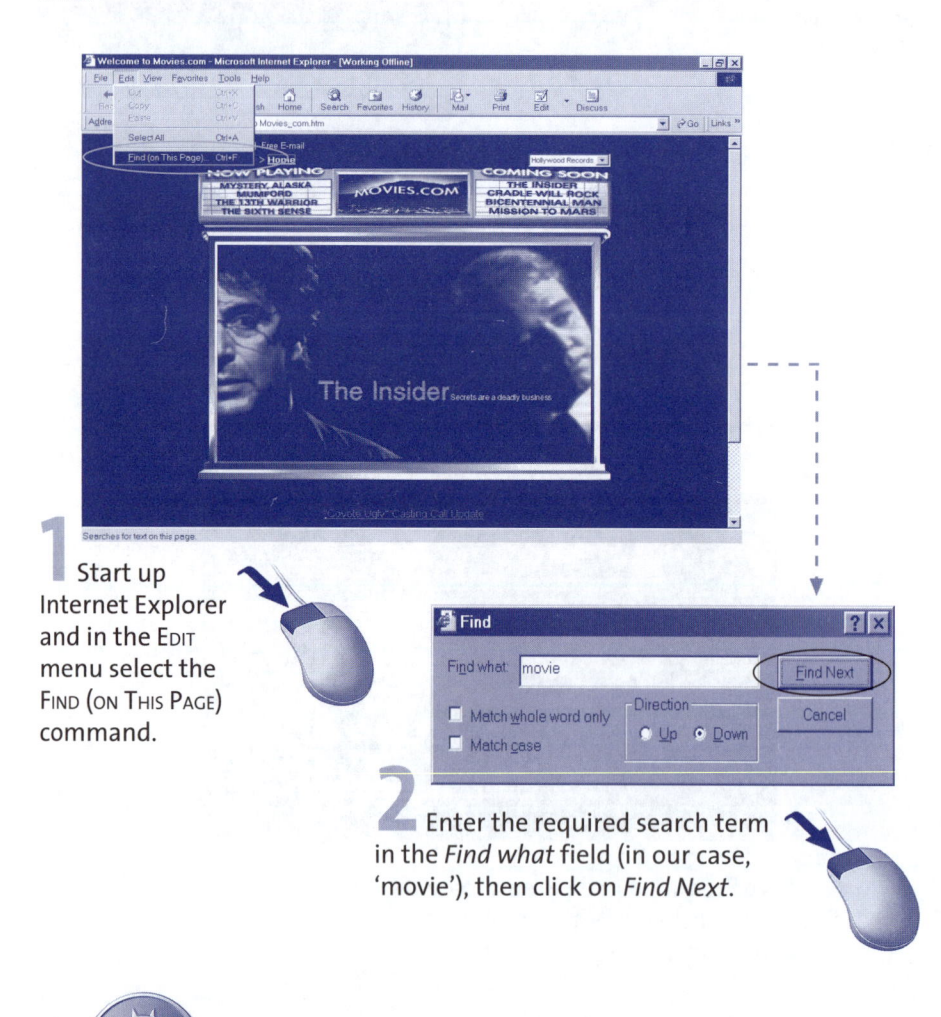

1 Start up Internet Explorer and in the EDIT menu select the FIND (ON THIS PAGE) command.

2 Enter the required search term in the *Find what* field (in our case, 'movie'), then click on *Find Next*.

Printing Web pages

You can instruct the computer to look out for *upper* or *lowercase spelling* by marking the *Match case* checkbox. Internet Explorer now searches through the whole document for the term you specified. If the search is successful, the Explorer will stop the search process and highlight the term in the document.

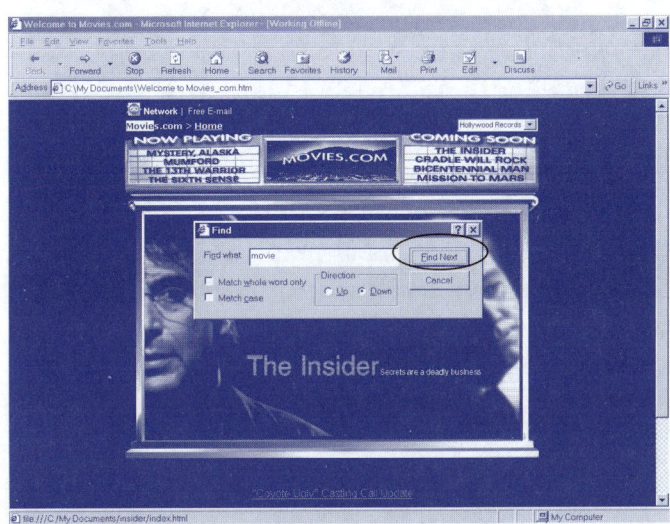

3 Click on *Find Next* to continue the search process.

Printing Web pages

You may decide that you want to **print** some pages from your Web archive.

> **WHAT'S THIS?**
> **HTML** is the programming language in which Web pages are written.

Microsoft has thought of this as well. With Internet Explorer, you have the choice of either printing Web pages directly from the Internet, that is, when you are online, or printing documents from your **hard disk**.

Start up your Internet Explorer and load a saved HTML page into the browser.

1 Select the FILE/PRINT menu command.

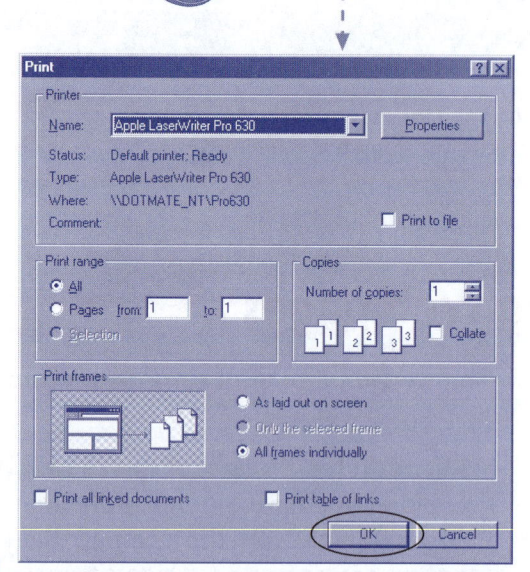

2 Click on *OK*, and your Web page will be printed out (provided you have installed an appropriate printer under Windows 98).

If you don't like the basic settings which determine how a Web page is put on paper, you can change them to what you want. To do this, open the FILE menu in Internet Explorer and select the PAGE SETUP command.

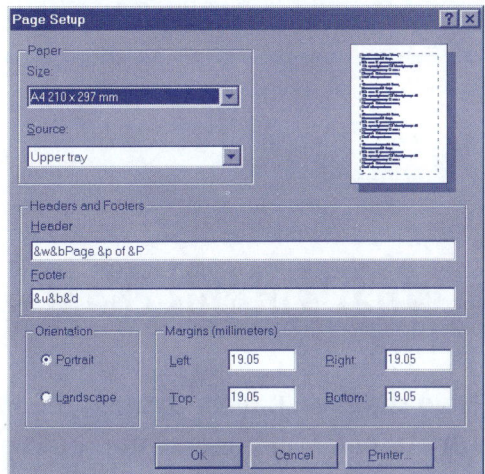

3 Here you can specify page format, margins and paper size. Confirm your adjustments by clicking on *OK*.

You have to laugh – the best computer messages

If one only knew what the heck of an error the machine is talking about!

91

3
On the hunt for Information

What's in this chapter:

Now that you have mastered the basic functions of Microsoft Internet Explorer, you are ready to learn how to use a search engine on the WWW. You will then closely study one particular example of this. You will also learn about the differences between a search engine and a Web catalogue, and how they can be put to most efficient use when searching the Internet.

You already know about:

Modems & Co.	10
The importance of software	16
Updating to Internet Explorer 5	63
Taking your first steps in the World Wide Web	67
Browsing and printing Web pages	88

You are going to learn about:

How a search engine works	94
Using the Lycos search engine	98
The primeval Internet: Gopher	104

How does a search engine work?

As you already know, the Internet is so huge that it is getting steadily more difficult to find the exact piece of information you are looking for. To get a grip on this problem, tools for searching the World Wide Web, called **search engines**, have been developed. These search engines are also called **Web crawlers** by those in the know because of the way they crawl through the Internet seeking out the requested information. Search engines are the most frequently visited sites on the Internet and, as a rule, are the best starting point for any 'Web excursion'. You will also see the term **Web spider** used in conjunction with search engines. Spiders are programs that hunt through the WWW for documents by following hyperlinks in Web pages.

A search engine will frequently use such a spider, which follows set rules when searching through the Internet. When a spider locates a homepage containing the requested information, a so-called **software agent** is instructed to collect the URLs and the document and to send the information to some indexing software. The indexing software then receives the documents and the URLs from the agent. Subsequently, the program extracts particular pieces of information on the topic in question and puts them all in a list – the data is indexed. The various search engines differ where this process is concerned. Some index every single word in the document, others index only specific words. Yet others only use the title and the headlines of the various Web pages. All this information is then saved in the search engine's database.

> **WHAT'S THIS?**
> A **software agent** hunts through the Internet for information, which you, the customer, have requested.

When using a search engine to find certain information, you usually enter keywords that outline your area of interest. When you have done this, your search engine's database will be searched for the information you have entered. If the search engine is successful, the results will be sent back in the form of an HTML page. Again, the various search engines work differently in this respect. Some of them weight the results to decide which Web sites correspond most accurately to your search terms. Many search engines show the first few lines of the document so that you can see immediately what you will find on the corresponding Web server.

If you now click on the link of one of the listed documents, a connection will be opened to this document or Web server.

What are the differences between search engines and Web catalogues?

It's quite simple: a catalogue system offers you weighted pages, sorted according to subject.

> An **index** is a table of data found during a search process.

Your hunt for information about a particular subject, firm or organisation is made much easier by a clear system of structuring and **indexing**. Hidden behind every Web catalogue is a whole host of industrious daemons. These daemons are constantly searching for new Web servers, which are then sorted according to subject and added to the catalogue with a short accompanying description. This type of editorial process greatly simplifies your search. In this way, a Web catalogue does not need to search the entire Internet for the search terms you supplied. Instead, it draws on its own vast data store to find Web page addresses, rather like the catalogue of a mail order firm.

In comparison, a search engine hunts through the entire Internet for every single word you specify. For this reason it is extremely important that you use the most exact search terms possible.

You will see that many search engines advertise themselves on the basis of the number of registered entries – which can sometimes be in the millions. Don't let yourself be taken in by this. A well-organised and properly edited Web catalogue will produce significantly fewer results than a search server (also known as a **robot-generated** index), but these results will be much closer to your original search terms.

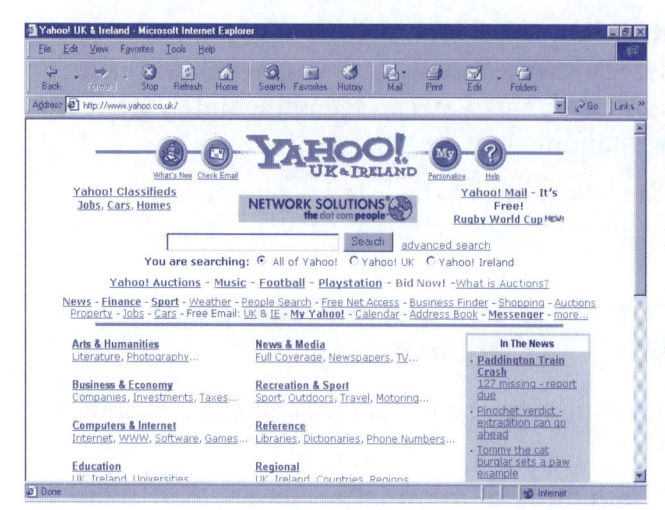

A Web catalogue is well suited to searching for a given topic or subject area. However, it is not so good at finding explanations for a specific question. Some well-known search servers are Lycos and Yahoo!, both of which present you with a summary table divided into sections about the various different aspects of everyday life.

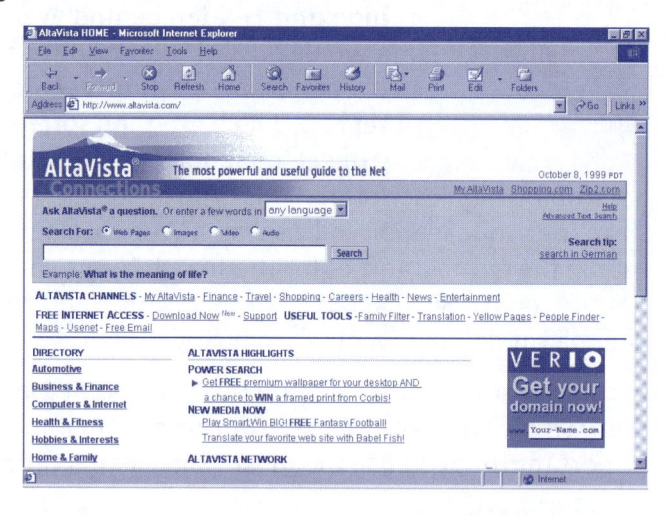

You can use these to isolate your chosen topic and then move more and more into the hierarchy of the Web catalogue. The more you limit your topic, the more exact the results from the Web catalogue will be. Some Web catalogues offer you a way of linking two or more of your search terms together. For example, if you want to find information about the history of the Internet, you must link the two terms – history and Internet – by means of an **'AND' operation**. Not all Web catalogues offer this possibility; it makes sense to find out which ones do.

A search engine is essentially made up of three parts. The first part is the actual information gatherer, the so-called 'robot', 'spider' or 'crawler', which moves through the Internet, automatically searching through pages. The mountain of information it finds is then sent to a central control point, the 'index'. The second component is the **indexing software**, which is responsible for structuring the gathered data and making it searchable.

The third component evaluates the search requests and sends them to the data computer, from where the search results are presented to the user.

A few search tips

You will certainly have heard the saying that 'all roads lead to Rome' – well, if not all, at least quite a lot – and experienced Internet users in particular go on all the time about it.

> There are various WWW servers on the Internet which have links to all the major search engines. When using these, you only need to enter your search term once and it is then sent to every search server and catalogue. This saves you from manually working your way through all of them individually. In particular, colleges and universities have set up this kind of service.

When searching for a particular piece of information on the Internet, you will need to revise the way you think. Think like a computer: the logical connection between search terms becomes all-important, while the factual overall content of the chosen topic shifts to the background. This means that you need to think of particular, generic terms for the topic. With this purpose in mind, you should make use of the extended search options offered by the search engines. For example, it would be pointless to search for the words 'Internet' or 'salt'. The **hit list** would include hundreds of thousands of results. What you really need to do is define a context area for your chosen subject. For example, if you want to find out about salt extraction in the Red Sea, you should not use terms such as 'chemistry', 'minerals' or 'mining' in your search list, as these will produce little of any use.

Rather, it would be better to include the search terms 'salt', 'nutrition', 'Red Sea' or similarly relevant expressions.

Be careful, however, where you use the 'AND' connection: too many such connections may produce no results at all, as the search server's database simply isn't big enough. It is more sensible to delimit and vary your terms one step at a time.

Generally speaking, you can use '+' or 'AND' to link words together. Using these **operators** tells the search engine that all the terms listed must appear in the results list. In the same way, a minus sign, '–', or the word '**NOT**' will make sure the word that follows is excluded: this word must not appear in the results list. You can link several words together by using quotation marks, for example, 'Tony Blair', 'Italian pop music'.

How this is written differs from server to server. Most search server operators, however, will tell you how their system works.

Using the Lycos search engine

After wading through all that theory, it is now time to put what you have learnt into practice.

Please imagine for a minute that you are interested in searching the Internet for photos of the last Mars mission.

Start up Internet Explorer and open an Internet connection. Then enter the Web page of our Web catalogue, for example *http://www.lycos.com*, and type in the search terms 'NASA' and 'Mars'. Connect the terms with 'AND'.

USING THE LYCOS SEARCH ENGINE

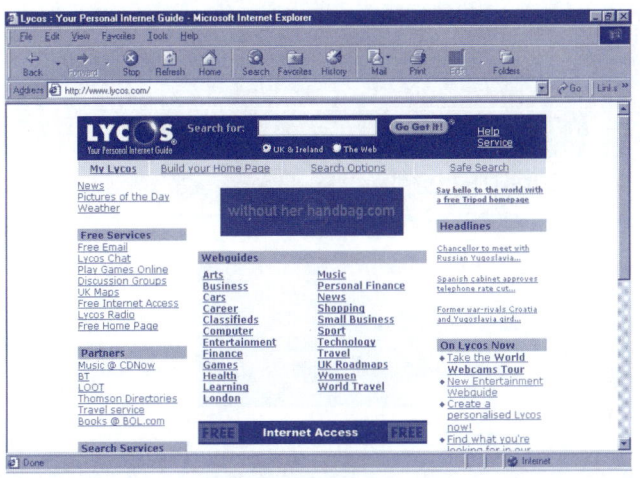

1 Here is the Lycos Web catalogue with the URL *http://www.lycos.com*.

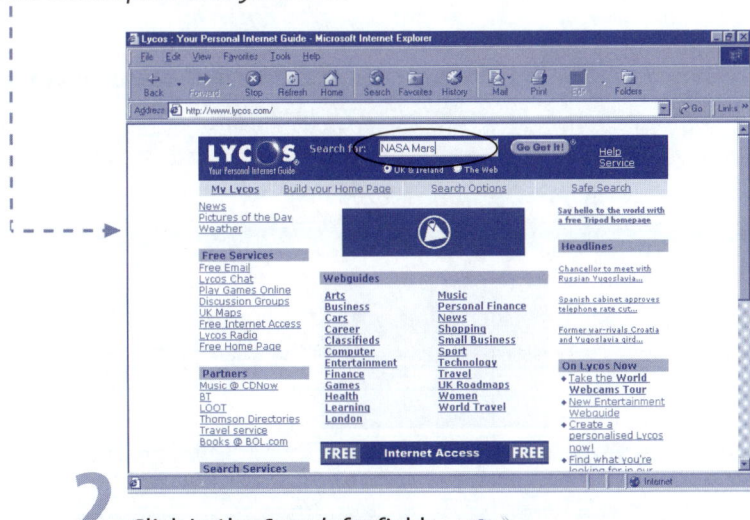

2 Click in the *Search for* field and type in the terms *NASA* and *Mars* with a space in between.

After a while, the Web catalogue produces every page that contains both of these terms and puts them into a list. You can use your mouse to move directly to the Web page containing the required information.

99

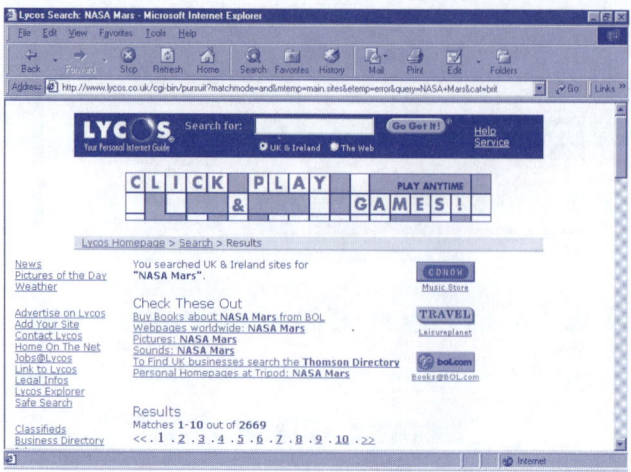

3 Many results of your search request will appear.

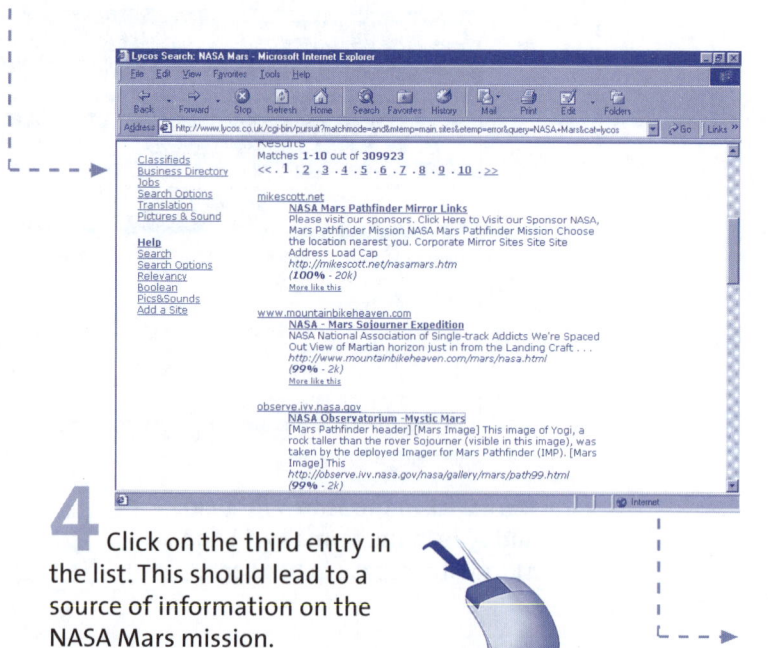

4 Click on the third entry in the list. This should lead to a source of information on the NASA Mars mission.

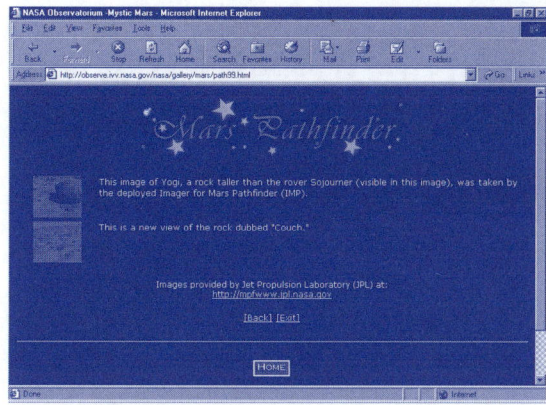

5 The page you requested is now shown.

The catalogue

Up to now, you have directly entered a **search term** to find your required document. You are now going to use the catalogue run by 'Web.com'.

Start up Internet Explorer and enter the address *http://www.Web.com*.

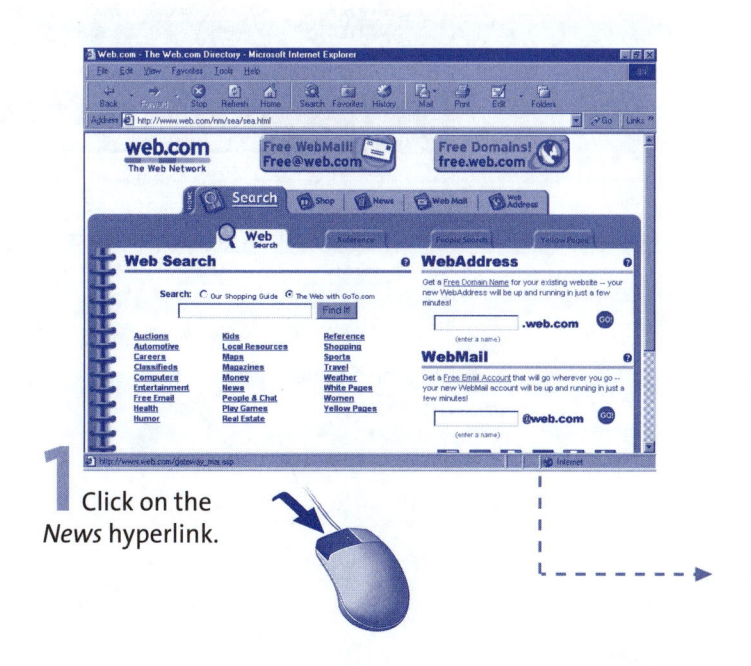

1 Click on the *News* hyperlink.

2 Click on the *News Guide* hyperlink.

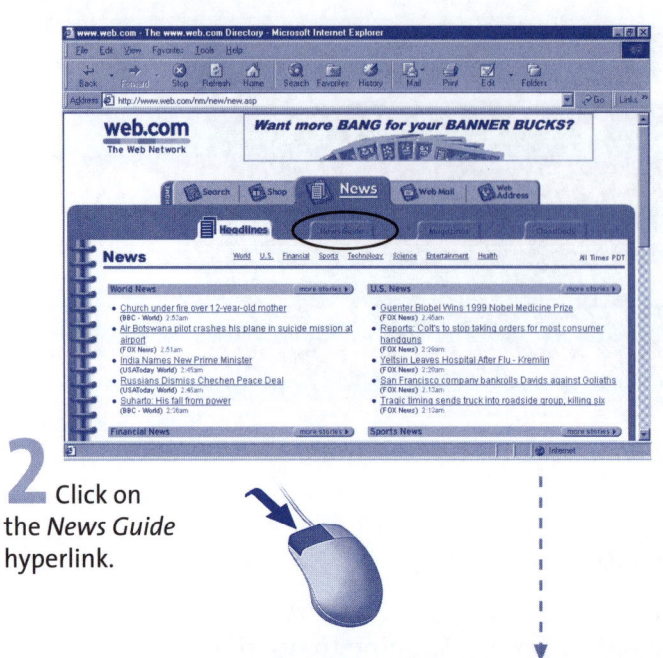

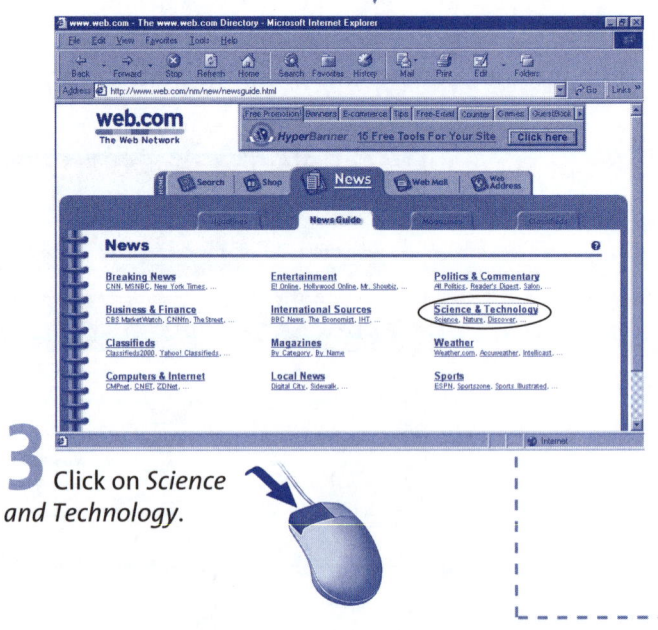

3 Click on *Science and Technology*.

Using the Lycos search engine

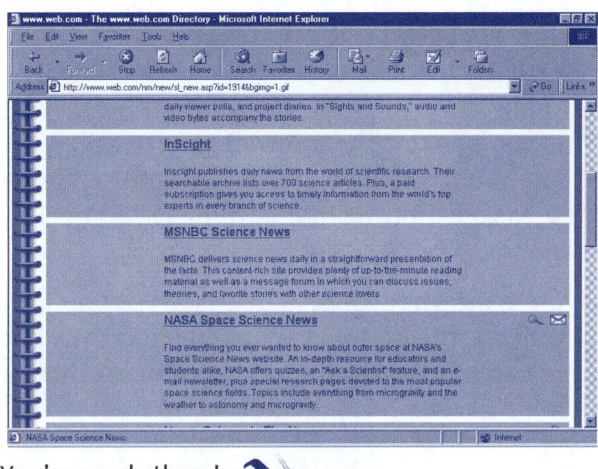

4 You're nearly there! Click on *NASA Space Science News*.

The deeper you move into the Web catalogue, the closer you will get to your goal. You will find yourself here almost at the very end of the directory structure – all the hyperlinks concerning space science are listed here. From here you can move directly to the WWW servers which deal with the subject of space.

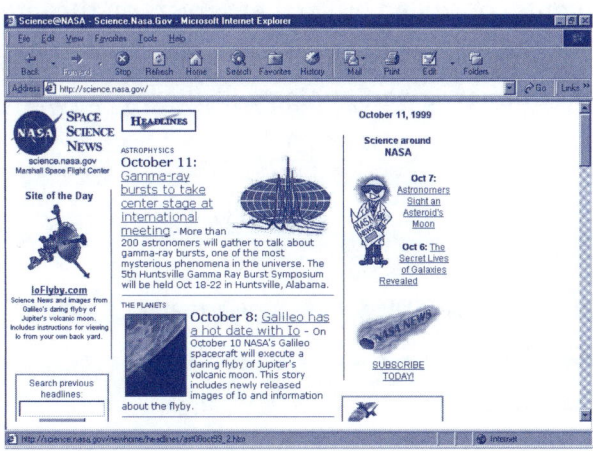

5 And there you are, everything you need to know about current space science.

103

Primeval Internet: Gopher

A somewhat older, but still interesting, way of retrieving documents from the Internet is to use the Internet service called Gopher. Gopher first came to light at the University of Minnesota in 1991. Its objective was to develop a tool, that would permit easy access to various Internet resources.

In contrast to the Internet services discussed so far, Gopher does not need any detailed information, such as file names or host addresses, for it to find a particular piece of information. All that is needed to launch a successful search is the Internet address of the chosen Gopher server.

Using a **Gopher server** is easy: Gopher provides the Internet surfer with a menu system, where the various Internet resources are summarised. You access these resources directly via the Gopher user interface.

Most of the Gopher servers on the Internet are connected to each other. This means that every search term entered is forwarded from one Gopher server to another, until every possible site has been searched. During your Gopher expeditions on the Internet, you will often come across the term **Gopher space**. This refers to the totality of documents controlled by Gopher servers on the Internet.

In the following table you will find the Internet addresses of a few important Gopher servers, which will allow you to access the Gopher space.

Gopher	Place
GOPHER.IC.AC.UK	UK
GOPHER.TH-DARMSTADT.DE	Germany
FINFO.TU.GRAZ.AC.AT	Austria
GOPHER.TORUN.EDU.PL	Poland
CAT.OHIOLINK.EDU	USA
GOPHER.SUNSET.SE	Sweden

There are still many Gopher servers on the Internet. Once you have registered with one Gopher server, you can switch from one server to another.

To take an active part in the Gopher system, you will need an appropriate Gopher client. You can find hundreds of these programs on the Internet, most of which are free. The program called **WSGopher** is best suited to our purposes. In the past few years this program has become very popular in the Internet community and so has spread rapidly. A particularly nice point about the program is its extensive collection of various interesting Internet addresses in Gopher space, which are filed according to subject and can be opened with just one click of the mouse.

Downloading WSGopher from the Internet

Like other programs, you can get everything you need for this off the Internet. Open an Internet connection and enter the following URL in Internet Explorer:

http://www.lib.utk.edu/PCarchive/IBMtype/WSgopher/

You will find many useful and helpful programs on this Web server, for which you won't need to pay a penny – here you can download the information for free. Start up your Web browser and open an Internet connection. Enter the URL shown above.

1 Click on the hyperlink entitled *WSG-11.exe*.

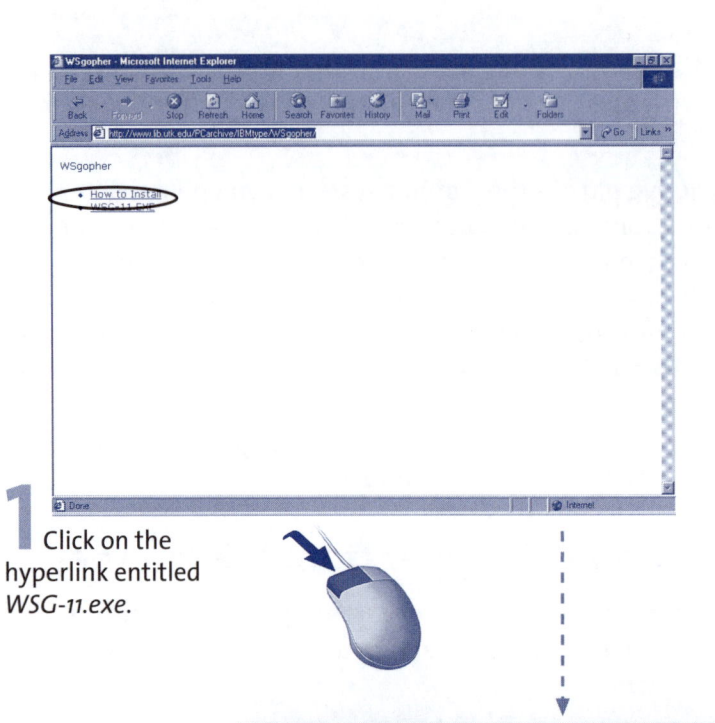

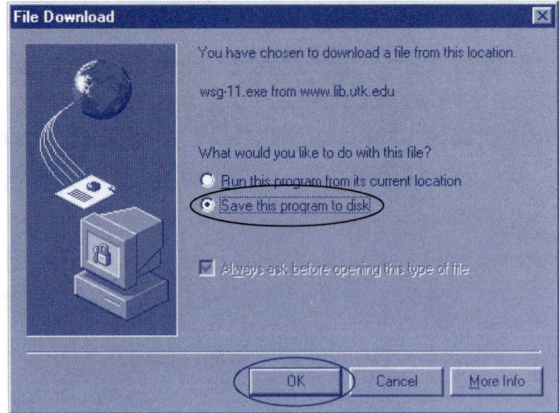

2 Check the radio button *Save this program to disk* and click on *OK*.

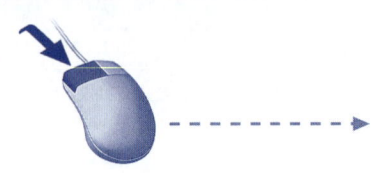

PRIMEVAL INTERNET: GOPHER

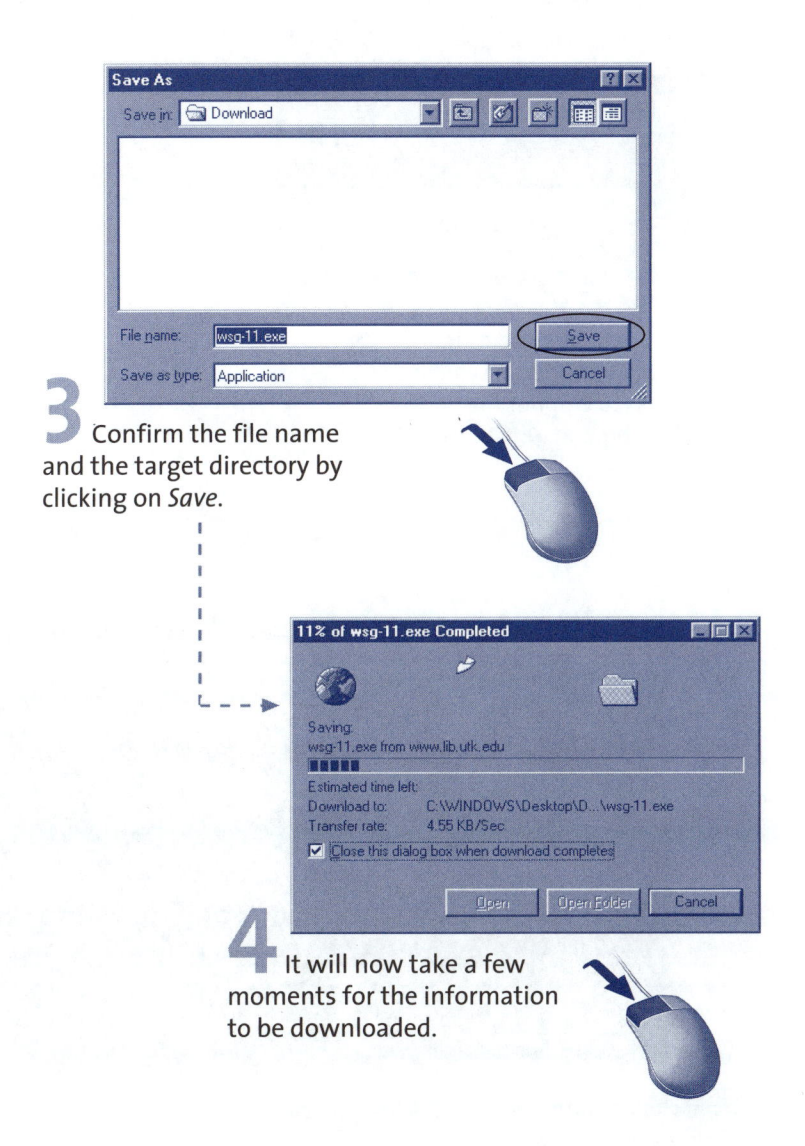

3 Confirm the file name and the target directory by clicking on *Save*.

4 It will now take a few moments for the information to be downloaded.

When the downloading process is over you will find a file in the target directory on your hard drive that will now need to be **decompressed**. The type of file used in our example will decompress itself automatically when it is opened. After this you need to establish a link to your Windows 98 desktop. You will need to do this manually, as the Gopher program does not carry out any installation itself.

107

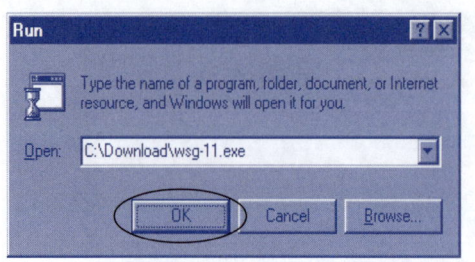

1 Here you will need to enter the name of the folder in which the compressed Gopher file is stored. Then type in *wsg-11.exe* and click on *OK*.

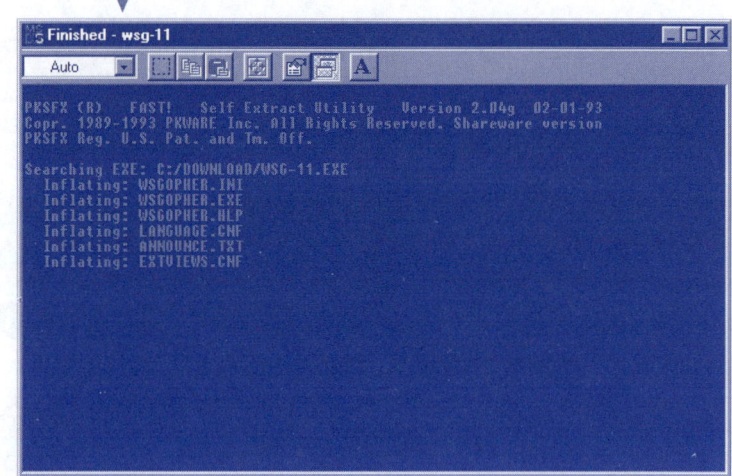

2 The compressed Gopher file is now decompressed.

Primeval Internet: Gopher

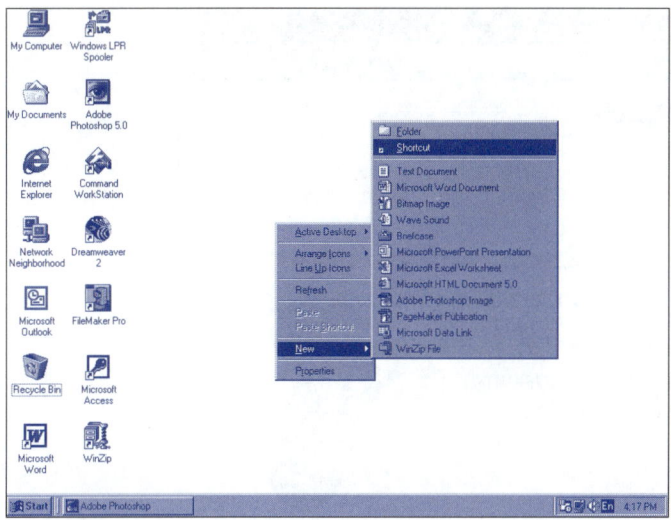

3 Right-click anywhere in the Windows 98 desktop. In the context menu, open the NEW submenu and click on the SHORTCUT entry.

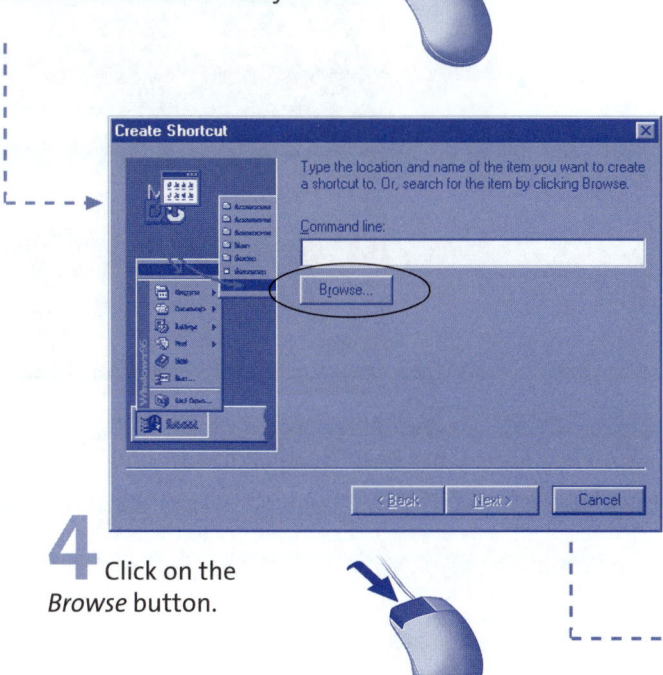

4 Click on the *Browse* button.

109

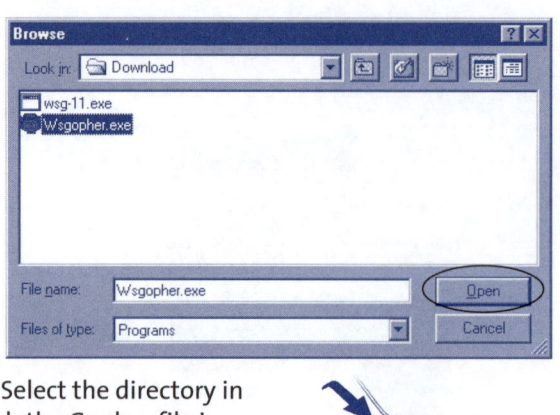

5 Select the directory in which the Gopher file is stored, then click on *Open*.

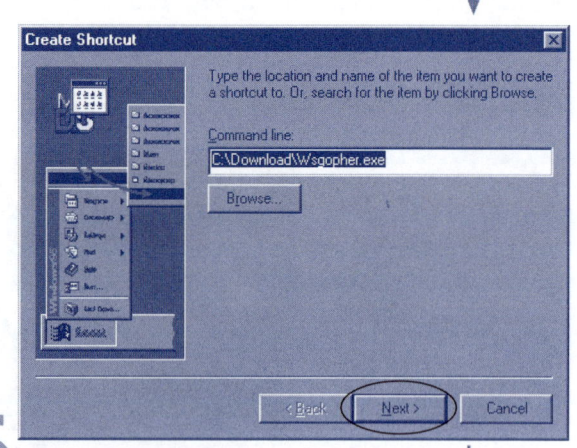

6 When the program has been located, click on *Next*.

7 Click on *Finish*.

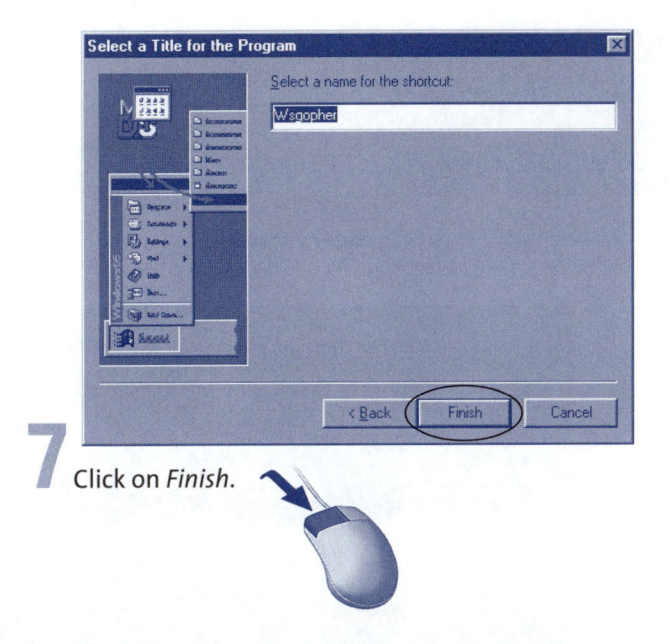

When you have completed this final step you will notice a new icon on your Windows 98 desktop. You are now ready to open the program and start using it.

Your first steps in Gopher space

When you have installed the Gopher program on your PC, you are then ready to set off on the road into Gopher space. To do this, open a connection to your Internet Service Provider. Once this connection is successfully opened, double-click on the Gopher icon on your Windows 98 desktop. As soon as the application is opened, you will need to specify a Gopher home server – the first Gopher server to be chosen whenever the program is started.

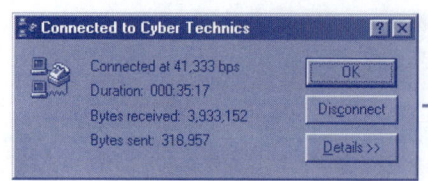

1 Open a connection to your Internet Service Provider.

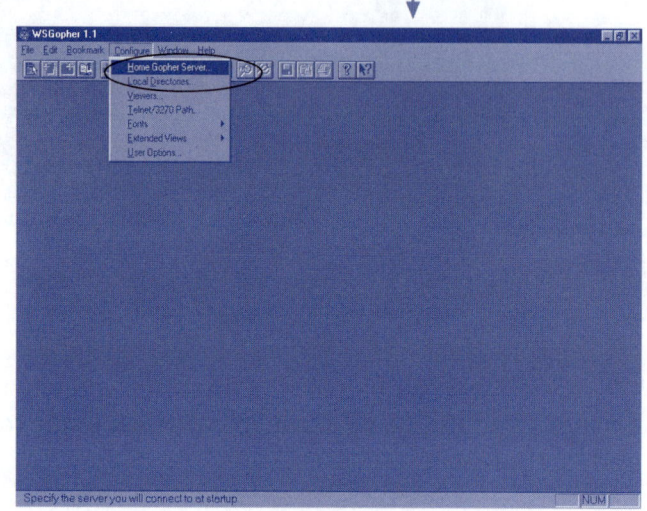

2 In the CONFIGURE menu, choose the HOME GOPHER SERVER command.

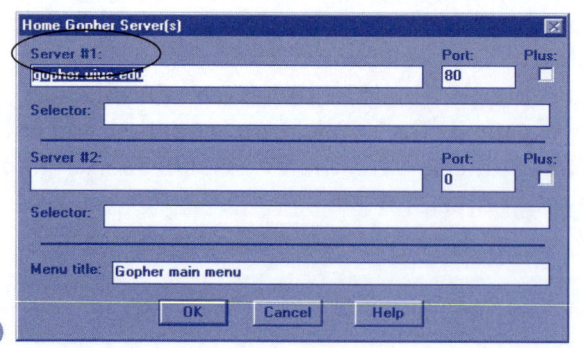

3 In the *Server #1* entry field, enter the name of the Gopher server which is to be called up first at every program start.

PRIMEVAL INTERNET: GOPHER

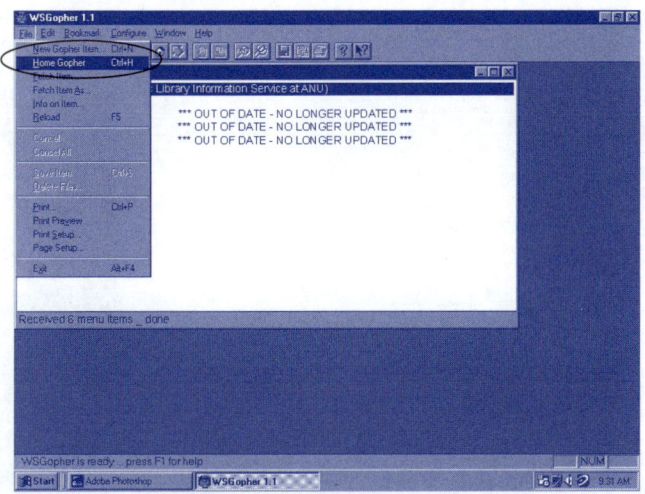

4 In the FILE menu select the HOME GOPHER command to connect to the specified Gopher server.

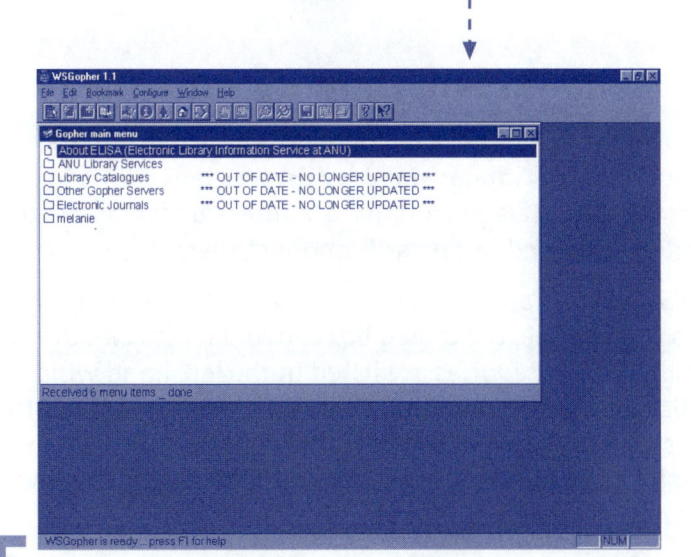

5 After a few moments you will be connected to the Home Gopher Server.

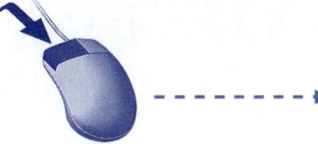

113

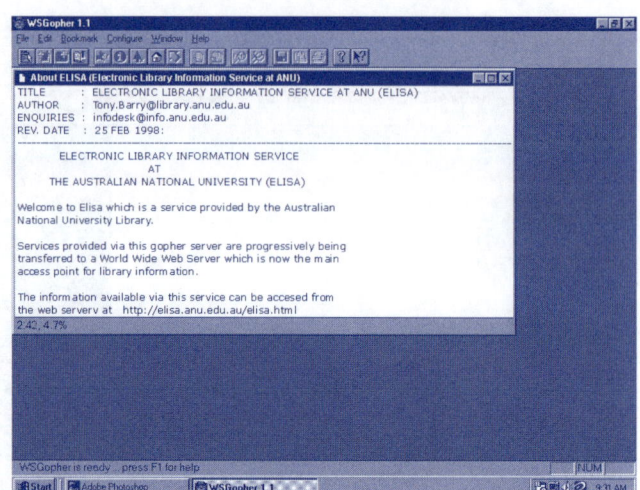

6 You can use your mouse to scroll through the various menus.

Bookmarks will simplify your life

During your journeys into Gopher space you will soon acquire a multitude of **Gopher server addresses** on various topics. If you want to, you can use a personalised 'address book' to save the most interesting and important amongst them.

WSGopher is already set up with an extensive **bookmark collection**. As you can see, the dialog box is divided into two areas. All the individual categories are listed in the left-hand window. When you click on a particular entry in this field, all the entries that are saved inside it will appear in the right-hand field. Every subcategory in the right-hand field represents an individual Gopher server which you can reach over the Internet.

In order to access a different Gopher server, you will need to click on another entry in the left-hand bookmark list.

Primeval Internet: Gopher

To view the whole **bookmark list** available, please perform the following steps:

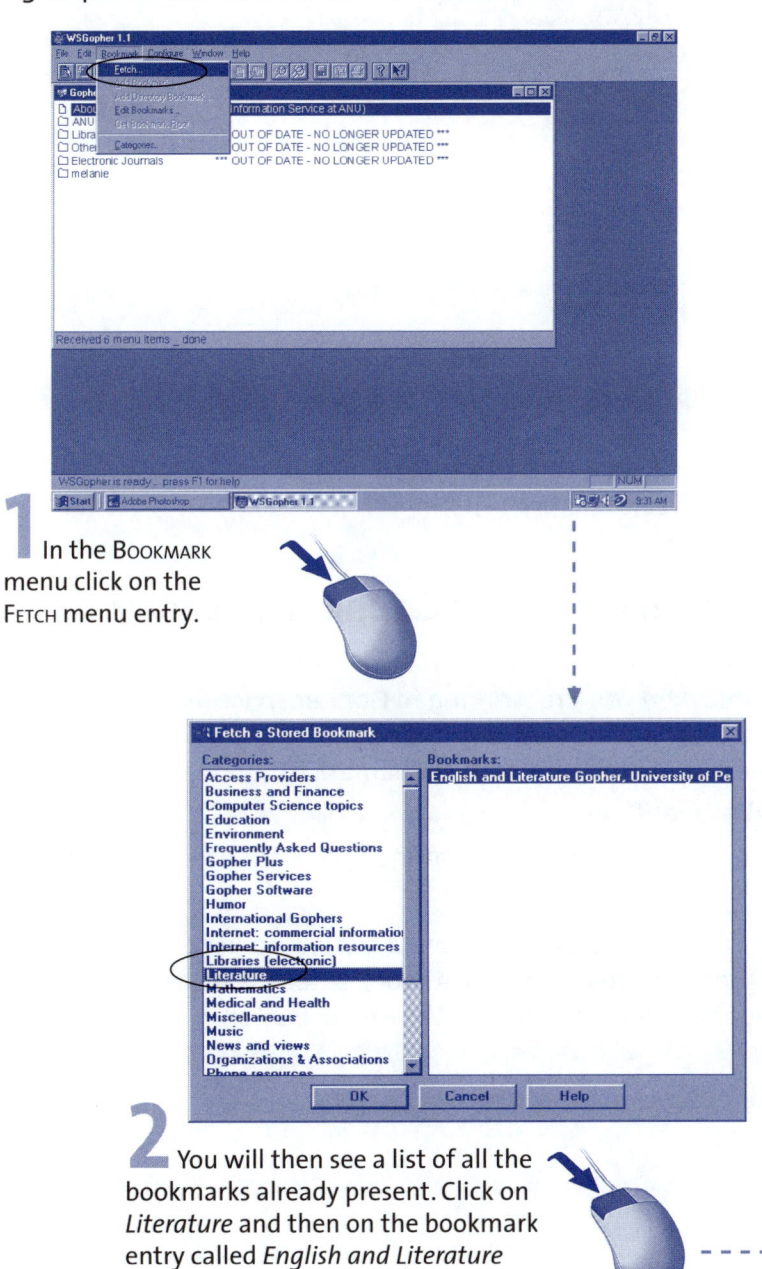

1 In the BOOKMARK menu click on the FETCH menu entry.

2 You will then see a list of all the bookmarks already present. Click on *Literature* and then on the bookmark entry called *English and Literature Gopher*.

115

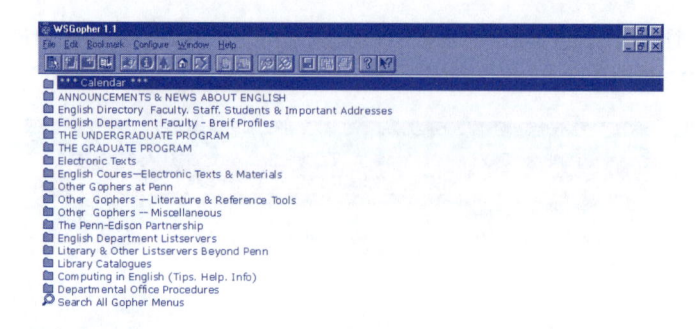

3 Using this bookmark list, you will be able to move quickly from one Gopher server to another.

Creating your own Gopher bookmark entries

Of course, you can also create bookmarks yourself. This is particularly useful when you are working in Gopher space and come across lots of interesting addresses. You can save these addresses initially in a generalised directory in the bookmark list and then arrange them properly later on.

To create a new bookmark category, choose the CATEGORIES entry in the BOOKMARK menu.

The window that is then opened contains a list of every available category. To create a new category, enter the desired name in the input box and then click on the *Create* button.

PRIMEVAL INTERNET: GOPHER

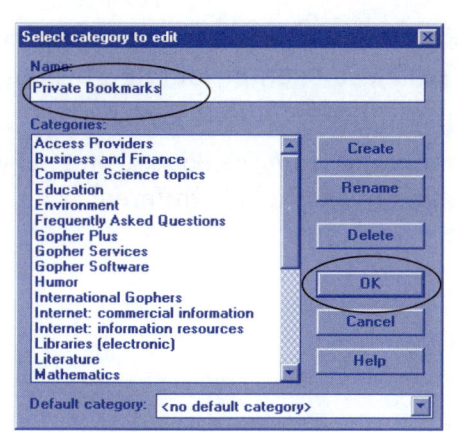

1 Type in *Private Bookmarks* – the name of the new bookmark category – and click on *OK*.

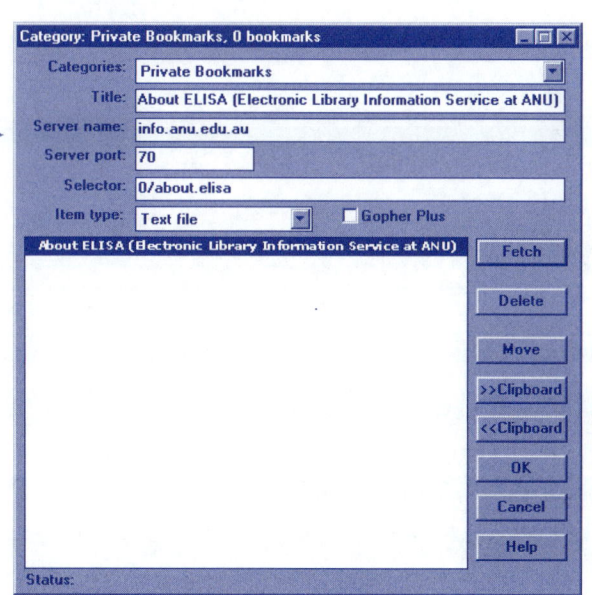

2 Here you can edit your bookmark entries and move them to other categories.

When you have saved all the addresses which you found during this particular Gopher session, you will need to enter your new bookmark group into the drop-down menu entitled *Default category*.

By choosing the EDIT BOOKMARK command from the BOOKMARK menu, you will be able to edit your entries and move them to different categories.

You have to laugh –
the best computer messages

To see this cartoon and others like it, go to *www.macworks.com*.

4

Internet access via an online service

What's in this chapter?

Many roads lead to Rome, and also to the Internet. It is not absolutely necessary for you to have an Internet Service Provider in order to access the Internet.
In this chapter you will see how you can get onto the Internet with AOL and BT.

You already know about:

Modems & Co.	10
The importance of software	16
Taking your first steps in the World Wide Web	67
Loading saved pages	86
Searching through and printing Web pages	88
How a search engine works	94
Using the Lycos search engine	98
The primeval Internet: Gopher	104

You are going to learn about:

Accessing the Internet with AOL	122
Accessing the Internet with BT Click	141

Accessing the Internet with AOL

Online services also offer their members Internet access. The private user can profit here from the good-value tariffs offered by online services, such as AOL and BT. Internet Service Providers are usually not able to compete with such offers.

> **WHAT'S THIS?**
>
> In contrast to the Internet, an **online service** is a closed system, which contains a continually revised and edited stock of information on every aspect of life. In this way it can be seen almost as a small Internet, without the associated chaos. To use an online service, you will first need to register with it. AOL and BT entice new members with a multitude of free offers, which can all be found on CD-ROMs in the many computer magazines around. All of the online services available in Great Britain now offer their members a gateway to the Internet. The member can then use the online service instead of an Internet Service Provider to access the Internet.

Installing the AOL software

You can find the AOL installation program on one of the countless CD-ROMs supplied with computer magazines. The following steps take you through the installation process:

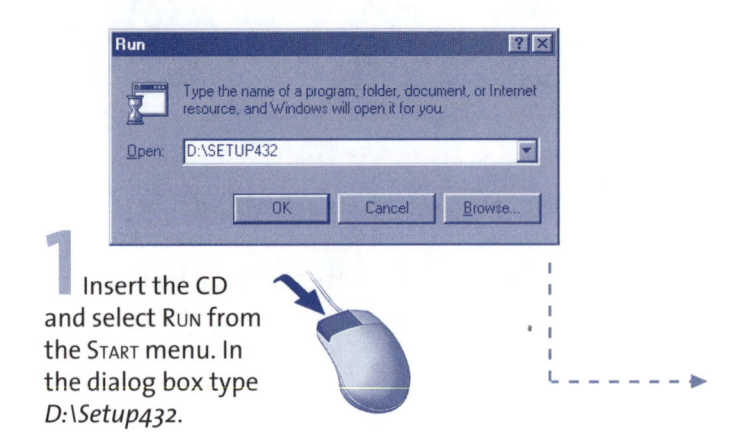

1 Insert the CD and select RUN from the START menu. In the dialog box type *D:\Setup432*.

ACCESSING THE INTERNET WITH AOL

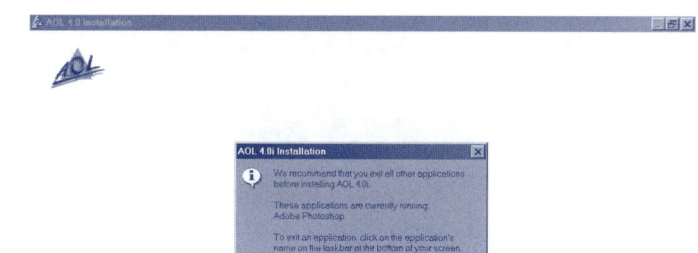

2 If the installation procedure detects other running applications, a warning box will tell you to close these applications. Follow the instructions, then click on *OK*.

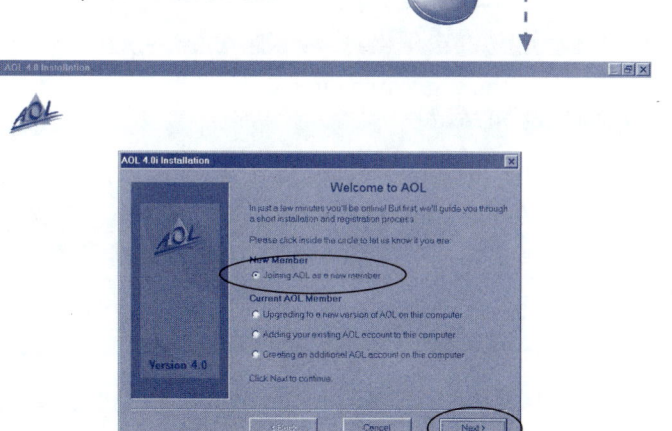

3 Select the *Joining AOL as a new member* radio button and click on *Next*.

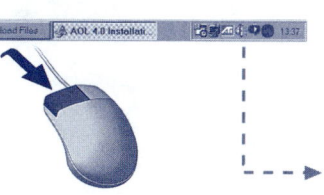

123

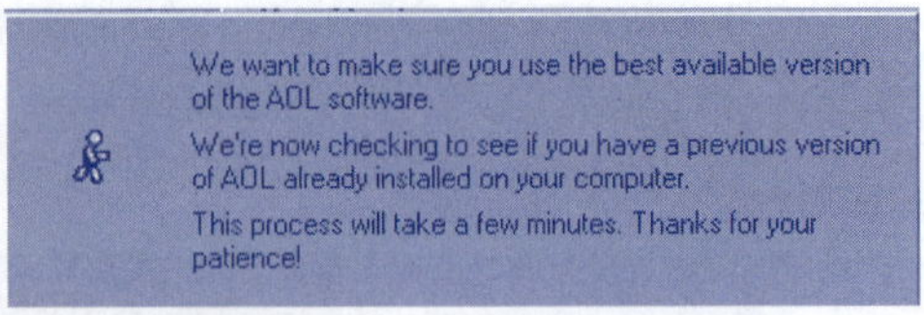

We want to make sure you use the best available version of the AOL software.

We're now checking to see if you have a previous version of AOL already installed on your computer.

This process will take a few minutes. Thanks for your patience!

4 The AOL installation process then searches your computer for any possible older versions of AOL.

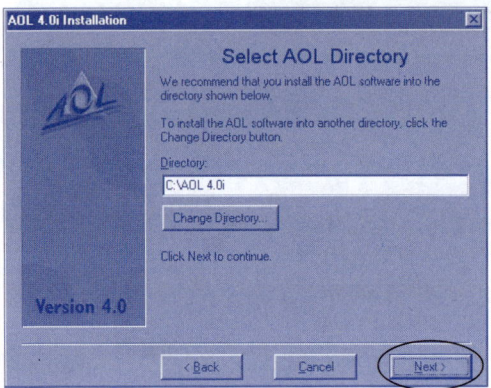

5 Accept the suggested directory by clicking on *Next*.

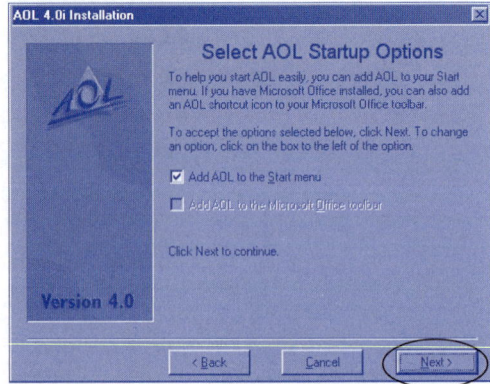

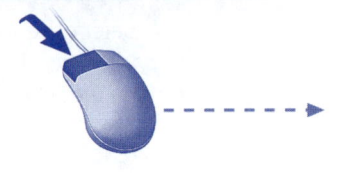

6 Click on *Next*.

ACCESSING THE INTERNET WITH AOL

AOL 4.0i Installation

Disk Space Check

Disk space available: 7658.1 MB
Disk space required: 13.5 MB

Your hard drive has enough free disk space to install all of the AOL 4.0i software.

Click Next to begin installation.

Version 4.0

< Back   Cancel   Next >

7 Click on *Next*.

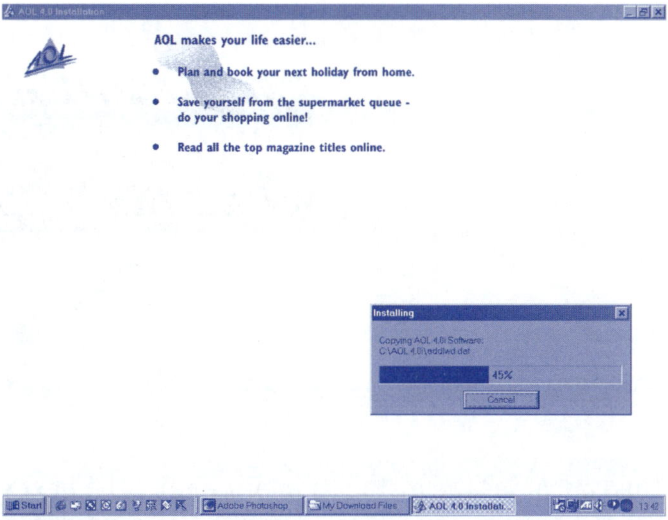

AOL 4.0 Installation

AOL makes your life easier...

- Plan and book your next holiday from home.
- Save yourself from the supermarket queue - do your shopping online!
- Read all the top magazine titles online.

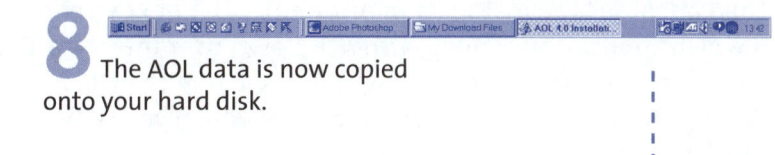

Installing

Copying AOL 4.0i Software:
C:\AOL 4.0i\saddled.dat

45%

Cancel

8 The AOL data is now copied onto your hard disk.

125

10 Click on *Finish*.

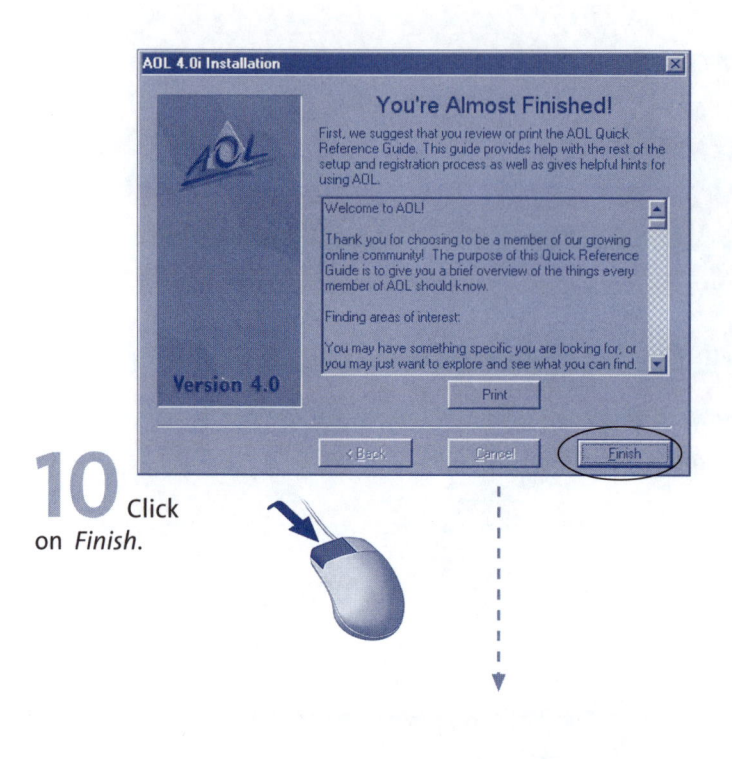

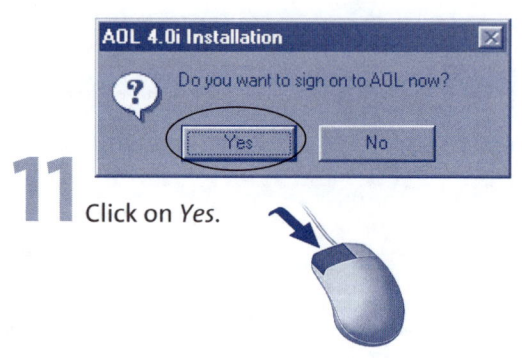

11 Click on *Yes*.

This concludes the installation procedure. The next screen you see is the AOL application screen, with AOL's own user interface. On this screen you are now presented with a 'Welcome to AOL' dialog box asking you to select the setup procedure which you will be using to configure AOL with your personal data.

Accessing the Internet with AOL

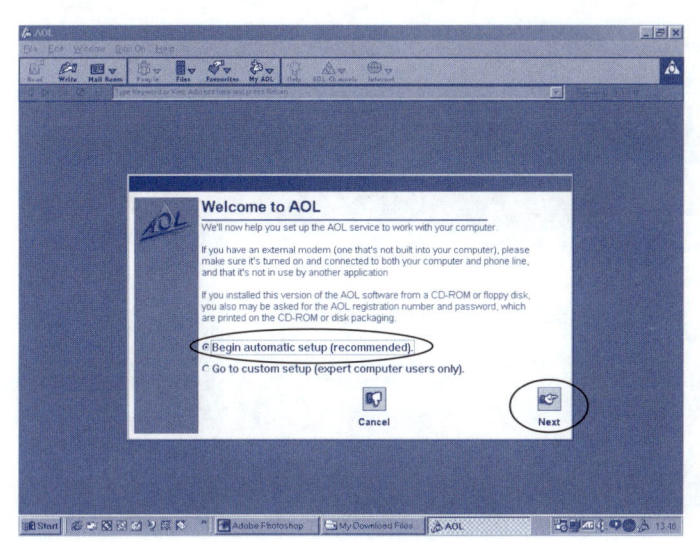

1 Select the *Begin automatic setup (recommended)* radio button, then click on *Next*.

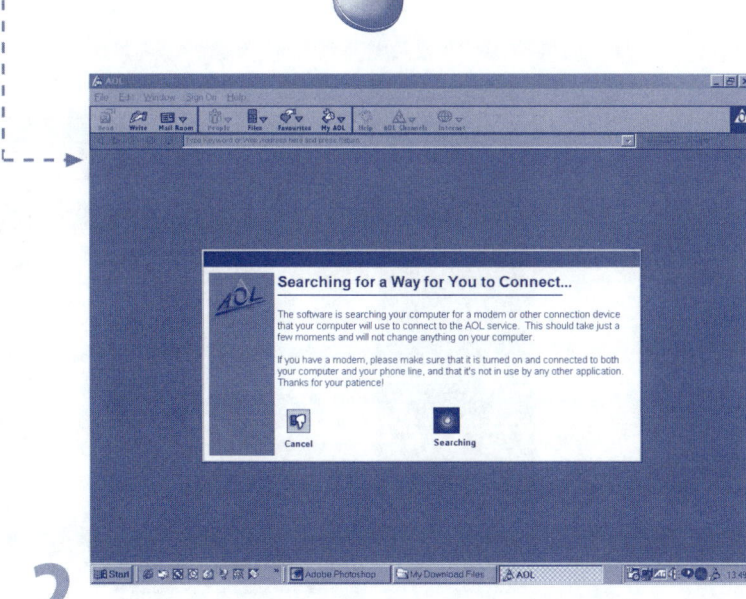

2 The computer searches for a suitable way to establish a connection to AOL.

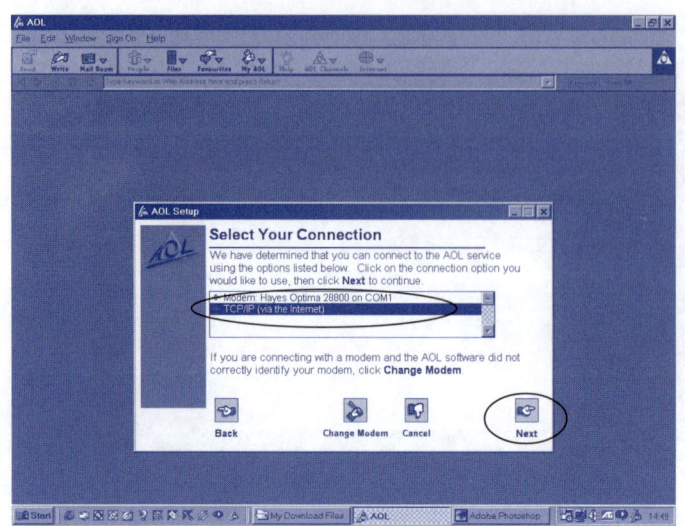

3 The computer has found a modem and an existing TCP/IP connection to an Internet Service Provider. Select the TCP/IP connection, then click on *Next*.

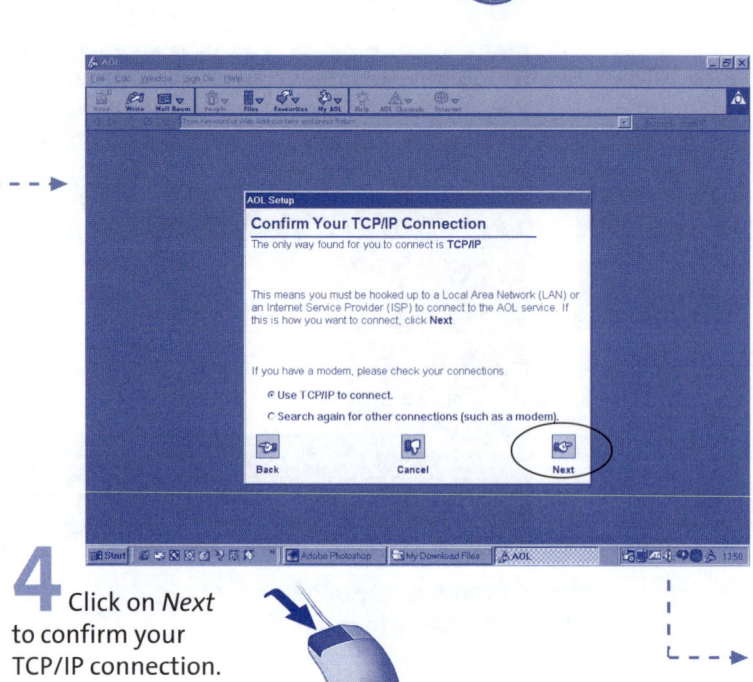

4 Click on *Next* to confirm your TCP/IP connection.

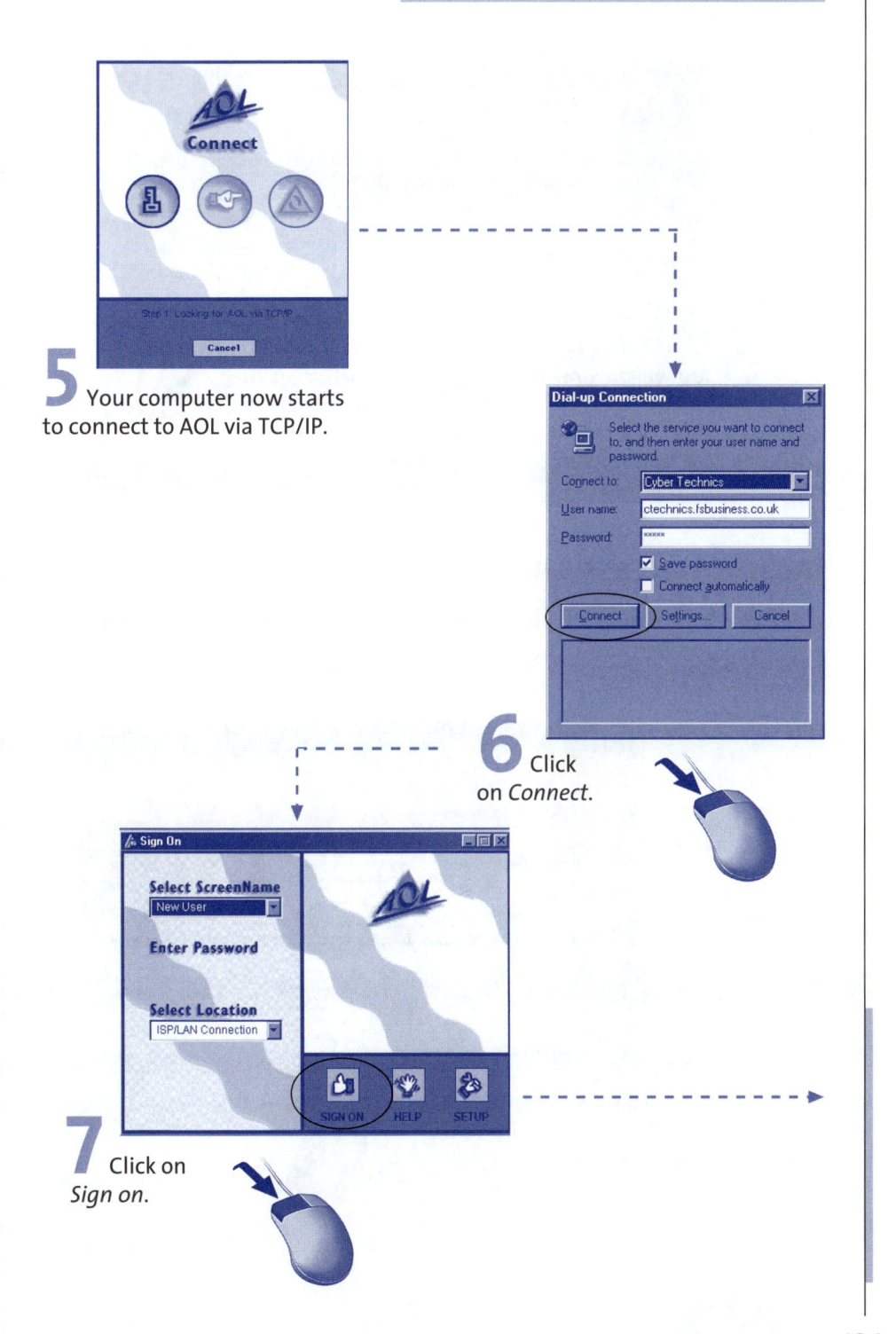

ACCESSING THE INTERNET WITH AOL

5 Your computer now starts to connect to AOL via TCP/IP.

6 Click on *Connect*.

7 Click on *Sign on*.

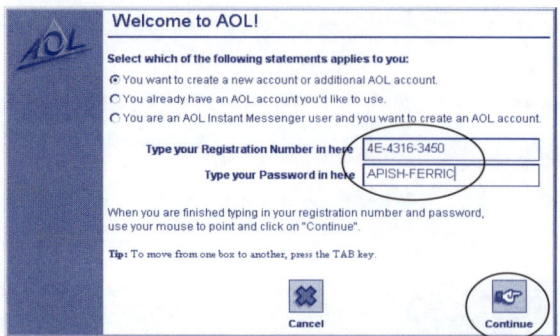

8 You will now need to enter your *Registration number* and *Password*. You can find this information either on the cover sleeve of the AOL CD-ROM or in the accompanying letter. Then click on *Continue*.

Internet access with AOL

Once you have successfully entered all the necessary information, you will soon be able to access AOL.

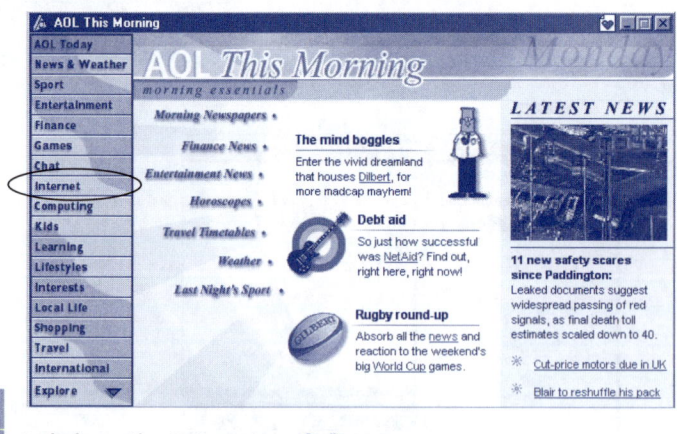

1 A click on the *Internet* button takes you into the Internet zone.

ACCESSING THE INTERNET WITH AOL

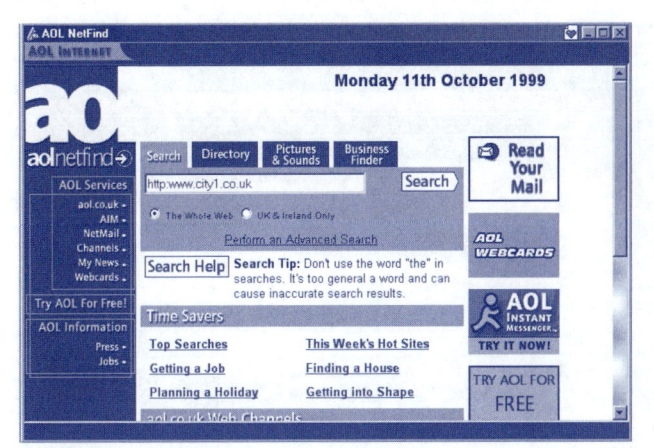

2 Enter the URL of your chosen Web site in the entry field, then click on *Search*.

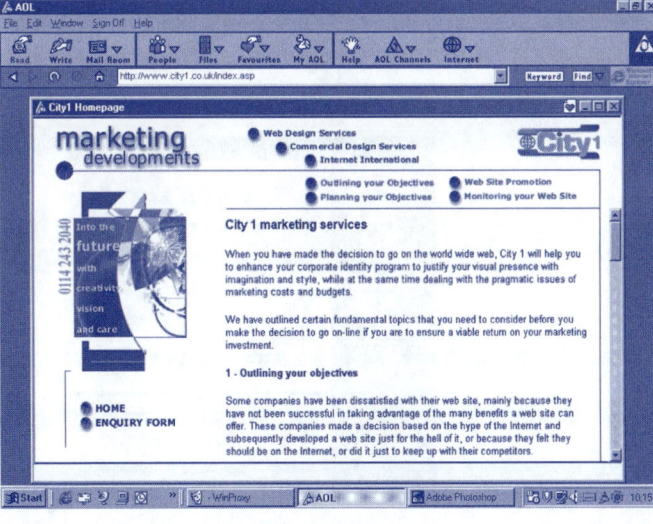

3 The Web site you requested will appear after a few moments.

131

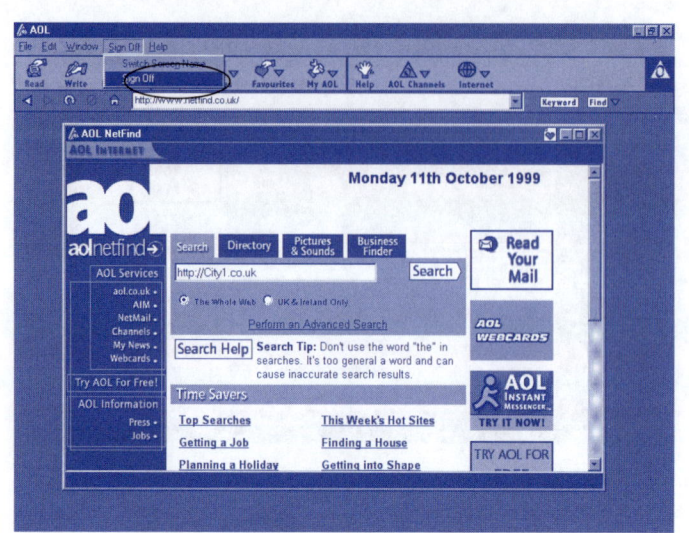

4 To leave AOL click on the SIGN OFF entry of the SIGN OFF menu.

5 To terminate your AOL session, click on *Exit Application*.

Using an existing AOL account

It may be the case that you don't have test access, but that you already possess a full AOL membership account.

To use this, open up the AOL software by double-clicking on the AOL icon on your desktop, and do the following:

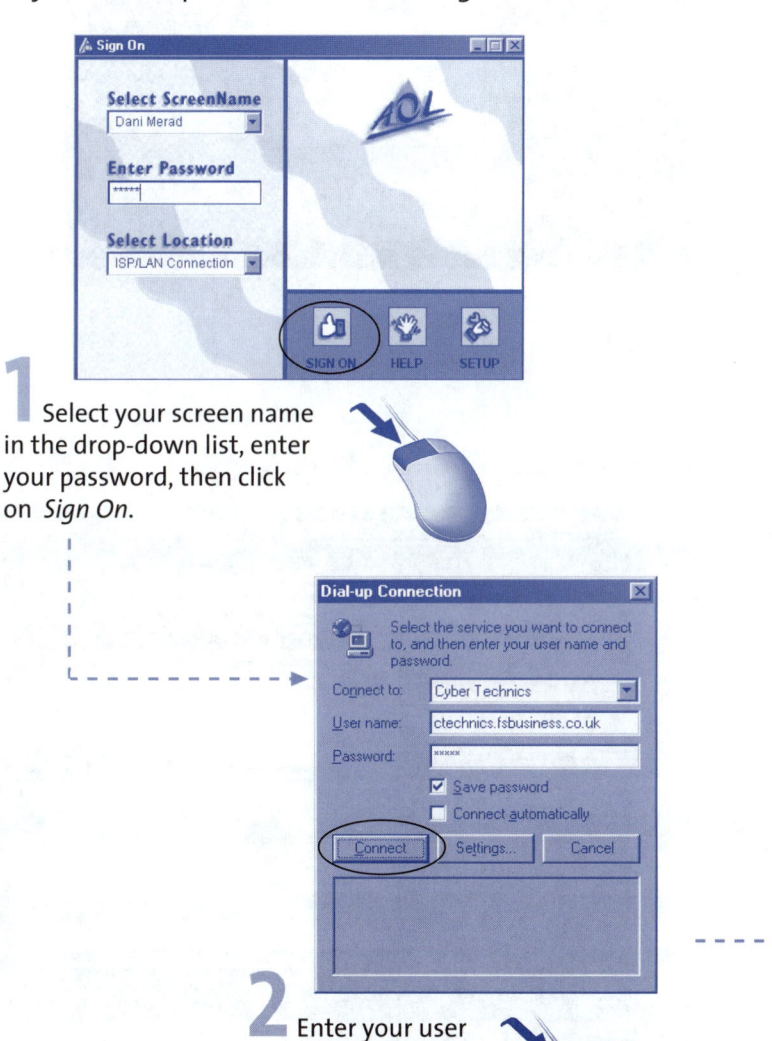

1 Select your screen name in the drop-down list, enter your password, then click on *Sign On*.

2 Enter your user name and password, then click on *Connect*.

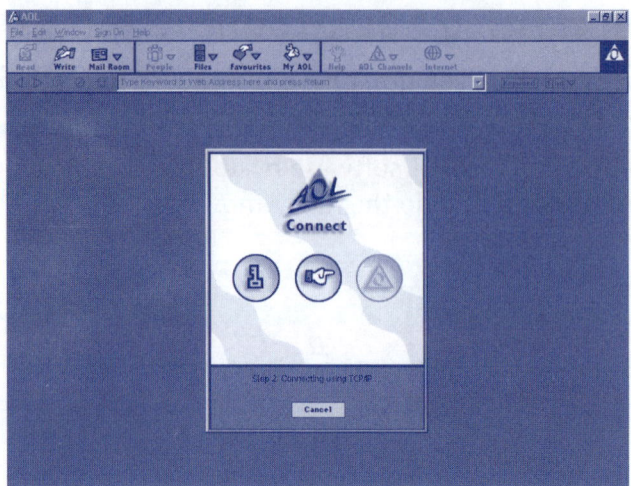

3 Your computer is now connecting to AOL.

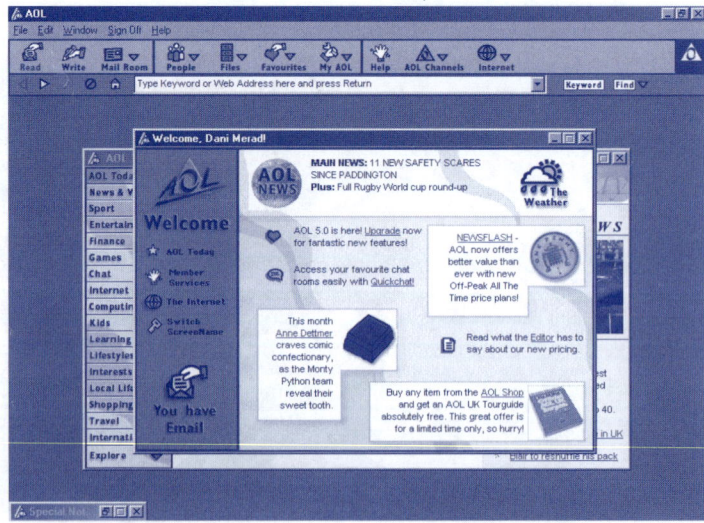

4 A few moments later the AOL homepage will appear.

Configuring a direct modem connection with AOL

If you don't have an Internet account with an Internet Service Provider, you can still dial into AOL directly via a modem or ISDN. The AOL software will automatically take over the configuration task for you.

Open up the AOL software as usual:

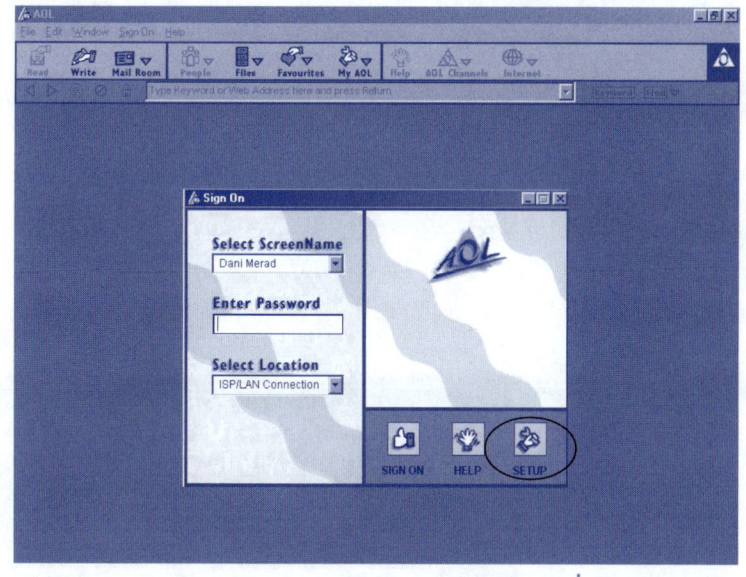

1 Click on *Setup*.

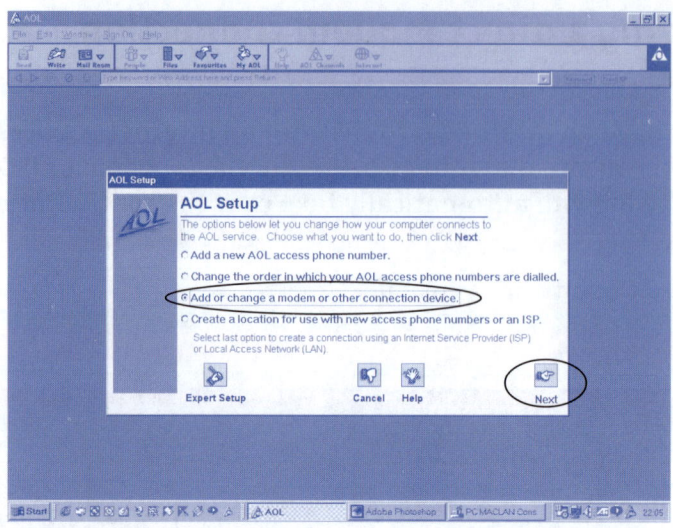

2 Select the *Add or change a modem...* radio button and click on *Next*.

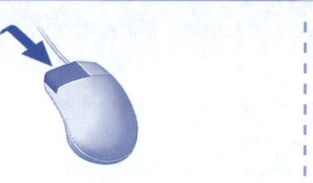

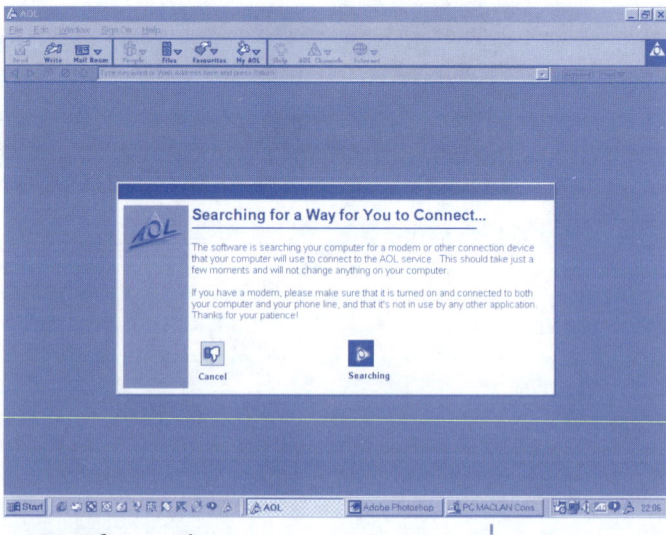

3 The AOL software then looks for a modem.

ACCESSING THE INTERNET WITH AOL

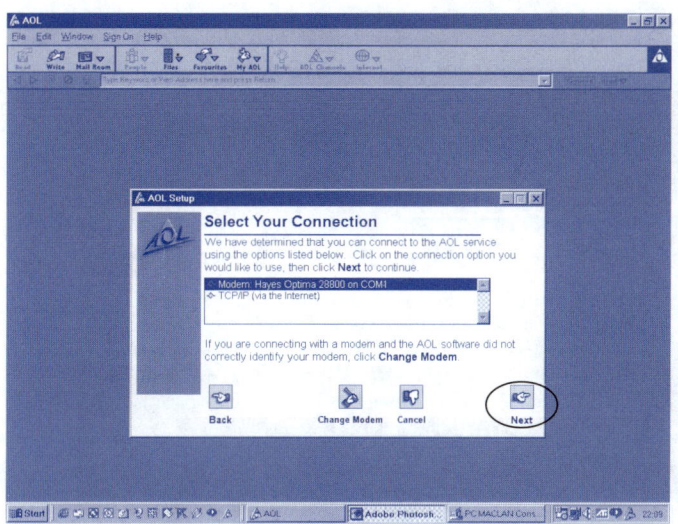

4 Once a modem has been found, click on *Next*.

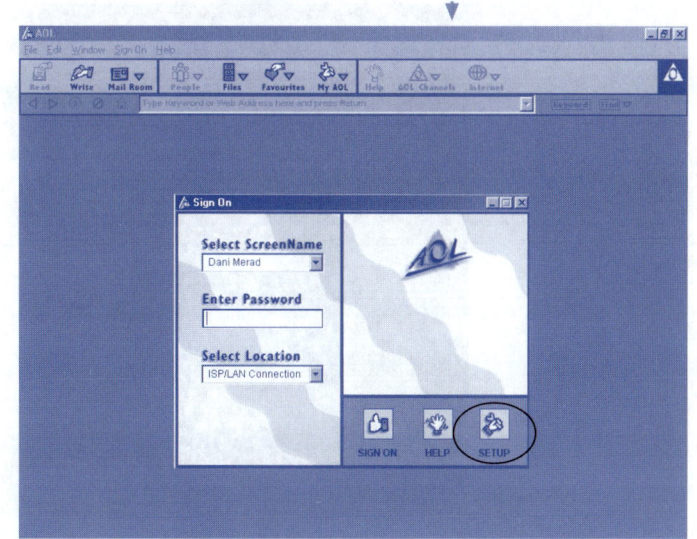

5 This takes you back to the *Sign On* dialog. Do not sign on yet, but click once again on *Setup* to configure your modem connection.

137

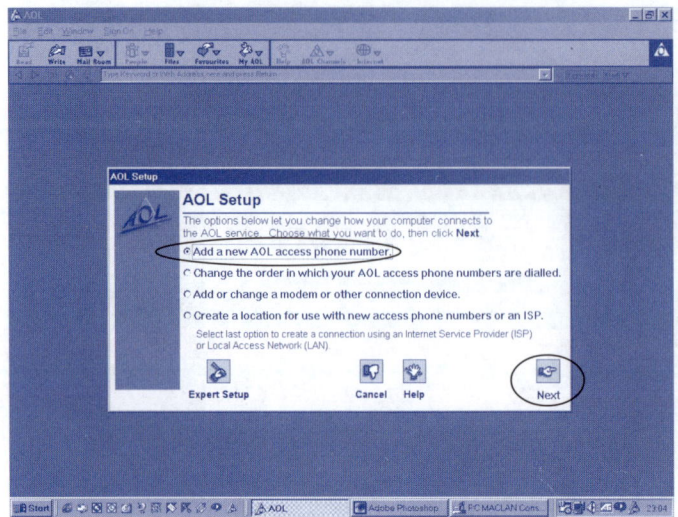

6 Select the *Add a new AOL access phone number* radio button, then click on *Next*.

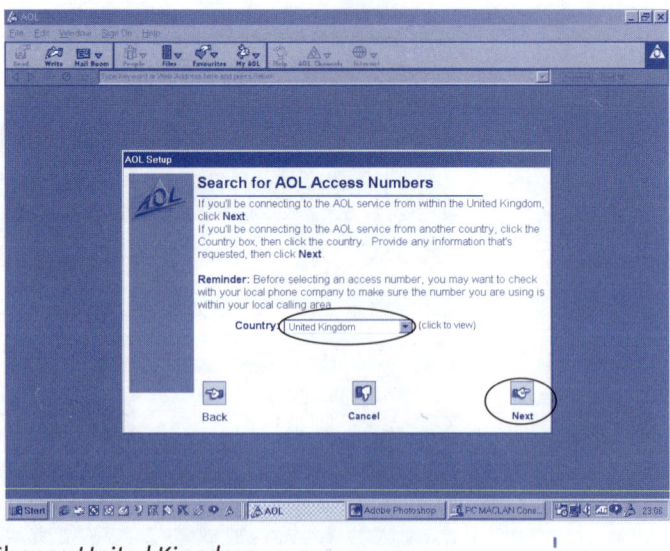

7 Choose *United Kingdom* in the drop-down list, then click on *Next*.

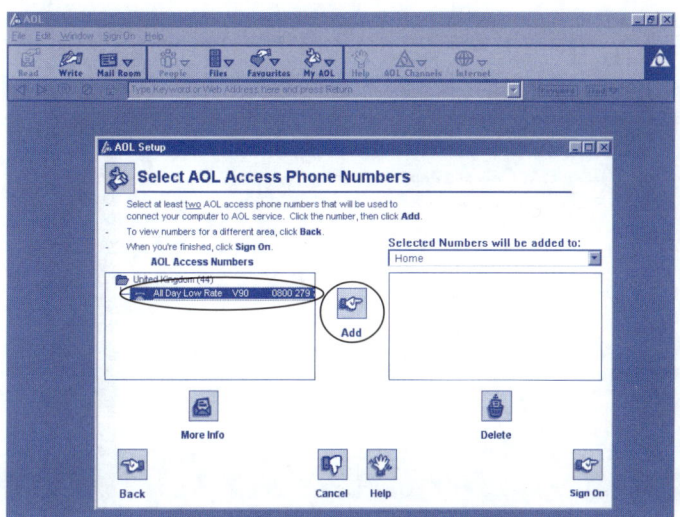

Accessing the Internet with AOL

8 In the left-hand list box select *All Day Low Rate*, then click on the *Add* button.

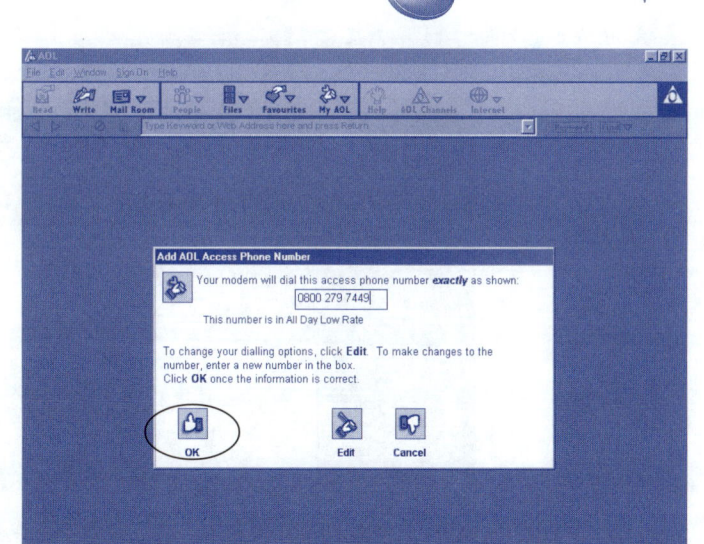

9 Click on *OK*.

139

10 Click on *Sign On*.

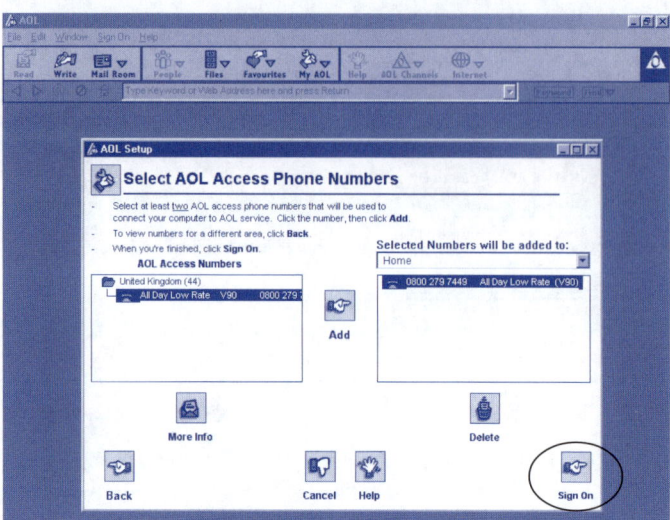

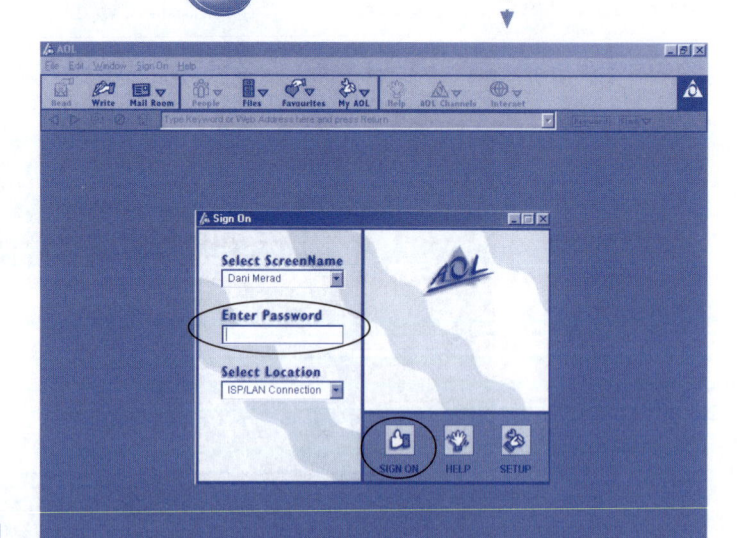

11 Enter your password, then click on *Sign On*.

140

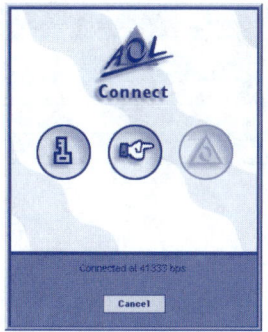

12 A connection to AOL is then established via your modem.

Accessing the Internet with BT Click

Alongside AOL, British Telecom is one of the success stories in the area of online services in the United Kingdom. As with AOL, BT also offers its members an Internet gateway, which they can use to get onto the Internet. To use BT to access the Internet, you will first of all need to install the appropriate software on your computer. You can find this software on almost every CD-ROM supplied with computer magazines.

Installing the BT Click software

Insert the CD-ROM containing the BT Click software into your CR-ROM drive where, in many cases, it will start up immediately. Otherwise, you will need to look for the BT Click setup file on the CD-ROM.

1 On your Windows desktop, double-click on the *My Computer* icon.

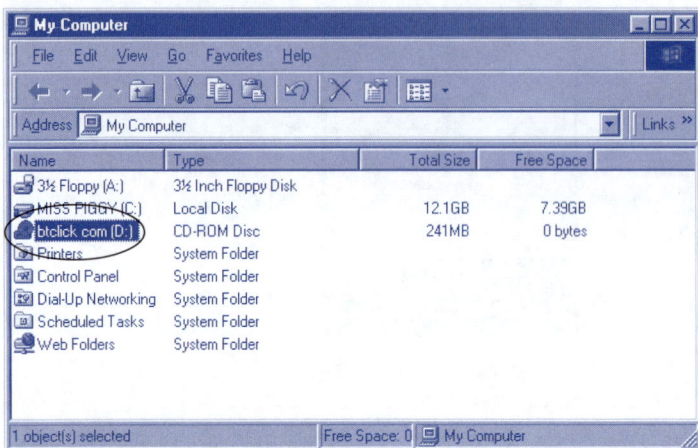

2 In the window that appears, double-click on the entry for the CD-ROM drive.

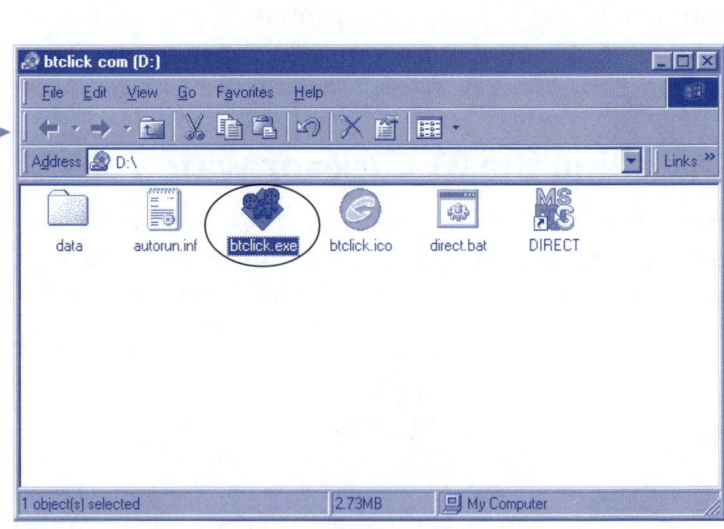

3 Then double-click on the icon entitled *btclick.exe*.

ACCESSING THE INTERNET WITH BT CLICK

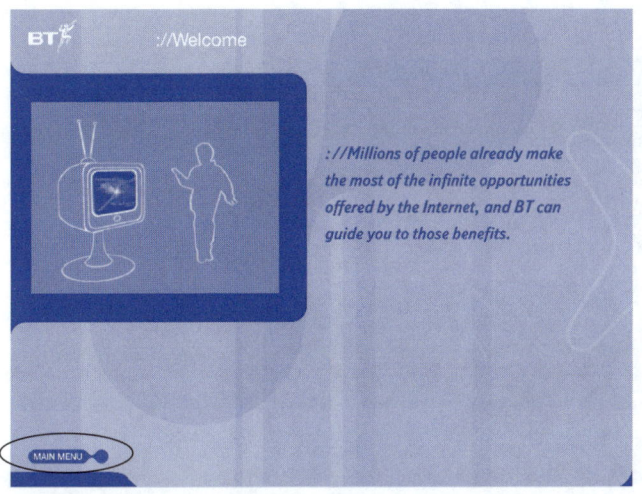

4 When the Welcome screen appears, click on *Main Menu*.

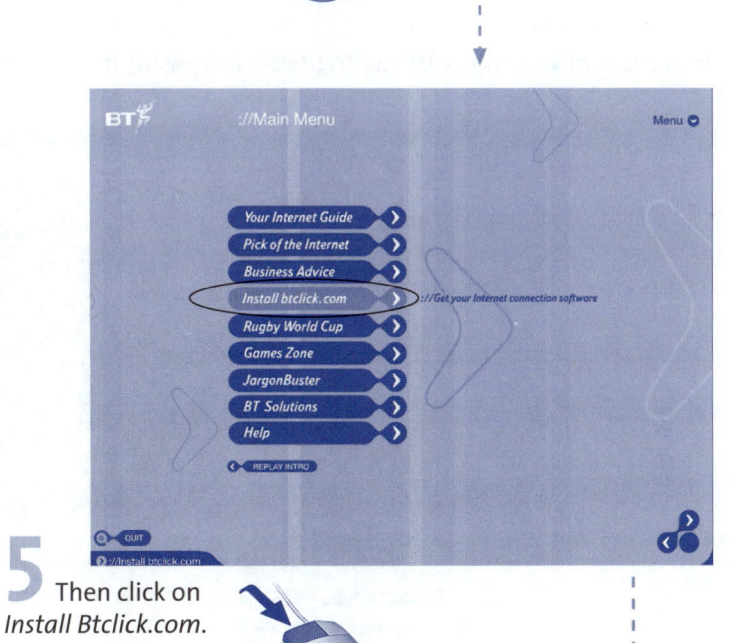

5 Then click on *Install Btclick.com*.

143

6 Click on *Install*.

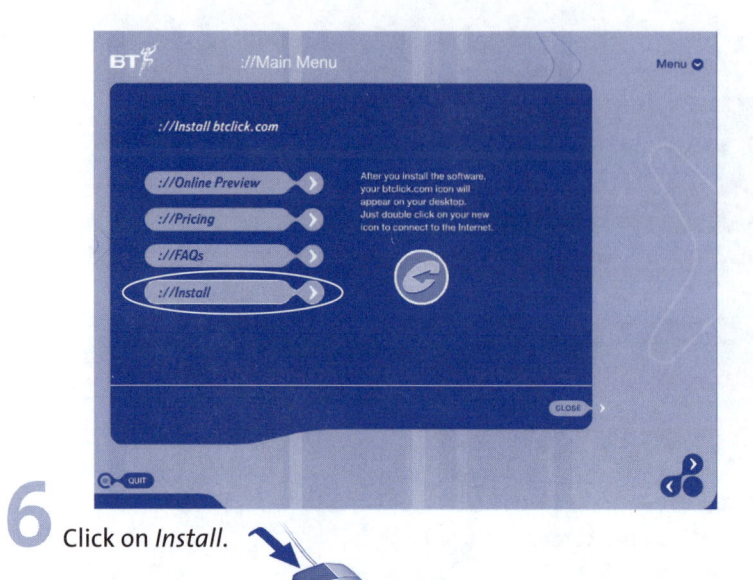

In the next step you will install the BT Click software. You should also make use of this opportunity to install Microsoft Internet Explorer 5.

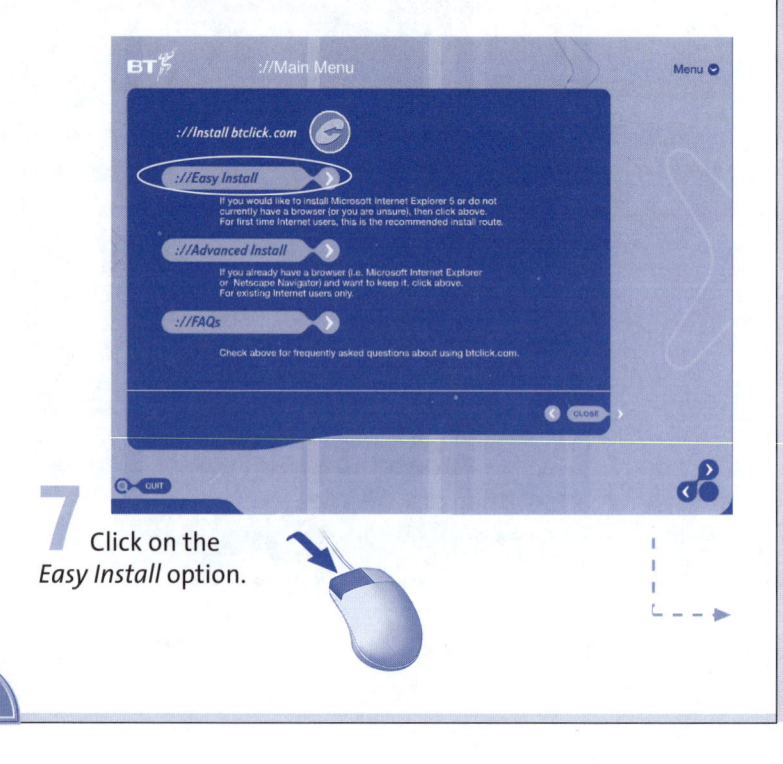

7 Click on the *Easy Install* option.

Accessing the Internet with BT Click

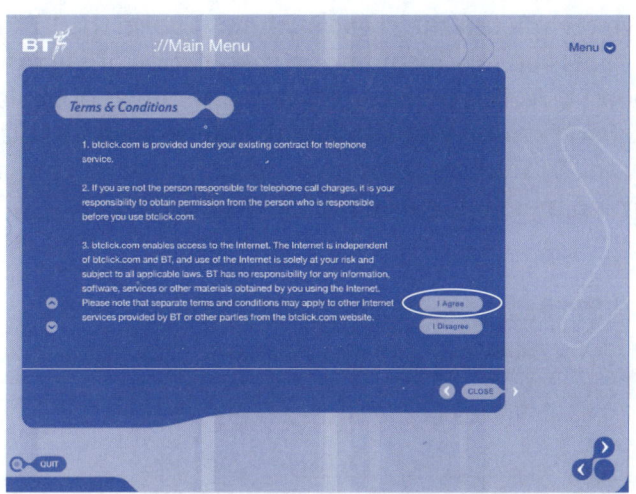

8 Agree to the terms and conditions by clicking on *I agree*.

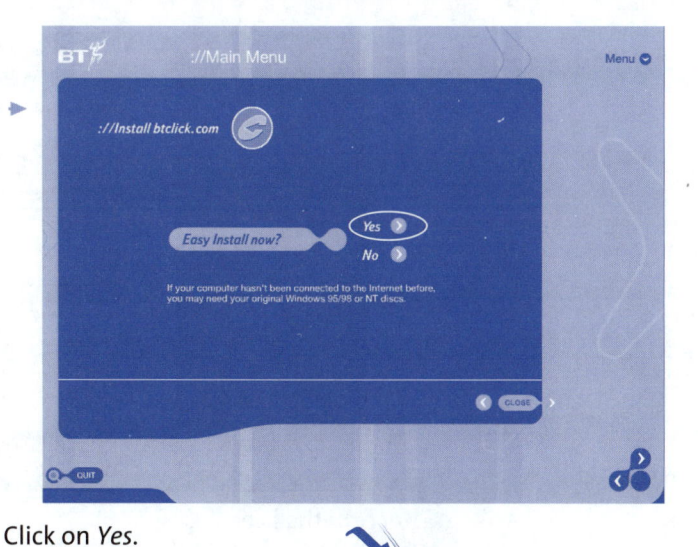

9 Click on *Yes*.

145

Once you have completed the steps outlined above, the BT Click installation process begins, including an installation of Microsoft Internet Explorer 5. As this procedure is not a Windows or Explorer update through a Microsoft Web site, but an independent installation performed by the BT Click installation procedure, you will probably receive a warning message, which you can safely ignore.

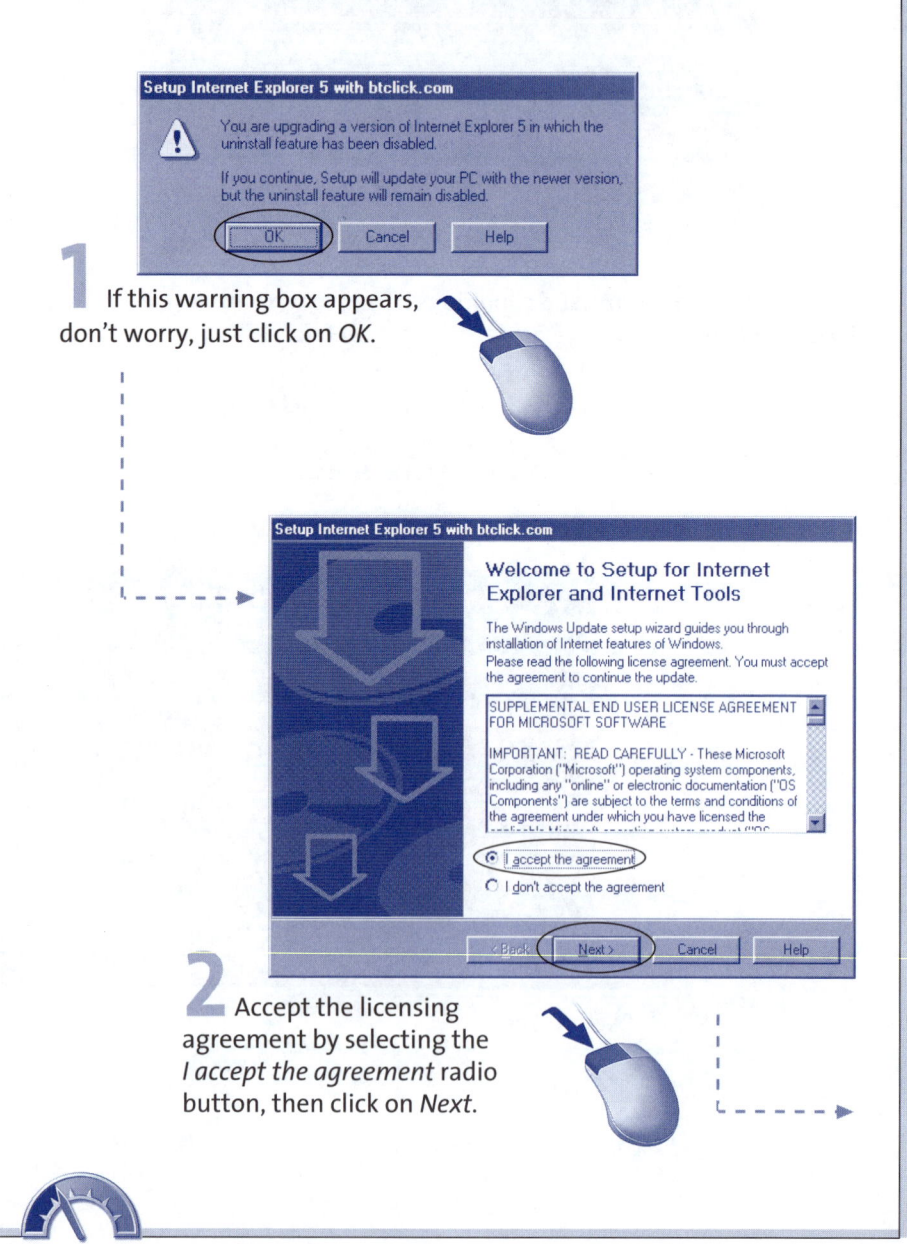

1 If this warning box appears, don't worry, just click on *OK*.

2 Accept the licensing agreement by selecting the *I accept the agreement* radio button, then click on *Next*.

Accessing the Internet with BT Click

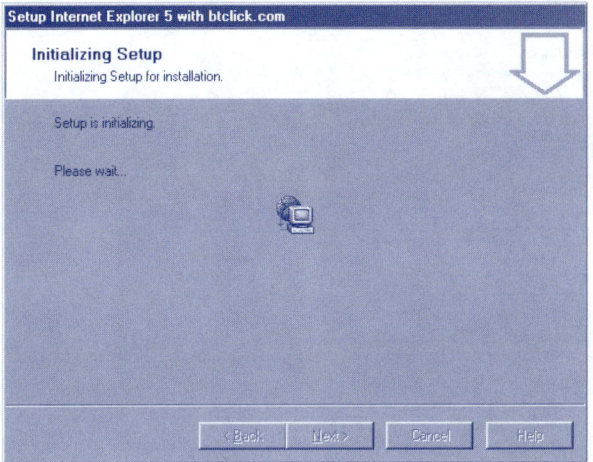

3 Wait for the initialisation process to finish.

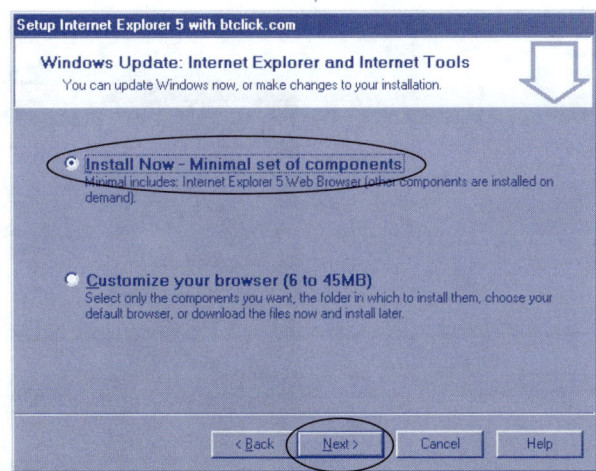

4 Accept the *Install Now – Minimal set of components* default setting, then click on *Next*.

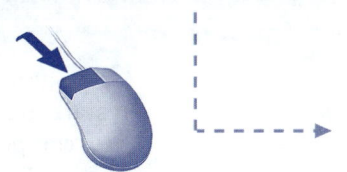

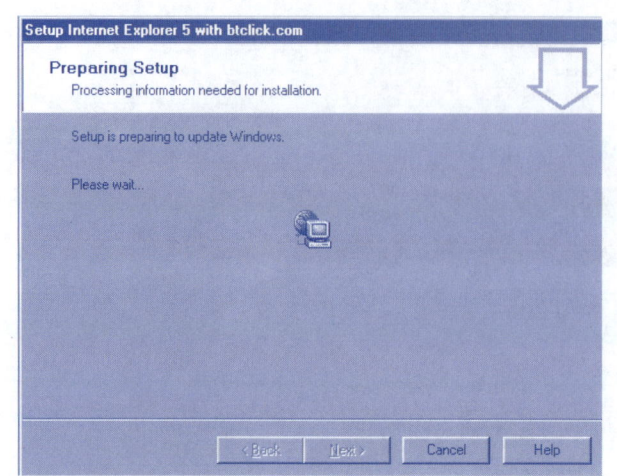

5 The setup procedure now updates your Windows configuration. Just wait...

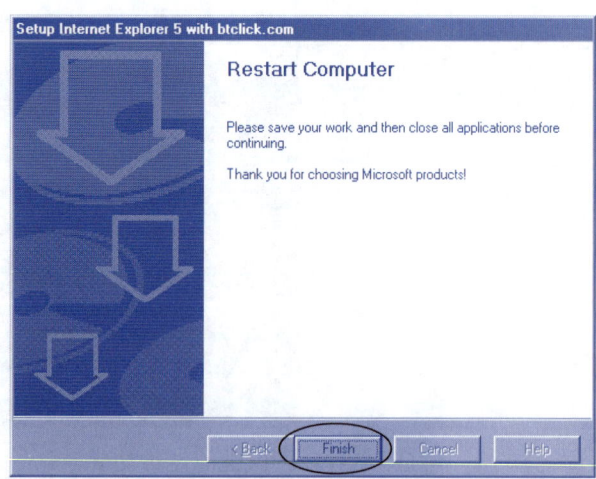

6 The setup procedure will now need to restart your computer to make sure all the new components are properly activated. Click on *Finish*.

ACCESSING THE INTERNET WITH BT CLICK

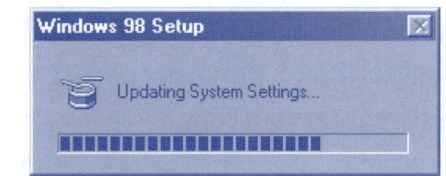

7 After restarting, the computer updates your system settings. This may take several minutes.

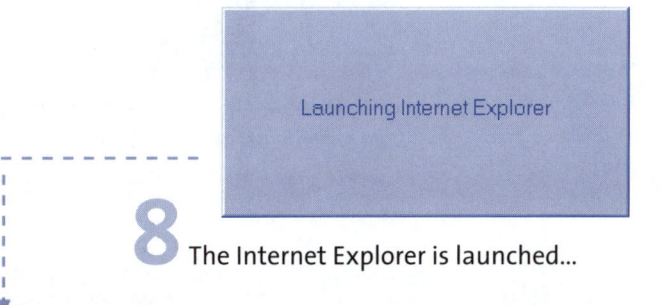

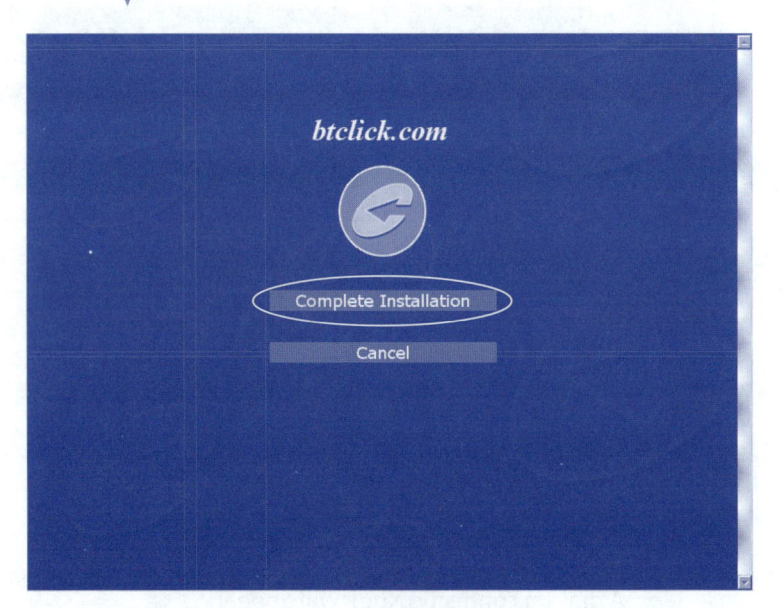

8 The Internet Explorer is launched...

9 ... and the *btclick.com* installation screen appears. Click on *Complete installation*.

149

Configuring your BT Click access data

Once the installation is complete, you will be returned to your desktop and will now be able to register your copy.

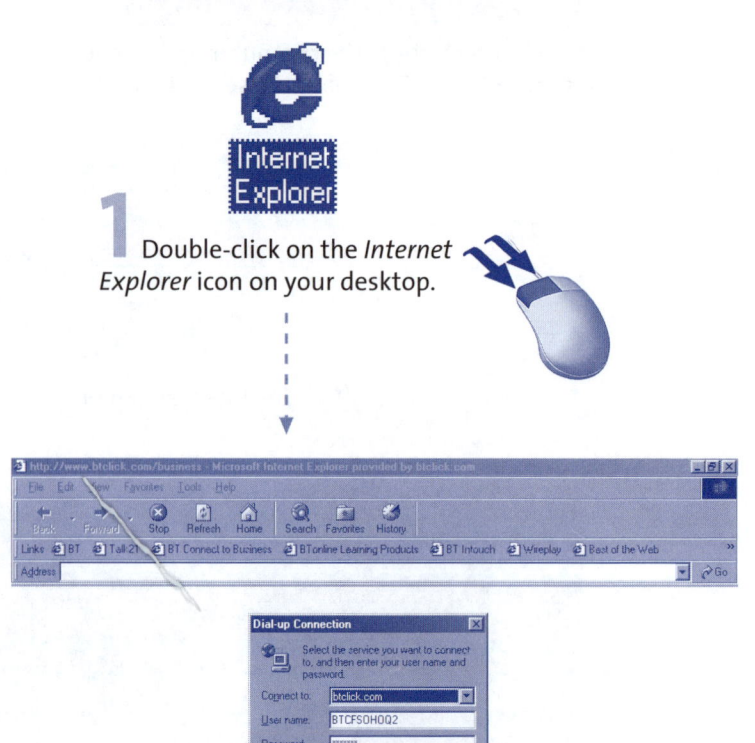

1 Double-click on the *Internet Explorer* icon on your desktop.

2 A dial-up connection box will appear. Select the BT Click connection, then click on *Connect*.

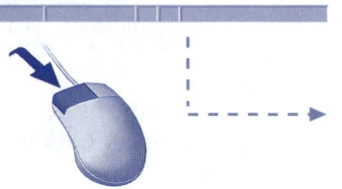

ACCESSING THE INTERNET WITH BT CLICK

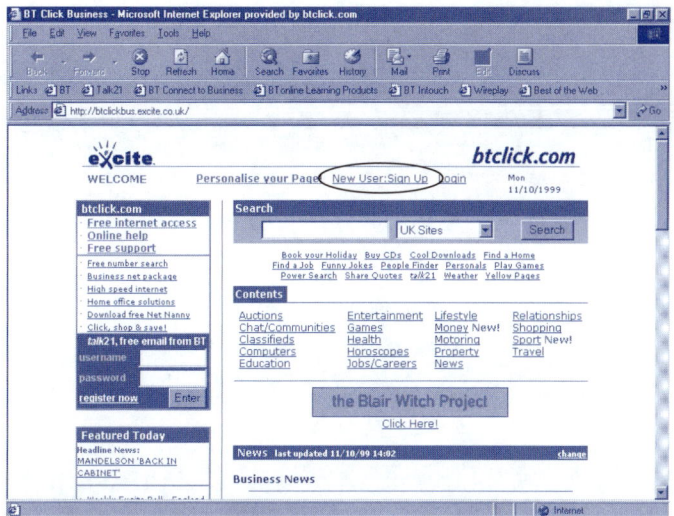

3 The BT Click Web page will now appear. To register as a new user, click on the *New User: Sign up* hyperlink.

4 Enter your personal details. Those marked with an asterisk are obligatory.

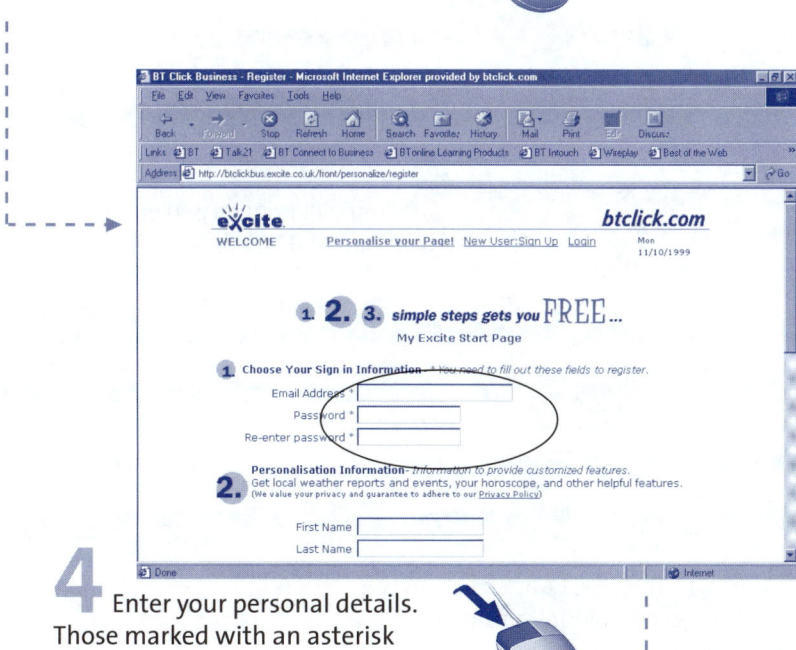

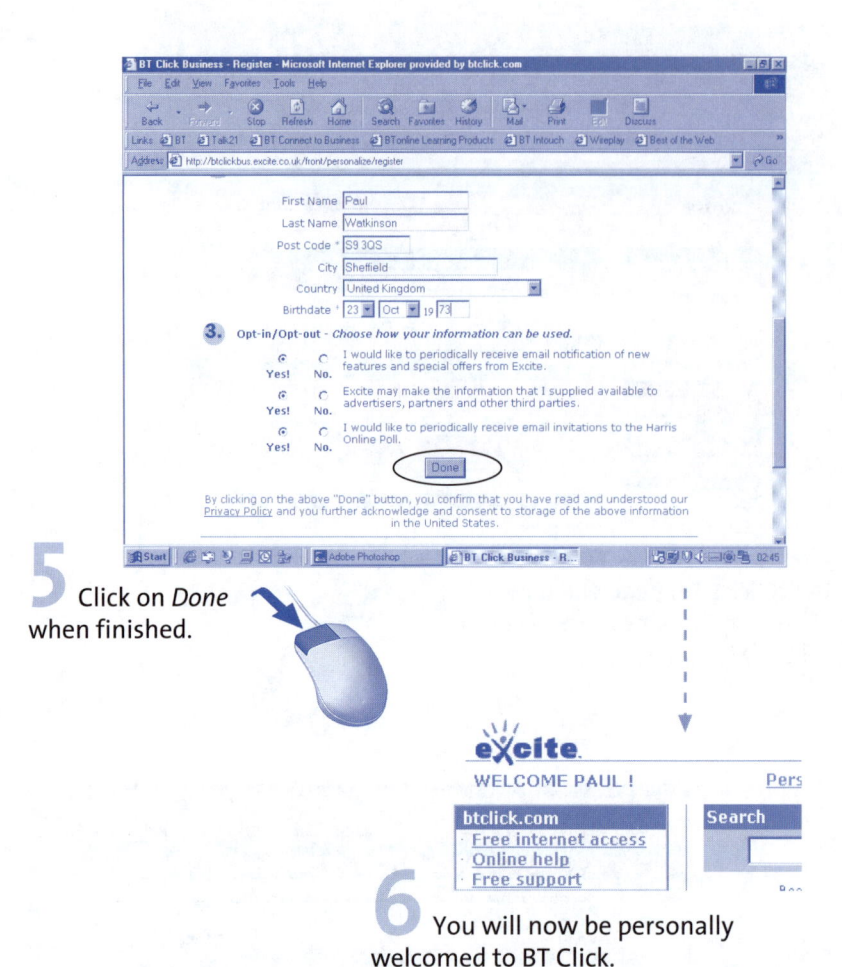

5 Click on *Done* when finished.

6 You will now be personally welcomed to BT Click.

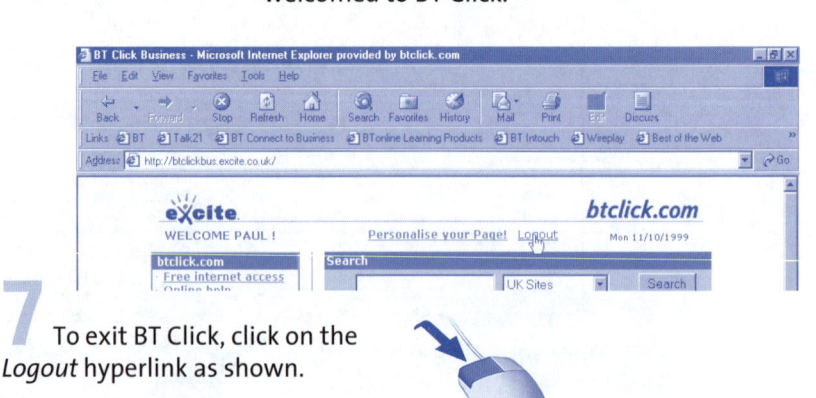

7 To exit BT Click, click on the *Logout* hyperlink as shown.

ACCESSING THE INTERNET WITH BT CLICK

In the next few steps, we will set up a free e-mail account with BT Click, through their associated e-mail service provider, Talk21.

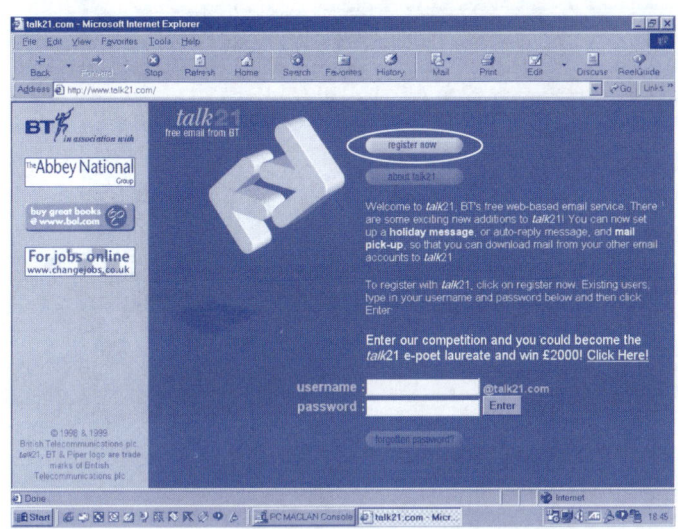

1 In your Web browser's *Address* field, enter the following URL: *http://www.talk21.com*. Click on *Register now*.

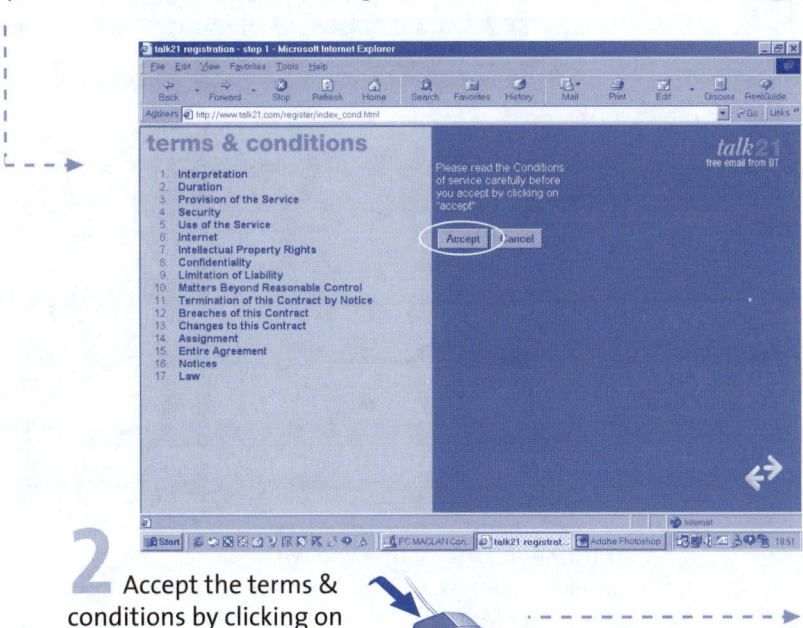

2 Accept the terms & conditions by clicking on *Accept*.

153

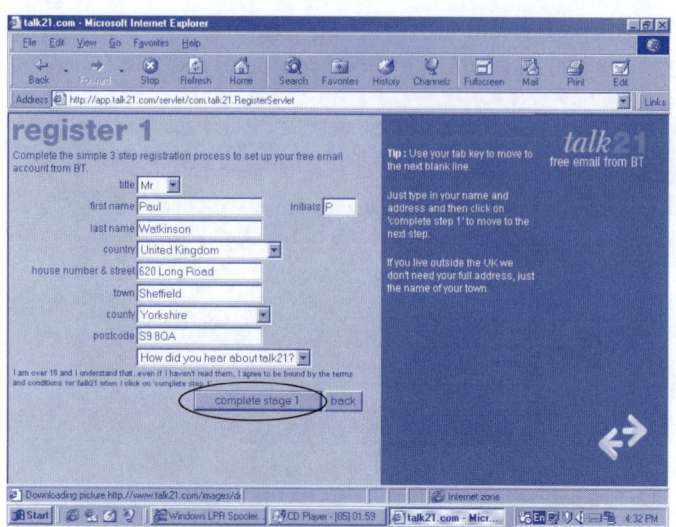

3 Fill in the entry fields as required. Then click on *complete stage 1*.

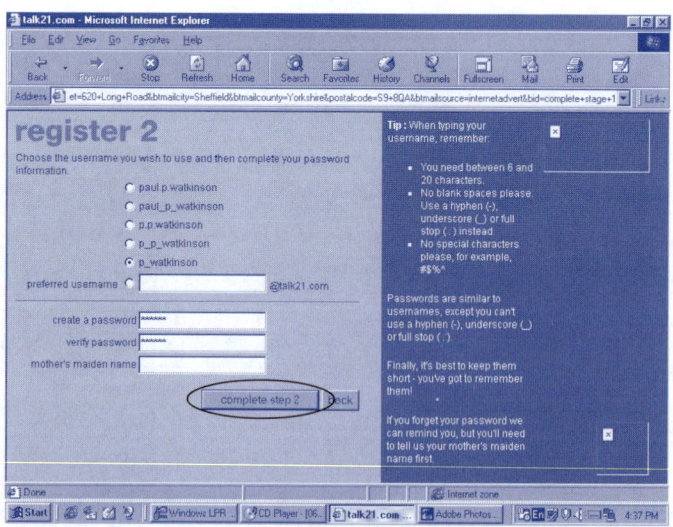

4 Choose the user name you wish to use, and provide your password information. Then click on *complete step 2*.

ACCESSING THE INTERNET WITH BT CLICK

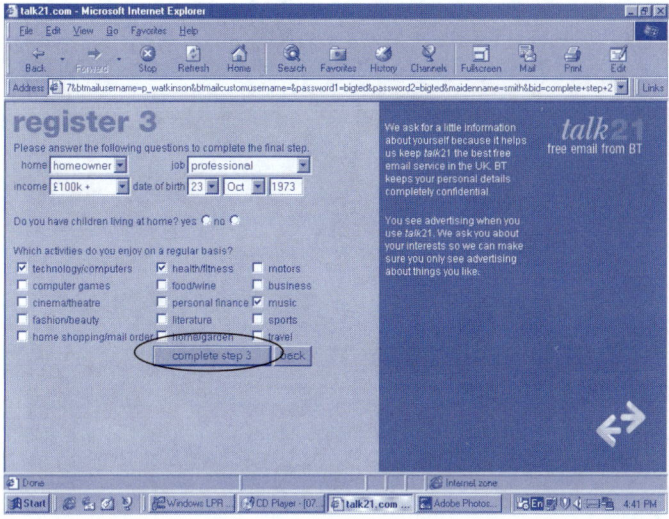

5 Provide the supplementary information required (you may specify what you like, but you must not leave any field empty). Then click on *complete step 3*.

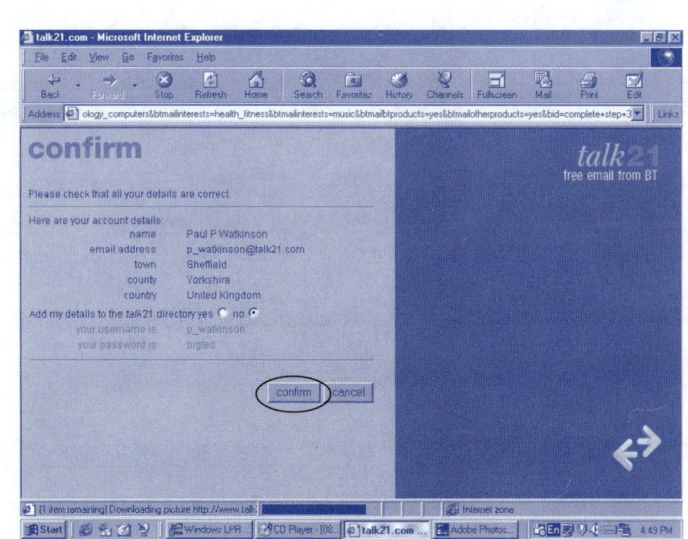

6 After a few moments, you will be presented with a summary of the information you provided. Click on *confirm*. This concludes your registration.

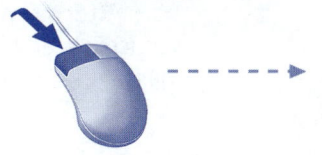

155

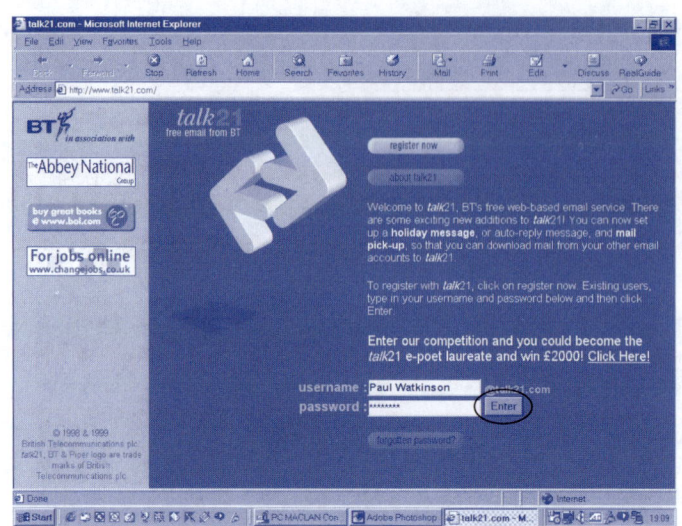

7 When you next call in to *talk21.com*, you can use the e-mail service. Enter your user name and password, then click on *Enter*.

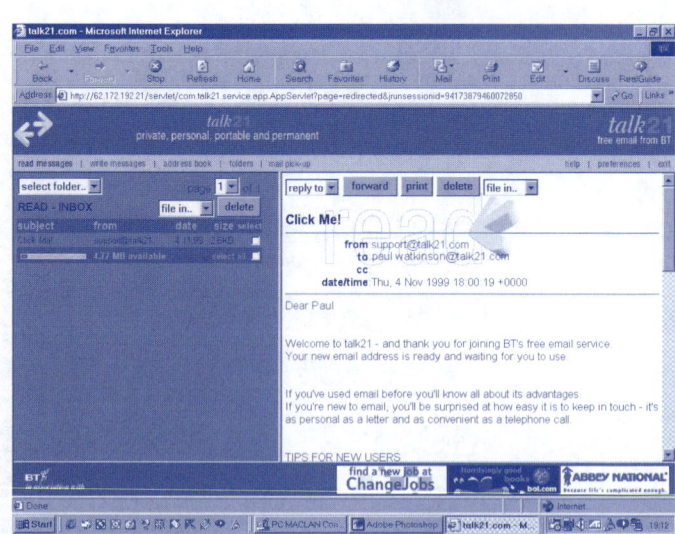

8 After a few moments, your e-mail service is ready for reading and sending messages.

Using BT Click to access the Internet, without calling the BT Click software

To access the Internet with BT Click, you really need to call up the BT Click software every time. However, there is a little trick you can use to get round this. To do this in Windows 95/98, you will need to consult the **Make New Connection wizard**, in order to set up a new dial-up networking connection.

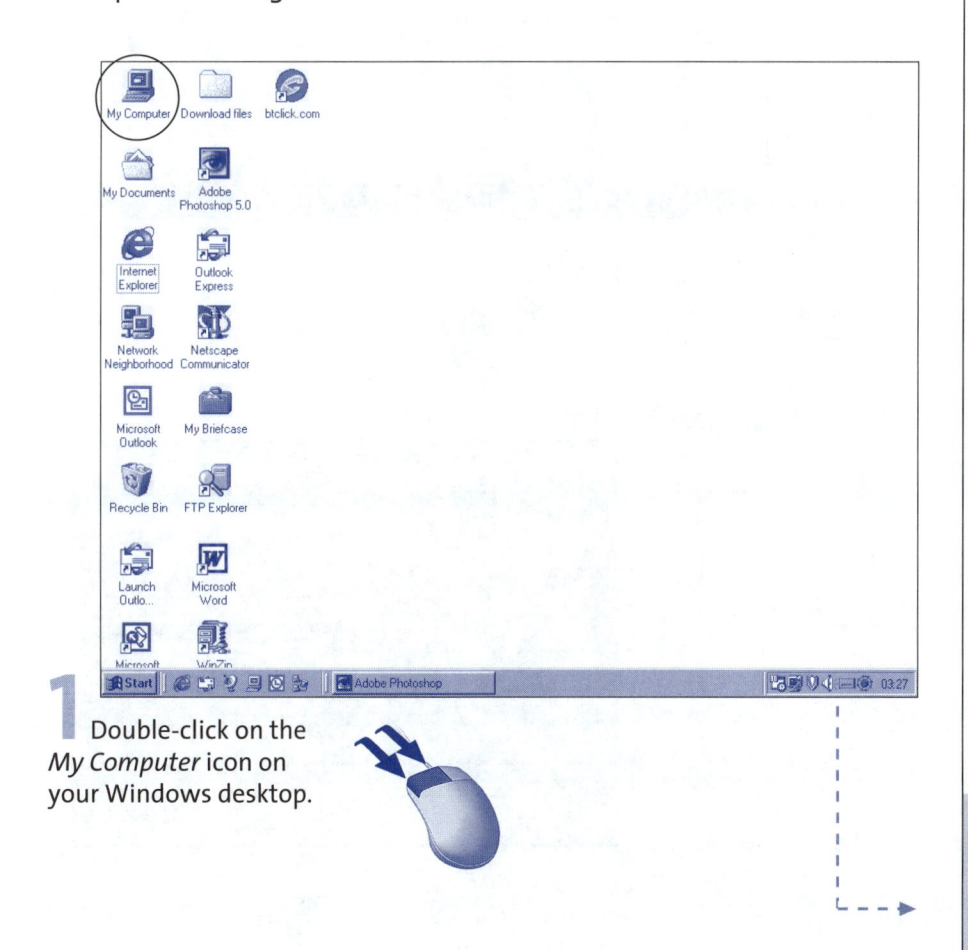

1 Double-click on the *My Computer* icon on your Windows desktop.

2 Double-click on the *Dial-Up Network* icon.

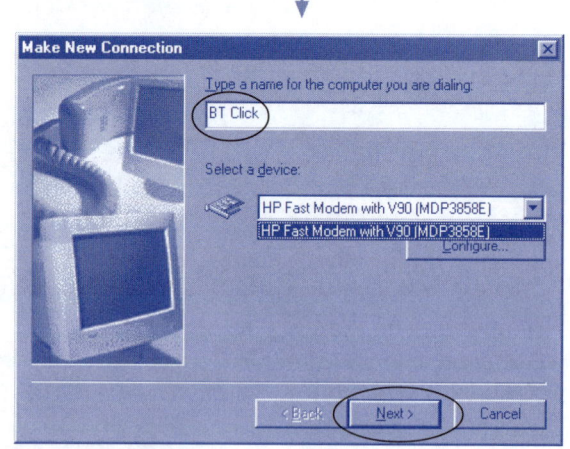

3 Enter a name for the connection and choose a modem which is connected to your computer. Then click on *Next*.

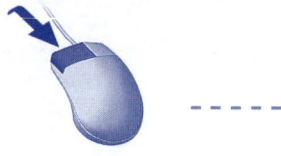

ACCESSING THE INTERNET WITH BT CLICK

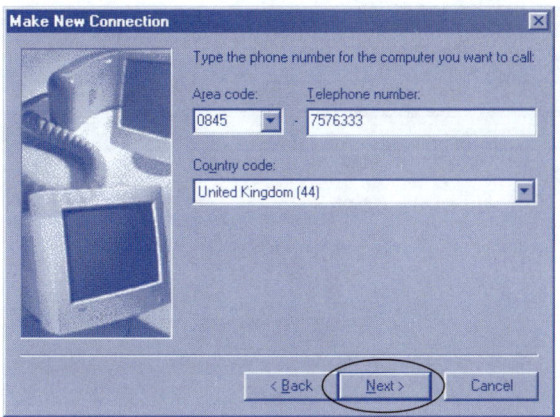

4 In the appropriate fields enter the local dialling code (0845) and then the countrywide access number for BT Click (757 6333). Confirm your input by clicking on *Next*.

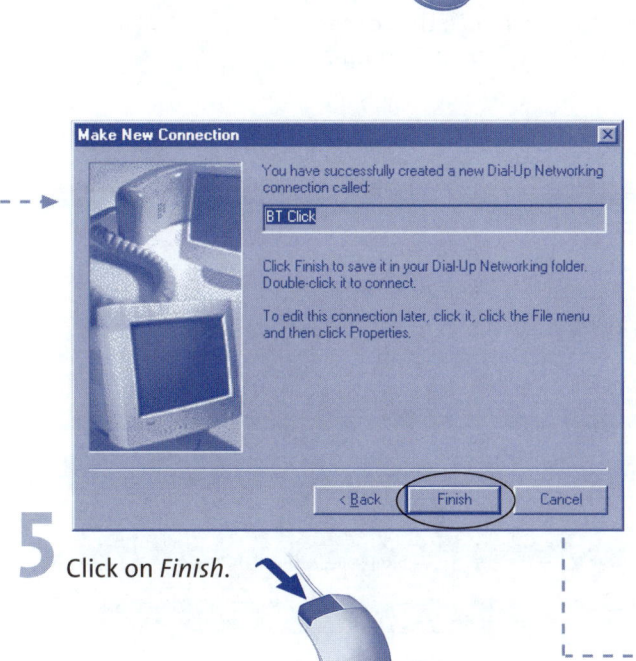

5 Click on *Finish*.

159

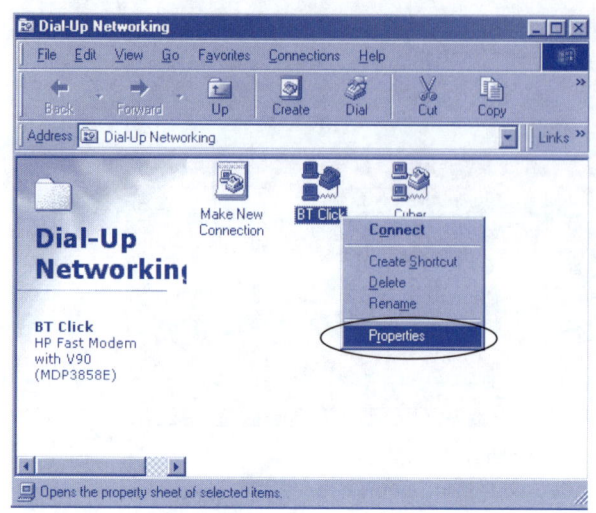

6 To configure the connection, right-click on the icon of the newly created connection. In the context menu, open the PROPERTIES command.

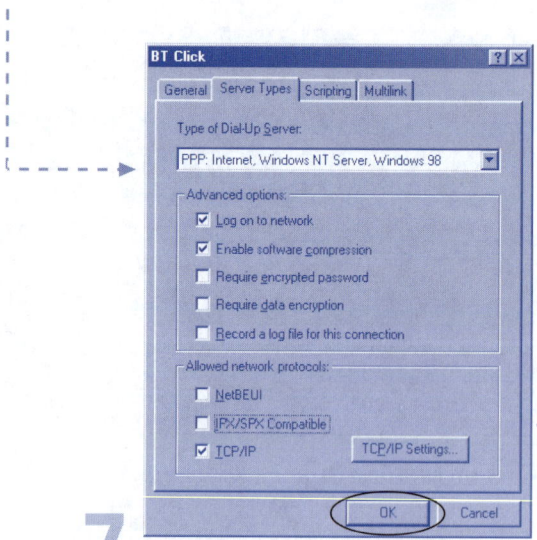

7 Follow the picture above to activate or deactivate the same checkboxes on the *Server types* tab. Then click on *OK*.

160

ACCESSING THE INTERNET WITH BT CLICK

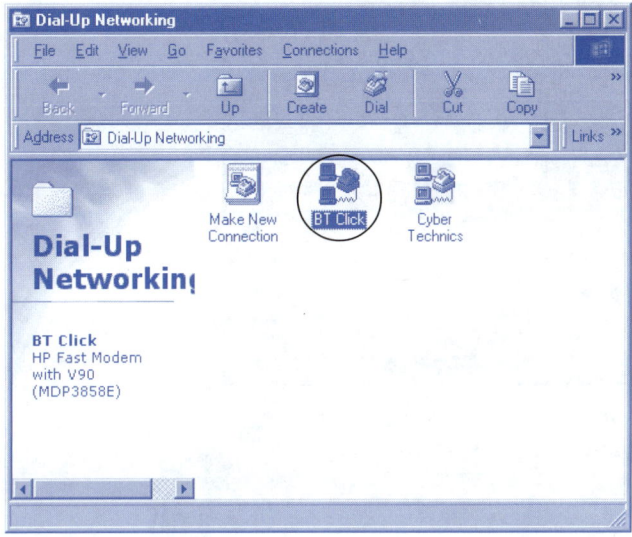

8 Double-click on the new connection.

In the next step you will need to supply your user name and password. Your user name will be the same one you specified when configuring your BT Click software. Your password is your BT Click password.

If you do not want to enter your password every time you establish an Internet connection via BT Click, mark the *Save password* checkbox in the following *Connect To* dialog.

161

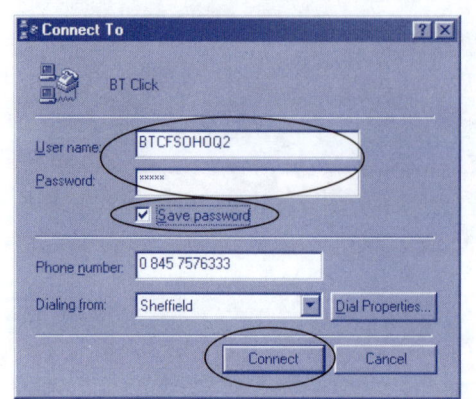

9 When you have entered your user name and password, click on *Connect*.

10 An Internet connection is opened via BT Click.

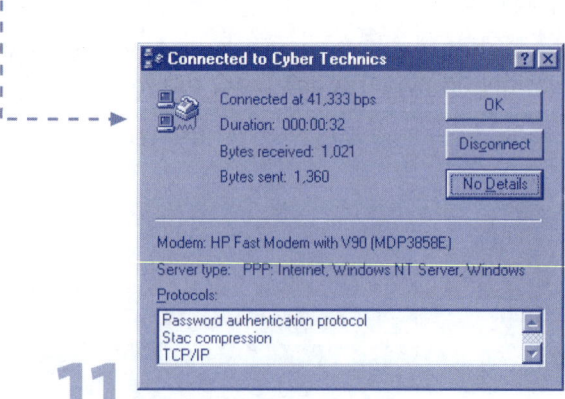

11 The Internet connection via BT Click is now ready.

You have to laugh

The Year 2000 problem has many guises...

"Your personal computer will still work on January 1, 2000... until a malfunctioning satellite falls on your house."

5

The Netscape Communicator

What's in this chapter:

Besides the Microsoft Internet Explorer, there are many alternatives available in the area of WWW browsers. The most well-known 'rival' is Netscape's Communicator. In the following chapter you will get acquainted with the essentials of Netscape Communicator 4.7. You will see how the Communicator is installed and used. Later on we will show you how to send and receive e-mail using the Communicator and how you can find and subscribe to newsgroups.

Your progress meter

You already know about:

Modems & Co.	10
The importance of software	16
Browsing and printing Web pages	88
How a search engine works	94
Using the Lycos search engine	98
The primeval Internet: Gopher	104
Getting onto the Internet with AOL...	122
... and with BT Click	141

You are going to learn about:

Installing Netscape Communicator 4.7	166
Configuring Netscape Communicator	172
The Communicator's postman – the Messenger	177
Newsgroups with the Netscape Messenger	183

165

Installing Netscape Communicator 4.7

Like Microsoft's Internet Explorer, you can get hold of a copy of **Netscape Communicator** either by downloading it free from the Internet or from one of the countless CD-ROMs given away in various computer magazines.

Insert the appropriate CD-ROM in your CD-ROM drive and look for the start-up file (for example cc32e47.exe), which is usually to be found in a folder named *Netscape*.

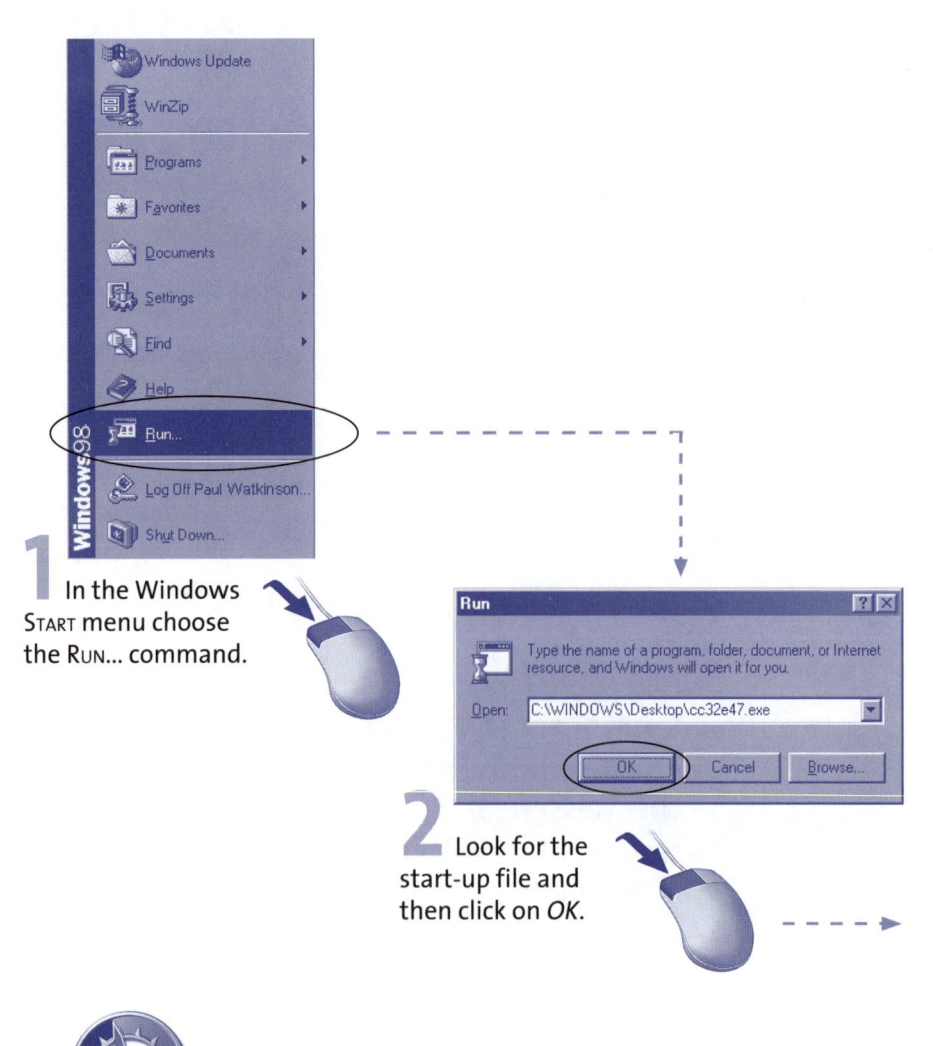

1 In the Windows START menu choose the RUN... command.

2 Look for the start-up file and then click on *OK*.

INSTALLING NETSCAPE COMMUNICATOR 4.7

3 The installation files are prepared.

4 Click on the *Next* button.

5 Accept the license agreement by clicking on *Yes*.

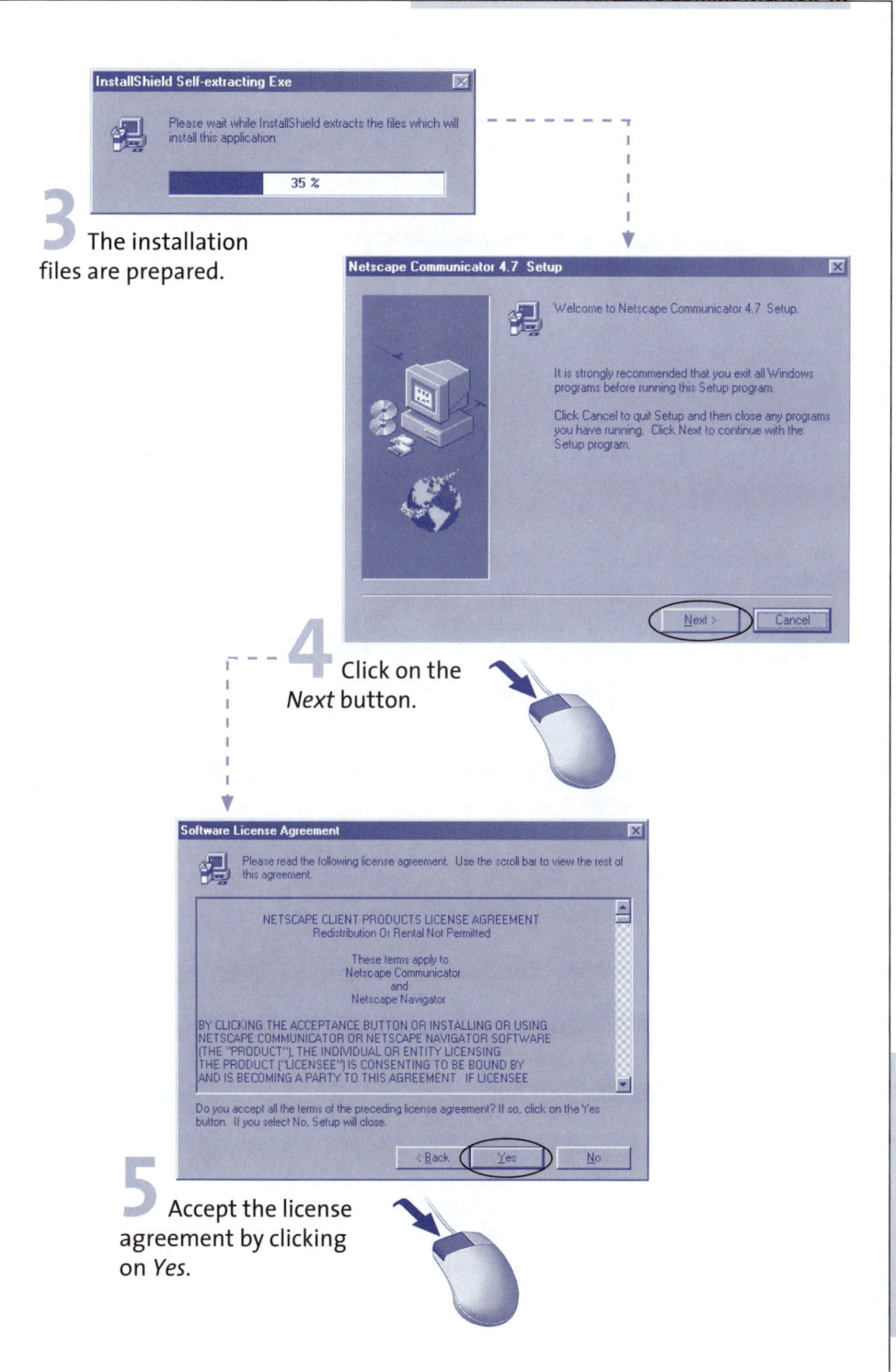

167

Netscape Communicator then offers you the choice of two different setup methods. The 'Typical' setup is the quickest and easiest and will automatically install all components needed to run the program.

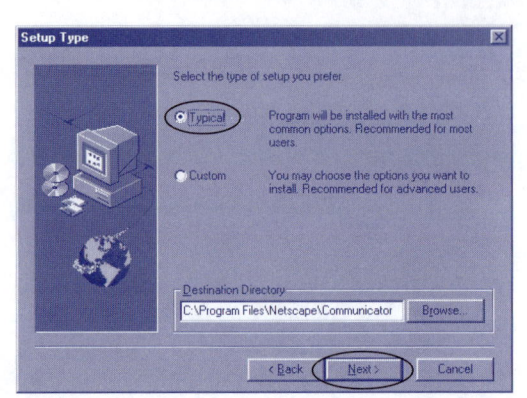

1 Select the *Typical* setup and accept the suggested destination directory by clicking on the *Next* button.

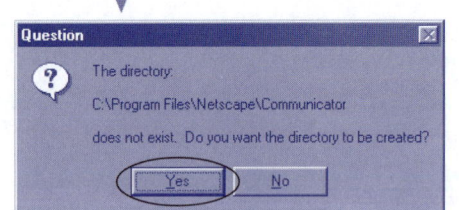

2 The setup procedure will ask you if you want the new destination directory to be created. Click on *Yes* to confirm this.

INSTALLING NETSCAPE COMMUNICATOR 4.7

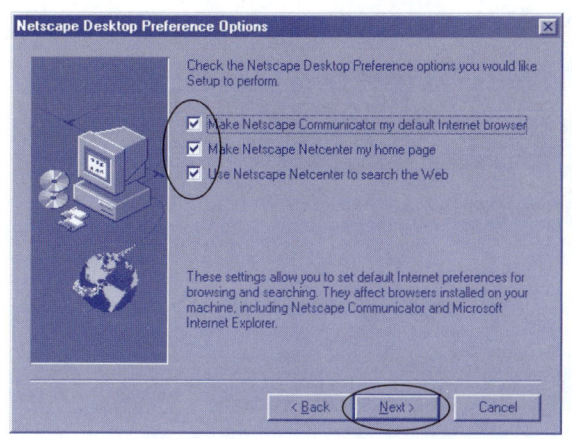

3 Select all of Netscape's desktop preference options and click on *Next*.

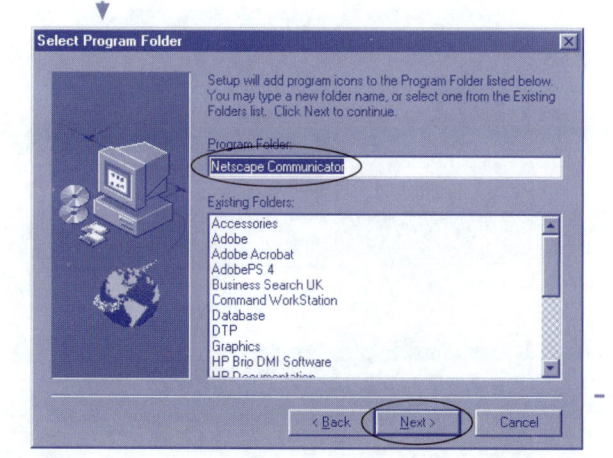

4 Accept the suggested folder, which will be created in the PROGRAMS submenu of the START menu. Click on *Next*.

169

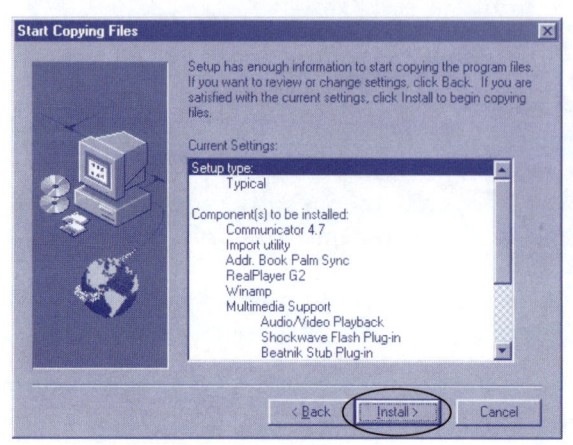

5 A summary then displays the final list of the currently selected Communicator components which are going to be installed. Click on *Install*.

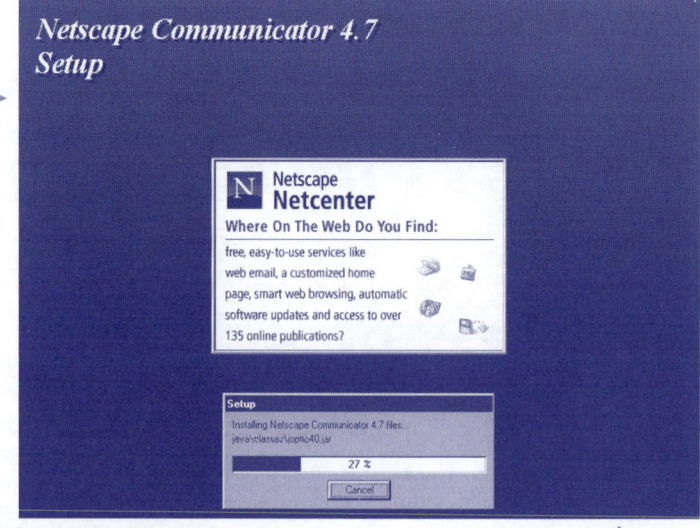

6 The installation procedure now copies all the files into the appropriate folders on your hard disk.

INSTALLING NETSCAPE COMMUNICATOR 4.7

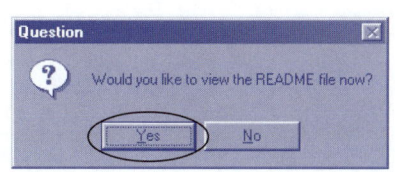

Question
Would you like to view the README file now?
[Yes] [No]

7 By clicking on the *Yes* button you can view the README file included with the installation, which contains additional, late-breaking information.

Information
Setup is complete. You may run Netscape Communicator 4.7 by double-clicking on one of the icons in the folder.
[OK]

8 Confirm the completion of the installation process by clicking on *OK*.

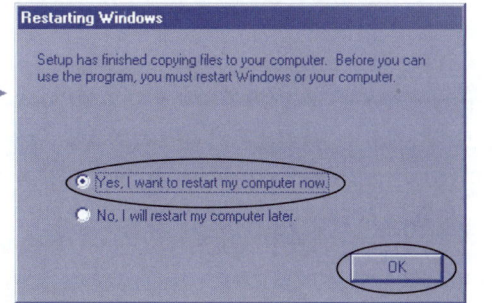

Restarting Windows
Setup has finished copying files to your computer. Before you can use the program, you must restart Windows or your computer.

● Yes, I want to restart my computer now.
○ No, I will restart my computer later.
[OK]

9 You will now need to restart your computer to activate all the newly copied and installed files. Click on *OK*.

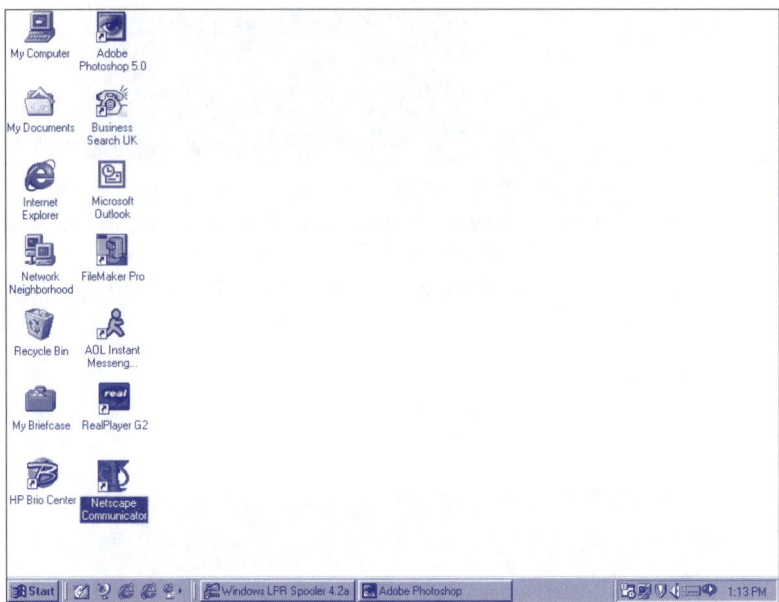

10 After restarting the computer you will find three new icons on the desktop as well as a new directory in the PROGRAMS submenu of the START menu.

Configuring the Netscape Communicator

Once Netscape Communicator has been installed on your hard disk, and is integrated into Windows 95/98, only a few more steps are required in the configuration process. Double-click on the *Netscape Communicator* icon on your desktop. First of all you will need to set up a **user profile** on the screen which appears so that the Communicator knows the person it is dealing with. Later on you will also be asked about the e-mail and newsgroups server of your Internet Service Provider.

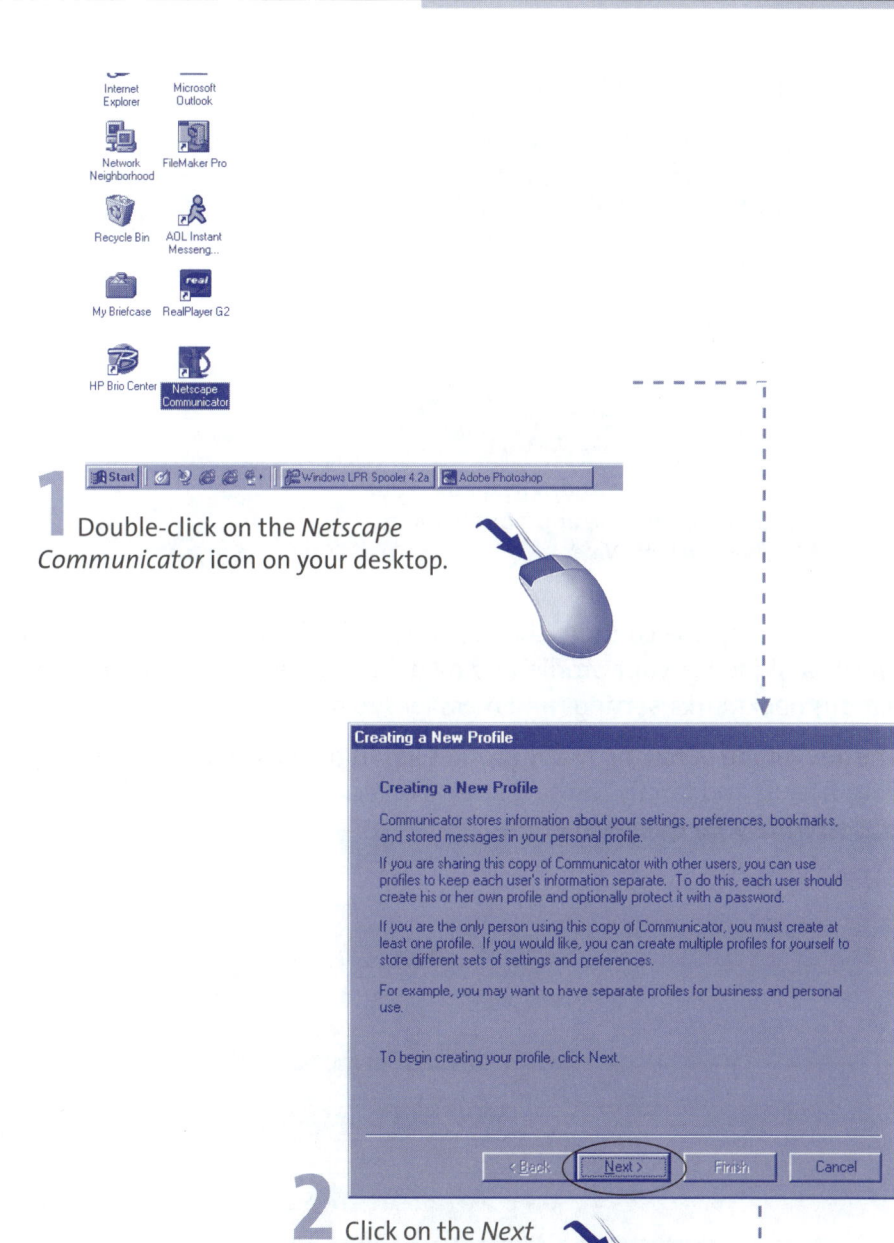

CONFIGURING THE NETSCAPE COMMUNICATOR

1 Double-click on the *Netscape Communicator* icon on your desktop.

2 Click on the *Next* button to create a user profile and thus enable the Communicator to start.

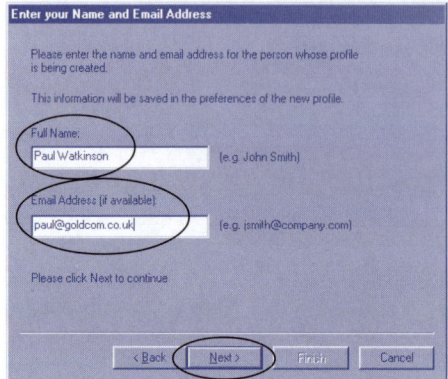

3 Enter your name and, if available, your e-mail address into the appropriate input fields. Then click on *Next*.

In the next step, the configuration routine will ask you for a name, which will be assigned to your profile, and for a directory, where you wish your various bookmarks, settings and messages to be saved.

The advantage of having many profiles lies in the fact that, for example, your friends and family can save their own access data without having to overwrite your data every time.

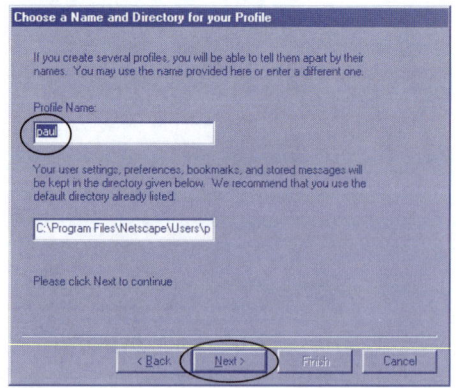

4 Enter the respective data and click on *Next*.

CONFIGURING THE NETSCAPE COMMUNICATOR

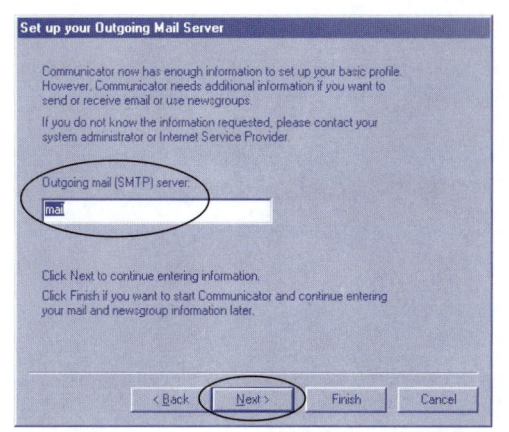

5 You will now need to register the mail server of your Internet Service Provider by name, so that the Communicator knows where to send all your outgoing mail. Then click on *Next*.

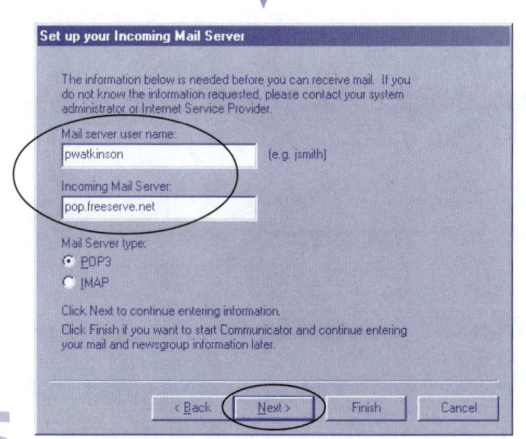

6 Now enter your user name for the mail box (you can find this out from your Internet Service Provider), and also the name of your mail server, which will forward all incoming e-mail to your PC. Then click on *Next*.

Since Netscape Communicator is also capable of displaying newsgroups, you will need to provide the name of your Internet Service Provider's newsgroup server in order to receive this source of information as well.

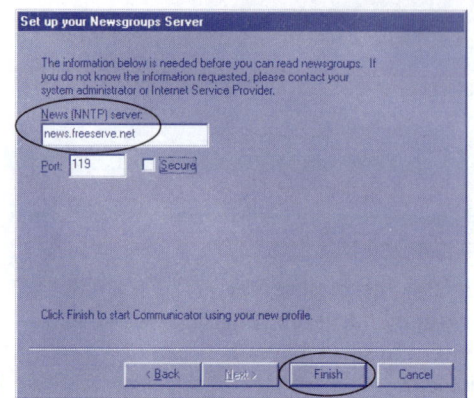

7 Enter the name of your Internet Service Provider's newsgroup server and then click on *Finish*.

Once all the data has been entered, it will take a few moments for the Communicator to start and display the usual screen of establishing a connection with the Internet.

1 Click on *Connect* to tell the Netscape Communicator to establish a connection with the Internet.

176

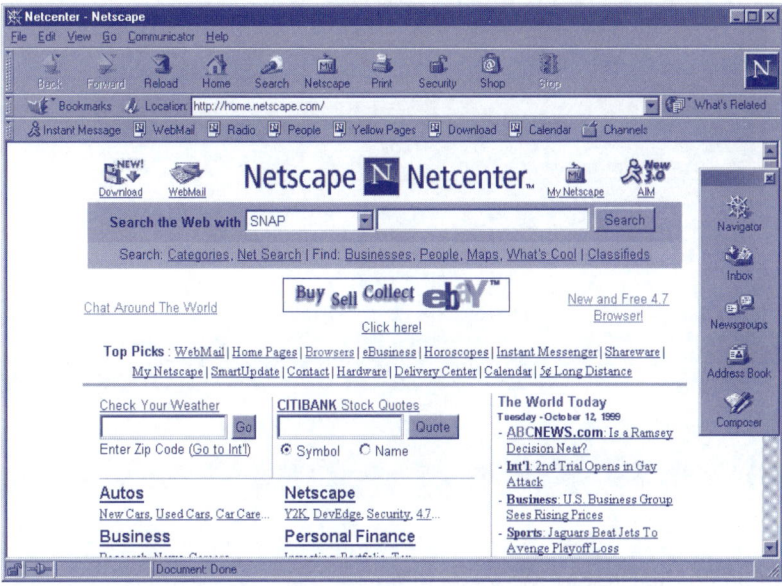

2 And here it is – the Netscape Communicator.

The Communicator's postman – the Messenger

With the installation of the Netscape Communicator you will have received a component called Netscape Messenger. This component is responsible for the sending and receiving of e-mail messages by means of the Communicator.

Receiving an e-mail message

In order to receive an e-mail message via the Netscape Communicator or its Messenger you will need to do the following:

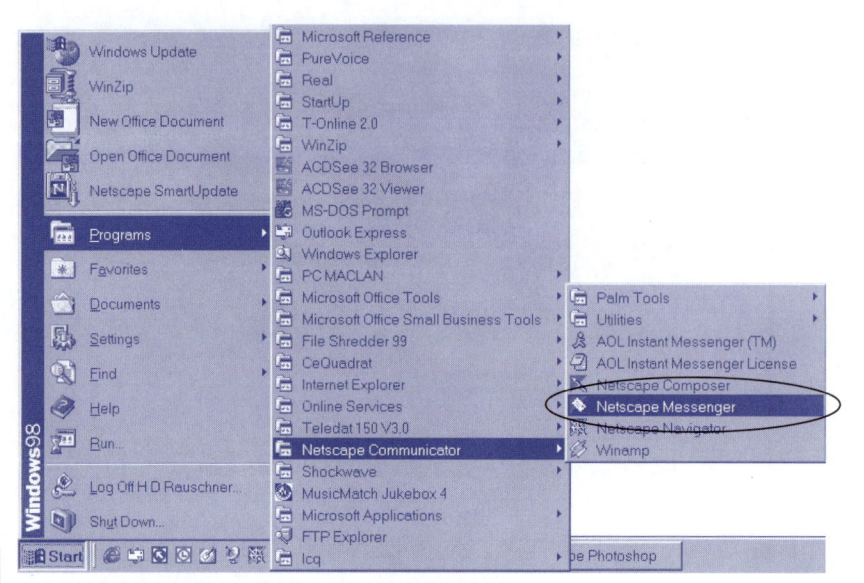

1 Call up the NETSCAPE MESSENGER entry from the START/PROGRAMS/ NETSCAPE COMMUNICATOR menu.

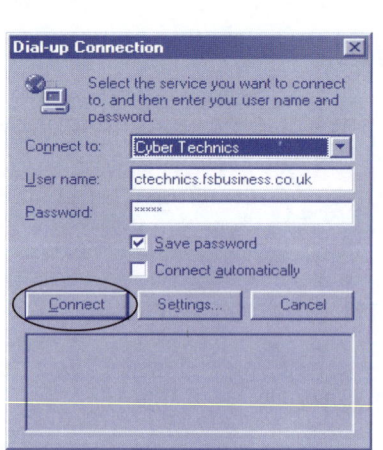

2 Click on *Connect* to allow the Messenger to connect to the Internet and establish a link with the Internet Service Provider's mail server.

THE COMMUNICATOR'S POSTMAN – THE MESSENGER

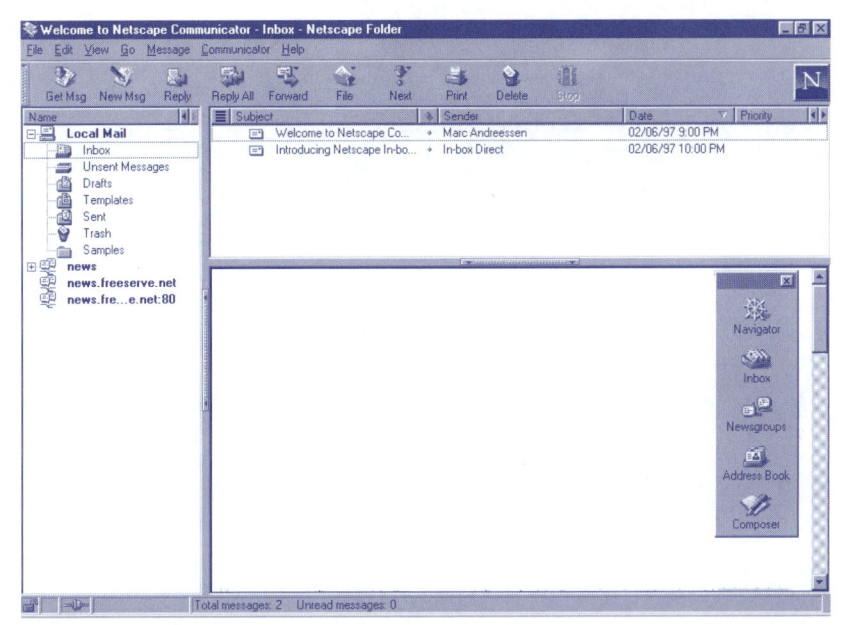

3 As soon as the Messenger is started, it contacts the mail server to see if there is any post for you. The first time you use it, it will ask you for the password to access your mailbox. Click on one of the newly received e-mail messages.

New e-mail messages are indicated in the form of bold type message headers in the top right-hand window. Double-clicking on one of these message headers will open the corresponding e-mail message.

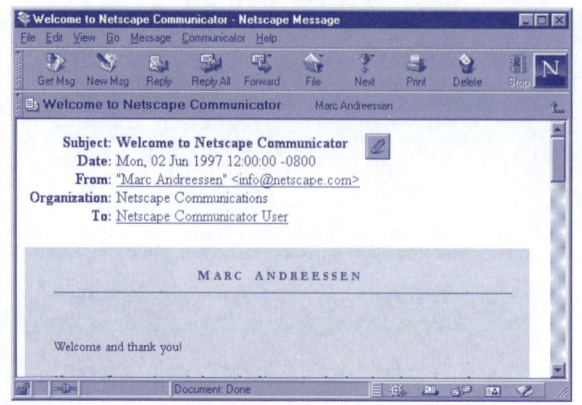

4 An e-mail message from Netscape welcomes you as a new user of Netscape Communicator and its various components.

Sending an e-mail message

You can also use the Messenger to send e-mail messages. Call up the Messenger as usual, and then do the following:

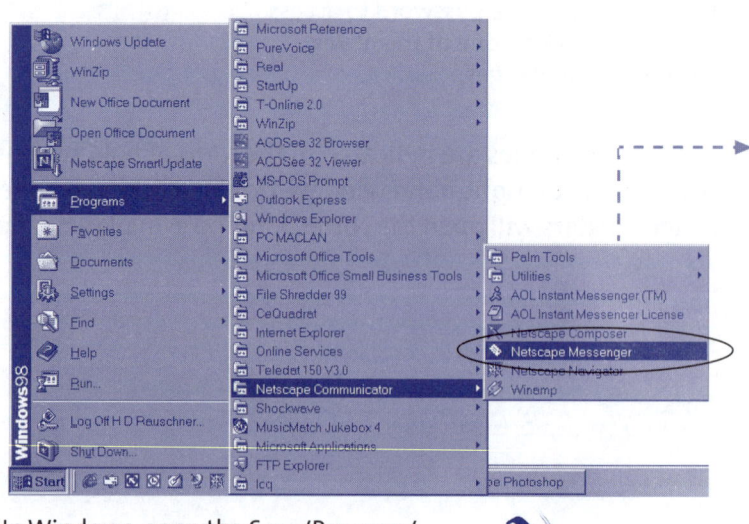

1 In Windows, open the START/PROGRAMS/ NETSCAPE COMMUNICATOR menu and select the NETSCAPE MESSENGER command. Open a connection to the Internet.

THE COMMUNICATOR'S POSTMAN – THE MESSENGER

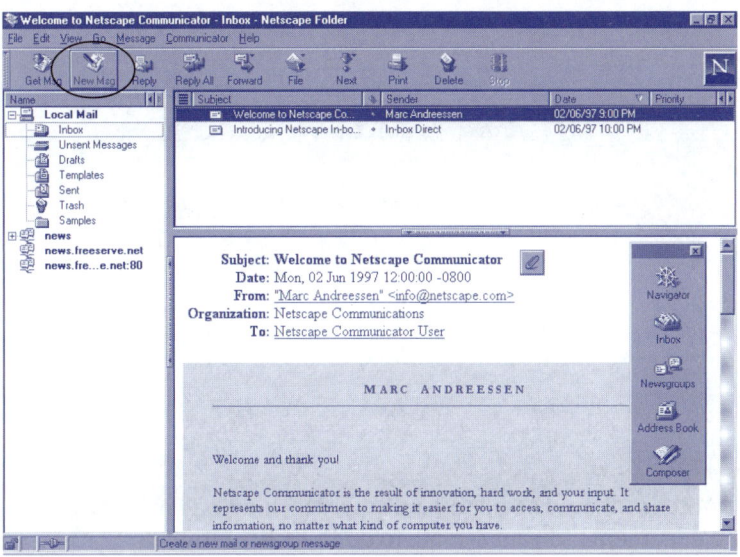

2 Click on the *New Msg* button in the Messenger's toolbar.

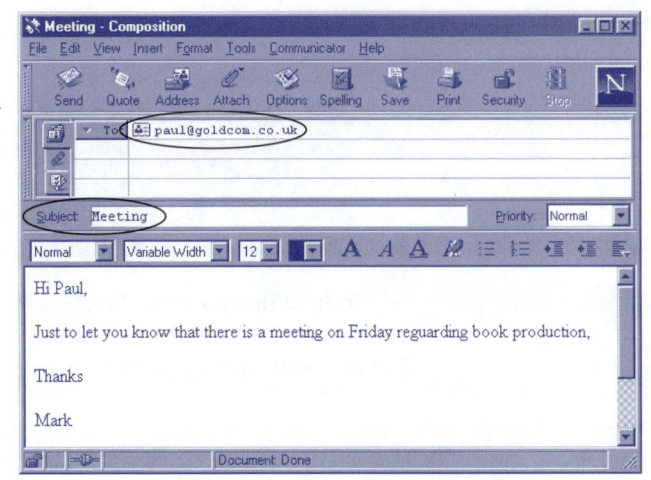

3 In the *To:* field enter the e-mail address of the person you are writing to. In *Subject* enter a short description of the message, and then compose the e-mail message itself in the text box.

181

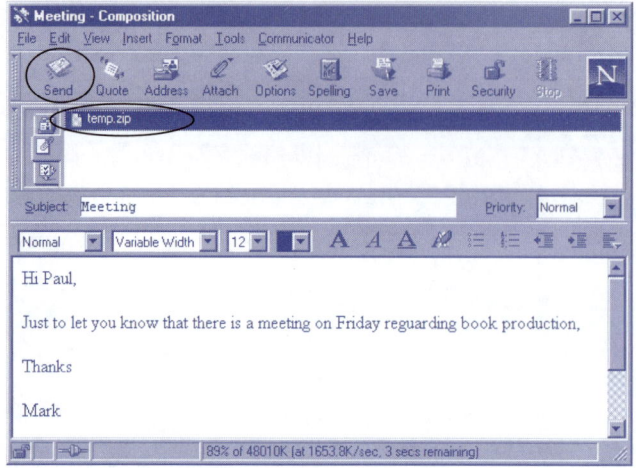

4 You now have the opportunity of attaching one or more documents to your e-mail. To do this, click either on the *Attach* icon in the toolbar or on the second tab beneath the e-mail address, and then select the required document from your hard disk.

Finally, click on the *Send* button in order to send your message out via the Internet.

5 Your computer then looks for the mail server of your Internet Service Provider and sends your e-mail.

Newsgroups with the Netscape Messenger

Like Microsoft's Outlook Express, Netscape Messenger is also capable of handling newsgroups. Call up the Messenger as usual and open a connection to the Internet.

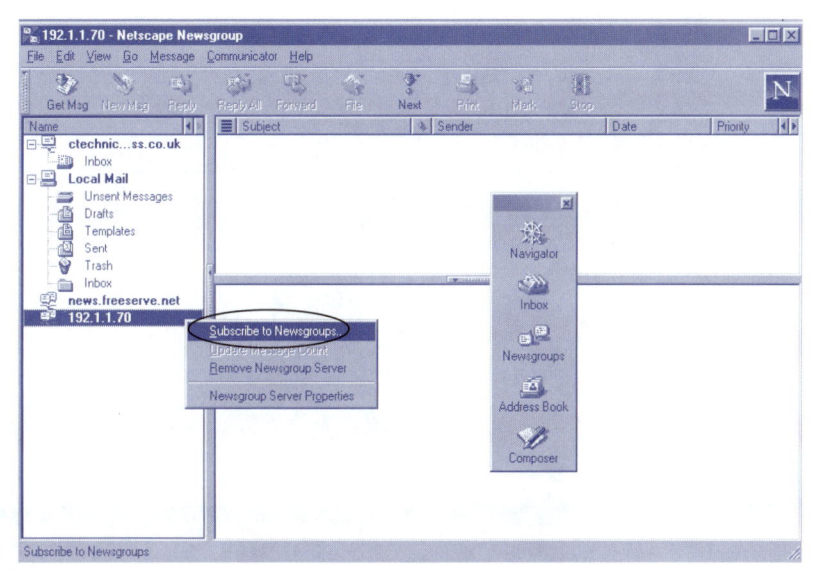

1 With the right mouse button, click on the entry for your news server and, when the context menu appears, choose the SUBSCRIBE TO NEWSGROUPS entry.

It will now take a few minutes for all the newsgroups to be loaded. You will then be able to choose which of the numerous newsgroups you wish to subscribe to. To do this, make use of the help offered by the *Search* tab.

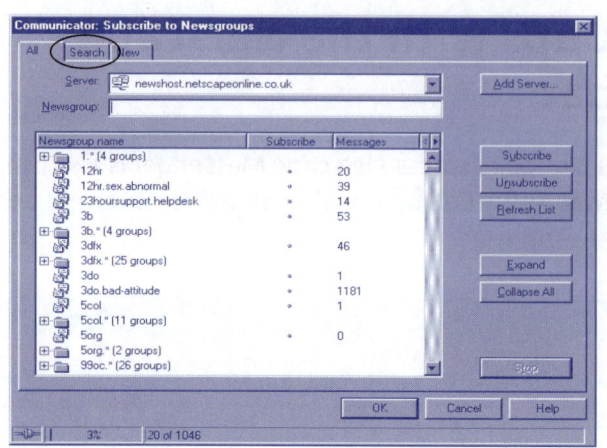

2 Activate the *Search* tab to help you find newsgroups on a particular subject.

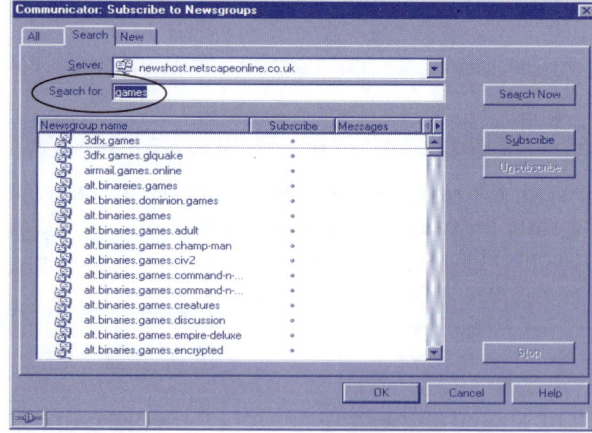

3 In the *Search for* field enter an appropriate search term.

NEWSGROUPS WITH THE NETSCAPE MESSENGER

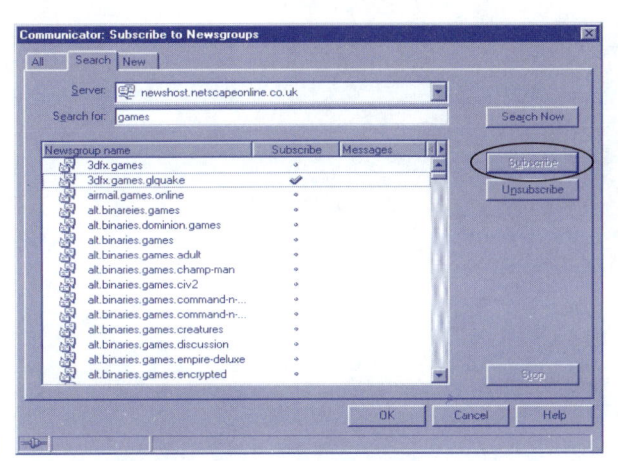

4 If you have found an interesting newsgroup, click on the *Subscribe* button.

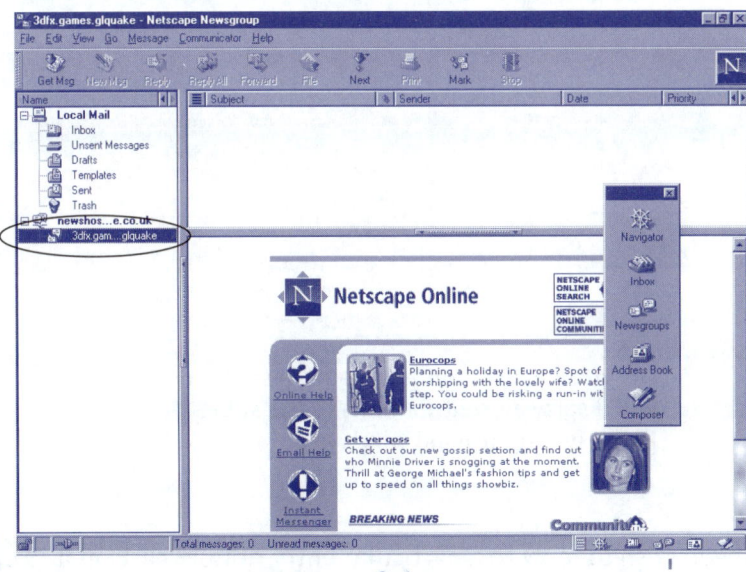

5 Now click on the newsgroup to which you have subscribed in the left-hand window of the Messenger, underneath your news server.

185

6 Click on the *Download* button.

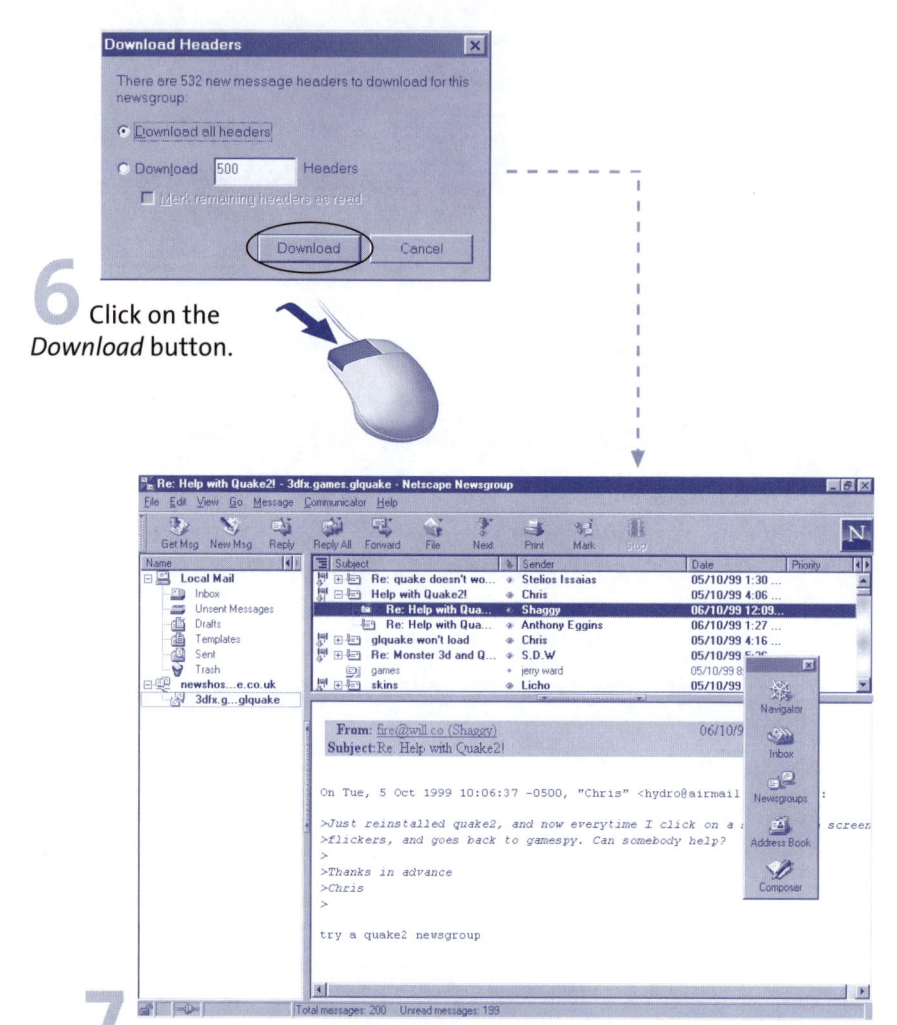

7 After a few moments your Messenger will display all contributions to the subject in the two right-hand windows.

If you wish to reply to a particular entry, double-click on it to open the corresponding mail window.

NEWSGROUPS WITH THE NETSCAPE MESSENGER

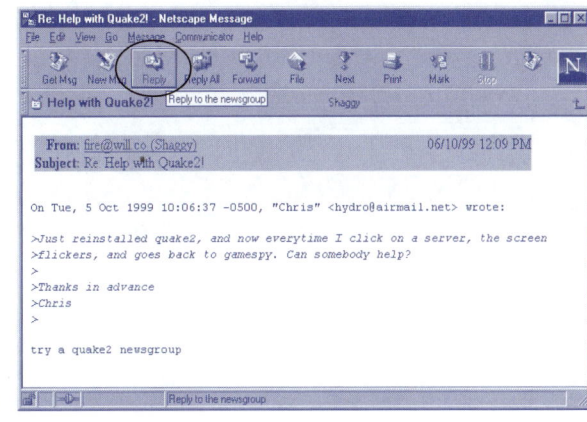

8 All you have to do to answer a question or reply to a remark is click on the *Reply* button.

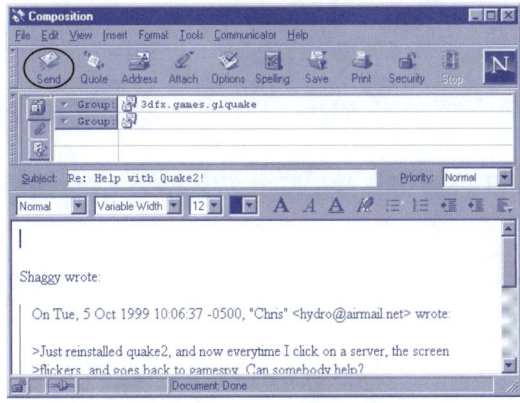

9 Enter the text of your answer and then click on the *Send* button in order to send your message.

Writing your own articles

You will, of course, be able to send your own questions to a particular newsgroup. You do it like this:

187

Open up the Messenger, connect to the Internet and choose the desired newsgroup out of the list of subscribed newsgroups shown underneath the newsgroup server.

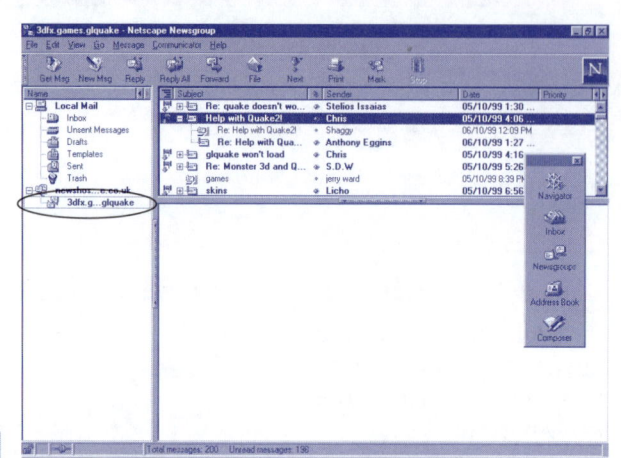

1 Click on the newsgroup you require in the list shown underneath the newsgroup server.

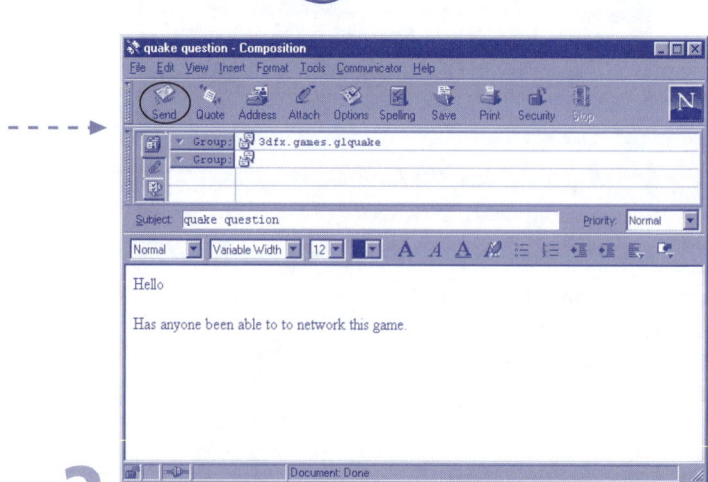

2 Compose your message for this particular newsgroup and, once you are done, click on the *Send* button.

A nice feature of the Messenger is its spell checker, which checks your e-mail messages for possible spelling mistakes. You activate the spell checker by clicking on the *Spelling* button.

You have to laugh

Jimmy's found a great way of speeding up his old 386…

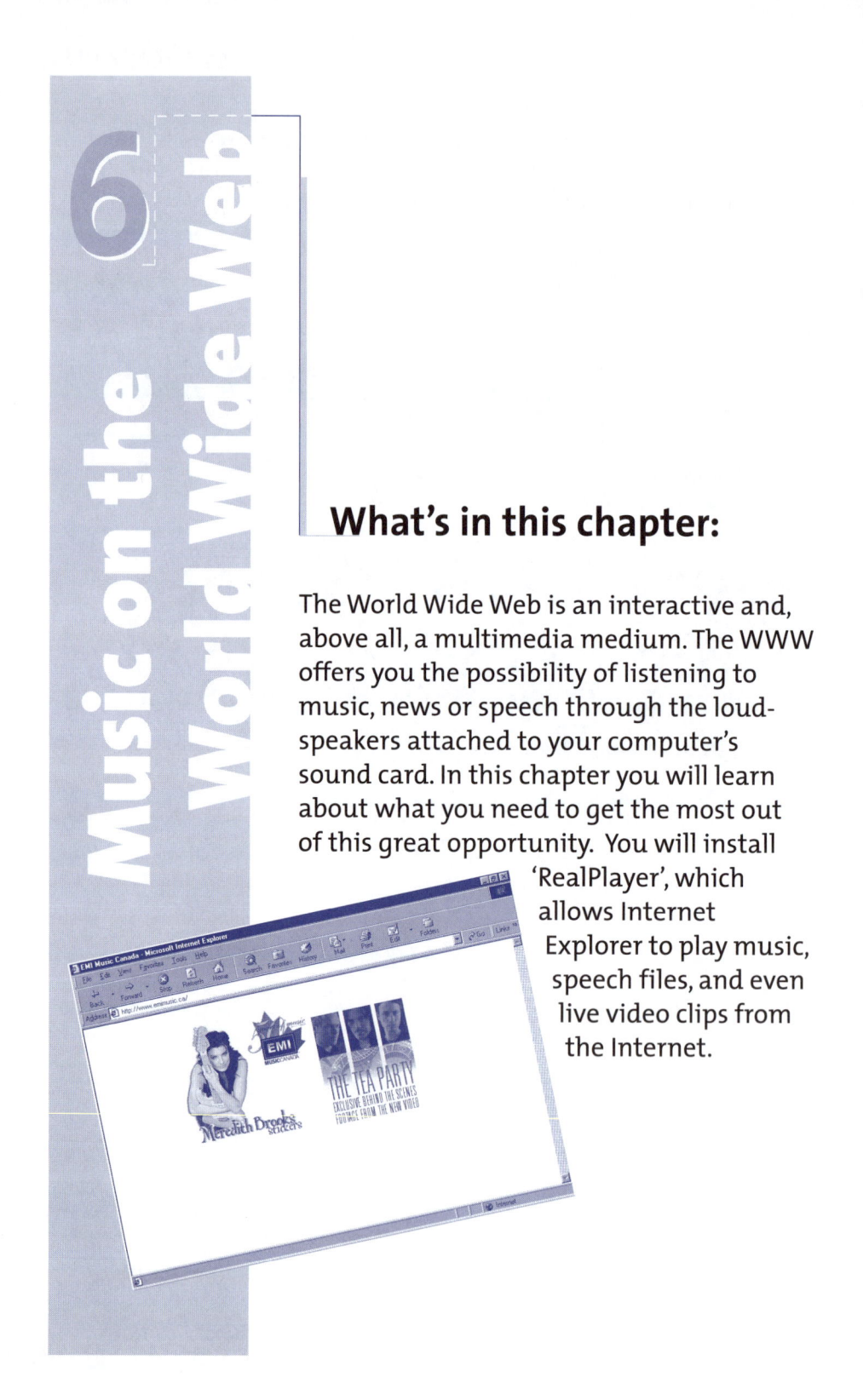

6

Music on the World Wide Web

What's in this chapter:

The World Wide Web is an interactive and, above all, a multimedia medium. The WWW offers you the possibility of listening to music, news or speech through the loudspeakers attached to your computer's sound card. In this chapter you will learn about what you need to get the most out of this great opportunity. You will install 'RealPlayer', which allows Internet Explorer to play music, speech files, and even live video clips from the Internet.

You already know about:

Taking your first steps in the World Wide Web	67
Loading saved pages	86
Browsing and printing Web pages	88
How a search engine works	94
Using the Lycos search engine	98
Accessing the Internet with AOL	122
Accessing the Internet with BT Click	141
Installing Netscape Communicator 4.7	166

You are going to learn about:

Rock, pop and classical music on the Web	192
Internet Explorer and its 'Players'	194
Getting started with RealPlayer	201
RealPlayer in detail	203
CD quality music – MP3	206

Rock, pop and classical music on the Web

We perceive the world around us by using our many different senses, but our eyes and ears play a particularly important role. The Internet, a truly modern way of communicating, has offered our ears an extra something since the invention of the World Wide Web.

Sounds, voices and music have now become everyday components of the Internet and their use ranges from radio stations, interviews and music on the Web to sound files and entire live concerts being transmitted over the WWW.

WHAT'S THIS?

Digitisation: analogue data such as speech or video must be converted into a sequence of zeros and ones so that the computer can understand the information. This conversion process is known as digitisation.

On the Internet there are many different types of audio data. They all have in common the fact that they have been digitised so that they can be transmitted over the Internet. You will almost certainly have seen files ending in .WAV or .AU already. These are files which contain audio data, such as music or speech. In order to play these files on your computer you will need to use a particular program, called an AudioPlayer or MediaPlayer, which is already included in Windows 95/98.

Audio files are usually very large and you must first download them from the Internet onto your computer. You will not be able to listen to these files until they are fully downloaded onto your hard disk. As you can see, this is an arduous task – it is not unusual for a file containing one minute's worth of music to take more than 20 minutes to download!

But don't panic! There is a much better and more modern way of using audio data on the Internet, called Streaming Audio. This process treats audio data in an intelligent way. You will no longer need to wait until an entire file is downloaded before you can listen to it. Instead, you will be able to hear the sounds as they are being downloaded. To use this function you will need a particular program which is automatically called up by your Web browser as soon as you click on a hyperlink which contains an appropiate sound file. The program you need at this point is called 'RealPlayer', and is, of course, freely available on the Internet.

How does RealAudio work?

When you are in a Web page and click on a link to a RealAudio file, this link does not lead directly to the required file itself. Instead, your browser sends a request to the WWW server, which in turn sends back a **RealAudio metafile**. This is a small text file which contains the address (URL) of the file. Furthermore, this file also contains instructions which tell the Web browser to start RealPlayer automatically if and when needed.

As soon as **RealPlayer** is started up it tries to connect to the URL specified in the metafile. This URL, however, is not located on the usual Web server, but on a special RealAudio server, specifically designed to supply Real-Audio files.

*WHAT'S THIS? A **RealAudio server** hosts music and sound files, which are available for you to retrieve on the Internet.*

The **RealAudio server** uses the RealPlayer to find out the speed at which your computer is working with the Internet. If it sees that you have a slow Internet connection it will send a file with low sound quality. With a fast connection the sound quality is high, and correspondingly more data needs to be transferred.

*WHAT'S THIS? A **buffer** is a particular memory zone where your computer stores temporary data.*

RealAudio files ready to be transmitted are compressed so that they can be transferred more quickly. At the receiver's end, all incoming data packets are stored in a particular memory zone, also known as a **buffer**. As soon as this buffer is full, all data is sent to the RealPlayer.

With RealAudio you can fast forward or rewind within an audio file. When doing this, the Player tells the server the new position and then the RealAudio server sends the file from this new starting point.

Internet Explorer and its 'Players'

Now here's something for Internet Explorer users: in less recent versions of IE4 or IE5, the audio and video player installed by Microsoft used to be the RealPlayer, so some of you will have either a RealPlayer plug-in or a full RealPlayer Plus installation.

More recent versions (including online upgrades via Microsoft's Web server), instead, are supplied with Microsoft's proprietary player, called Windows Media Player, current version 6.4. Any support for the RealPlayer has been discontinued – it is no longer included in the list of WIndows-compatible software.

Why this is so shall be left to your imagination. What needs to be said, however, is that anybody who has worked with the user-friendly interface and the many features of RealPlayer will certainly miss it.

Therefore, you will have to install RealPlayer yourself if you want to be able to really enjoy sound transmissions and video clips from the Internet. Like many other things, you can obtain this software freely from the manufacturer's Web site.

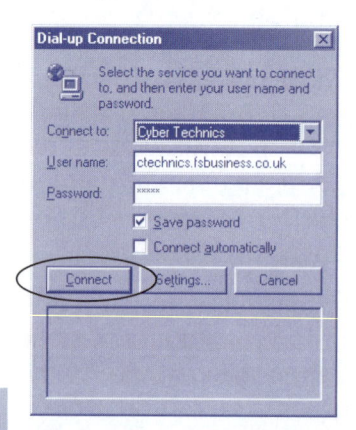

1 On the desktop click on the *Internet Explorer* icon and open a connection to the Internet. Enter your user name and password, then click on *Connect*.

INTERNET EXPLORER AND ITS 'PLAYERS'

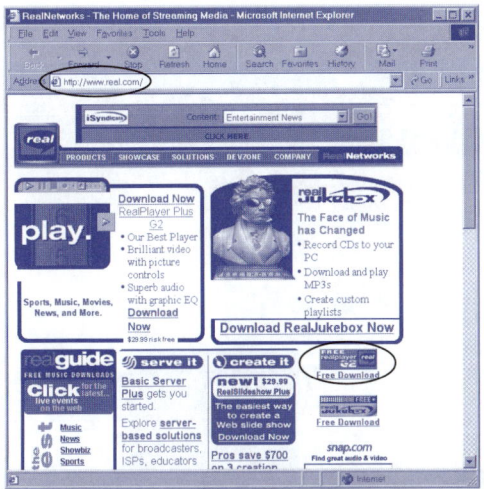

2 In the *Address* field, enter the following URL: *http://www.real.com/*. Then click on the *Free Download* hyperlink showing 'Free RealPlayer G2'.

Don't get tempted by the many other *Download Now* hyperlinks – most of them lead to chargeable software products.

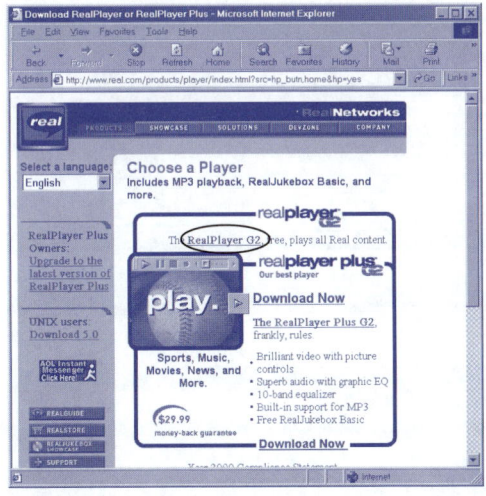

3 Click on the hyperlink named *RealPlayer G2*. Once again, do **not** click on any of the *Download Now* links.

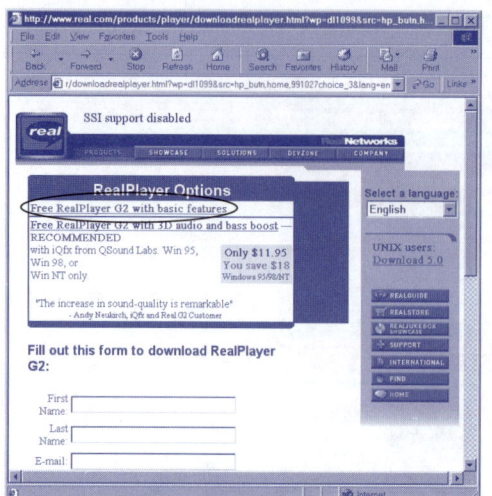

4 Click on *Free RealPlayer G2 with basic features*.

The next screen will present you with a form to be filled in before you can actually download RealPlayer G2. On this screen, click on the *Minimum requirements for RealPlayer G2* hyperlink to make sure that your computer is powerful enough to handle the application.

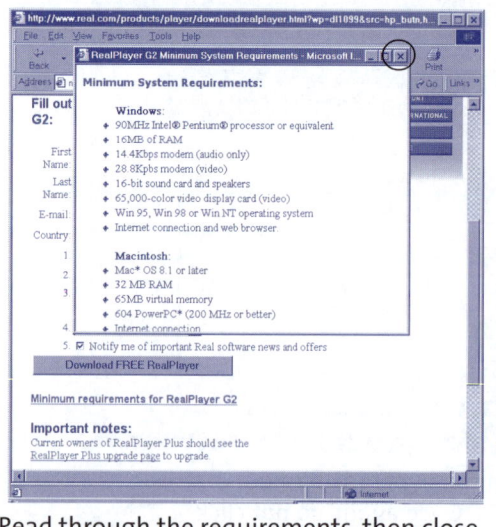

5 Read through the requirements, then close the window by clicking on the small cross icon.

196

INTERNET EXPLORER AND ITS 'PLAYERS'

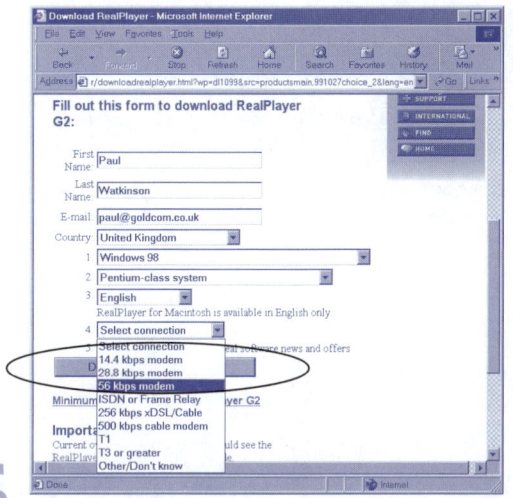

6 Fill in all the fields of the form by typing your first and last name, your e-mail address, and selecting the other items from the corresponding drop-down lists such as the *Select connection* list shown above. Then click on the *Download FREE RealPlayer* button (it appears as soon as you close the list box).

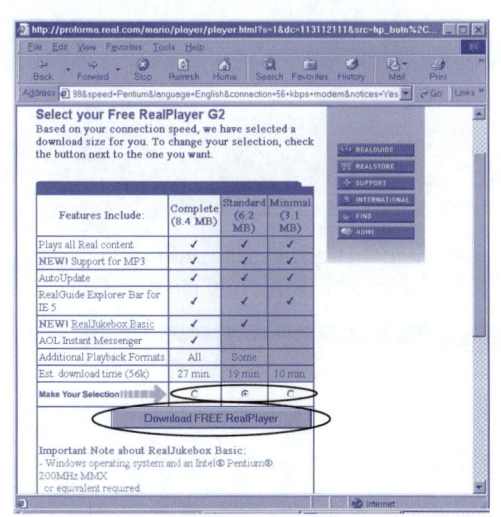

7 Select the configuration you wish to download, then click on the *Download FREE RealPlayer* button.

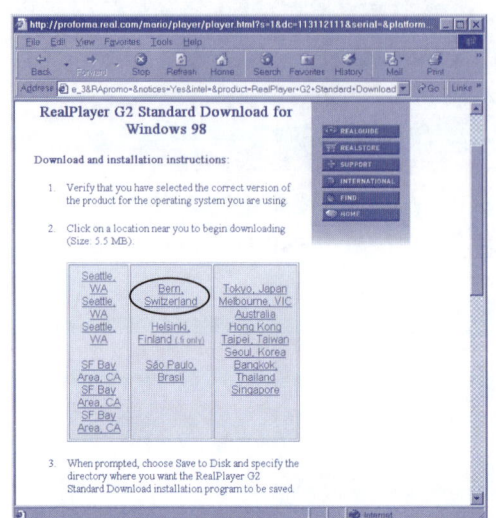

8 Click on the connection you wish to use for loading RealPlayer. From the UK, this should be Bern, Switzerland.

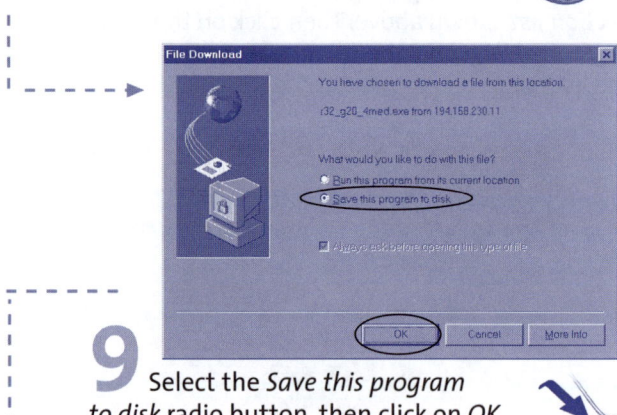

9 Select the *Save this program to disk* radio button, then click on *OK*.

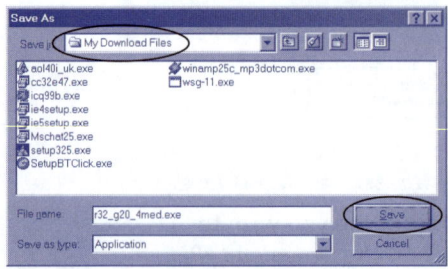

10 Select a folder in which the setup program will be saved, then click on *Save*.

198

INTERNET EXPLORER AND ITS 'PLAYERS'

11 Enter the name of the setup file you just saved in the START/RUN dialog, then click on *OK*.

12 Click on *Accept* to accept the license agreement and begin the installation process.

13 Enter your e-mail address in the appropriate field, select the folder in which you want RealPlayer to be installed, then click on *Finish*.

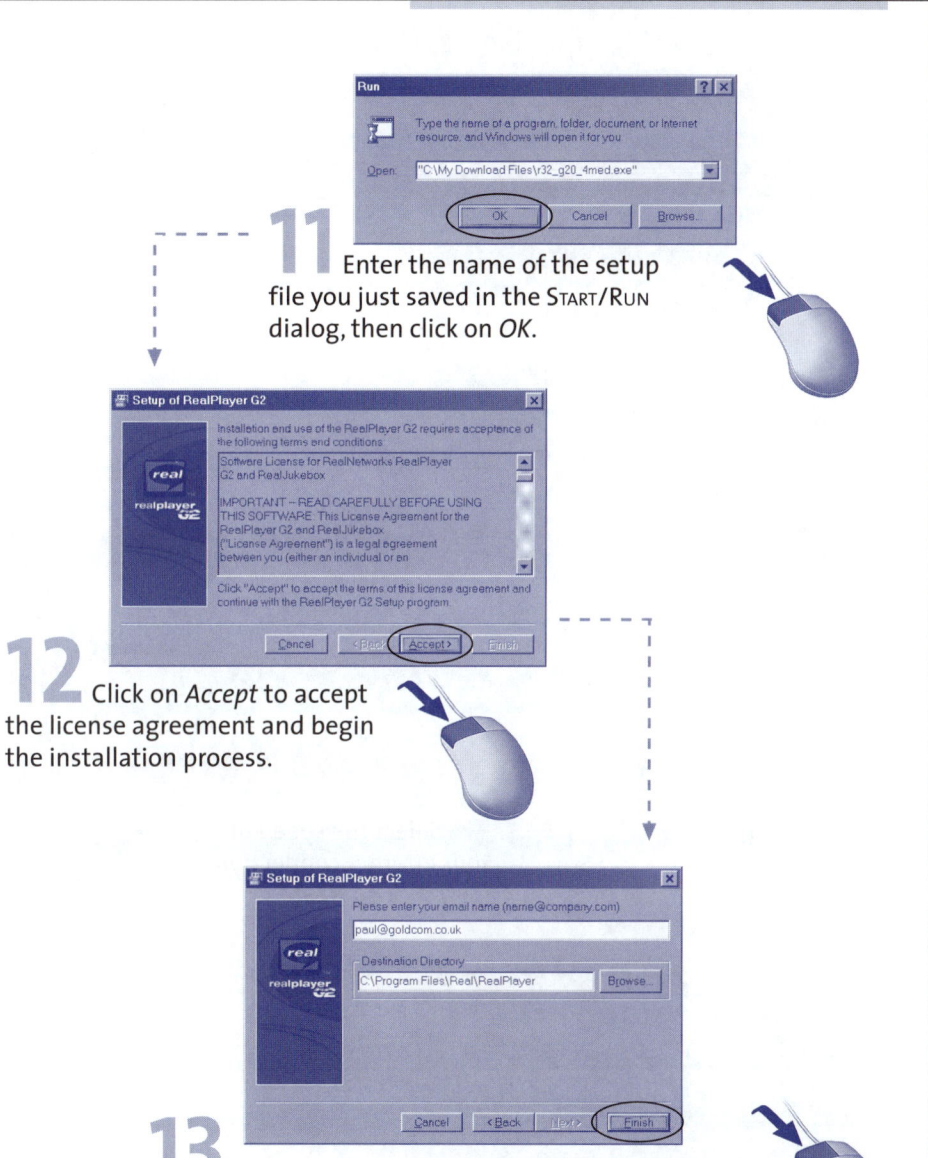

This concludes the installation. A new icon named *RealPlayer G2* is created on your desktop. Double-click this icon to launch the RealPlayer. On the first launch, you will need to answer a few questions about your preferred setup – refer to the online help function for more information.

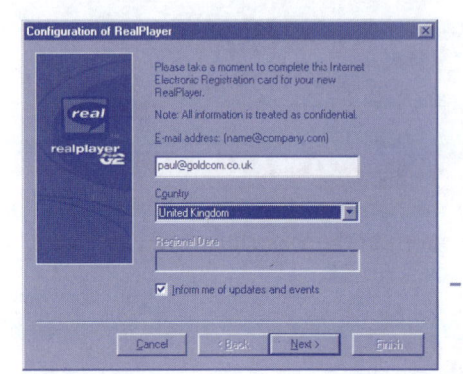

1 Enter your e-mail address and select your country, then click on *Next*.

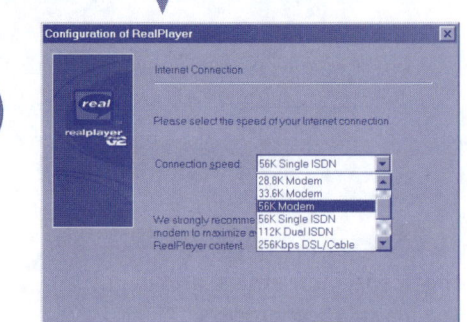

2 Select the speed of your Internet connection, then click on *Next*.

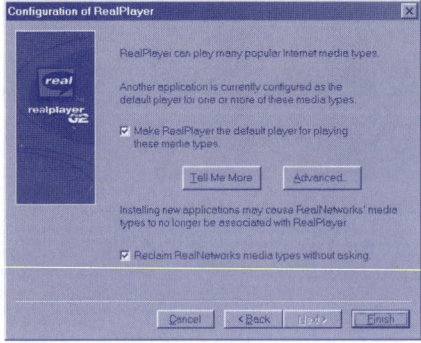

3 Make sure that the two checkboxes are marked, then click on *Finish*.

Getting started with RealPlayer

Start up the Explorer and enter the URL: *http://www.emimusic.ca*. This is a well-designed Web page, which contains a lot of information about music and, of course, many RealAudio files.

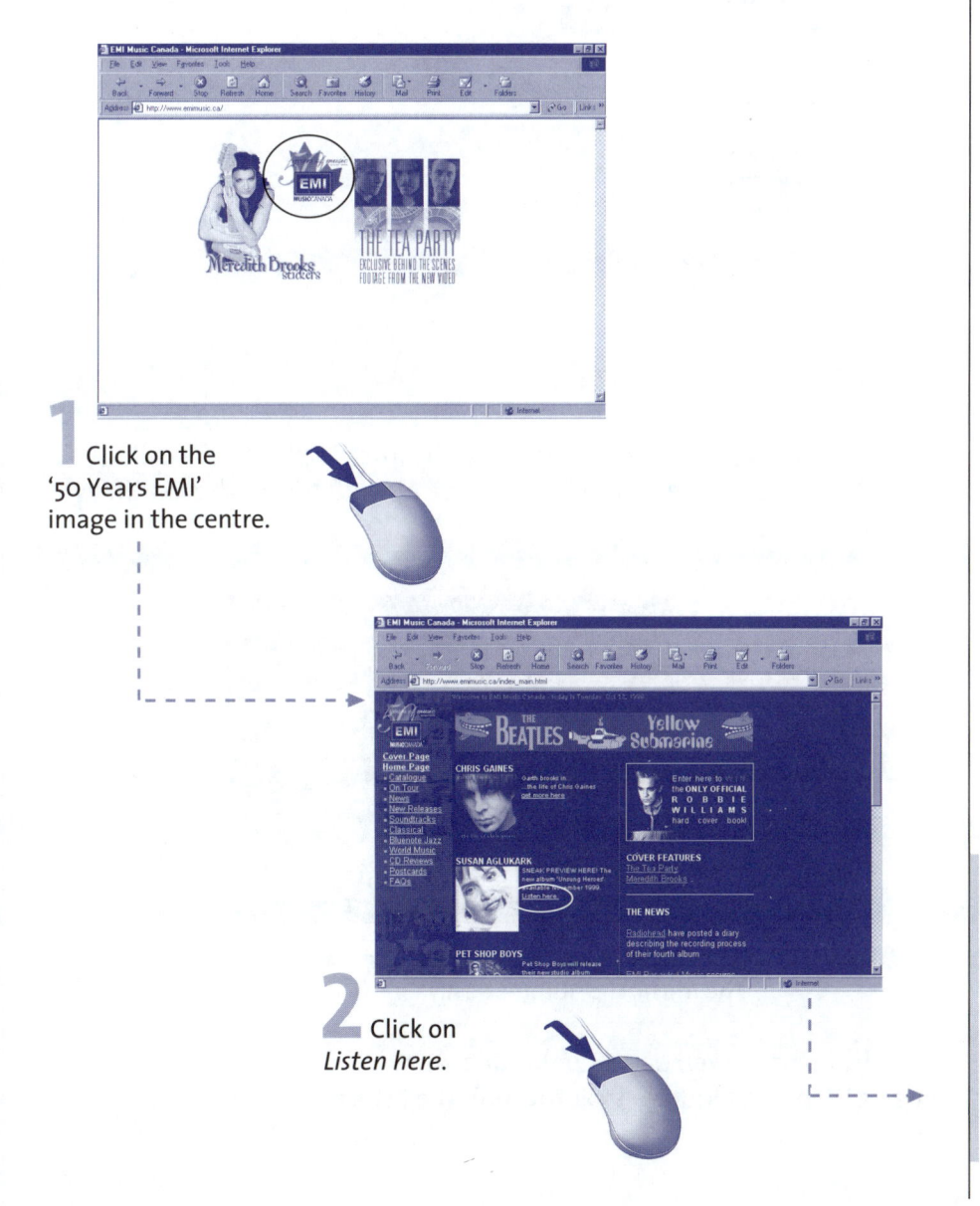

1 Click on the '50 Years EMI' image in the centre.

2 Click on *Listen here*.

201

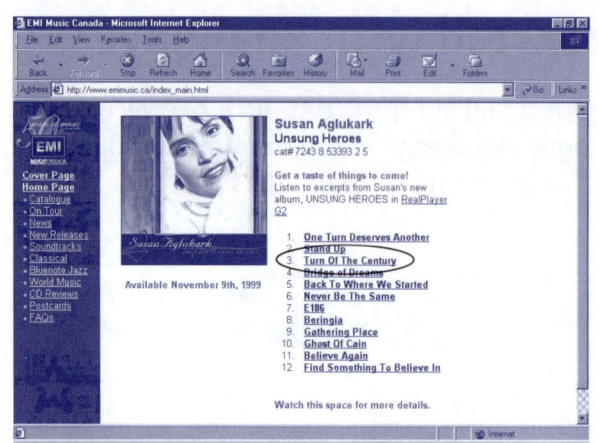

3 Click on the song that you want to listen to.

Once you have activated a music clip, Internet Explorer will call up RealPlayer G2 and the sound file will be played during the loading process.

4 RealPlayer G2 begins playing the music clip automatically.

There are many Web pages containing Real-Audio files on the Internet. Use a Web catalogue to look through the Internet for the required search terms.

RealPlayer in detail

Now that you have seen how RealPlayer works when called automatically by Internet Explorer to play an audio clip, it is time to take a closer look at RealPlayer G2 and its various functions.

1 Double-click on the *RealPlayer G2* desktop icon.

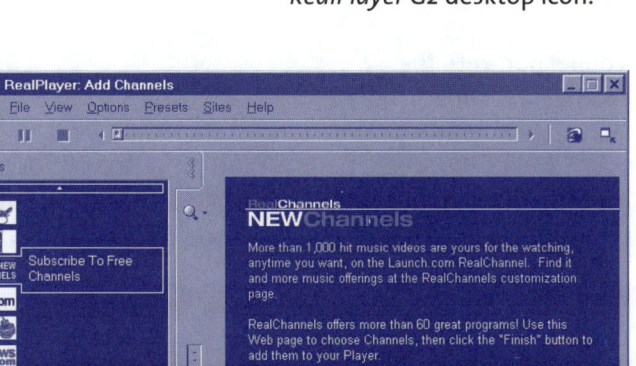

2 The RealPlayer is opened. Click on *Add New Channels*.

As you can see, the RealPlayer displays a window containing two large areas, a selection area to the left and a display area to the right.

The selection area shows all the channels to which you have subscribed, automatically scrolling the list every couple of seconds. You can also scroll manually using the two arrows at the top and bottom of the selection area.

3 Open a connection with the Internet by clicking on *Connect*.

Clicking on *Add New Channels* opens a Web page that allows you to subscribe and unsubscribe to hundreds of free channels, subdivided into several categories, such as News, Science, Sports, and so on.

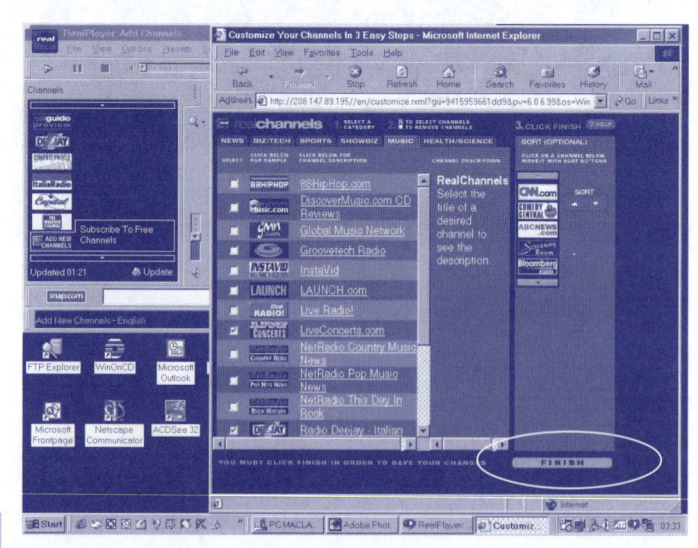

4 Make your selections and confirm your choices by clicking on *Finish*.

REALPLAYER IN DETAIL

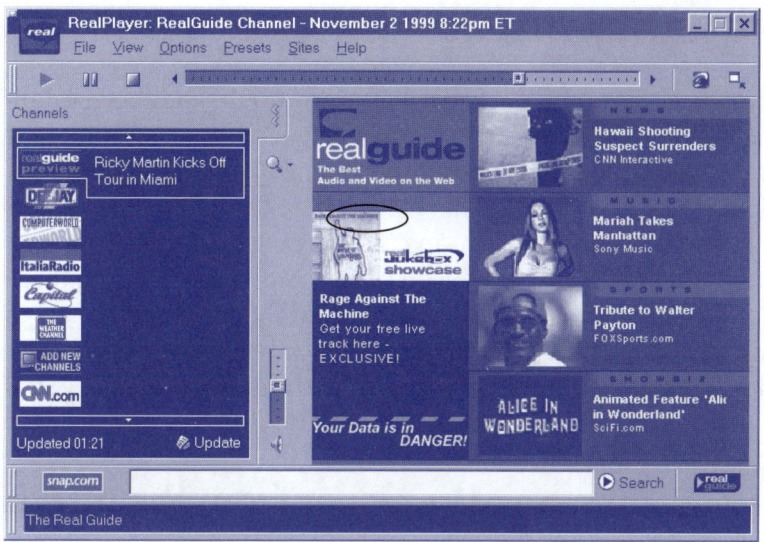

5 The RealPlayer has a home page of its own, optimised for display and interaction inside the RealPlayer, without any need to activate a Web browser.

6 Or, activate Fox News to watch the daily news (more about this in the next chapter).

CD quality music – MP3

Besides RealAudio, a new standard of music quality has been established in the past few months – MP3. This is a special compression method, whereby frequencies out of our hearing range are removed from the particular pieces of music. This means that the sound files are much smaller and better suited for transmission over the Internet. In this way, a complete song takes up between 5 and 7 Mb, whereas using the *.wav* format the same song would arrive at a stately size of more than 30 Mb. To play these Mp3 files you will need a special MP player, which you can find for free on the Internet. If you want to burn MP files onto CDs you will need an MP3 decoder, which you can also find free on the Internet.

Downloading an MP3 player from the Internet

At the Web address *http://www.mp3.com* you will find a central point of call for every aspect of MP3. There you will find MP3 players, MP3 decoders and, of course, many MP3 sound files. The MP3 player we are going to download and install is Nullsoft's Winamp 2.5. Netscape 4.7 users will be glad to know that this MP3 player is automatically installed and can be accessed via START/PROGRAMS/NETSCAPE COMMUNICATOR/WINAMP.

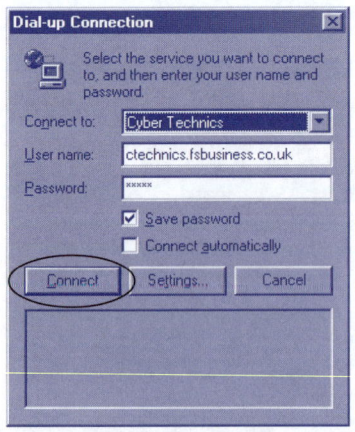

1 Open a connection with the Internet by clicking on *Connect*.

CD QUALITY MUSIC – MP3

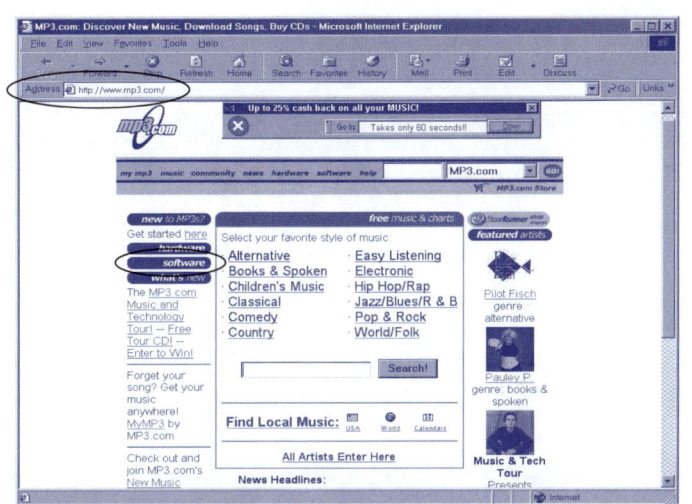

2 In the *Address* field enter the URL *www.mp3.com*. Once the page has been loaded, click on the *Software* hyperlink.

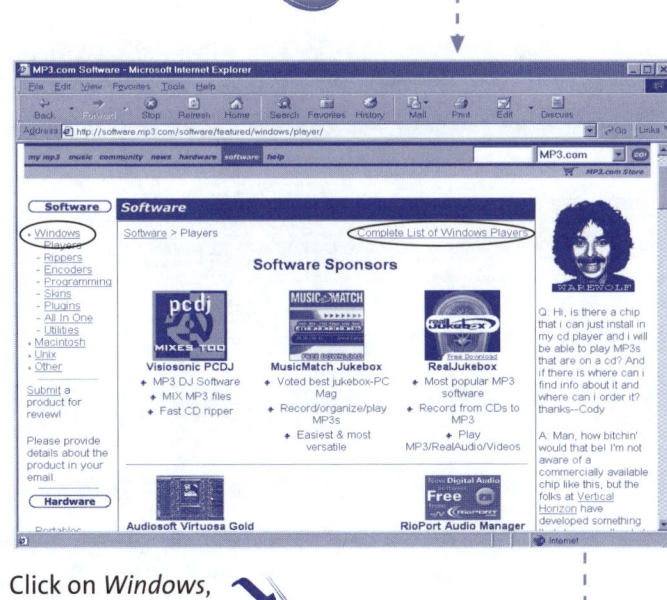

3 Click on *Windows*, then on *Complete List of Windows Players*.

207

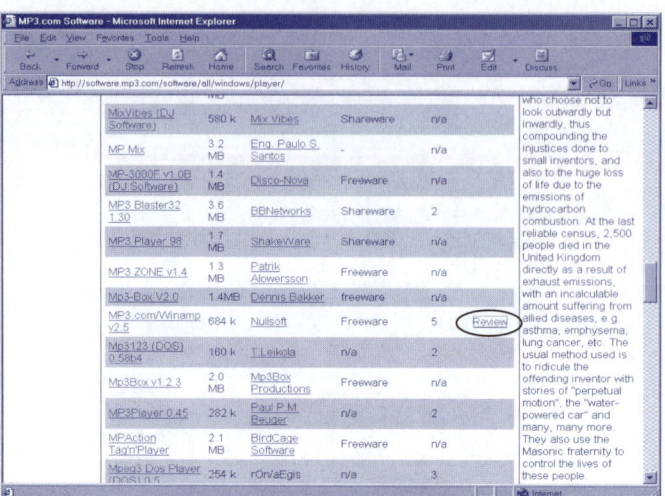

4 Scroll down the list until you can see the entry *MP3.com/Winamp v2.5*. Click on *Review*.

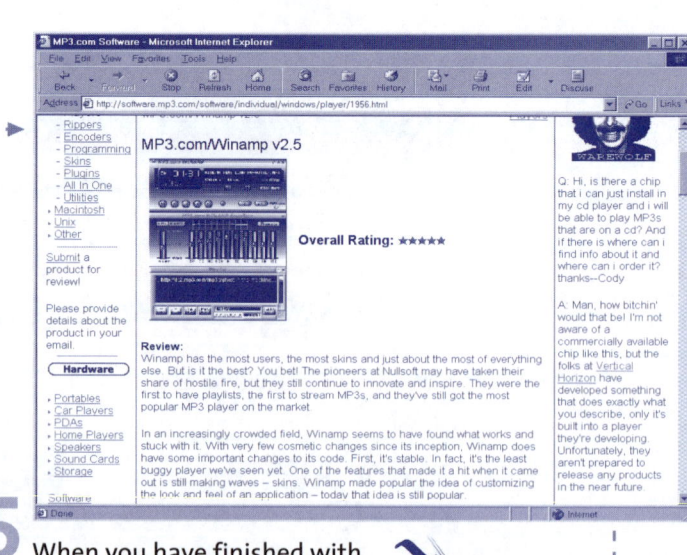

5 When you have finished with the review, click on your browser's *Back* button and, on the previous screen, click on *MP3.com/Winamp v2.5* to download the player.

208

CD QUALITY MUSIC– MP3

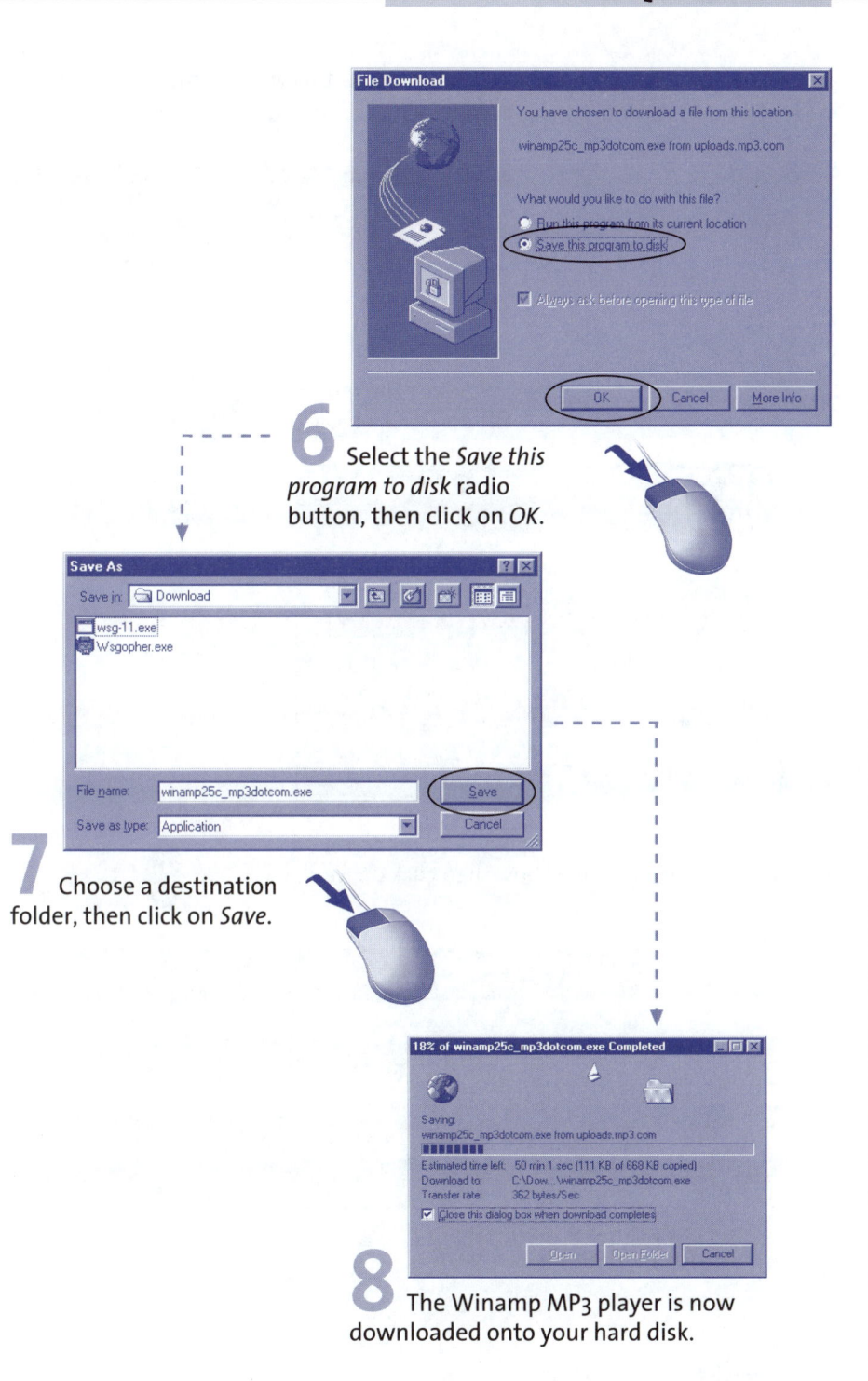

6 Select the *Save this program to disk* radio button, then click on *OK*.

7 Choose a destination folder, then click on *Save*.

8 The Winamp MP3 player is now downloaded onto your hard disk.

209

After the MP3 player has been downloaded to your computer, it will need to be installed. In the Windows START menu click on RUN.

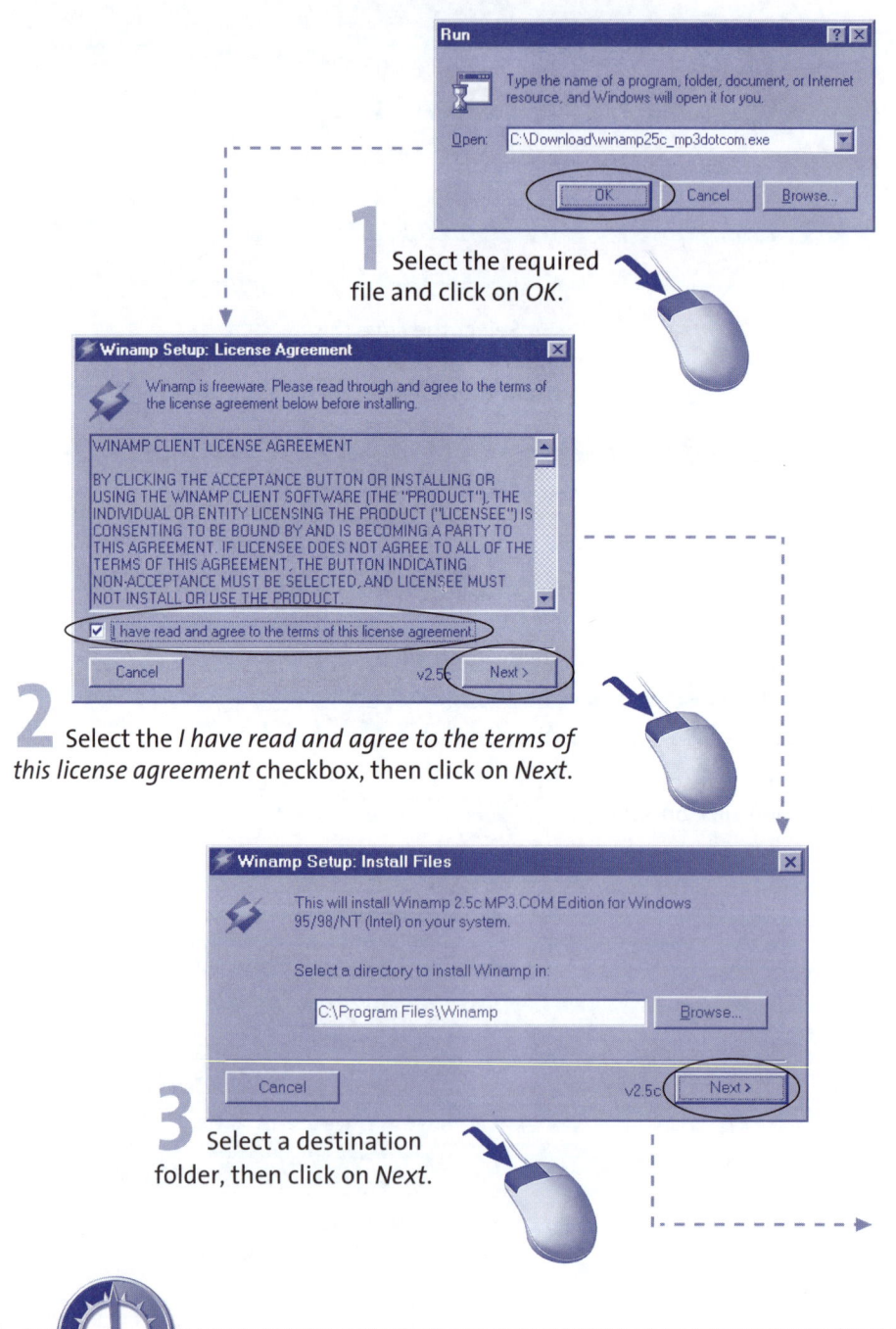

1 Select the required file and click on *OK*.

2 Select the *I have read and agree to the terms of this license agreement* checkbox, then click on *Next*.

3 Select a destination folder, then click on *Next*.

CD QUALITY MUSIC – MP3

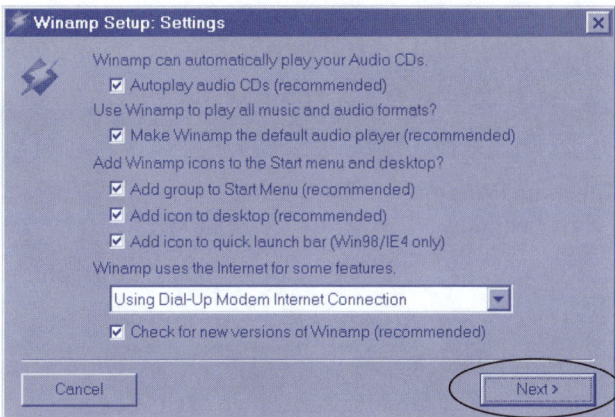

Winamp Setup: Settings

Winamp can automatically play your Audio CDs.
☑ Autoplay audio CDs (recommended)
Use Winamp to play all music and audio formats?
☑ Make Winamp the default audio player (recommended)
Add Winamp icons to the Start menu and desktop?
☑ Add group to Start Menu (recommended)
☑ Add icon to desktop (recommended)
☑ Add icon to quick launch bar (Win98/IE4 only)
Winamp uses the Internet for some features.
Using Dial-Up Modem Internet Connection
☑ Check for new versions of Winamp (recommended)

[Cancel] [**Next >**]

4 Make sure that all checkboxes are selected and that the correct Internet connection is selected (usually via modem). Then click on *Next* to finish the installation.

The Winamp installation procedure will have added a new menu entry to the START menu in the taskbar and created a new shortcut icon on your desktop.

Winamp

1 Start Winamp by double-clicking on the corresponding desktop icon.

Winamp opens four new windows on your desktop which 'stick' together as a group and can be moved together by dragging the title bar of the window entitled *MP3.com WINAMP*.

211

1 The main Winamp MP3 player window.

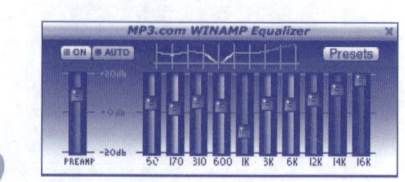

2 The graphic equalizer window.

3 The Winamp playlist window.

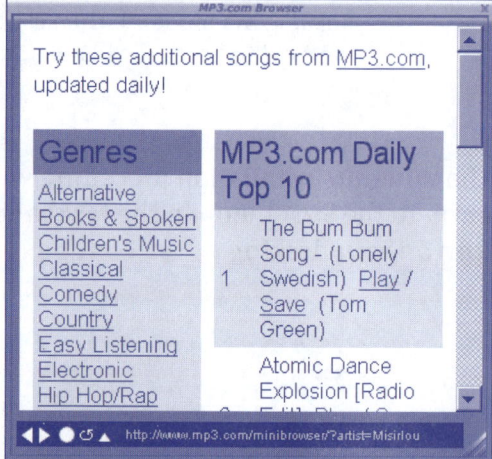

4 Winamp's own mini-browser window.

Loading an MP3 file from the Internet

Now you have an **MP3 player** at your disposal, you will need to 'feed' it with MP3 sound files. Obviously, these can also be found on the Internet. The Web page where you found the MP3 player, http://www.mp3.com, is a good starting place for this. So, open up a connection with the Internet and visit this Web site.

CD QUALITY MUSIC – MP3

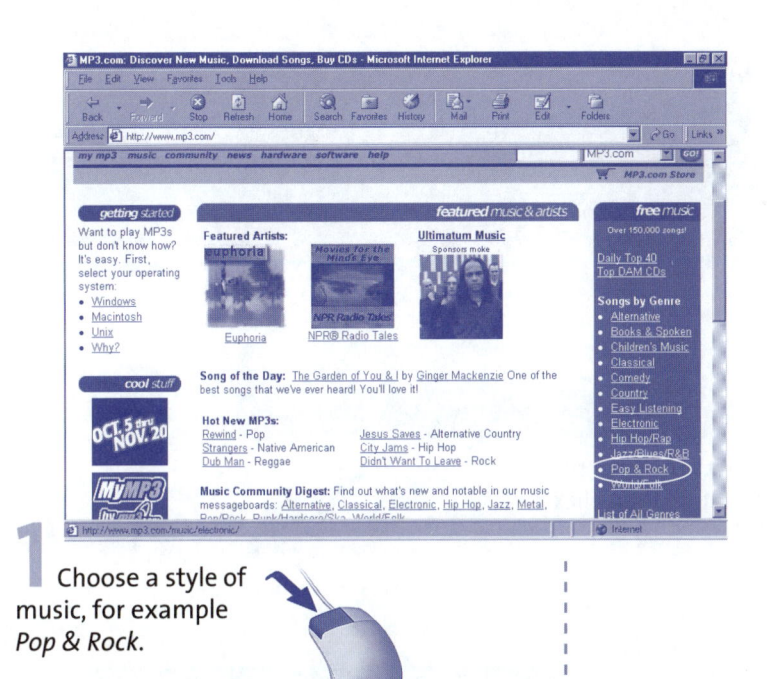

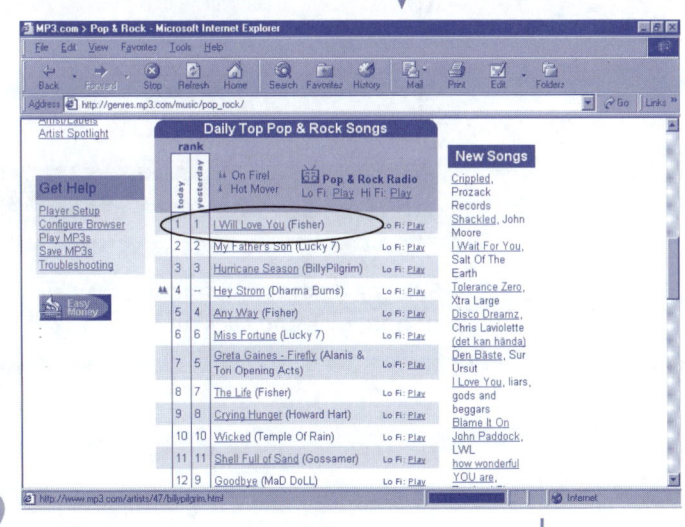

1 Choose a style of music, for example *Pop & Rock*.

2 Click on a title that interests you.

213

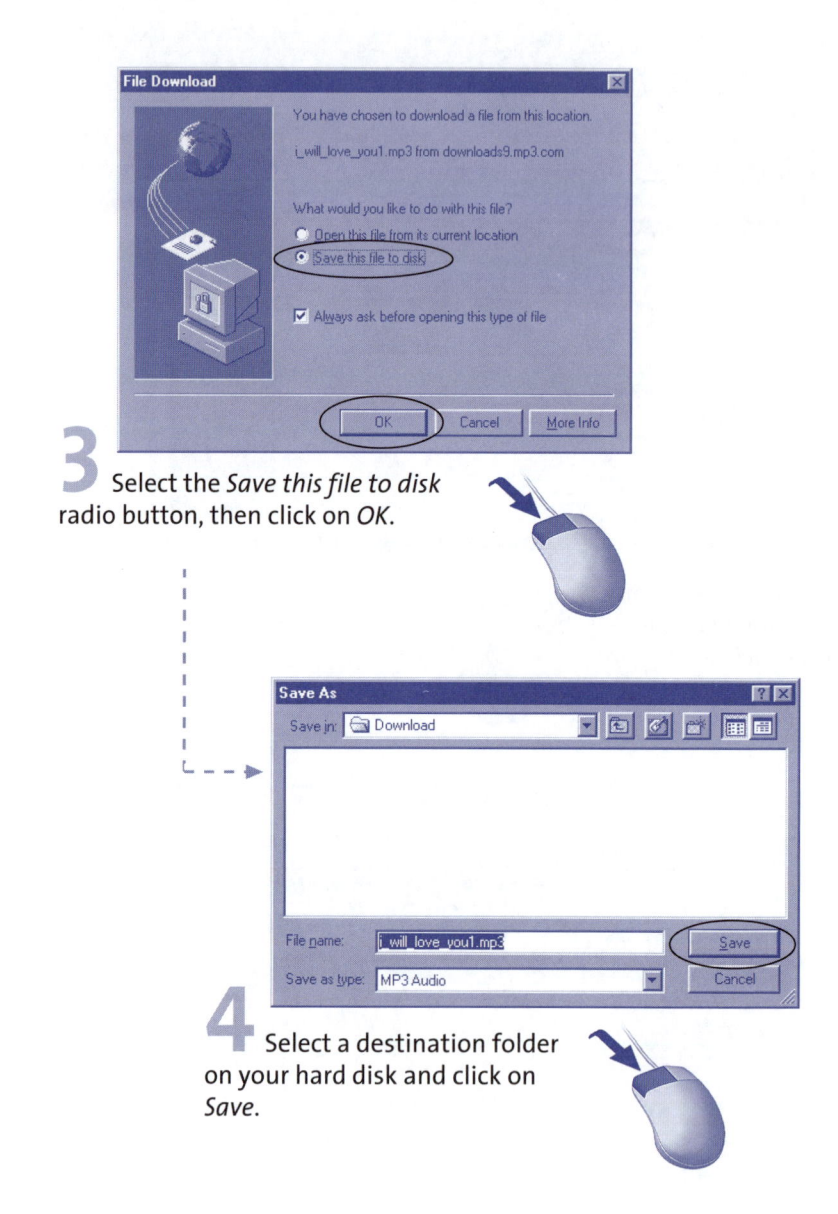

3 Select the *Save this file to disk* radio button, then click on *OK*.

4 Select a destination folder on your hard disk and click on *Save*.

After a few minutes you will see a file with the extension *.mp3* on your hard disk. You can use any appropriate MP3 player to play this file.

Playing an MP3 file

Once you have loaded the MP3 file onto your computer, you will be able to play it by using your MP3 player.

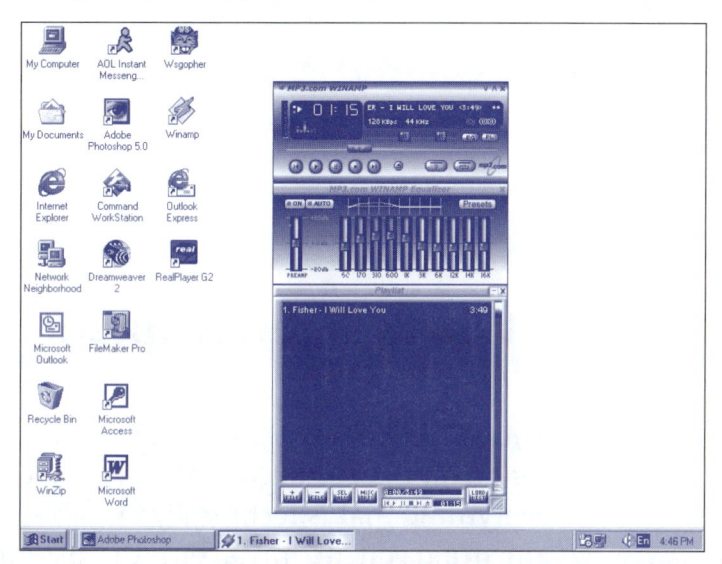

1 Click on the *MP3* icon on your desktop and load the required MP3 file into the player. To find out how to do this, consult the MP3 player's instructions.

You have to laugh – the best computer messages

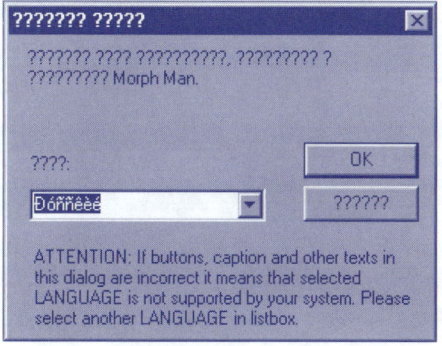

7

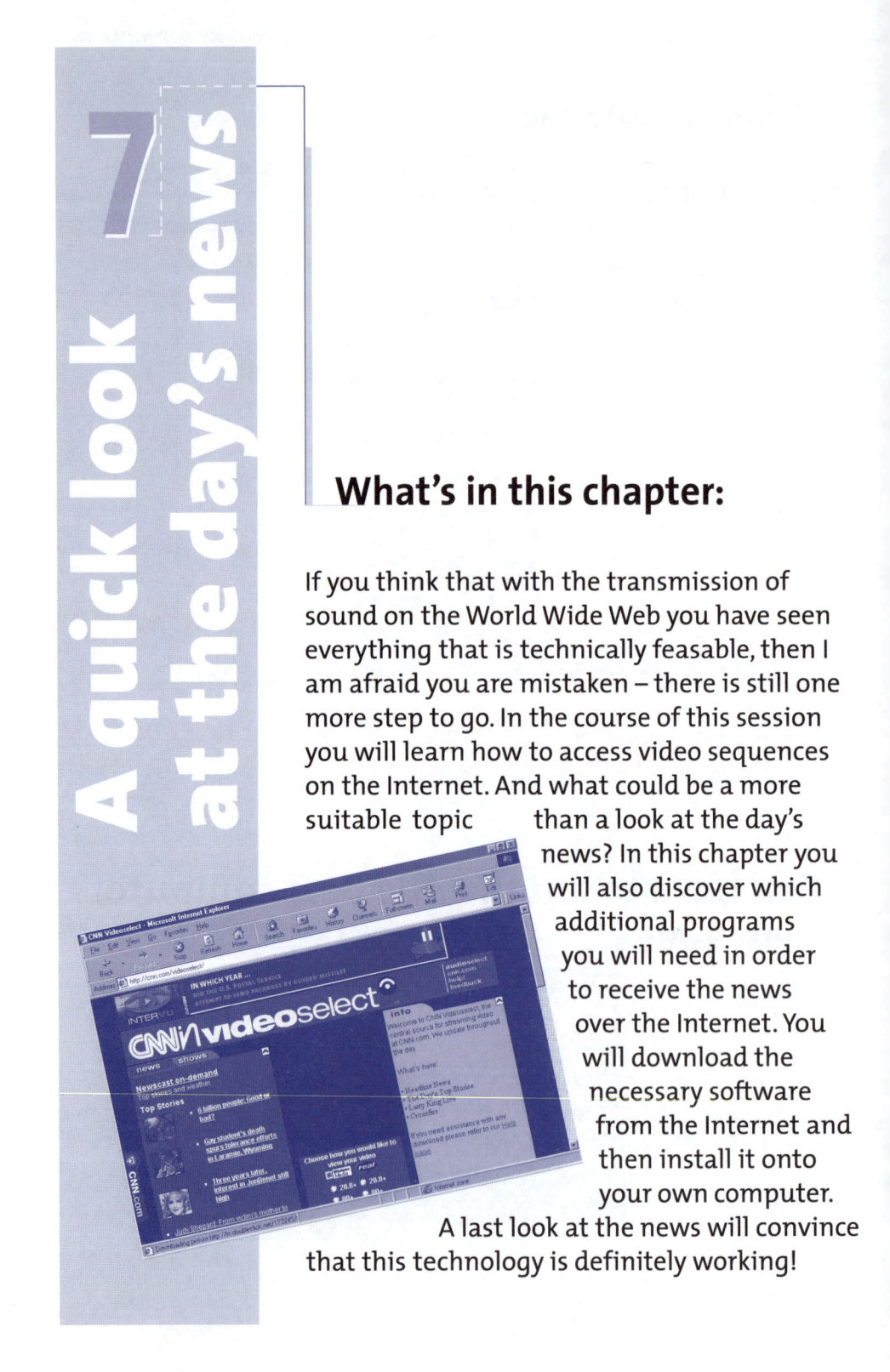

A quick look at the day's news

What's in this chapter:

If you think that with the transmission of sound on the World Wide Web you have seen everything that is technically feasable, then I am afraid you are mistaken – there is still one more step to go. In the course of this session you will learn how to access video sequences on the Internet. And what could be a more suitable topic than a look at the day's news? In this chapter you will also discover which additional programs you will need in order to receive the news over the Internet. You will download the necessary software from the Internet and then install it onto your own computer. A last look at the news will convince that this technology is definitely working!

You already know about:

Browsing and printing Web pages	88
How a search engine works	94
Using the Lycos search engine	98
Accessing the Internet with AOL	122
Accessing the Internet with BT Click	141
Installing Netscape Communicator 4.7	166
Rock, pop and classical music on the Web	192
IE4 and RealPlayer	194
Using RealPlayer	201
CD quality music – MP3	206

You are going to learn about:

Video on the Internet	218
Looking at the day's news	219

Video on the Internet – how does it work?

WHAT'S THIS
Video sequences are short pieces of animated film which you can retrieve from the Internet.

In the course of a few decades, the Internet has changed from being a pure text transmission system (e-mail and telnet) to a graphical system (World Wide Web). The next logical step in this process is being able to transmit **video sequences**, or even whole films and documentaries over the World Wide Web.

However, this is all just pie in the sky. At the moment, there are many small video clips jerking through the Web, which give a taste of how things might be in ten years' time.

Developers and engineers are, however, working round the clock to find a solution to this problem. The key piece of technology which has recently come into use is **streaming video**. Streaming video's main task is to counter the basic problem: as videos usually contain a large amount of data, so their corresponding video files on the Internet are equally large. It used to take hours to download all the video data.

Streaming video solves this problem in two ways. Firstly, the video files are highly compressed so that less data needs to be transmitted over the Internet. Secondly, videos can actually be played during the transmission process.

So, how does it work? Using streaming video allows you to watch videos live on the Internet. There is no need to wait for the whole video to be copied onto your hard disk. An example of streaming video is the RealPlayer, a program you will need if you want to watch daily news services from, for example, the BBC, ITV or CNN. Before the video is transmitted, it is compressed and encoded. This process is carried out with the help of a special algorithm (a mathematical formula) which makes the video file much smaller.

As soon as you click on a hyperlink inside a Web page that leads to a video, a message is sent to a server. This message asks the server for the video and the required file is then sent over the Internet. The video data is saved in a special storage area on your computer, known as a **buffer**, which is usually between 5 and 30 Kb in size. By seeing how quickly the buffer fills up, the server can ascertain the transmission speed of the connection. With a **high speed** connection, more video data can be transmitted, which gives the video a 'live' look. With a lower transmission speed, the quality of the video will be correspondingly worse.

While the buffer continues to fill up, a process which only takes a few seconds, your computer will start up a **video player** which it uses to play the video clip. While you watch this clip, more files will be transferred to the buffer and, at the same time, video files will be forwarded from the buffer to the video player. Once all the video files have been transferred, the display is complete. The video files are not saved on your computer, but rather are deleted as soon as they have been played.

A look at the day's news

Open an Internet connection and, as an example, call up CNN news under the Web address *http://cnn.com/videoselect*.

> **TIP**
> Do not expect too much in the way of picture quality and speed. Even using an ISDN line the picture will still be somewhat jerky on the screen. This is mainly due to the narrow bandwidths and capacity on the Internet. But don't panic, the right people are working feverishly on solving this problem.

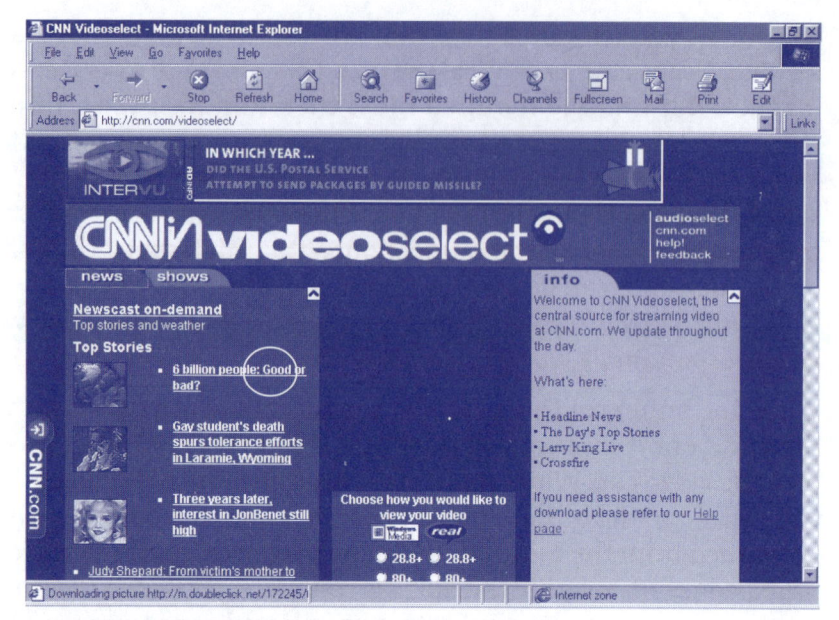

1 Next to the picture summary you will see a box offering a choice of video players and download speeds. Choose which player and speed is most suitable for your connection.

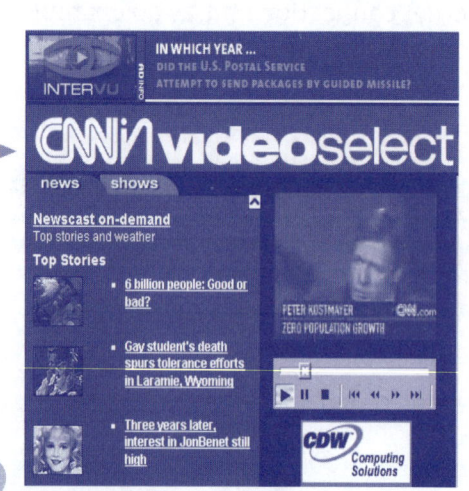

2 And there you are! The news story of the day from the Internet!

You have to laugh – the best computer messages

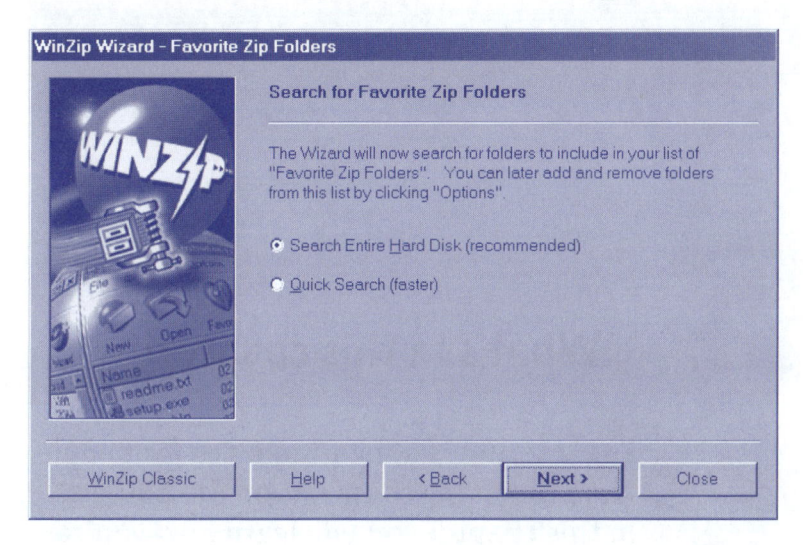

Is it not obvious that, in general, a quick search will be faster...?

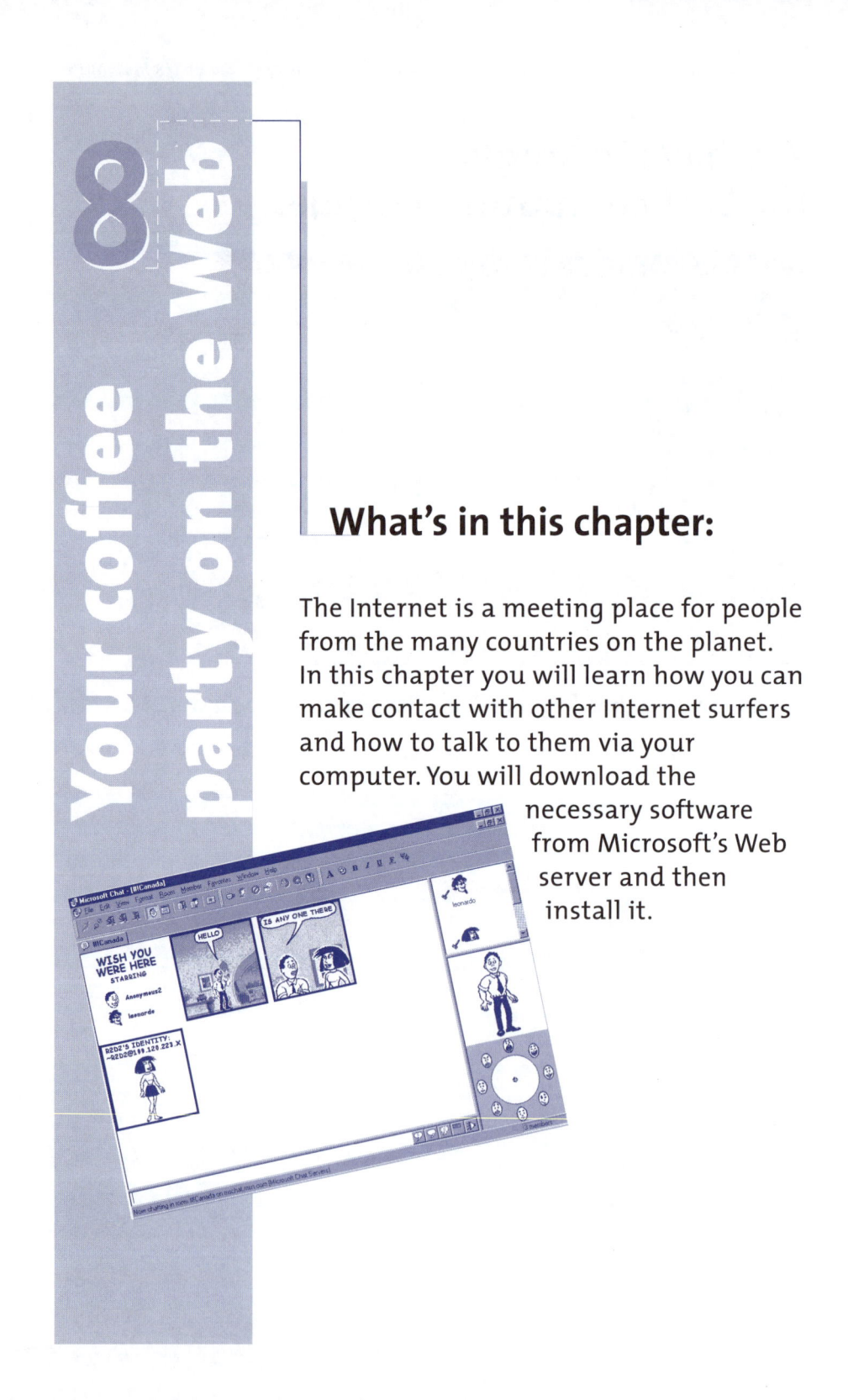

8

Your coffee party on the Web

What's in this chapter:

The Internet is a meeting place for people from the many countries on the planet. In this chapter you will learn how you can make contact with other Internet surfers and how to talk to them via your computer. You will download the necessary software from Microsoft's Web server and then install it.

You already know about:

Browsing and printing Web pages	88
How a search engine works	94
Accessing the Internet with AOL	122
Accessing the Internet with BT Click	141
Installing Netscape Communicator 4.7	166
Rock, pop and classical music on the Web	192
IE4 and RealPlayer	194
Getting started with RealPlayer	201
CD quality music –MP3	206
Video on the Internet	218
Looking at the day's news	219

You are going to learn about:

IRC chat	224
Installing Microsoft's Chat program	225
Finding out if anyone is there	231
Modifying the program	236

What is an IRC chat?

There is no more direct form of communication on the Internet than the **chat**. During an IRC (Internet Relay Chat) conversation, the users don't actually speak to each other as they do on the telephone, rather they use the keyboard to carry on a conversation. The words that you enter on your keyboard are seen in **real time** on the participants' screens, and vice versa. In this way you can converse with people from all over the world via your keyboard.

> **WHAT'S THIS?**
> **Real time** means an only marginally delayed transfer of files over the Internet. An example of this is using the Internet as a telephone, where there will usually be very few long pauses.

There are many ways of chatting with people on the Internet, the most popular being IRC. Thanks to IRC, many thousands of people all over the world can 'meet' every day to discuss all sorts of issues. Each topic has its own **channel**. As soon as you choose one of these channels you will see all the messages posted by the other participants. In this way, IRC has another advantage besides passing the time, as has been proved during crisis situations. For example, during the attempted Russian coup in 1993, eyewitnesses were able to post their messages directly on suitable news channels. The same thing happened during the Los Angeles earthquake of 1993.

> **WHAT'S THIS?**
> An **IRC Client** is a program that allows you to establish a Chat connection with other participants.

In order to participate actively in IRC you will need an appropriate program, an **IRC Client**, which receives and forwards all the messages to the IRC server on the Internet. Every word you type is forwarded to a particular IRC server. As a rule, IRC servers are not linked together. Your own IRC server sends the chosen message to another server and this one then sends the message to all the users who are currently either on the server or in the same channel.

Once you have set up a connection to an IRC server, you will need to choose a particular channel (subject area) as well as a name, which will make you 'legitimate' in the eyes of the other users. You will soon see that every server contains countless channels.

> **TIP**
> At first, limit yourself to just listening to the conversations, to get a feeling for the subjects and the participants.

As soon as you enter a particular channel, called a **chat room** by those in the know, you can start to participate in the current topic. When you enter a message, your chat program sends it to the IRC server to which you are currently connected. This, in turn, sends the message to all the participants in the chat room.

Installing the Microsoft Chat program

As you already know, you will need a special program to participate in a chat session. Like most of the other Internet tools available, you can find this program on the Internet. On the Microsoft Web server there is a program that allows **participants** to chat to each other in the form of a comic strip.

If this chat program does not yet exist on your computer, you can install it in the following way. Call up Microsoft's Web site at *http://www.microsoft.co.uk*, from where you will be redirected to the most recently updated Microsoft home page.

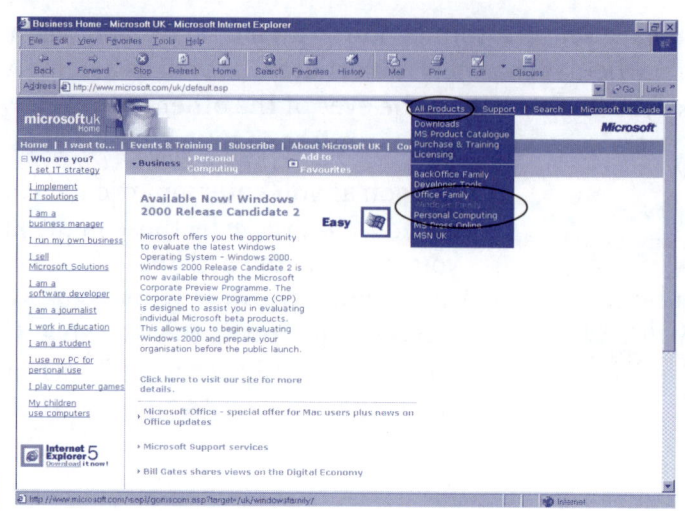

1 Click on the *All Products* hyperlink and select the *Windows Family* entry.

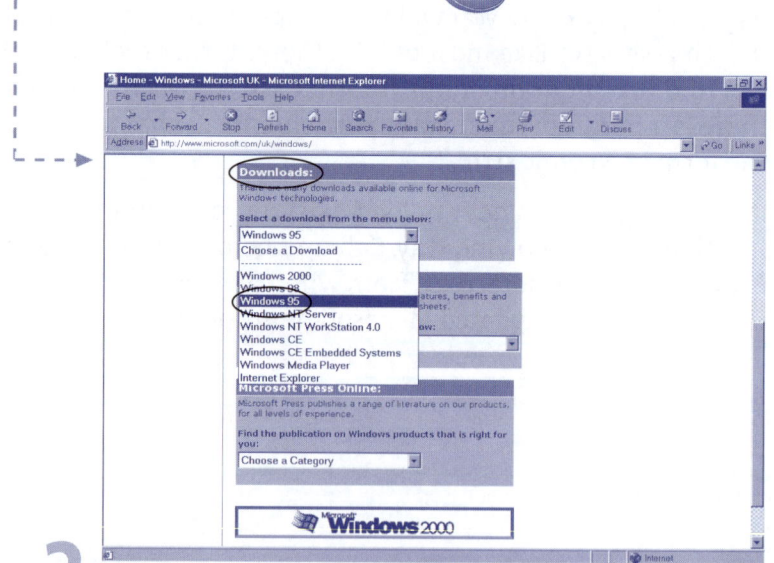

2 Open the list box under *Downloads* and select *Windows 95*.

INSTALLING THE MICROSOFT CHAT PROGRAM

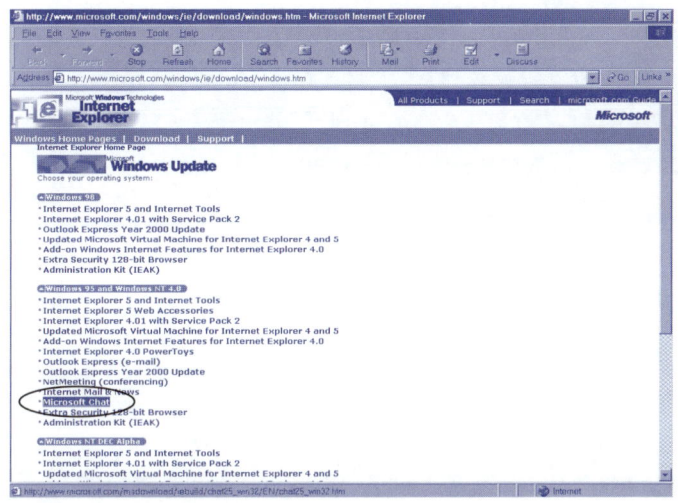

3 Click on *Microsoft Chat*.

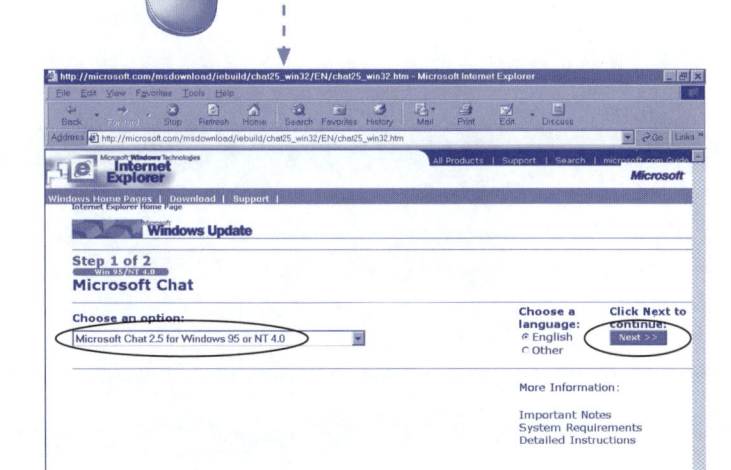

4 Choose the *Microsoft Chat 2.5 for Windows 95 or NT4.0* option, then click on *Next*.

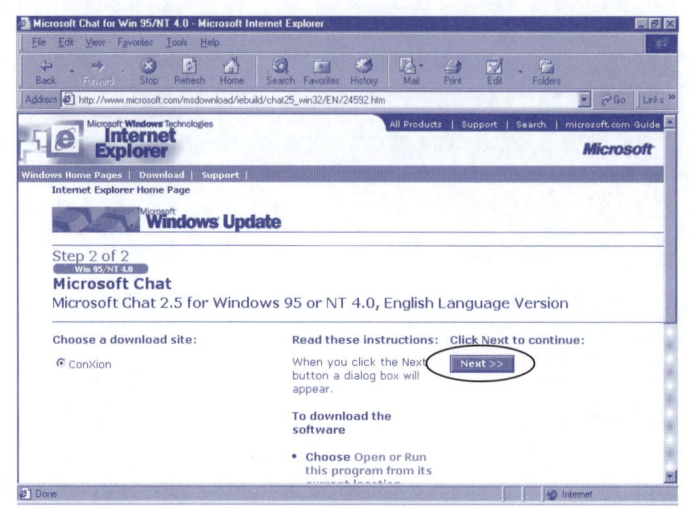

5 To download the program, click on *Next*.

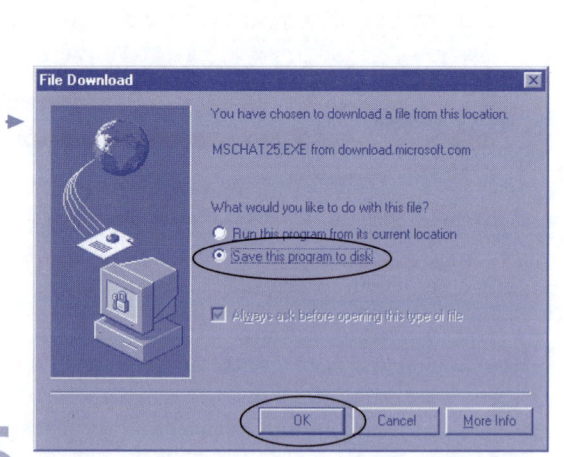

6 Click on the *Save this program to disk* radio button, then click on *OK*.

INSTALLING THE MICROSOFT CHAT PROGRAM

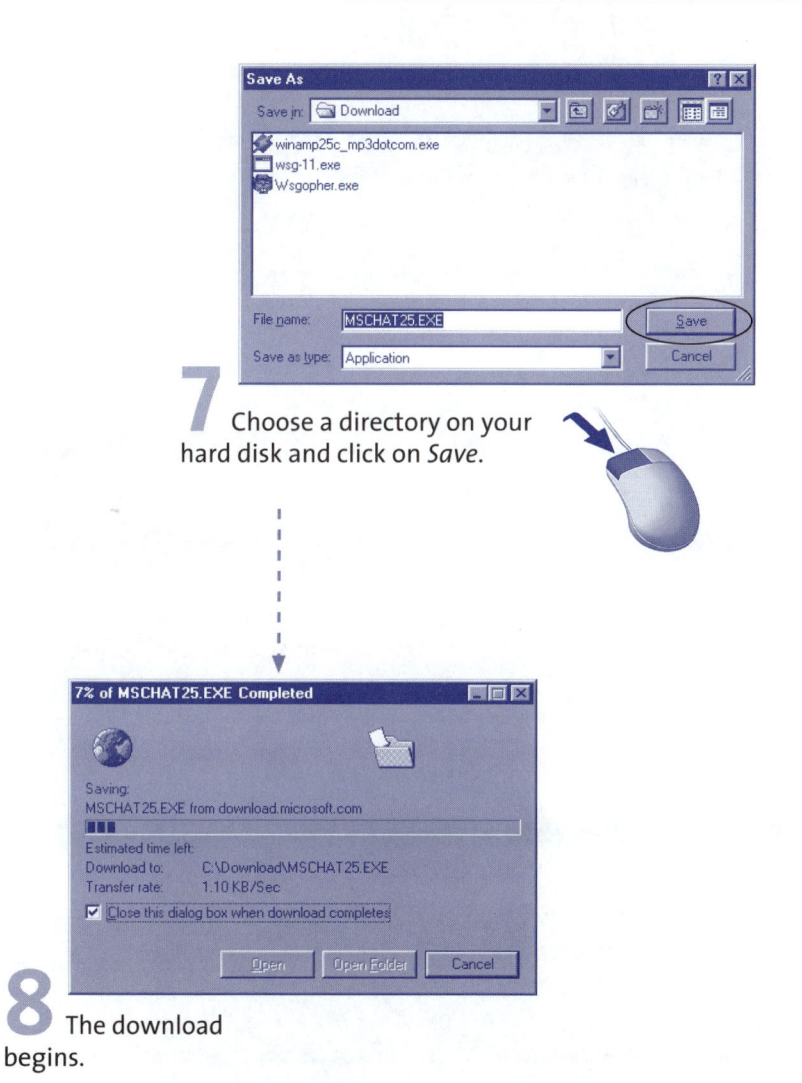

7 Choose a directory on your hard disk and click on *Save*.

8 The download begins.

Once the downloading process is complete, you will need to **install** the program on your computer. To do this, open the START menu on your Windows 98 taskbar and select the RUN menu entry. Look for the file in the folder where you saved it.

1 Click on *OK*.

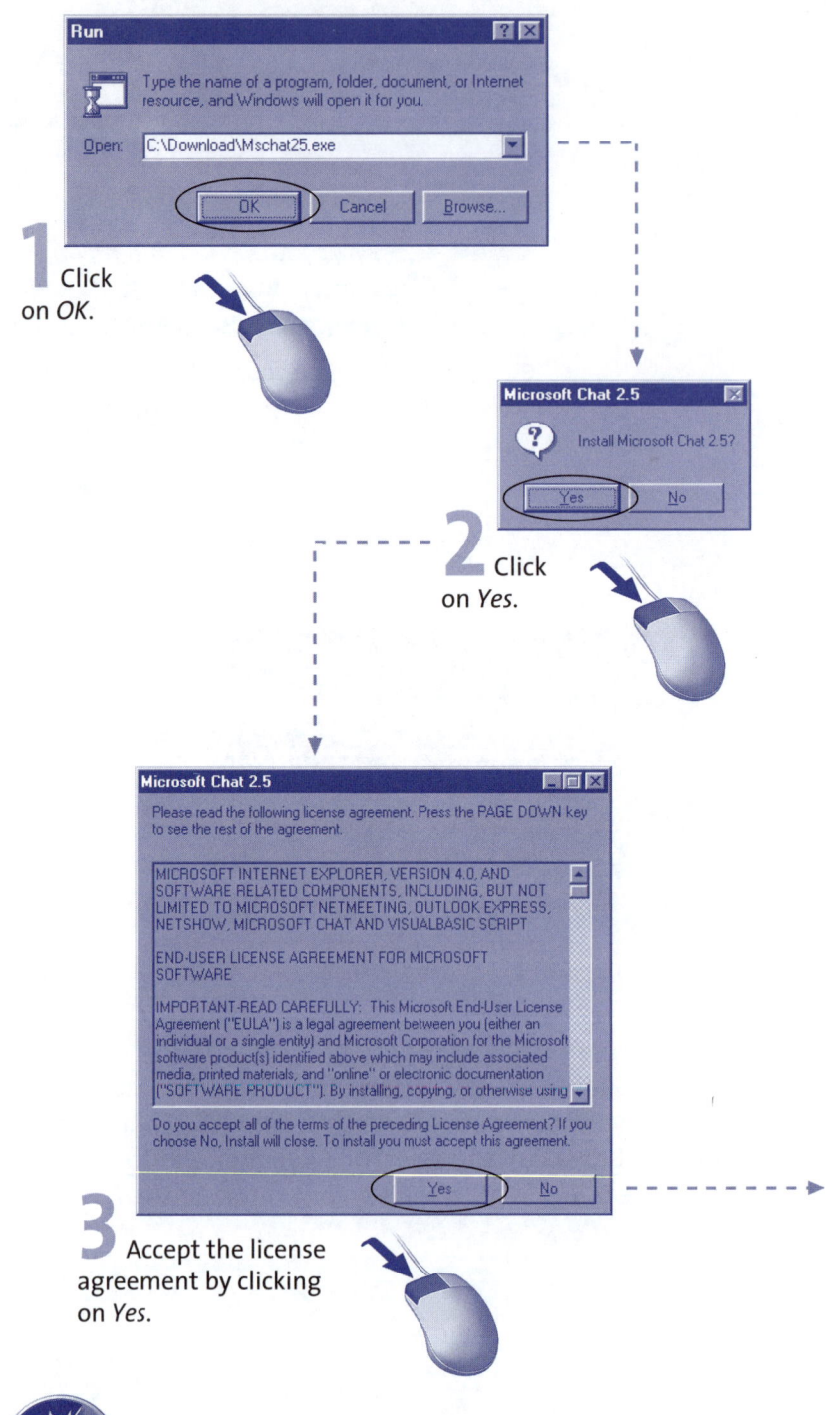

2 Click on *Yes*.

3 Accept the license agreement by clicking on *Yes*.

4 Accept the suggested folder and click on *OK*.

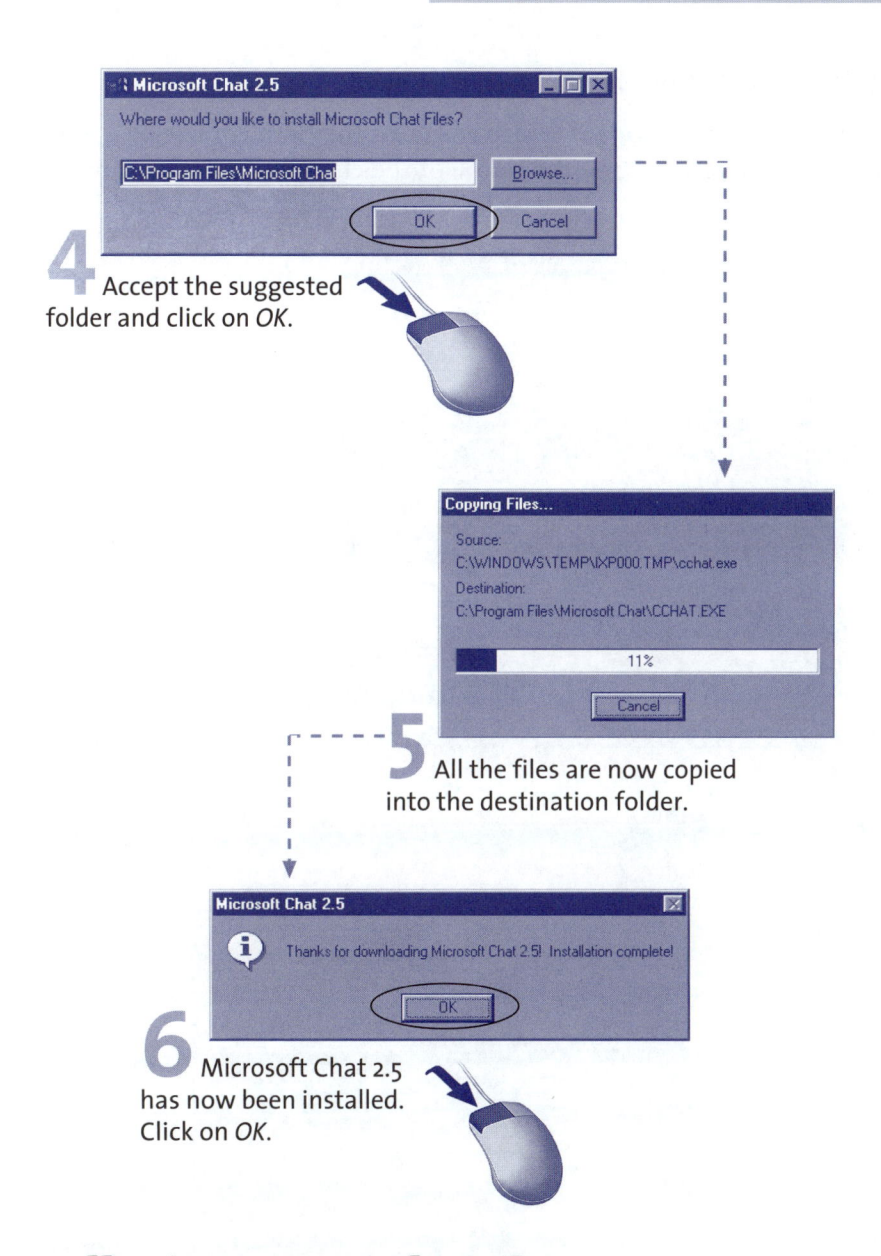

5 All the files are now copied into the destination folder.

6 Microsoft Chat 2.5 has now been installed. Click on *OK*.

Hello, is anyone there?

So, the program is now installed on your computer and is ready for use. You can find the corresponding entry in the Programs submenu of the Windows taskbar's Start menu.

In this menu, click on the MICROSOFT CHAT entry.

A window will then appear which contains the name of the IRC server. Furthermore, you will see the name of the **chat room** you are about to visit.

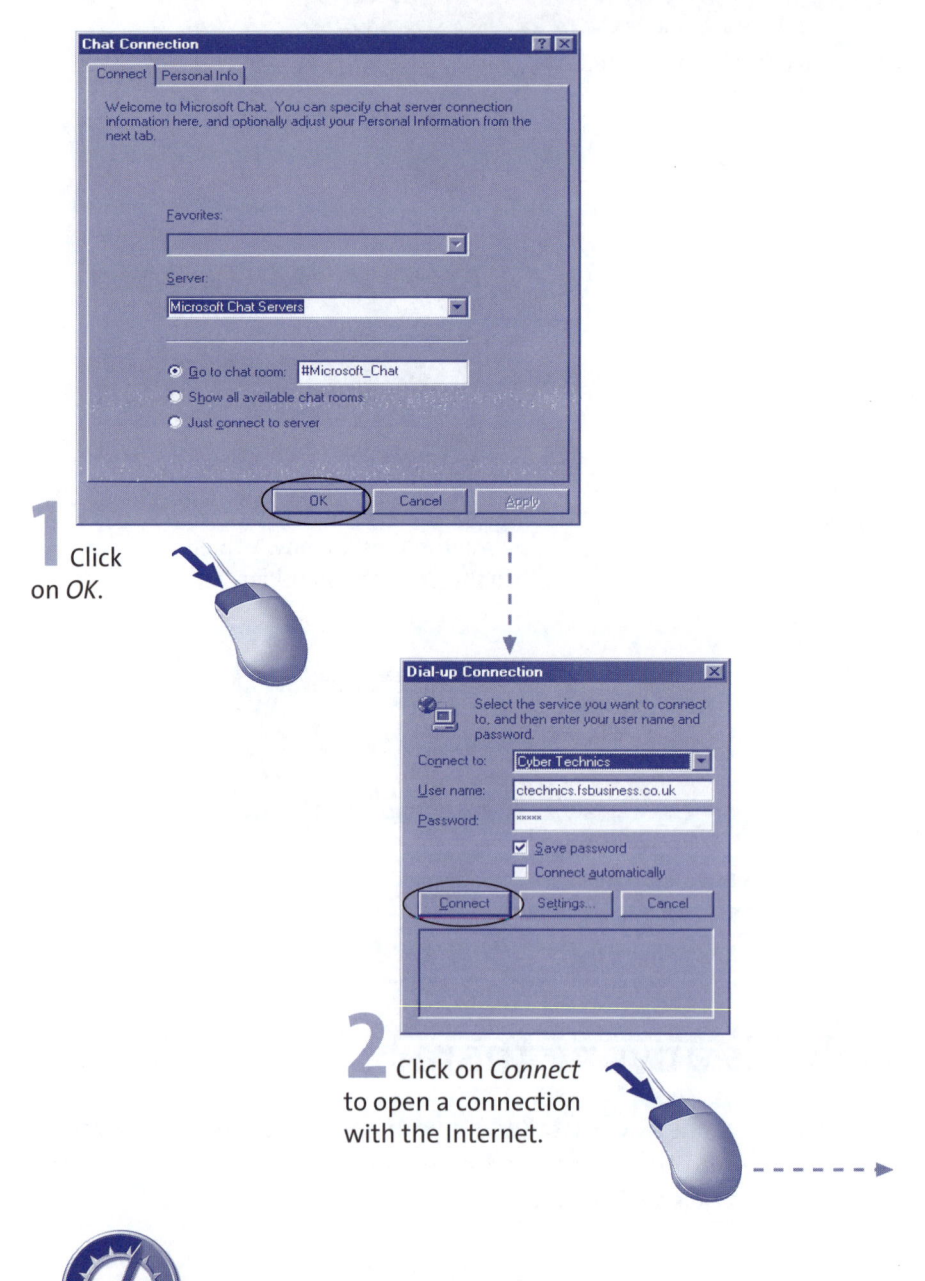

1 Click on *OK*.

2 Click on *Connect* to open a connection with the Internet.

HELLO, IS ANYONE THERE?

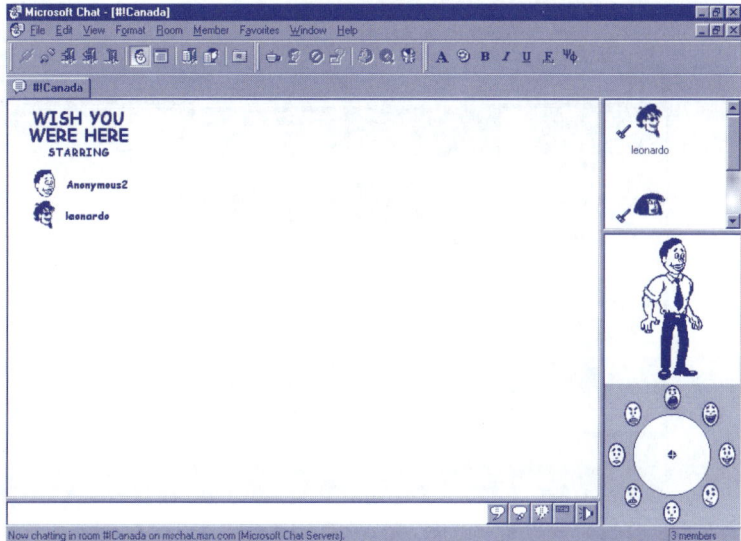

3 The program is now up and running.

WARNING: Under no circumstances should you give away any personal details, passwords, bank account numbers or PIN numbers to anyone in a chat room, even if you are convinced of their identity. If anyone asks for such information, you should stop the conversation immediately.

You will now find yourself in a chat room. Have a go at finding someone else in the room to whom you can talk.

Enter a few words in the bottom section of the window and greet the other **chat participants**.

233

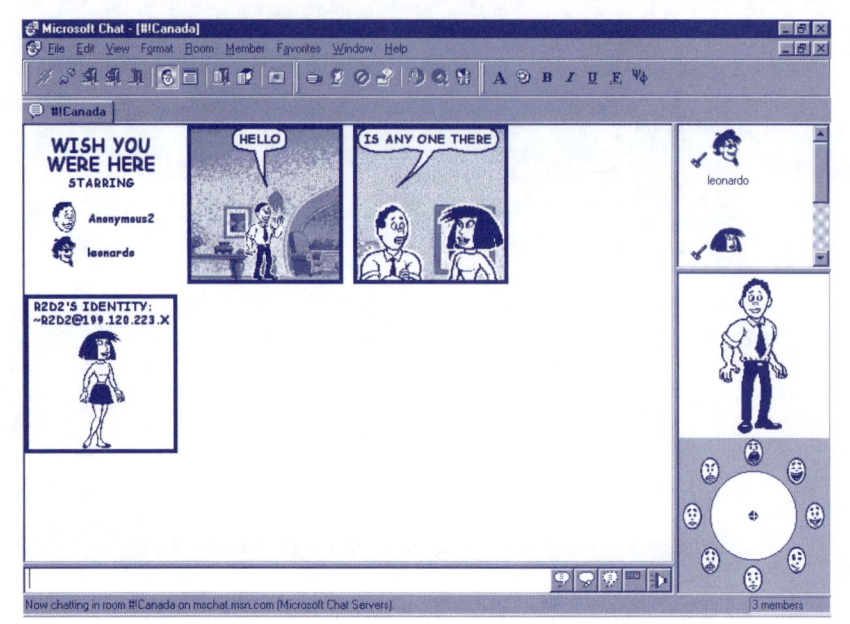

1 The words you write are represented by a cartoon figure and a speech bubble. As soon as someone replies to your message, a new cartoon picture will appear. In this way a cartoon develops which contains every message entered by the chat participants.

When you want to leave the chat room, you will need to choose the Leave room entry from the Room menu.

Now it is time for you to visit a few other chat rooms. First of all you will call up a list of every available chat room.

HELLO, IS ANYONE THERE?

1 Click on the ROOM LIST entry in the ROOM menu.

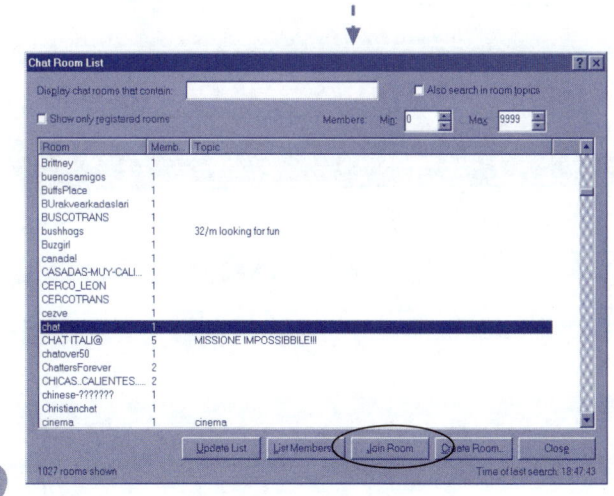

2 Click on a chat room and then on the *Join Room* button.

235

Modifying the program

Now that you know how to chat, perhaps you would like to modify the program a little. If you want to, you can add different cartoon figures, background pictures, or personal details.

Start up the Chat program.

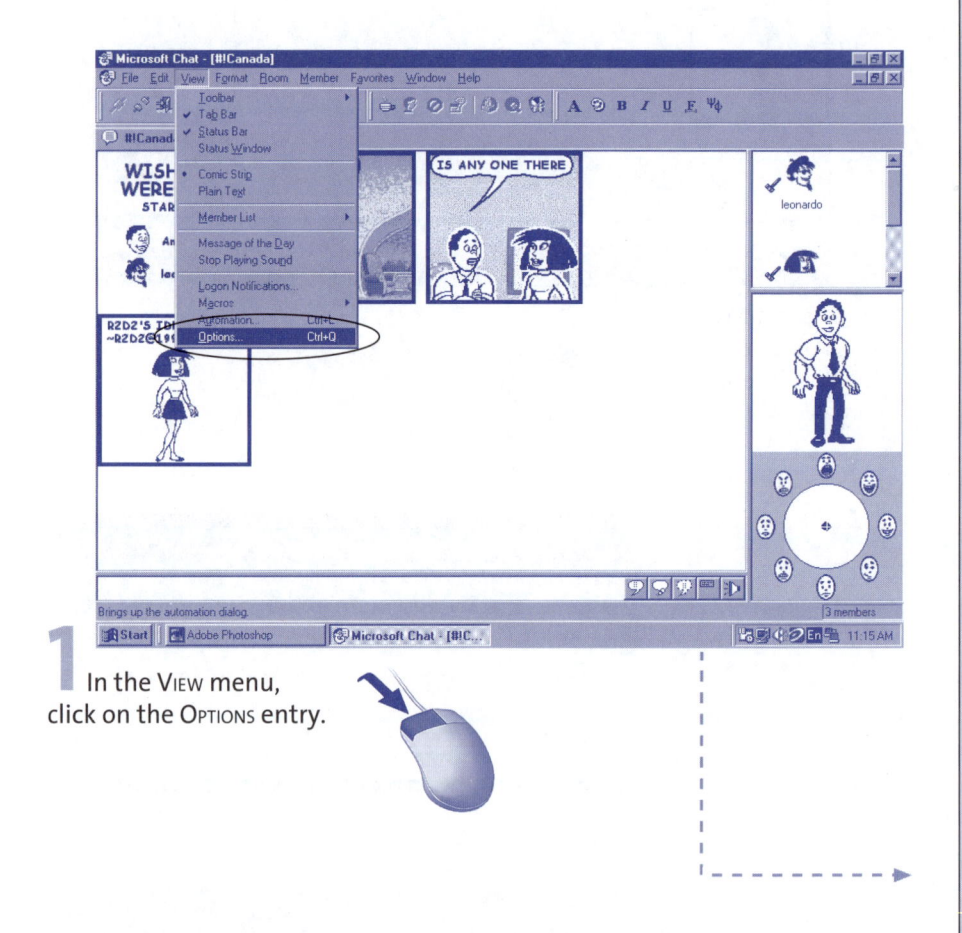

1 In the VIEW menu, click on the OPTIONS entry.

MODIFYING THE PROGRAM

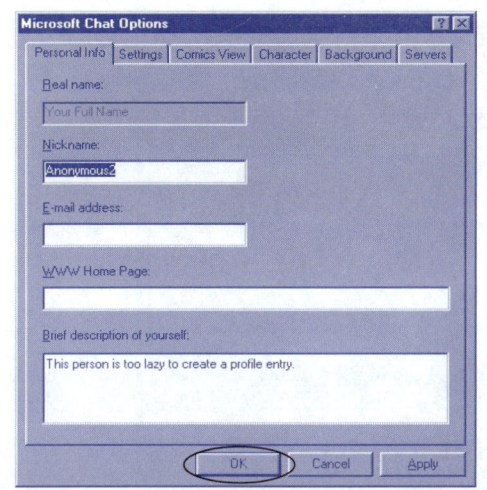

2 Now enter your personal details and confirm them by clicking on *OK*.

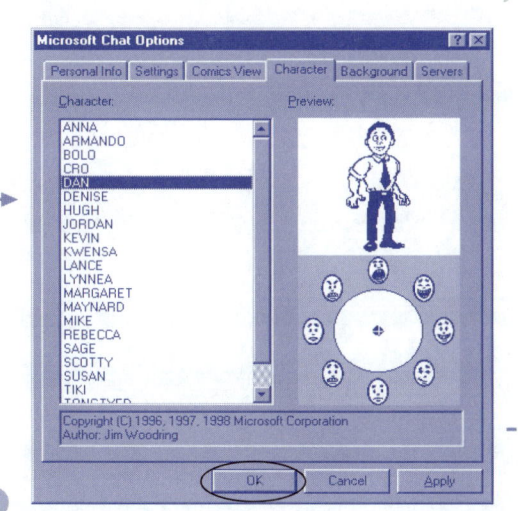

3 Choose a cartoon figure that you like the look of and then click on *OK*.

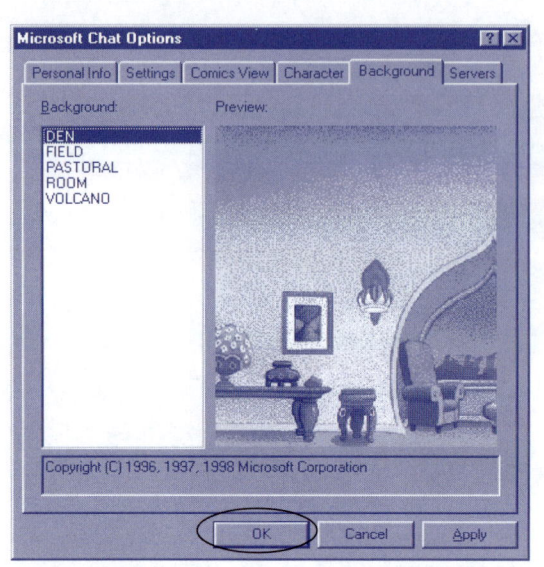

4 Now choose your favourite background for the cartoon and click on *OK*.

You have to laugh – the best computer messages

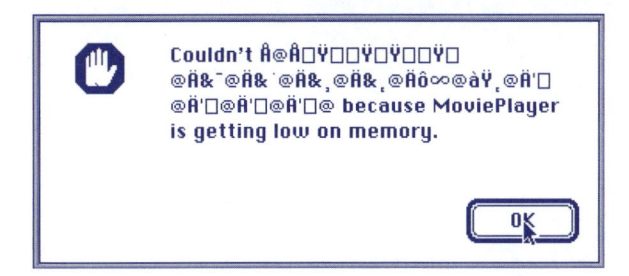

> Couldn't Å@Å□Ÿ□□Ÿ□Ÿ□□Ÿ□ @Ä&¯@Ä& ˙@Ä&ˌ@Ä&ˌ@Äô∞@àŸˌ@Ä'□ @Ä'□@Ä'□@Ä'□@ because MoviePlayer is getting low on memory.
>
> [OK]

Are we getting a bit nervous when we are running low on memory?

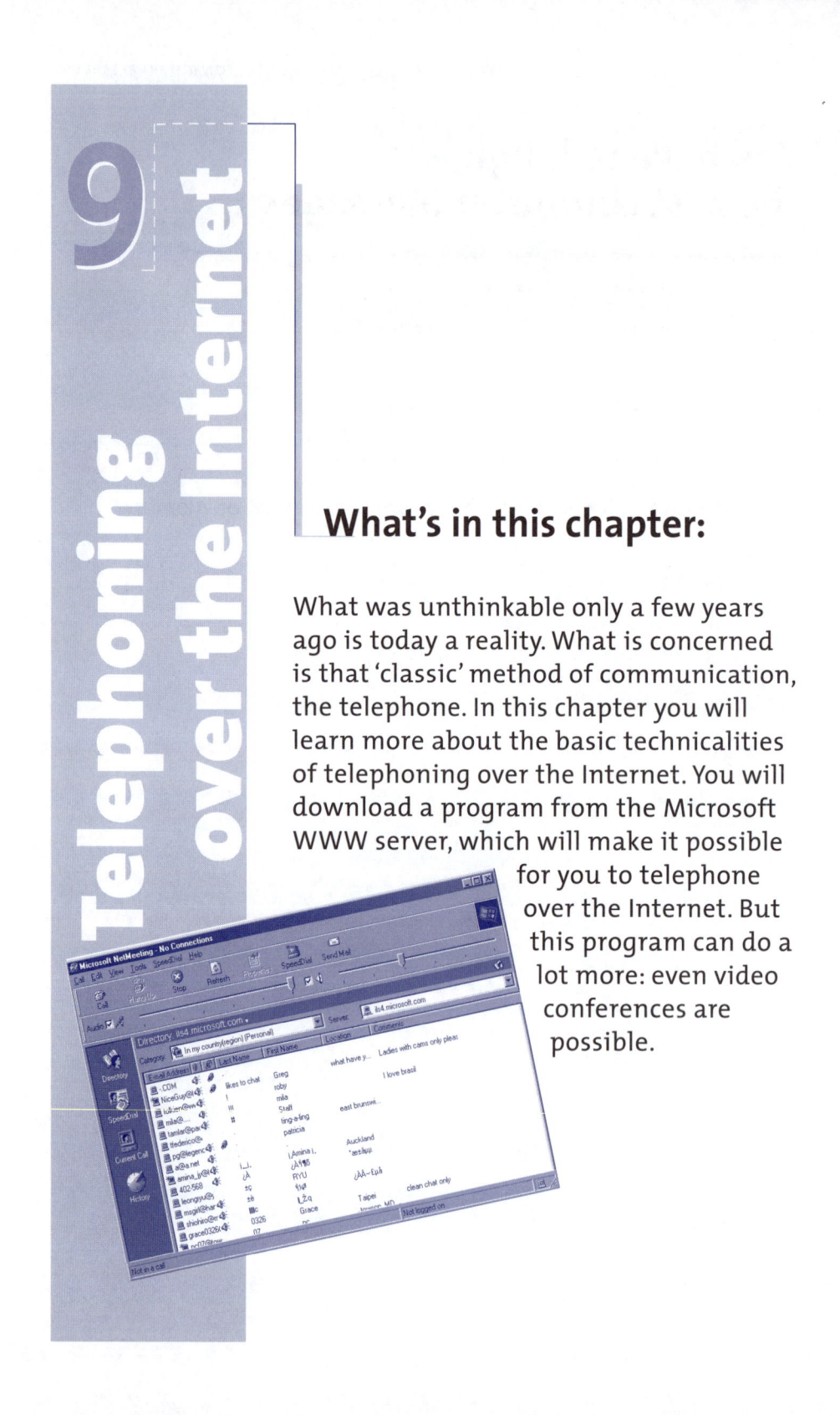

9 Telephoning over the Internet

What's in this chapter:

What was unthinkable only a few years ago is today a reality. What is concerned is that 'classic' method of communication, the telephone. In this chapter you will learn more about the basic technicalities of telephoning over the Internet. You will download a program from the Microsoft WWW server, which will make it possible for you to telephone over the Internet. But this program can do a lot more: even video conferences are possible.

You already know about:

Modems & Co.	10
The importance of software	16
Accessing the Internet with AOL	122
Accessing the Internet with BT Click	141
Installing Netscape Communicator 4.7	166
Rock, pop and classical music on the Web	192
IE4 and RealPlayer	194
Using RealPlayer	201
CD quality music – MP3	206
Video on the Internet	218
Looking at the day's news	219
IRC chat	224
Installing the Microsoft Chat program	225

You are going to learn about:

Using the Web to telephone	242
Making a call over the Internet	243

Using the Internet to telephone – how does it work?

The Internet has broken down the old methods of communication and has developed new ways for us to talk to each other – just think of e-mail, IRC chat or newsgroups (which you will learn about later). Even that classic tool of communication, the telephone, has not been spared the modernisation process. What is revolutionising the telephone system is that, unlike the conventional telephone, you will no longer need to pay any **long-distance call charges**. All you have to do is pay your Internet Service Provider for your normal telephone connection – nothing else. Even if you spend hours on the phone to Australia, which would normally cost a fortune, you will now be charged only the cost of a **local call** for the connection.

WHAT'S THIS?
A **sound card** gives your computer both ears and mouth, and enables you to play and record music and speech.

In order to use the Internet as a telephone you will need to install some particular software, which carries out the telephone's functions. You must also provide your computer with a sound card which has a **microphone input**. Speech is broadcast via loudspeakers connected to your sound card. You will find many programs available on the Internet, some of which you have to pay for, while others are free. For this particular session you will use Microsoft's Netmeeting program, which can be found for free on their server.

TIP
Do not expect miracles. The sound quality of an Internet conversation is substantially lower than that of a normal telephone conversation. However, there are solutions in the pipeline for supplying high quality lines that will not even have to fear competition from ISDN telephones.

At the moment, the number of people with whom you can have an Internet conversation is still limited. However, this situation will soon start to change substantially.

An Internet telephone conversation basically happens like this: when you are logged on and wish either to make or to receive a telephone call, you go to the address book of the corresponding program. Here you will find a list of all the people who also use that program. When you find the name of someone you wish to telephone, the program searches for the IP address of that person and forwards your call to them. If this person is currently logged on, the telephone will 'ring' at their end. Thanks to the sound card and the microphone you will now be able to talk to each other.

As soon as you speak into the microphone, the program converts your words into a series of 'zeros and ones', as these are the only signals the computer can understand. In addition, all the data is compressed so as to allow a quicker transport over the Internet. At the same time, the program ascertains the speed of the current Internet connection. If it is a fast connection, the program can relay the speech in high quality mode.

Next, your words are divided up into small 'packets', which are then sent out over the Internet. At the receiver's end these data packets are decompressed, so that the receiver can understand what you have said – so simple!

Making a call over the Internet

When you install IE5, Microsoft Netmeeting is automatically copied onto your computer.

When you open up Netmeeting, you will see that it offers a variety of **functions**. You can use it to send e-mails, chat to people, and even to set up a video connection, which will allow you to see the person you are speaking to. We will limit ourselves here to just using the telephone, as everything else would be outside the framework of this book.

Click on the START menu on your Windows taskbar and open the PROGRAMS and then the INTERNET EXPLORER submenu. There you will find an icon entitled *Netmeeting*.

You will then need to establish a connection with your Internet Service Provider.

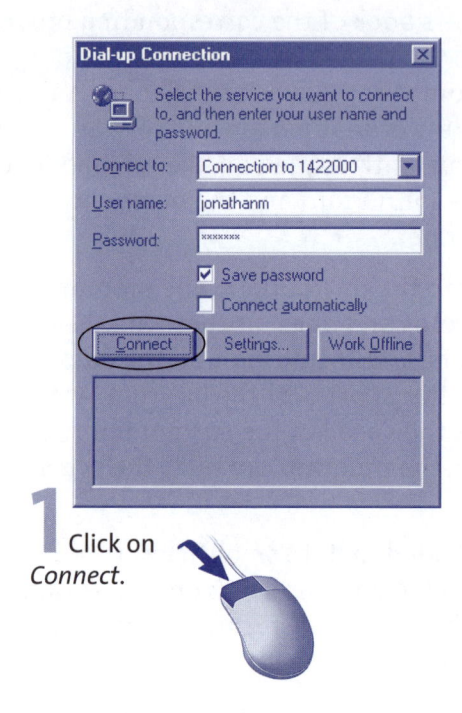

1 Click on *Connect*.

Netmeeting is started up as soon as the Internet connection is established. A connection is immediately opened to a Microsoft Internet server, which contains a directory of all the **users of Netmeeting**. This directory is then downloaded onto your computer.

You will see that many of the entries have a small red star on top of the computer icon. All this means is that this particular user is logged on and you can open a **telephone connection** with them.

In the upper third of the window you will see two slide rules. The one on the left is responsible for the sensitivity of the microphone. You can use the ruler on the right to control the volume of your **speakers.**

Making a call over the Internet

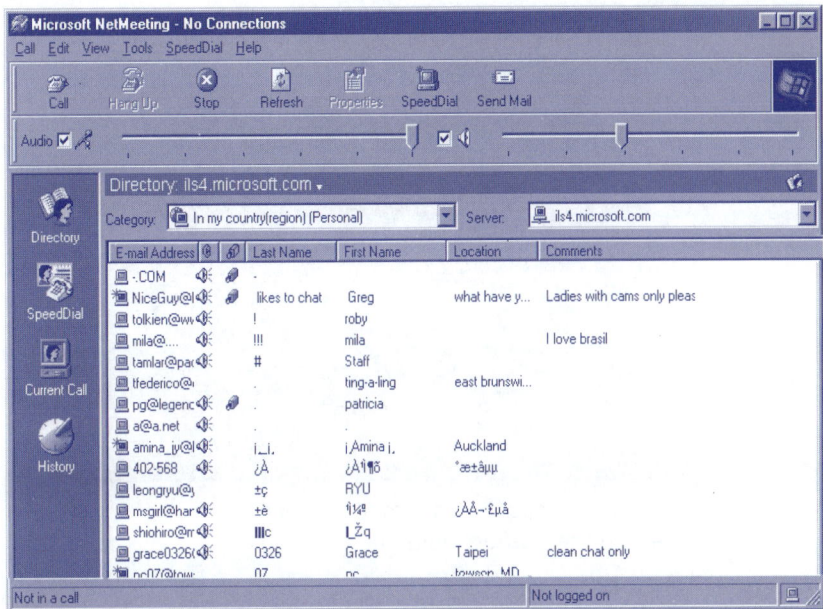

2 Double-click on any of the entries.

If the person you want to speak to is logged onto the Microsoft server, and if they want to speak to you, you can start to talk.

If your partner is online and you know their e-mail address, you can then enter this address directly. To do this, click on the *Call* icon.

245

New Call

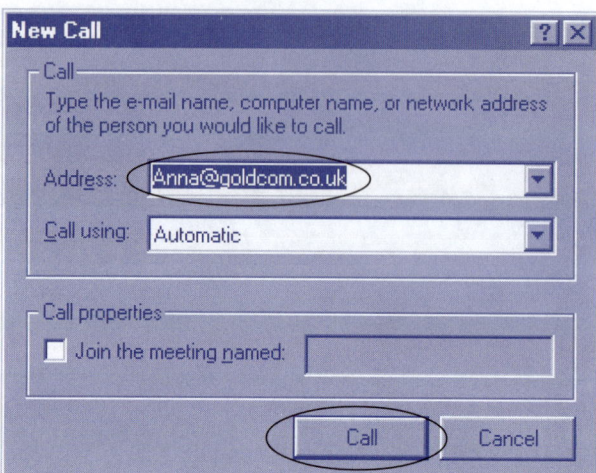

Call

Type the e-mail name, computer name, or network address of the person you would like to call.

Address: Anna@goldcom.co.uk

Call using: Automatic

Call properties

☐ Join the meeting named:

Call   Cancel

3 Enter your partner's e-mail address in the *Address* field, then click on *Call*.

You have to laugh – the best computer messages

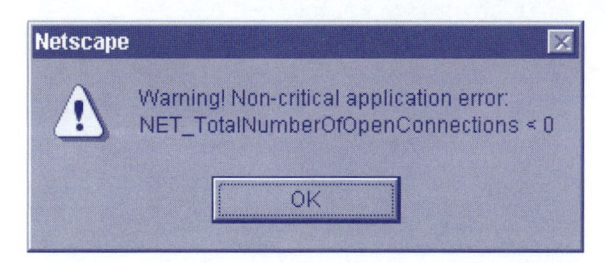

Netscape

⚠ Warning! Non-critical application error:
NET_TotalNumberOfOpenConnections < 0

[OK]

How many times must this user have hung up to have less than zero open connections...

10 Downloading files from the Internet

What's in this chapter:

In the previous chapters you have often seen how to download a file from the Internet to your own computer. There is another way, however – FTP. In this chapter you will work more closely with this Internet service: you will download an FTP program from the Internet and install it on your own computer. Following this, you will use FTP to download a file from the Internet. Later on you will learn a little about how to handle compressed files and how to decompress them.

You already know about:

Accessing the Internet with AOL	122
Accessing the Internet with BT Click	141
Using RealPlayer	201
CD quality music	206
Video on the Internet	218
Looking at the day's news	219
Installing the Microsoft Chat program	225
Using the Internet to telephone	242
Making a call over the Internet	243

You are going to learn about:

How FTP works	250
Finding an FTP program	251
Decompressing a file	254
Installing the FTP program	255
Using FTP to download a file to your computer	258
Adding a new FTP address	262

How does FTP work?

Downloading a file is one of the classic functions of the Internet. No other service is used by the Internet community more than FTP. You can use this service to download all the different types of files, such as programs, graphics, sounds, text files and much more.

WHAT'S THIS? An **FTP Client** is a program that enables you to connect to an FTP server.

As with all the other Internet services that you have been learning about, you will need a special program to operate FTP – a so-called **FTP Client**. This program contacts an FTP server, which in turn runs a small program to enable the transport of data.

In order to register with an FTP server and download files, you will need either an entry number or a user name as well as a password. This identifies you as someone who is allowed to receive data from the FTP server. However, this process has recently become less of a necessity. Most FTP servers allow access to everyone, but they still require a user name and password. If you want to access the files on these FTP servers you will need to give the word **Anonymous** as your user name and use your e-mail address as your password. For this reason, these FTP servers are also known as 'Anonymous FTP' servers.

FTP is easy to use. As soon as you have registered with an FTP server you will be able to look at every available folder and all the files in it. If you find what you are looking for, all you need to do is click on the required file and decide which folder you want to save the data in on your computer.

So how does FTP work exactly? To start up an **FTP session** you first need to open the FTP program on your computer and then establish an Internet connection. A special program, the FTP daemon, runs on the FTP server and is responsible for controlling all the transfer activities.

WHAT'S THIS?

The **FTP daemon** is a program that watches over and regulates all downloading activity on your computer.

As soon as you use your FTP program to contact an FTP server, the FTP daemon will ask for your user name and password.

Once you have registered, a **command connection** is set up between your computer and the FTP server. This connection enables the transfer of commands from your computer to the FTP server as well as receiving messages and information.

If you should want to change to another of the FTP server's files, your FTP program sends a corresponding command to the FTP daemon. This changes the path to the file and uses the command connection to send you a list of all the files contained in the new folder.

A second connection, the **data connection**, is established once you find a file that you would like to download. Files are loaded from the FTP server onto your computer via this file connection. This connection is automatically closed when all the data has been transferred. The command connection lasts a little longer, so that you can look at the folder's contents on an FTP server even after downloading.

Let's find an FTP program

There are many FTP programs available on the Internet, all of which are free. You will now visit the WWW server of a firm that offers one of these free programs.

Open an Internet connection and enter the following URL: *http://www.ftpx.com*.

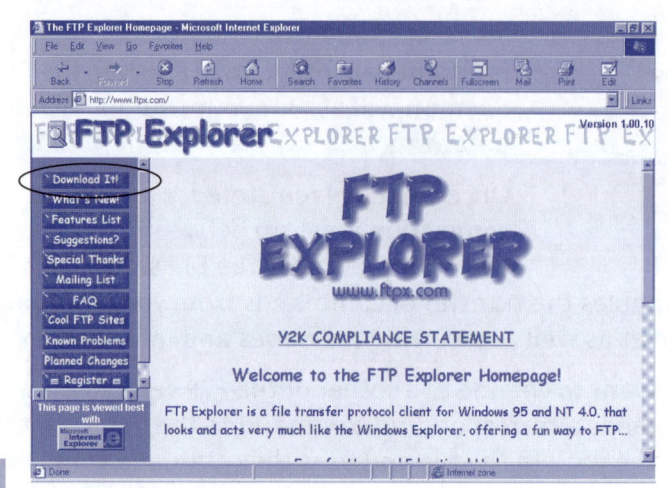

1 Click on the *Download It!* hyperlink on the left-hand side of the Web page.

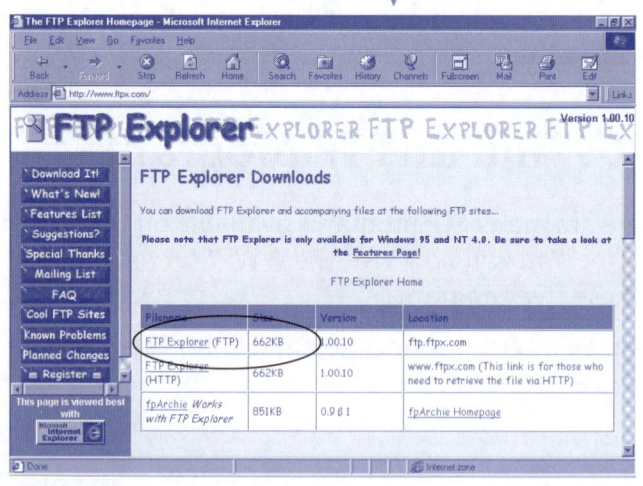

2 Click on the *FTP Explorer* hyperlink to download the file from the Internet.

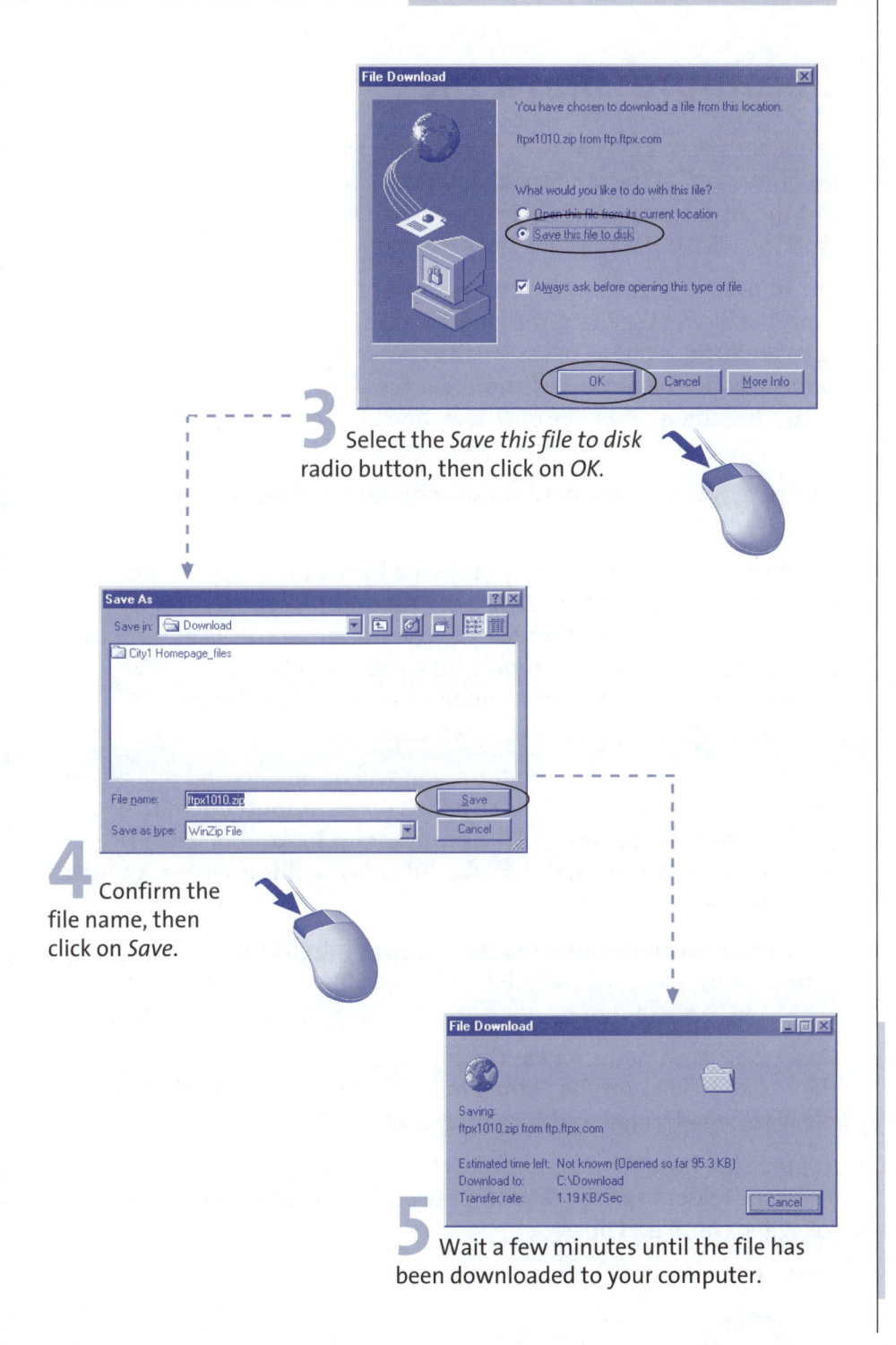

LET'S FIND AN FTP PROGRAM

3 Select the *Save this file to disk* radio button, then click on *OK*.

4 Confirm the file name, then click on *Save*.

5 Wait a few minutes until the file has been downloaded to your computer.

253

Decompressing a file

When the file has been moved to your computer, you will need to decompress it. In the previous chapters this all happened automatically, but the situation is slightly different here. You are now going to be working with a file that has the extension *.zip*.

The transfer of files from the Internet takes time, sometimes a lot of time. The bigger the file is, the longer it takes to download. In order to keep the surfer's phone bill as small as possible, some resourceful souls came up with the process of 'shrinking' files. Once a file has undergone such a treatment, it will be only a fraction of its original size. This smaller file can then be transferred, quickly and smoothly, over the Internet.

As a rule, you can recognise these compressed files, known as **archives**, by the file extensions *.zip*, *.arj* and *.lha*.

Since these files have been compressed by means of special programs (for example, PKZip or WinZip), a corresponding counterpart is required to restore the files back to their original size. Files with the *.zip* extension can be decompressed either by PKUnzip or by WinZip. If WinZip is installed in your Windows system, it will open automatically every time you download a *.zip* file.

If you do not own such a program, you will be able to find one either on one of the many CD-ROMs supplied with computer magazines, or by downloading it from an FTP server. Keep a lookout on the FTP servers for folders entitled 'tools' or 'utilities' – this is where you will find the program you need.

Once you have decompressed the file back into its individual components, you can safely delete the original, compressed file.

Now, decompress your newly downloaded file. In Winzip, select the OPEN ARCHIVE command, locate the file and then select OPEN. You will then need to click on the *Extract* button, specify a folder where the file is to be extracted and click on *Extract*.

If you do not have WinZip, open the MS-DOS Prompt under Windows, select the folder in which the compressed file is located and enter the following command line:

PKUNZIP FTPX.ZIP

Confirm your input by pressing the ⏎ key, and the file will be decompressed into it's individual components.

Installing the FTP program

In the previous step you broke down the compressed file into its individual files. Once you have done this, you can start the procedure to install the FTP program on your computer. To do this, click on the RUN command in the Windows START menu.

In the following window you will be asked to supply the name of the file to be executed. In case you cannot remember this, you can browse through your hard disk to find the correct component of the archive you just decompressed.

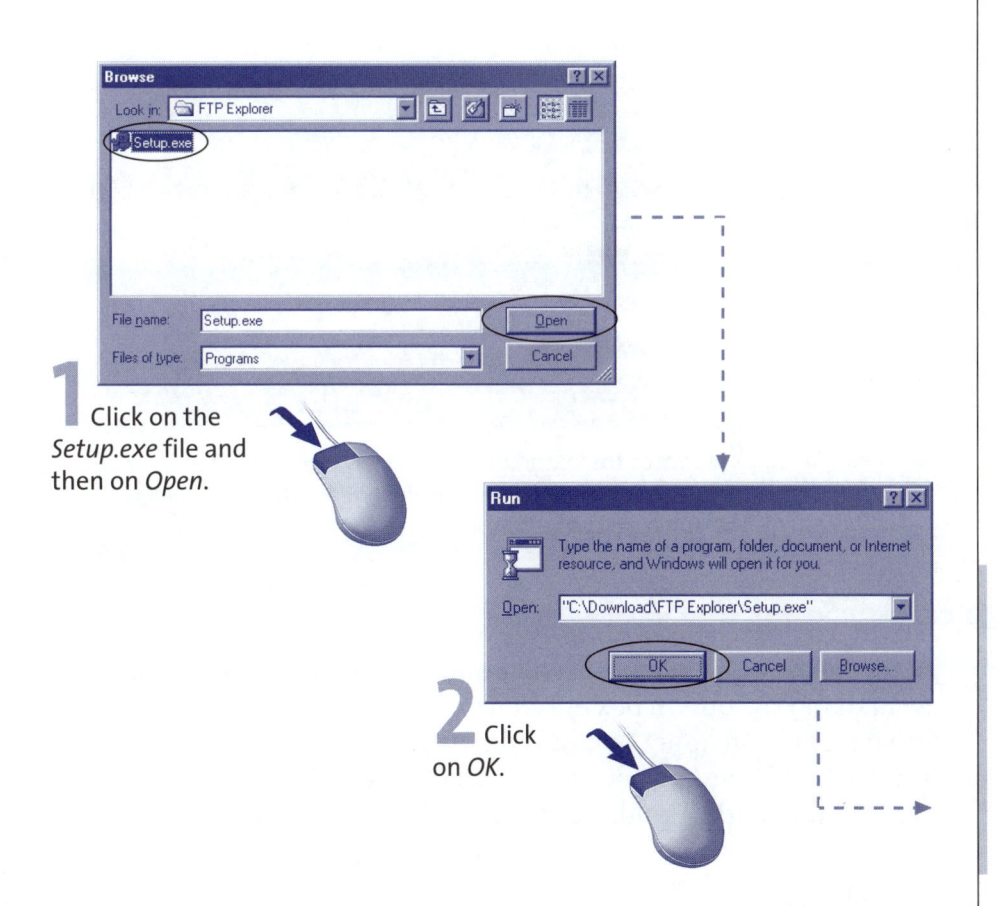

1 Click on the *Setup.exe* file and then on *Open*.

2 Click on *OK*.

255

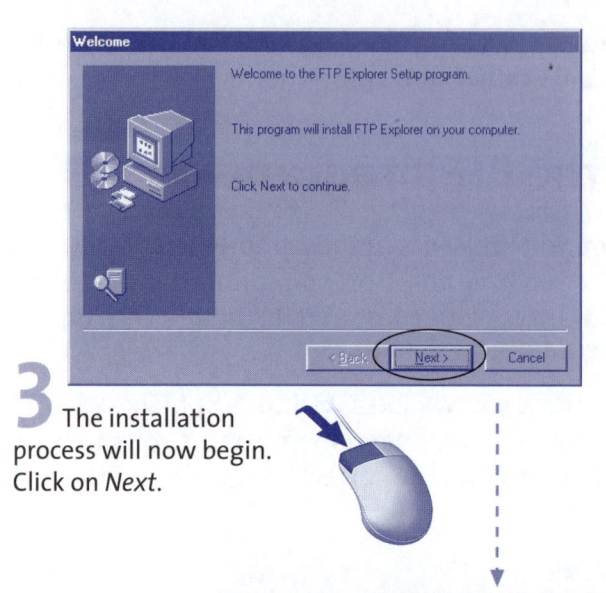

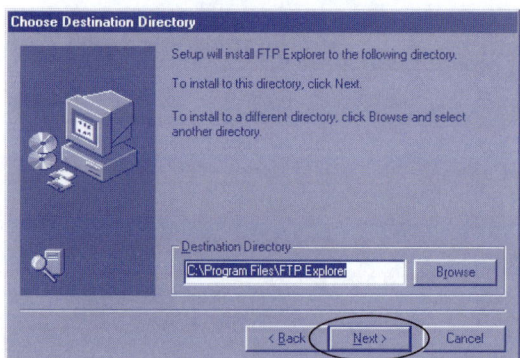

3 The installation process will now begin. Click on *Next*.

4 Enter the name of a folder where you wish the software to be installed, or accept the suggested one. Then click on *Next*.

In the following window you will be asked to make some decisions. By marking the option box entitled *Create Shortcut on Desktop*, you can have an icon appear on your desktop. Using this icon, known as a **shortcut**, will save you a lot of time as you won't have to search for the program in the Windows menu structure. If you mark the second

INSTALLING THE FTP PROGRAM

option box, entitled *Create Shortcut in Start Menu/Programs*, you will add a shortcut option to the PROGRAMS submenu of the Windows START menu.

By marking the last option box you will be able to view a README file containing additional information. The default setting is to have all the option boxes marked. Please keep these settings.

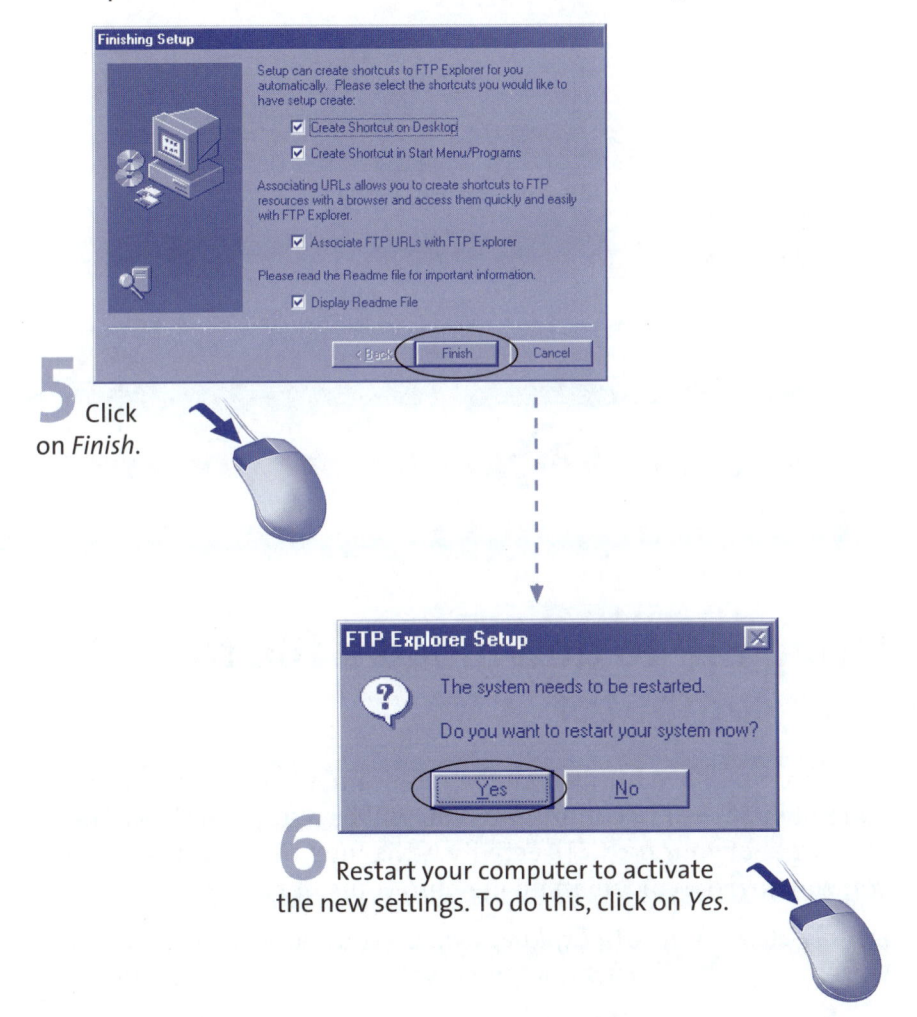

5 Click on *Finish*.

6 Restart your computer to activate the new settings. To do this, click on *Yes*.

Once your computer has restarted and Windows is back up, you will see a new icon on your desktop.

257

7 Double-click on the *FTP Explorer* icon on the Windows desktop.

Using FTP to download a file to your computer

Now that you have fulfilled all the requirements necessary for being a member of the FTP community, you will be ready to get stuck in. The target of your next FTP activity is the Intel FTP server, from where you will now download an image onto your computer.

Double-click on the *FTP Explorer* icon on your desktop. This will take you through the registration process the first time you use it.

USING FTP TO DOWNLOAD A FILE TO YOUR COMPUTER

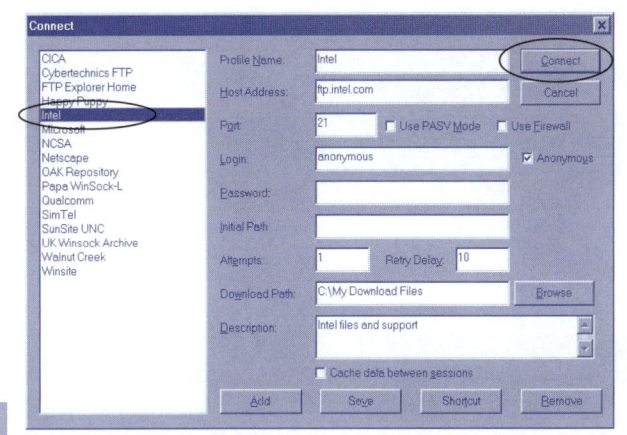

1 Click on *Intel* in the left-hand list box of the window, then click on *Connect*.

This will open an Internet connection (as was the case in all the other chapters). You will have noticed that our FTP program already contains the standard addresses of several FTP servers, so there is no need for you to enter an **FTP address** here.

> When you acquire a program via FTP, all you actually do is download the corresponding files onto your computer. However, by no means does this make the program ready to use. You will still need to decompress or install it. In most cases, you will find a file on your hard disk called *Setup* or *Install*. You will need to click on this after downloading, in order to set the program up on your computer.

As soon as the Internet connection is open, the FTP program will connect to the Intel FTP server. You are then connected to the server's **root directory**. From here you can move ever deeper into the server's structure until you find what you are looking for.

259

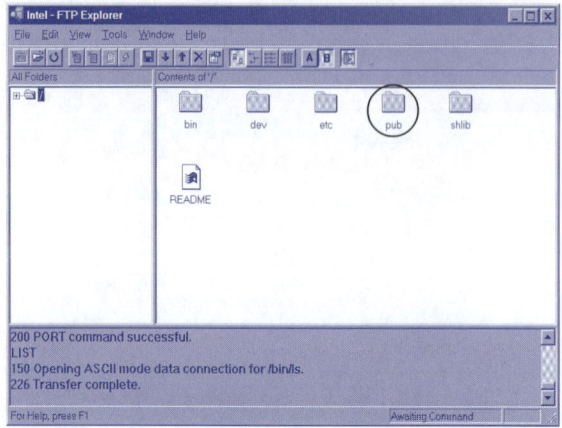

2 Double-clicking on the folder entitled *Pub* will open this folder.

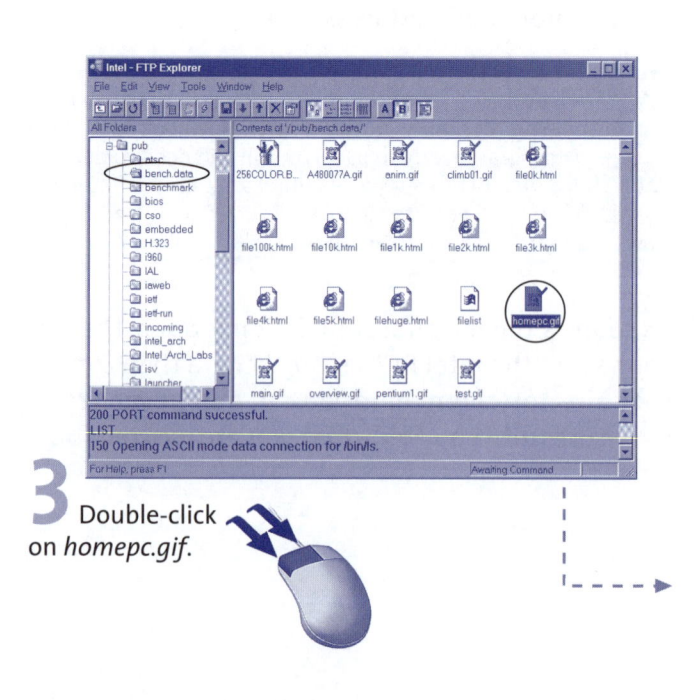

The file which you are going to download can be found in the folder *bench.data* and is called *homepc.gif*. Just keep 'clicking through' until you reach your goal.

3 Double-click on *homepc.gif*.

260

USING FTP TO DOWNLOAD A FILE TO YOUR COMPUTER

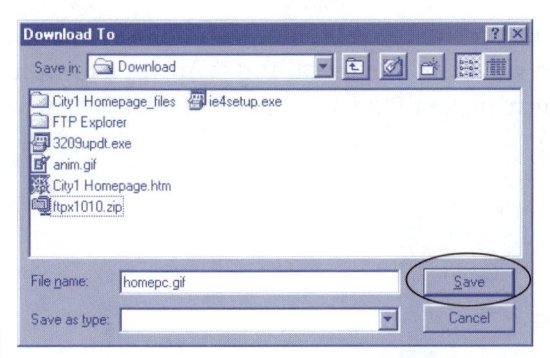

4 Choose a folder in which you wish to save the file, then click on *Save*.

When you have carried out this final step, your FTP program will start downloading the required file from the FTP server. This will take a few minutes or (as in this case) seconds to happen and you can then close both the FTP program and the Internet connection.

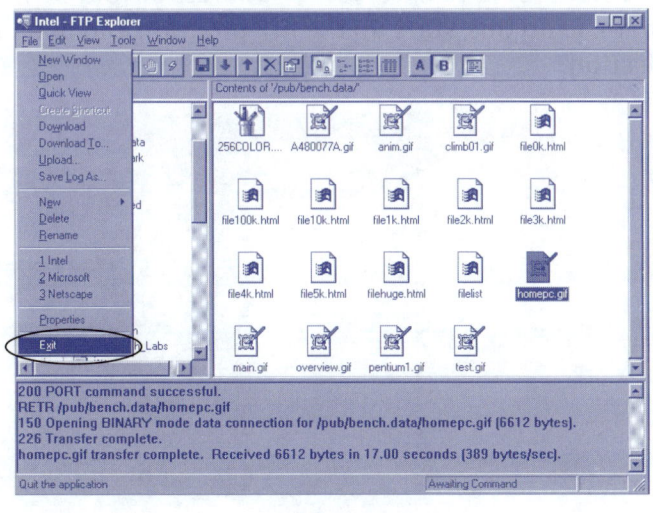

5 To end the program, click on EXIT in the FILE menu.

261

If you now have a look in the target folder, you will see the file named *Homepc.gif*. You can view this file by calling it up, for example, in Netscape Communicator, RealPlayer G2, or even in Paint (in START/ PROGRAMS/ACCESSORIES).

6 And here it is, the picture you downloaded from the Intel FTP server.

Adding a new FTP address

You are now going to enter an **FTP address** of your own into your FTP program. To do this, start up the FTP program and open an Internet connection.

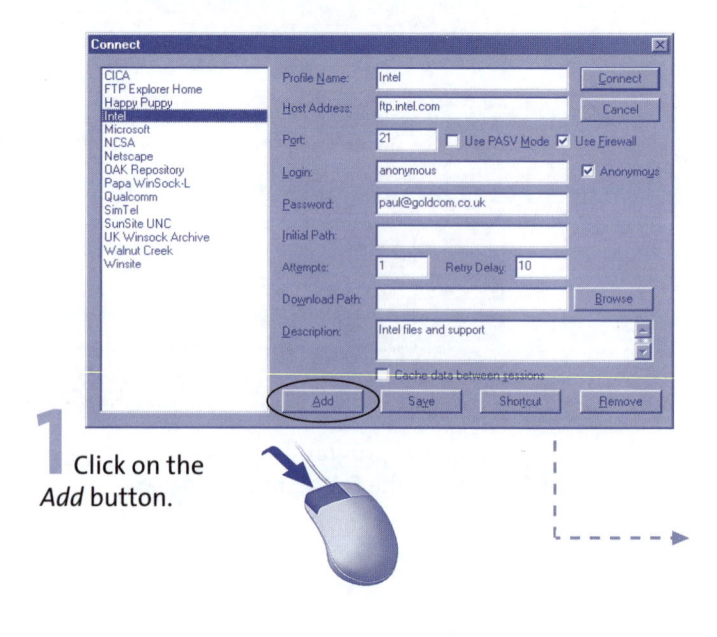

1 Click on the *Add* button.

262

ADDING A NEW FTP ADDRESS

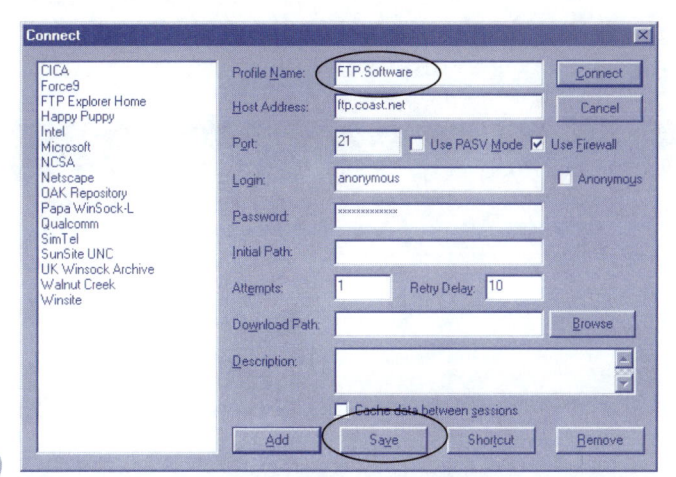

2 Now enter a name for the connection, the address of the FTP server and a password (your e-mail address) in the appropriate fields, then click on *Save*.

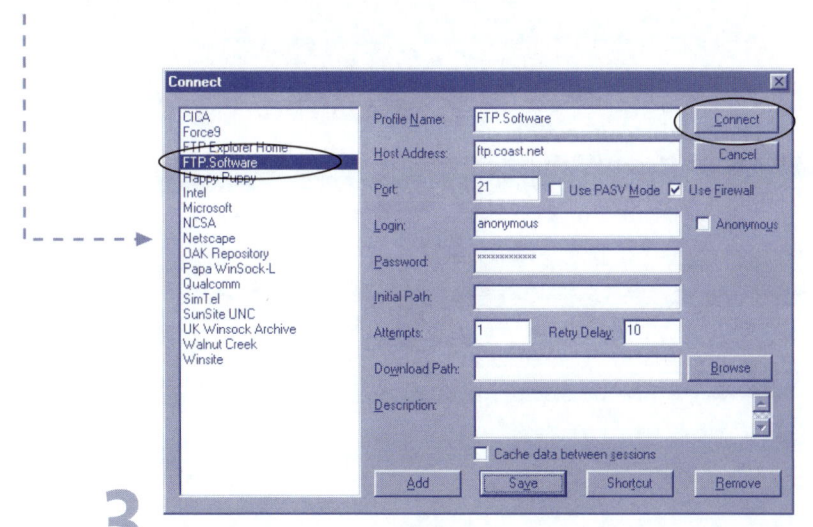

3 The new *FTP Software* entry.

263

When you now click on *Connect*, you will be connected to this FTP server.

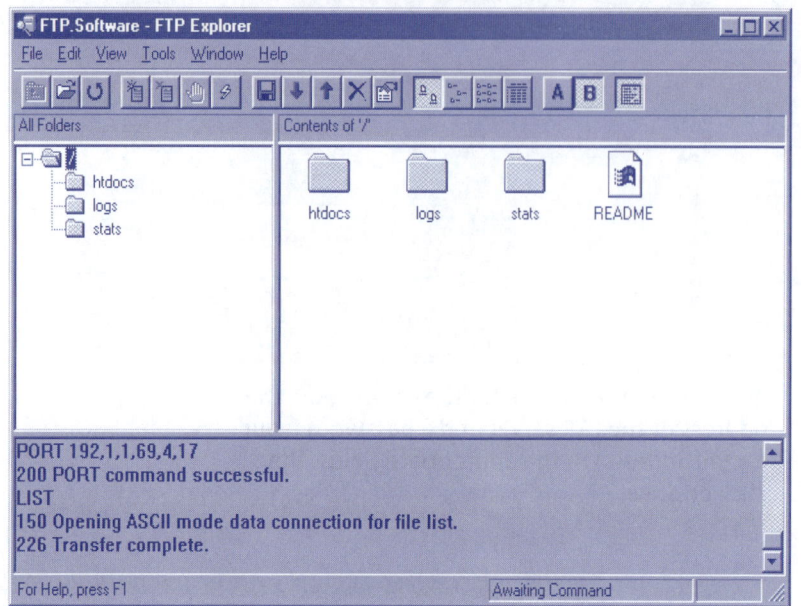

4 Here is the connection to the new FTP server and its contents.

You have to laugh – the best computer messages

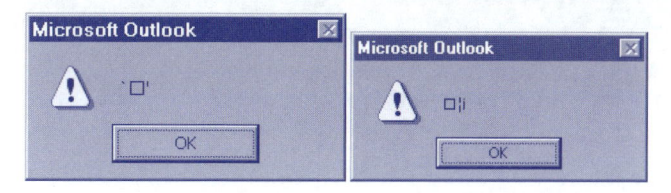

Is this still the same message... or does it change with the font size?

11

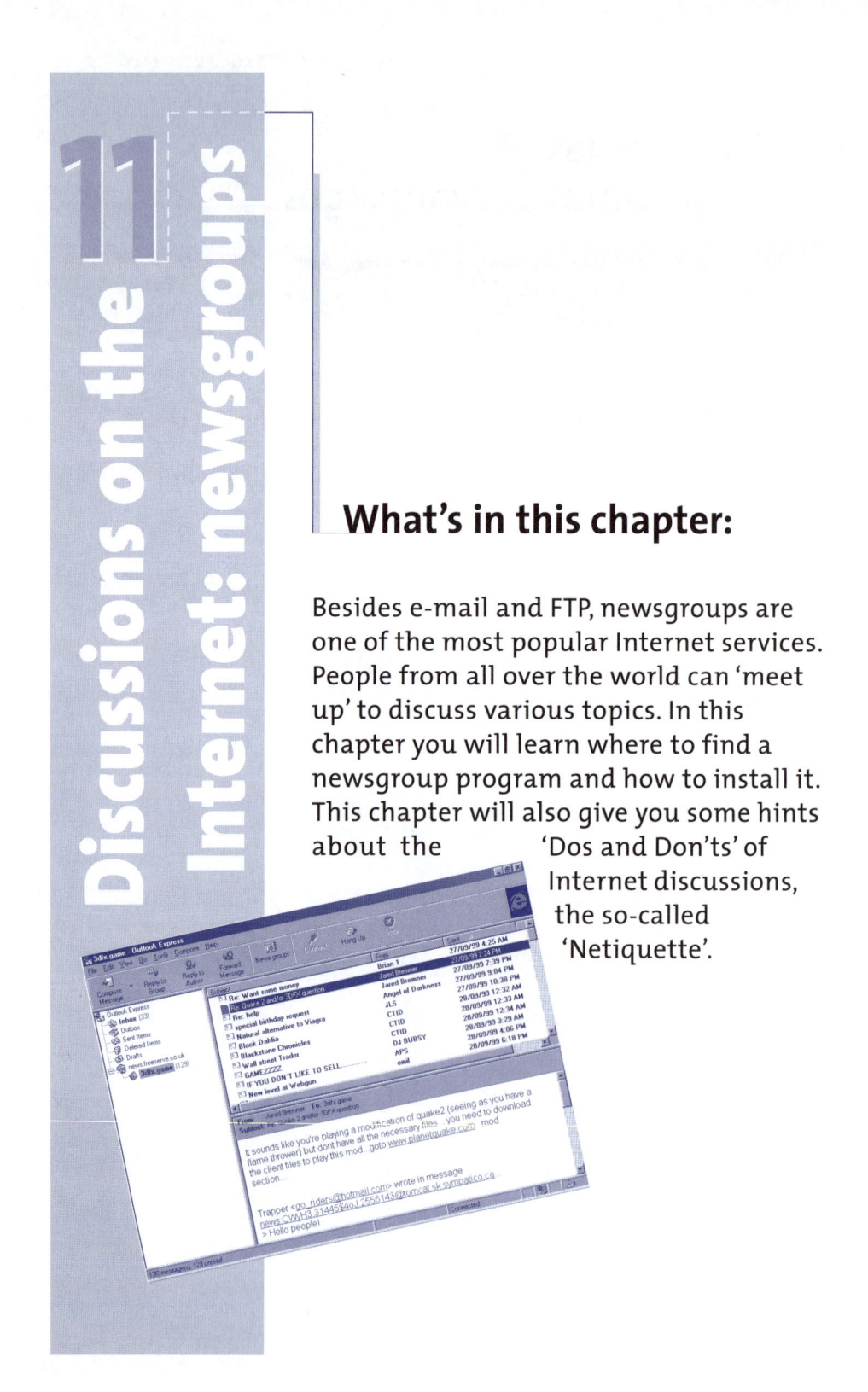

Discussions on the Internet: newsgroups

What's in this chapter:

Besides e-mail and FTP, newsgroups are one of the most popular Internet services. People from all over the world can 'meet up' to discuss various topics. In this chapter you will learn where to find a newsgroup program and how to install it. This chapter will also give you some hints about the 'Dos and Don'ts' of Internet discussions, the so-called 'Netiquette'.

You already know about:

Accessing the Internet with AOL	122
Accessing the Internet with BT Click	141
Newsgroups with the Netscape Messenger	183
Telephoning over the Web	242
How FTP works	250
Finding an FTP program	251
Decompressing a file	254
Installing the FTP program	255

You are going to learn about:

Newsgroups	268
Outlook Express and IE4	270
Configuring the newsgroup reader	276
Reading and subscribing to newsgroups	280
IE5 and Outlook Express 5	284
Netiquette	293

From A to Z – newsgroups have something for everyone

Humans love to talk. The Internet, with all its newsgroups, takes this human characteristic very much into account. The 'Usenet' is a worldwide electronic **discussion forum**. This information pool allows for the exchange of messages across the entire network. In practice this means that people from all over the world can take part in discussions on every subject imaginable. The communities inside the **Usenet**, which deal with particular themes, are called 'newsgroups'.

TIP: Groups whose names begin with a language code, such as *de.*, *it.* etc., are foreign language forums. The same usually applies to forums which include the full name of a country.

WHAT'S THIS?: A **newsgroup reader** is a program which allows you to contact a newsgroup, read the articles and then reply to them by writing your own contributions.

There are currently over 20,000 newsgroups covering every possible subject: cars, cinema, sexuality, computers etc. You will soon see how popular and well used this type of communication really is.

If you want to take part in a newsgroup, you will need a particular program, called a **newsgroup reader**.

There are both moderated and unmoderated newsgroups on the Internet. In a moderated newsgroup, all the messages received are checked over by a moderator. This person then decides whether or not to publish the message in that particular newsgroup. In an unmoderated newsgroup, all messages are automatically sent to everyone in the group.

Messages intended for publication are sent via **Usenet servers** to all the participants who have access to that particular newsgroup. Usually only the most recent messages are sent. As a rule, older contributions are archived and deleted at a later date. By subscribing to a 'mailing list', you will be able to receive the most recent additions to a newsgroup. Next time you visit the newsgroup you will automatically receive the new messages.

Multimedia: the term covers, for example, sound, graphics and video sequences.

Besides pure text, messages published in newsgroups may also contain pictures, sound and other **multimedia data**.

How the Usenet works

The Usenet is like a worldwide 'blackboard', which functions as a discussion forum. To participate actively in this forum, Internet users send and receive messages, which are then published in a newsgroup.

Newsgroups and their messages are managed by newsgroup servers, which are situated all over the world. These servers are first divided into **main categories**, which in turn are divided into subcategories. All newsgroup and Usenet servers can communicate with each other, which means that every message published on one server is available to all the other servers. You will soon see that not every server publishes every newsgroup. Each newsgroup server decides for itself which newsgroups it will support and which it won't.

Coding is a process that manipulates data in a particular way in order to prepare it for a specific method of transfer.

Many different types of data, for example pictures, sounds or other multimedia data, can be published in newsgroups. In order to use this data, a particular **coding** process must be carried out before the data can be published. If you then want to be able to view or play particular files, you will first need to transfer them to your computer and then use some special software to decode them.

269

Using the **newsgroup reader** allows you to read and then reply to published messages. You can use the software to subscribe to newsgroup lists, which means you will always receive the most recent messages. You can cancel your subscription to a group at any time.

The many newsgroups available are all organised according to the topic they discuss. This has the advantage of making it easier to find newsgroups you are interested in.

In this hierarchical system, newsgroups are first divided into main categories. The following main categories are currently available:

Title	Abbreviation
Computer	COMP.
Alternate	ALT.
Social	SOC.
Science	SCI.
Recreation	REC.
News	NEWS.

The main category is then divided into subcategories. For example, SCI.ASTRO is a subcategory of SCI and, in the same way, SCI.ASTRO.HUBBLE is a subcategory of SCI.ASTRO. This last newsgroup is for all those interested in the Hubble telescope.

In most cases, you can tell from a newsgroup's name what sort of subject it discusses.

Outlook Express and IE4

Now that you understand the basic theory, it is time to install a newsgroup reader on your computer. Internet Explorer 4 contains a program called Outlook Express, which has two parts – an e-mail program and a newsgroup reader. You may have already installed the newsgroup reader at the same time as installing Internet Explorer 4.

In any case, you will always be able to find a current version of this program on the Microsoft Web site.

Start up Internet Explorer and select the SOFTWARE UPDATES entry from the FAVORITES menu. This instructs Internet Explorer to access the update area on the Microsoft Web server and download the required components for Outlook Express.

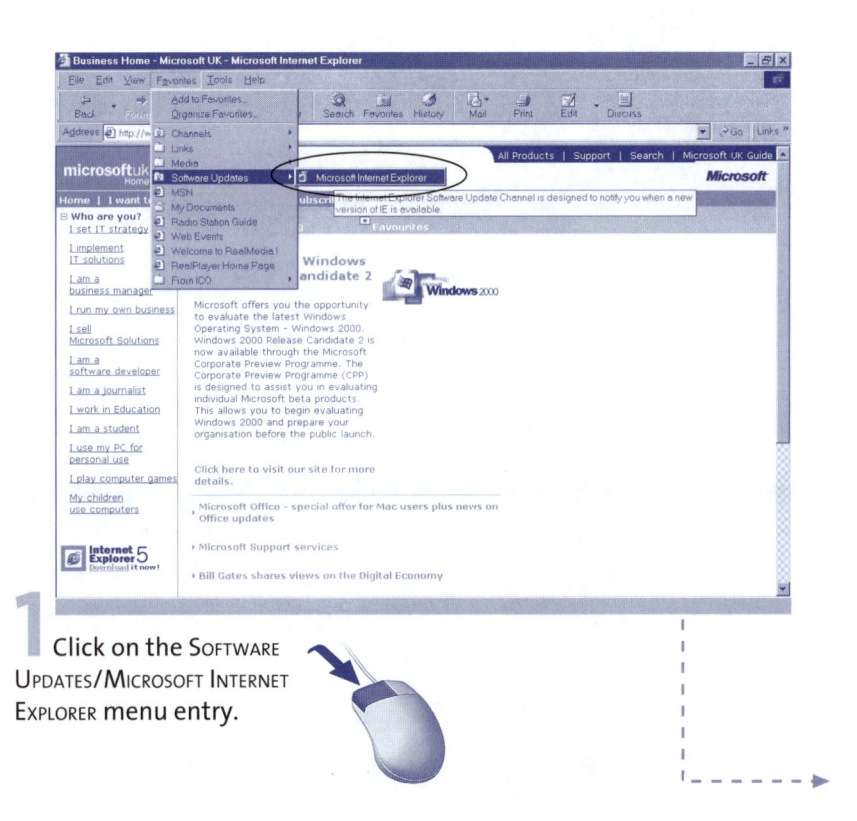

1. Click on the SOFTWARE UPDATES/MICROSOFT INTERNET EXPLORER menu entry.

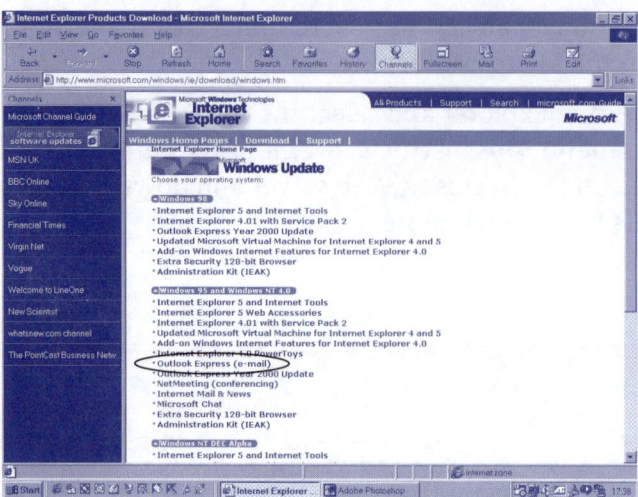

2 Click on *Outlook Express (e-mail)*.

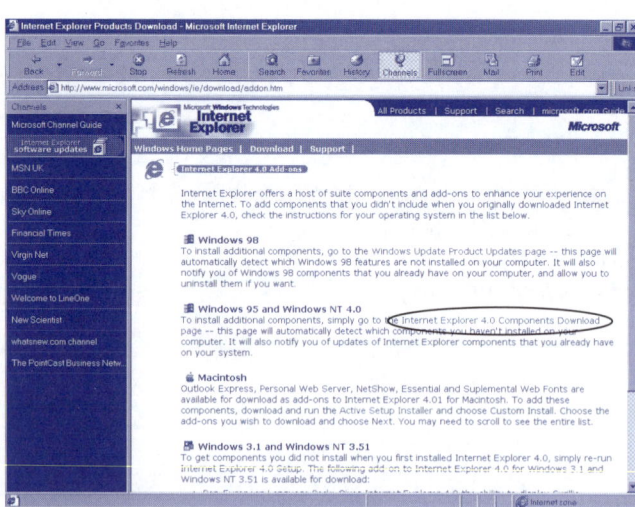

3 Click on the *Internet Explorer 4.0 Components Download* hyperlink.

272

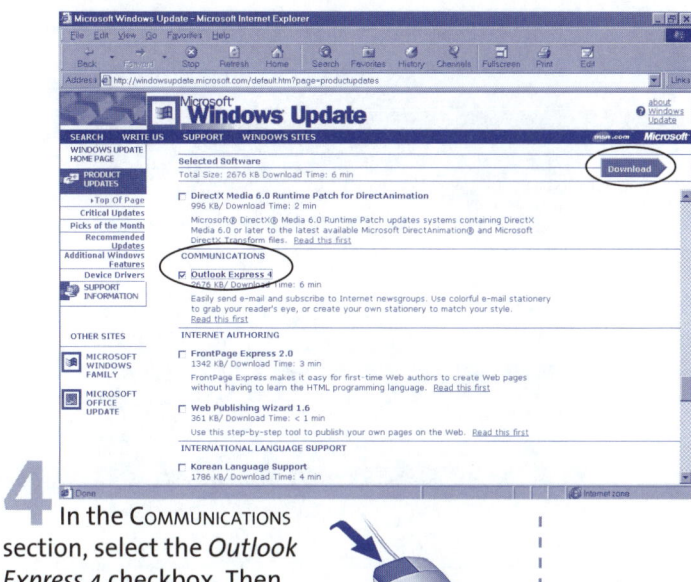

Outlook Express and IE4

4 In the COMMUNICATIONS section, select the *Outlook Express 4* checkbox. Then click on *Download*.

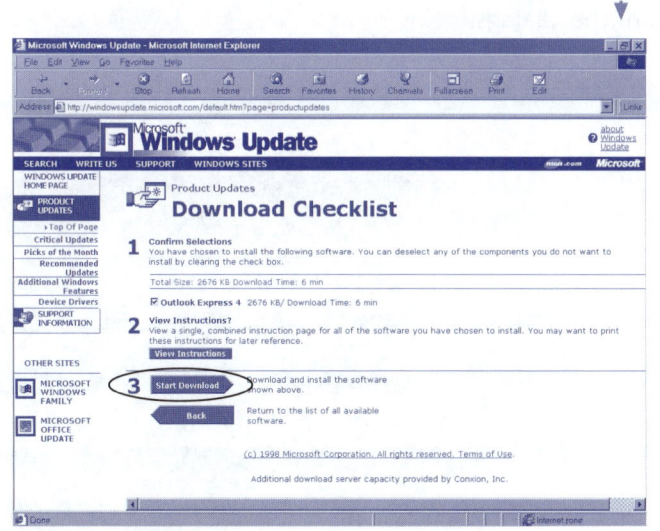

5 Confirm your choices in the Download Checklist by clicking on the *Start Download* button.

273

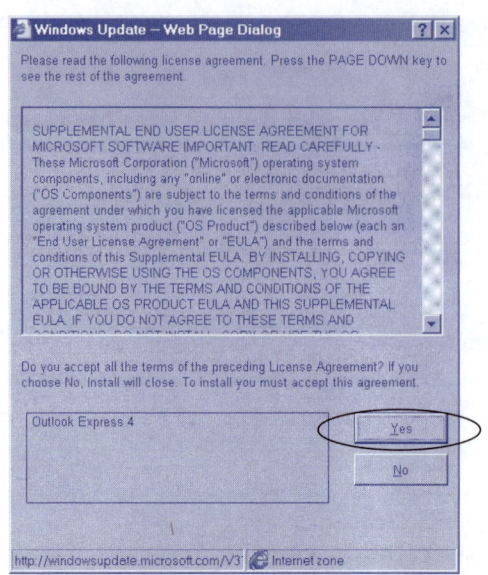

6 Click on *Yes* to accept the license agreement for Outlook Express. The download procedure will then start without further dialogs.

7 The appropriate data is downloaded onto your computer.

OUTLOOK EXPRESS AND IE4

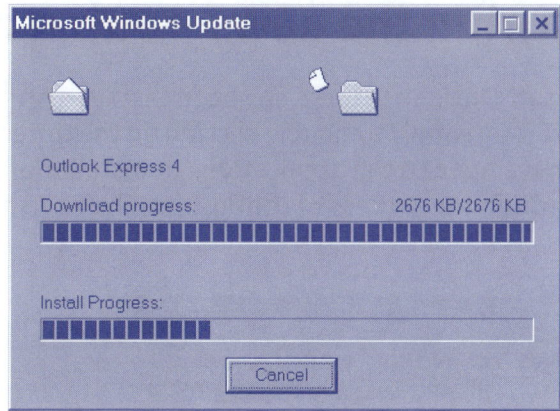

8 Once all the data has been copied to your computer, the Outlook Express installation procedure begins.

After a few minutes of installation and a restart of your computer:

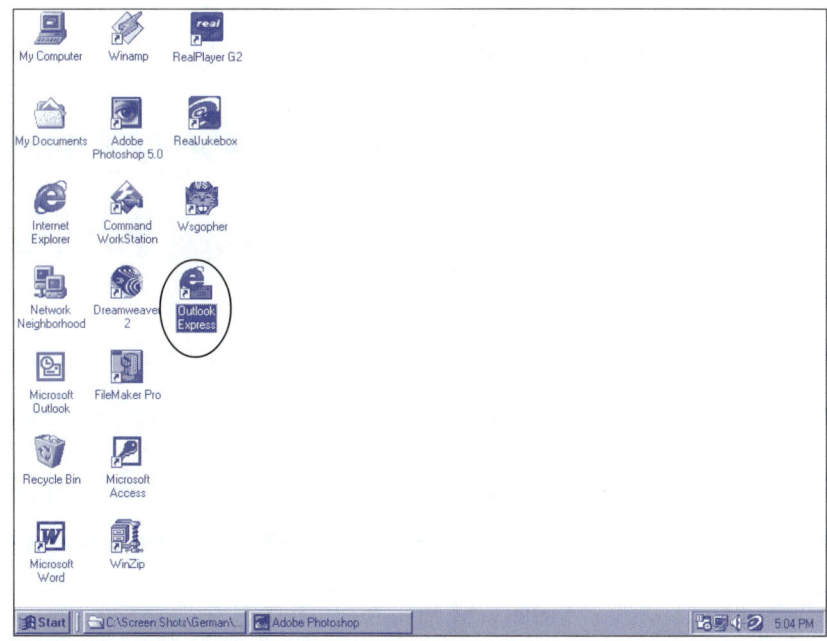

9 You will now see the new Outlook Express icon on your desktop.

275

Configuring the newsgroup reader

Once Microsoft Outlook Express has been installed on your hard disk, you can start it up simply by double-clicking on the corresponding icon. When you have opened the application, an installation wizard will lead you through the process of configuring the newsgroup reader.

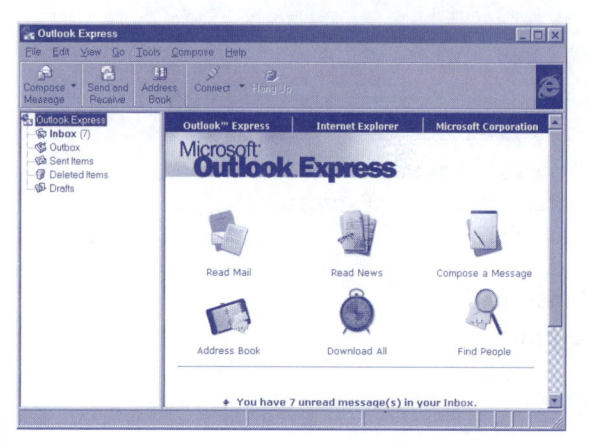

1 The user interface of Microsoft Outlook Express.

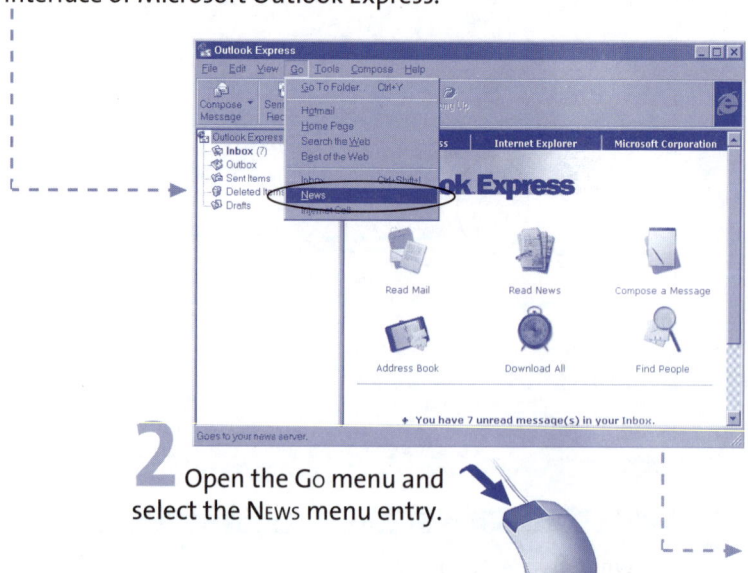

2 Open the Go menu and select the News menu entry.

CONFIGURING THE NEWSGROUP READER

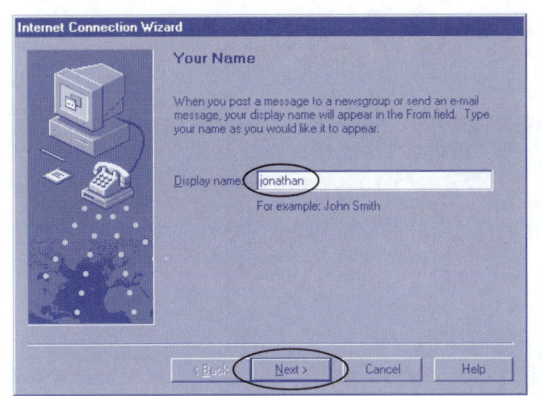

3 Enter the name under which you wish to appear in the newsgroups and click on *Next*.

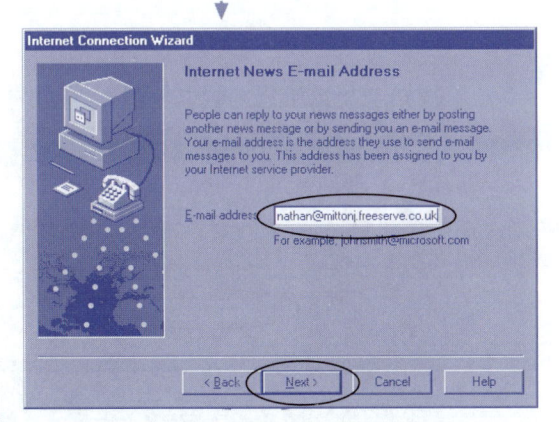

4 You will then be asked for your e-mail address. Type it in and click on *Next*.

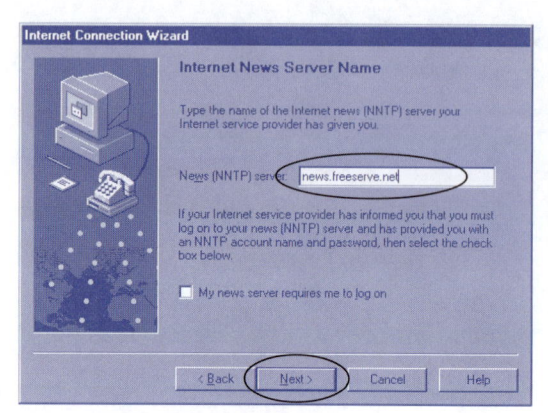

5 Now enter the name of your Internet Service Provider's news server (you will find it in your Internet account's records). Then click on *Next*.

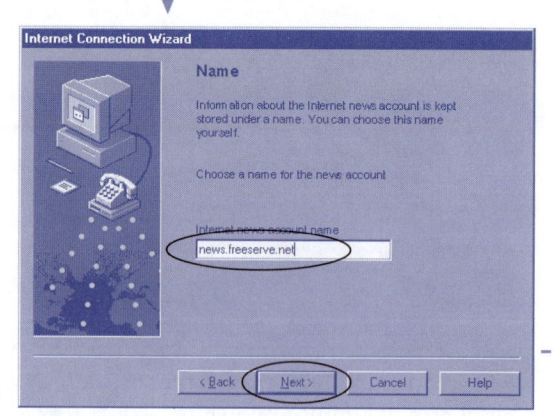

6 At this point you can either give your Internet news account a name or accept the suggested one. Then click on *Next*.

CONFIGURING THE NEWSGROUP READER

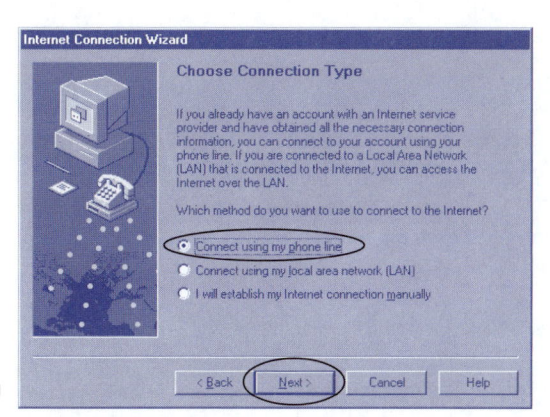

7 Click on the *Connect using my phone line* radio button, then click on *Next*.

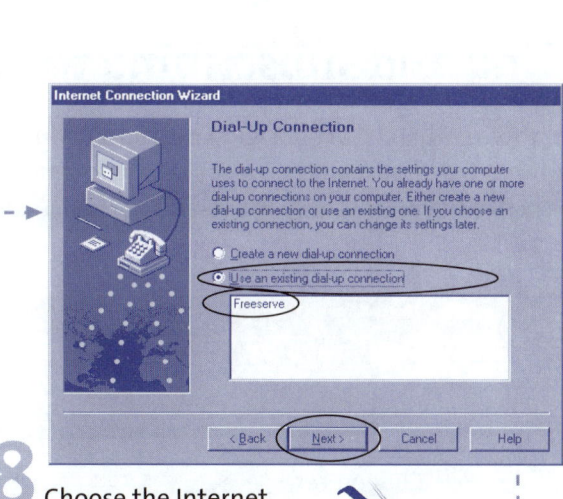

8 Choose the Internet connection that you already have installed and click on *Next*.

279

9 Click on *Finish* to conclude the installation.

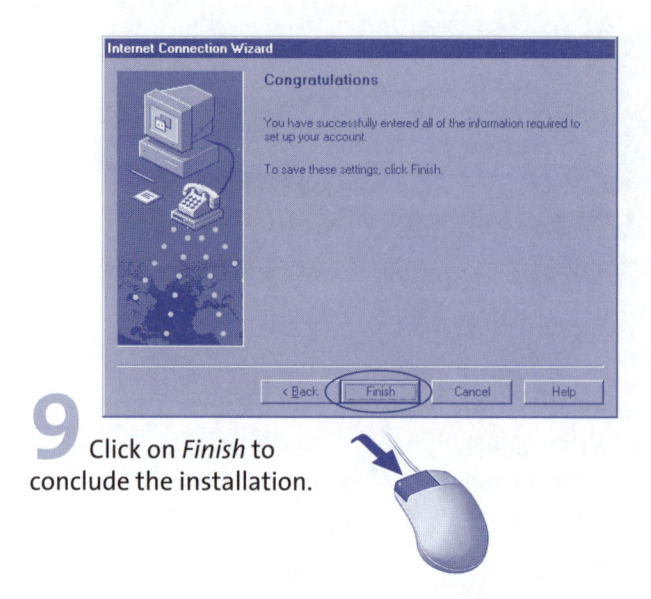

Reading and subscribing to newsgroups

You are now ready to start actively participating in newsgroups. After you have entered all the necessary information, Microsoft Outlook will ask you if you want to subscribe to any Internet newsgroups.

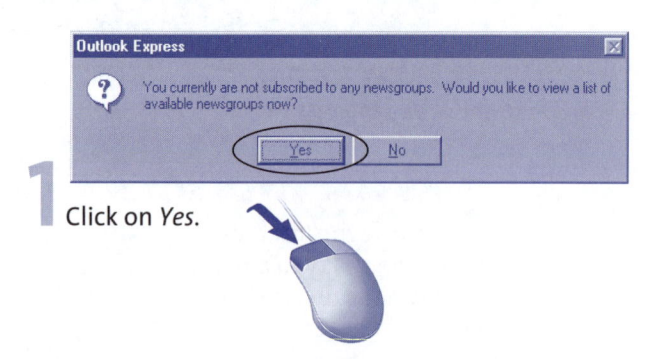

1 Click on *Yes*.

The newsgroup program then opens a connection to the newsgroup server and downloads all newsgroups or, more precisely, the names of all newsgroups into your newsgroup reader. You will then be able to subscribe to any groups that you find interesting.

2 Click on *Yes*.

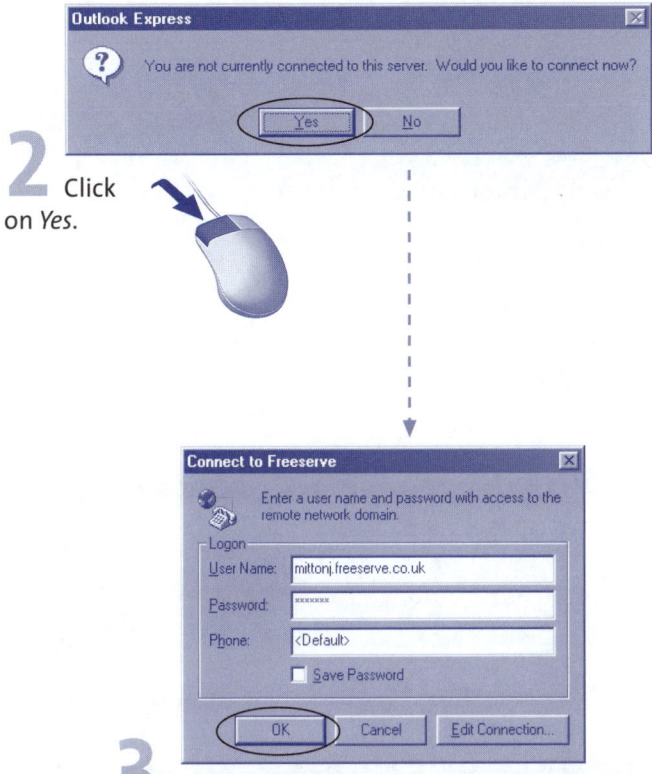

3 Enter your username and the password for your Internet connection. Then mark the *Save Password* checkbox to save the password. Confirm your choices by clicking on *OK*.

Clicking on *OK* will open an Internet connection. Once this **connection** has been successfully established, every available newsgroup is then downloaded from the newsgroup server. This will take some time as, according to which Internet Service Provider you use, 10,000, 15,000 or even more newsgroups will be loaded.

281

4 The list of available newsgroups is loaded.

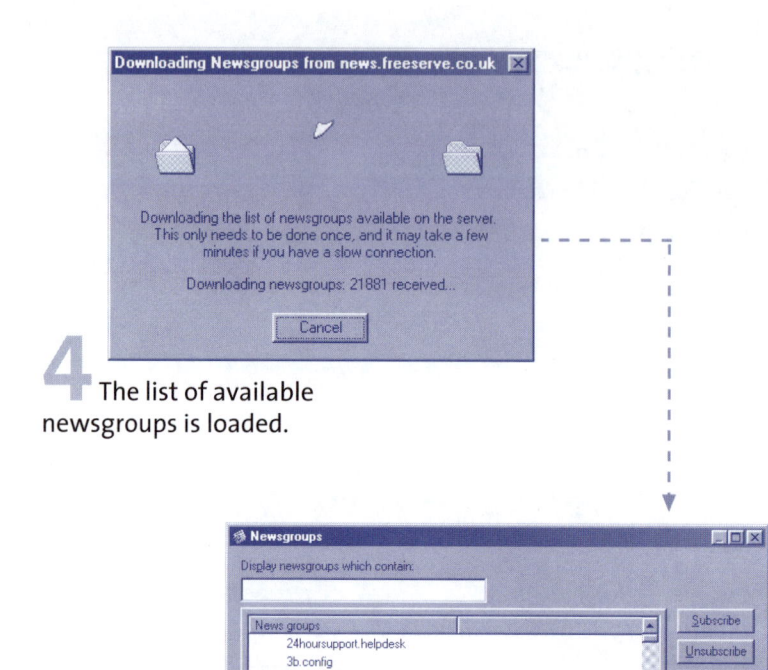

5 You now have all newsgroups to hand.

You now have a list of all the newsgroups saved on your computer. When you are looking for a particular group, you may do this by entering search terms.

You can subscribe to any newsgroups that you think might be interesting. To do this, just double-click on the required newsgroup.

READING AND SUBSCRIBING TO NEWSGROUPS

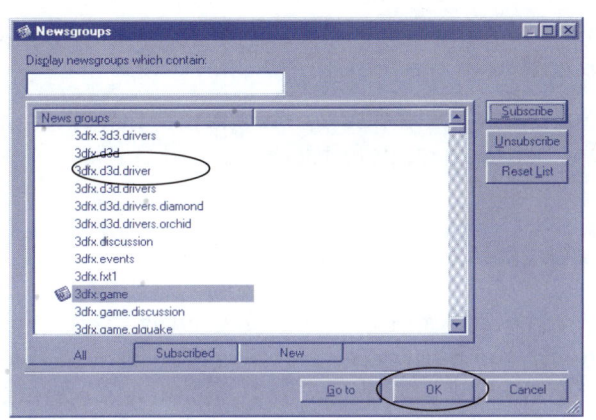

6 Double-click on your chosen newsgroup and confirm your subscription by clicking on *OK*.

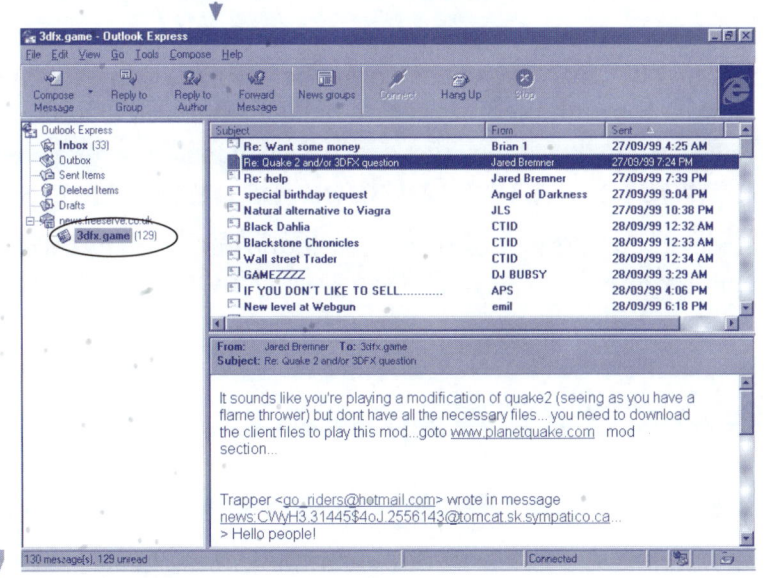

7 Click on any entry in order to view its content.

283

If you feel the need to reply to a particular entry, just open it up and click on *Reply to Author* in the toolbar.

To formulate your own question to a newsgroup, click on *Compose Message* in the newsgroup reader's toolbar.

IE5 and Outlook Express 5

The Outlook Express mail program, which has already been described, is also included with the most recent version of Internet Explorer, which differs from the preceding version by just a few cosmetic retouches.

However, I have decided to describe both versions in this book, as the older version still has a very strong market presence. Despite this, you should still have a look at Microsoft's most recent version – and if you are already running Windows 98, IE5 and Outlook Express 5 are the default browser and mail software anyway.

The installation of Outlook Express 5 happens automatically when you install IE5 and so needs no further explanation. We have already worked through the installation of IE5 in an earlier chapter.

Configuring the Outlook Express 5 newsreader

You can start Outlook Express 5 by clicking either on the corresponding icon on your desktop, or on the icon in your Windows taskbar.

1 Double-click on the *Outlook Express* icon on your Windows desktop.

IE5 and Outlook Express 5

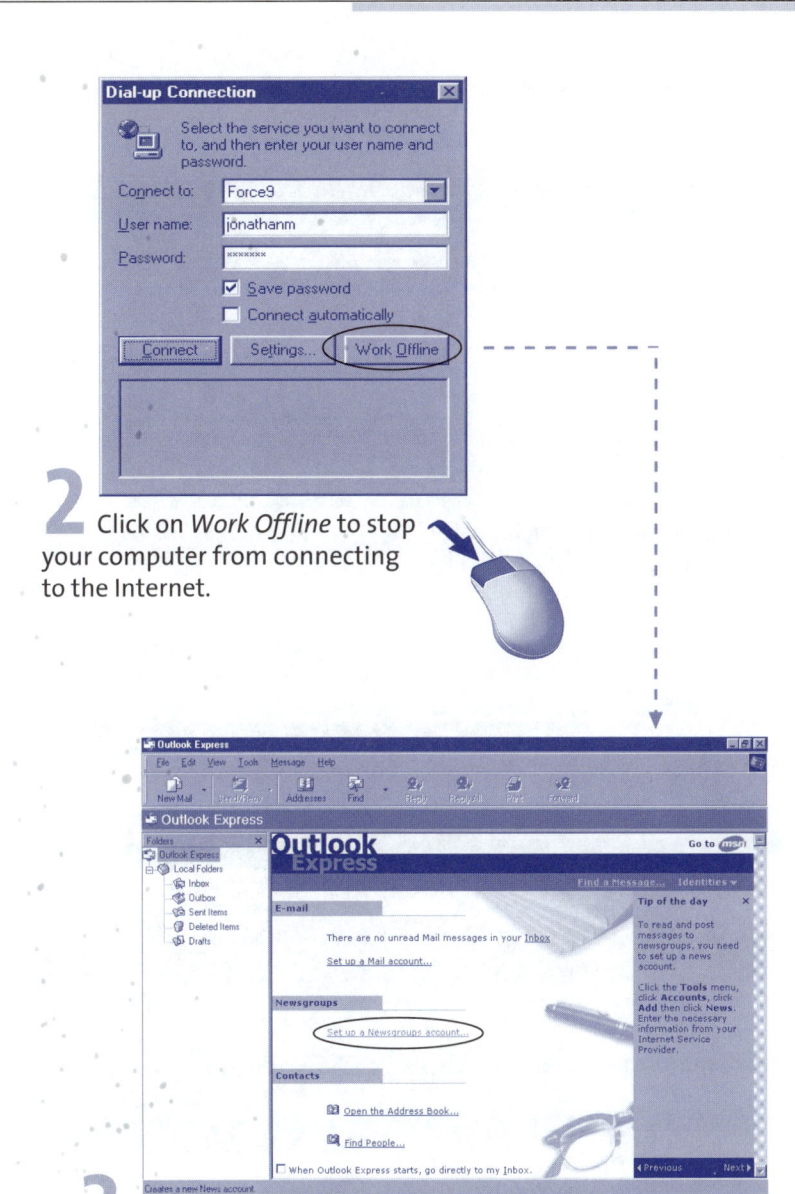

2 Click on *Work Offline* to stop your computer from connecting to the Internet.

3 In the *Folders* section, click on *Outlook Express*, then click on the *Set up a Newsgroups account* hyperlink in the right-hand part of the window.

285

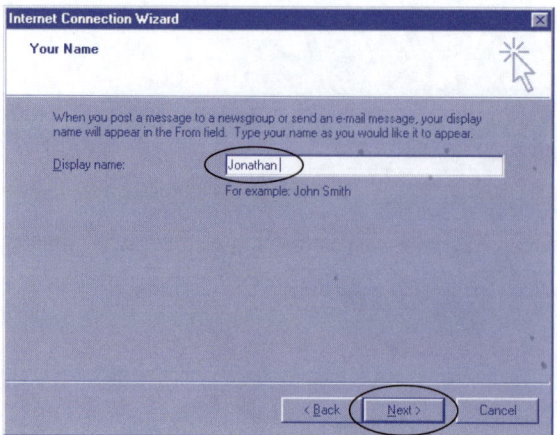

4 In the input field, enter your name as you would like it to be displayed, then click on *Next*.

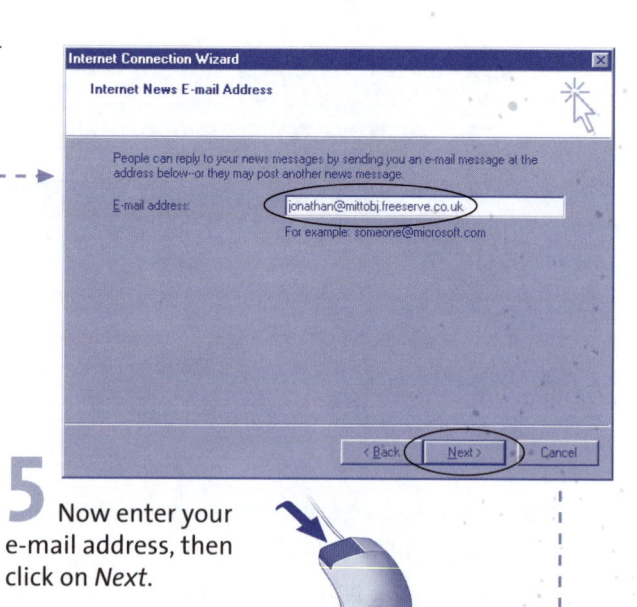

5 Now enter your e-mail address, then click on *Next*.

286

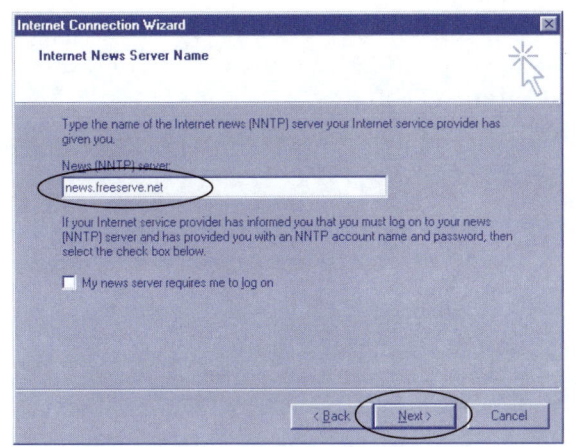

6 Now enter the name of your Internet Service Provider's news server, then click on *Next*.

7 Finally, click on *Finish*.

Now that you have entered all the necessary information, you will be able to call up all the newsgroups and hunt around in them until you find something that interests you.

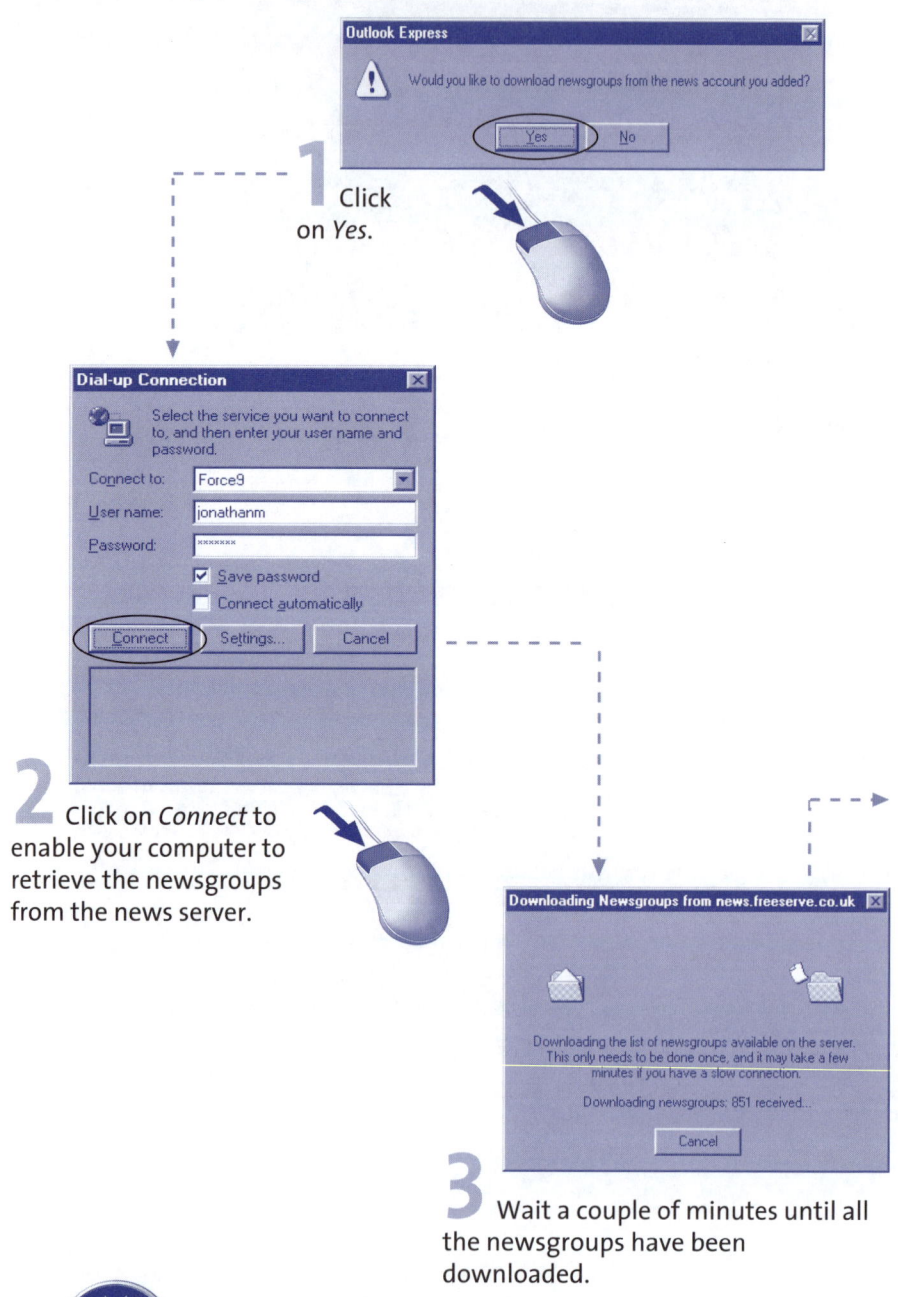

1 Click on *Yes*.

2 Click on *Connect* to enable your computer to retrieve the newsgroups from the news server.

3 Wait a couple of minutes until all the newsgroups have been downloaded.

IE5 and Outlook Express 5

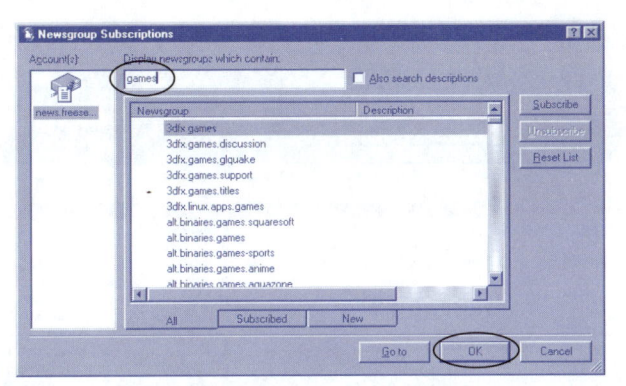

4 Enter a search term in the upper text box. Outlook Express will then search through all the newsgroups for this term and will supply a list of its results.

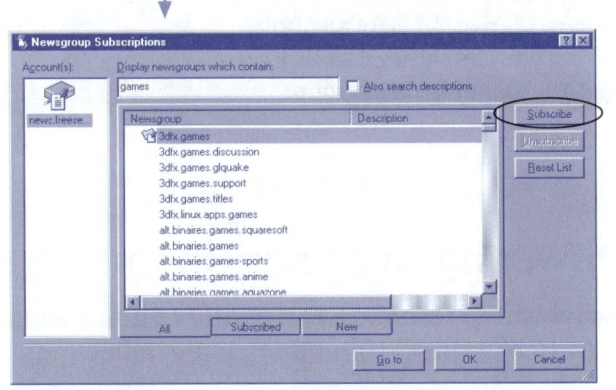

5 Select the required newsgroup, then click on *Subscribe*.

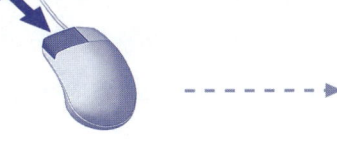

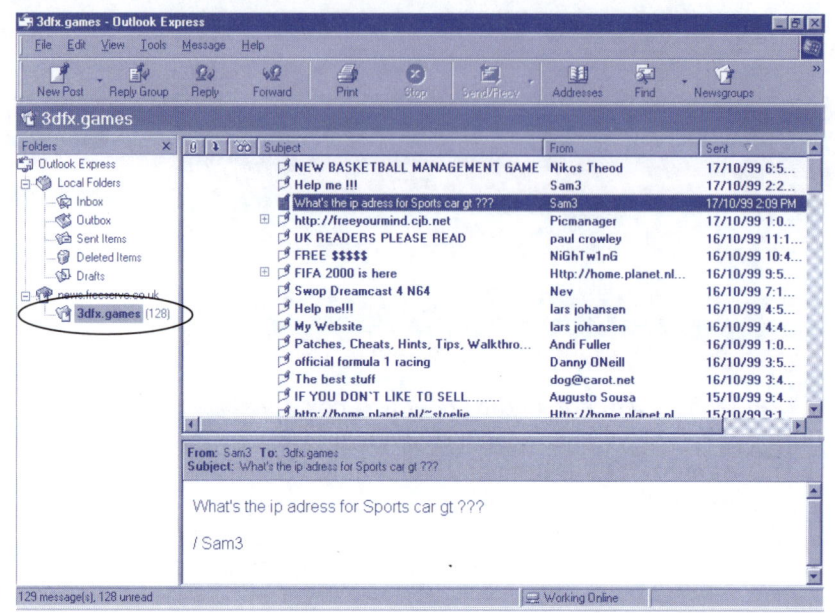

6 The newsgroup that you have subscribed to now lies underneath the news server. To view all of the entries, you simply need to click on the corresponding newsgroup.

Answering an enquiry in a newsgroup

If you want to respond to an enquiry published in a newsgroup, start up Outlook Express 5 and then do the following:

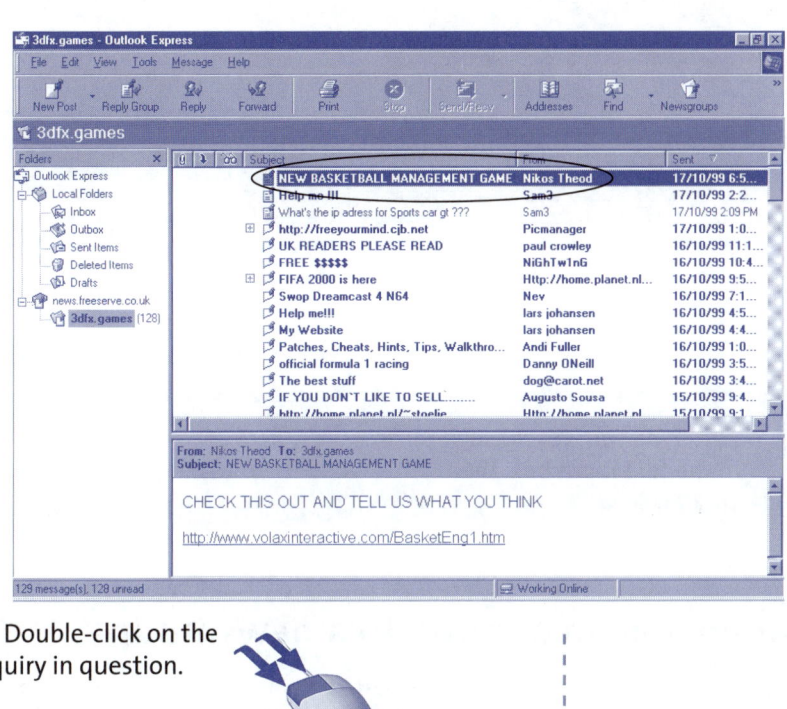

IE5 and Outlook Express 5

1 Double-click on the enquiry in question.

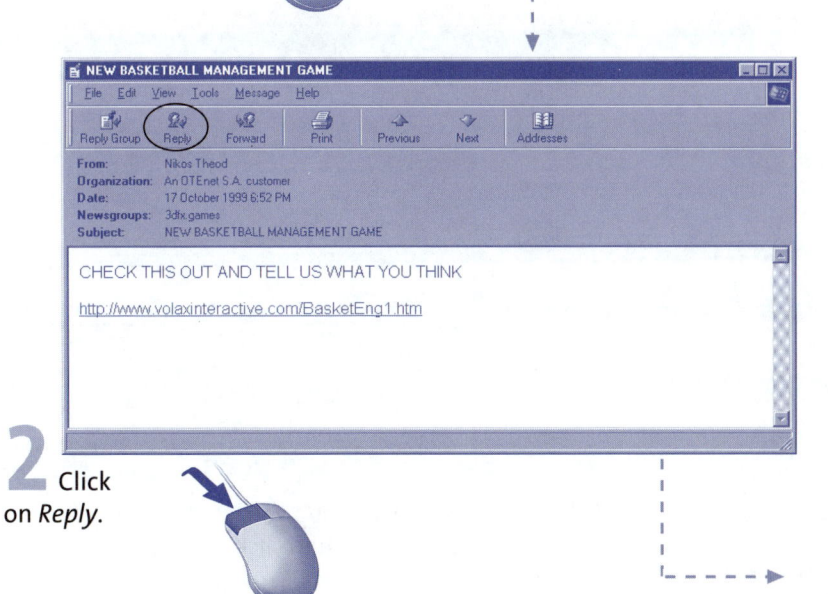

2 Click on *Reply*.

291

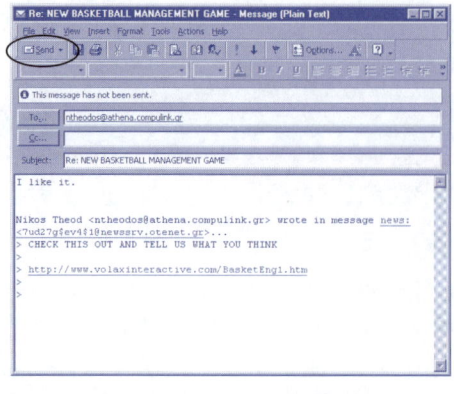

3 Type your response in the text input box, then click on *Send*.

Composing an enquiry to a newsgroup

If you want to submit your own enquiry to a particular newsgroup, start up Outlook Express and do the following:

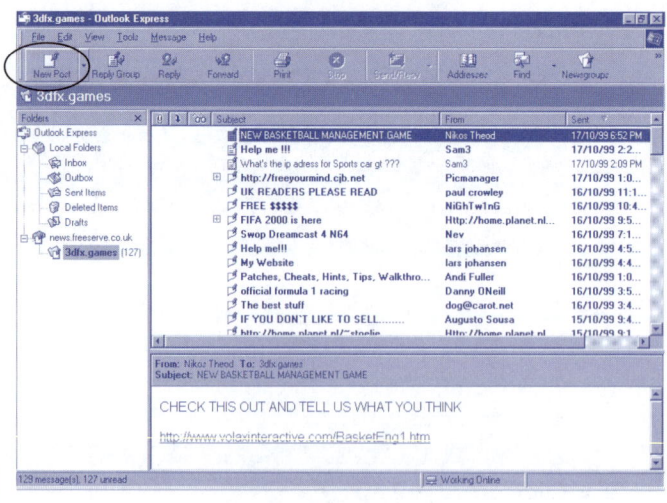

1 Click once on the newsgroup you want to send a message to. Then click on *New Post*.

292

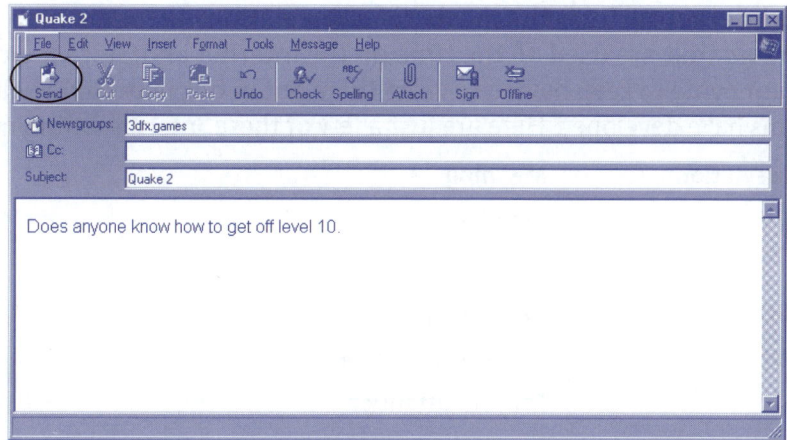

2 Enter your text, then click on *Send*.

Netiquette

'Manners maketh the man', even on the Internet. Here are a few tips to help you out with this way of communicating.

The Internet is an international network whose language of communication is English. International groups should only post messages of international interest. Content of a purely national nature has no place in the international forum. You can usually recognize national forums by a language code, such as *de.*, *it.* etc., prefixed to their names.

Where politeness is concerned, you should always remember to write your answer in the same way you would like to receive one.

So-called 'Smileys', also known as **Emoticons,** are often used on the Internet. These are combinations of letters and symbols that are used in e-mail, chat or newsgroup conversations to convey your feelings.

The Internet surfer is the master of abbreviation. There are many phrases that are used all the time on the Internet and, since it would be annoying to keep having to write them out in full, many abbreviated forms have developed. Here are just a few of these 'Internet acronyms':

Abbreviation	Meaning
(bg)	Broad grin
(g)	Grinning
EGBOK	Everything's going to be OK
ASAP	As soon as possible
FYA	For your attention
FYEO	For your eyes only
HHOJ	Ha, ha, only a joke
IDU	I don't understand
L8R	Later
LOL	Laughing out loud
PITA	Pyrrhic, Iambic, Trochaic, Anapestic (metaphorically for 'absolutely awful')
SCNR	Sorry, could not read
WDYW	What do you want?

There are more of these abbreviations. Have a look round the Internet and you will soon find lots of them.

You have to laugh – the best computer messages

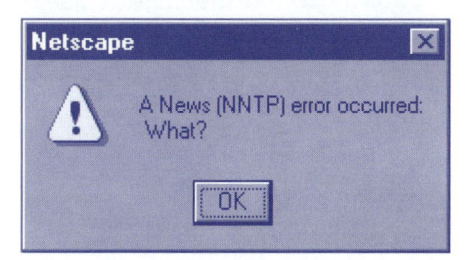

Netscape

A News (NNTP) error occurred: What?

OK

And 'what' about Netiquette?

12 Why not send an e-mail instead

What's in this chapter:

In this chapter you will get to grips with that classic of Internet services – e-mail. You will learn a little about the way e-mail works and about the various e-mail programs available. Finally, you will download an e-mail program from the Microsoft Web server which will then be installed under Windows.

You already know about:

Accessing the Internet with AOL	122
Accessing the Internet with BT Click	141
Installing Netscape Communicator	166
CD quality music – MP3	206
Newsgroups	268
Configuring the Microsoft newsgroup reader	276
Reading and subscribing to newsgroups	280
Netiquette	293

You are going to learn about:

E-mail	298
Configuring the Microsoft IE4 e-mail program	300
Sending e-mail	304
Using IE5 and Outlook Express 5 as an e-mail program	309

What is e-mail?

People have sent each other letters for as long as we can remember. Electronic mail, known as e-mail for short, is now rapidly overtaking the traditional way of sending a letter. There are many reasons for this: firstly, an e-mail message can reach the other side of the world in just a few minutes and, secondly, it costs very little to send. More and more people are now setting up electronic mailboxes, both at home and at work. Millions of e-mail messages circulate the globe every day. E-mail is an excellent way of communicating with friends, relatives and business associates.

> **WARNING**
>
> **E-mail messages** are an excellent transport medium for viruses. If you ever receive an e-mail message with a strange sequence of symbols in the subject or address fields, do not open it. It may contain a virus which is automatically activated when you open the message.

You can also attach all sorts of graphics, sounds and video clips to your e-mail messages.

This is how e-mail is actually sent. When you send an e-mail message, the message is broken down into smaller, individual **data packets**. Each one of these little packets is given a 'label', which contains the receiver's address. There are several **Internet routers** on the Internet, whose task is to send the packets to the receiver along the fastest route. It sometimes happens that the packets are sent to the receiver via several different routes. If a route becomes unavailable, the Internet router will find an alternative route and will then use it to transfer the rest of the data packets.

> **WHAT'S THIS?**
>
> An **Internet router** is a computer which forwards your outgoing and incoming data to and from the Internet. Every Internet Service Provider owns such Internet routers.

Once all the individual packets have been delivered to the receiver, they are then put back together into a complete e-mail. In actual practice, this process looks a little different. The e-mail messages arrive at an Internet Service Provider, which collects all the e-mails for a particular person.

When you open an Internet connection, all e-mail messages addressed to you will be downloaded onto your computer.

E-mail can be exchanged between all the major online services. This means that you can send e-mail messages to someone on a different online service, such as AOL or CompuServe.

E-mail addresses

In order to send and receive e-mail, you will need to have an e-mail address. E-mail addresses look different depending on which Internet Service Provider you use. The author's e-mail address, for example, is *ingol@lackerbauer.do.uunet.de*. The personal name comes before the strange-looking symbol known as an '*at*' sign, and is followed by the address, which is also called the domain. You are assigned your e-mail address by your Internet Service Provider and usually have no say as to how it is written.

All this address business looks quite different where online services are concerned. Every **CompuServe** user is given a user ID number as identification. This is made up of numbers, which are separated from each other with a comma, like this: 123456,789. To send an e-mail message within CompuServe, you will only need to use this number. However, if you wanted to send e-mail to a CompuServe user from somewhere else on the Internet, you would have to enter a different address, which would look something like *123456.789@compuserve.com*. The user ID number must be separated by a full stop rather than a comma.

If you are an **AOL** user, you can choose your own e-mail address, as long as it has not already been chosen by someone else. The author's AOL name, for example, is *ILackerbau*. Just as with CompuServe, this address is all you need to use when sending a message from inside AOL. However, if you wanted to send an e-mail message from somewhere else in the Internet, you would have to change the syntax. You can work this address out for yourself: *ILackerbau@aol.com*.

The e-mail service for **BT Click** users is run by Talk21, and is provided free of charge. Your user name will be similar to that supplied by AOL, for example *ILackerbau@talk21.com*. To access your e-mail, you need to use a Web browser and call up the URL *http://www.talk21.com*. This service has the advantage that you can call up your mail from anywhere in the world, just by using your name and password – that's all!

Configuring Microsoft's IE4 e-mail program

When you have installed Microsoft Outlook Express on your computer, you will still need to configure it.

On your Windows desktop, double-click on the Outlook Express icon.

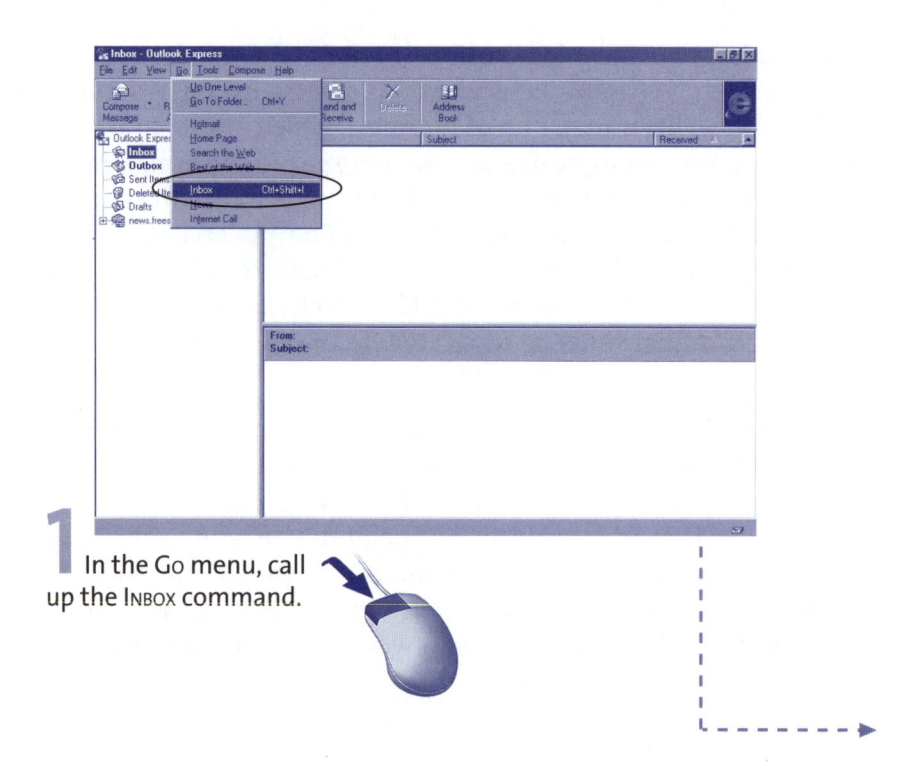

1 In the Go menu, call up the INBOX command.

CONFIGURING MICROSOFT'S IE4 E-MAIL PROGRAM

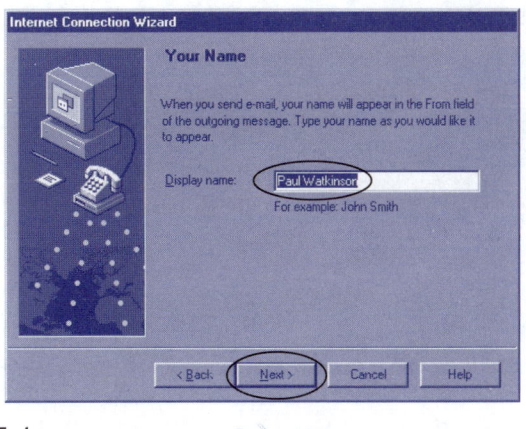

2 Enter your name, then click on *Next*.

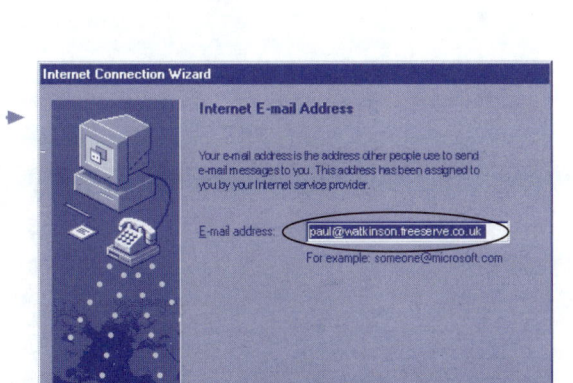

3 Now enter your e-mail address, then click on *Next*.

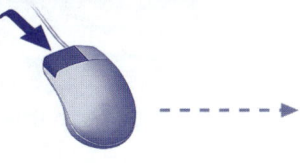

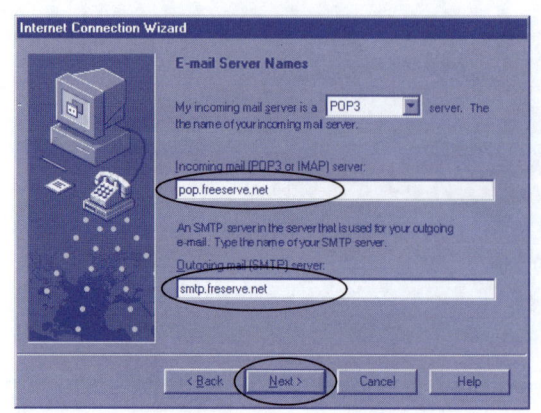

4 In the two input fields, enter the addresses of your e-mail server for incoming and outgoing mail. Then click on *Next*.

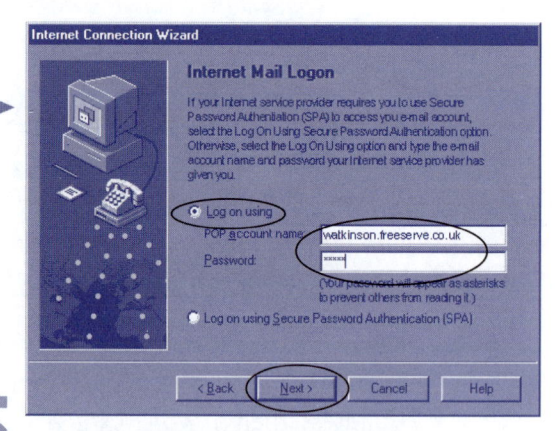

5 Enter your mail account name and your password. Then click on *Next*.

CONFIGURING MICROSOFT'S IE4 E-MAIL PROGRAM

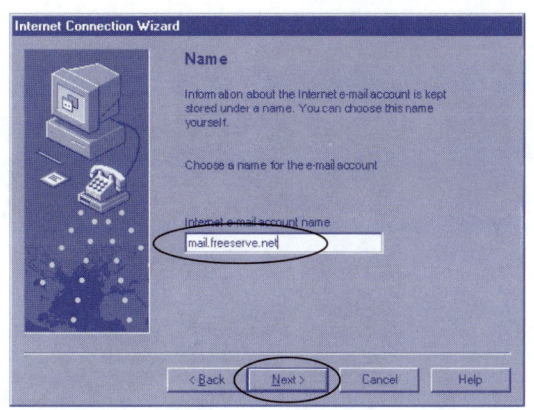

6 Accept the suggested account name by clicking on *Next*.

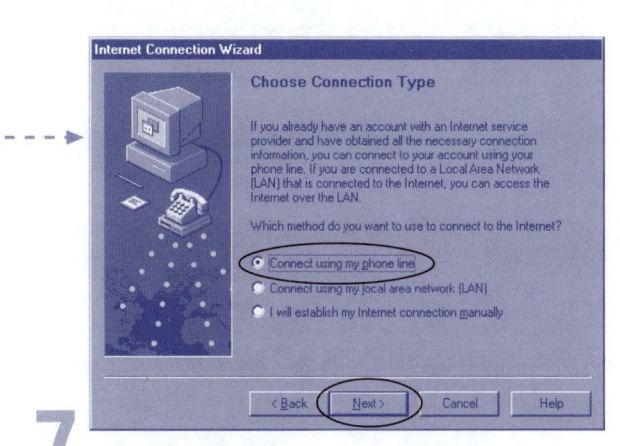

7 Click on the *Connect using my phone line* radio button, then click on *Next*.

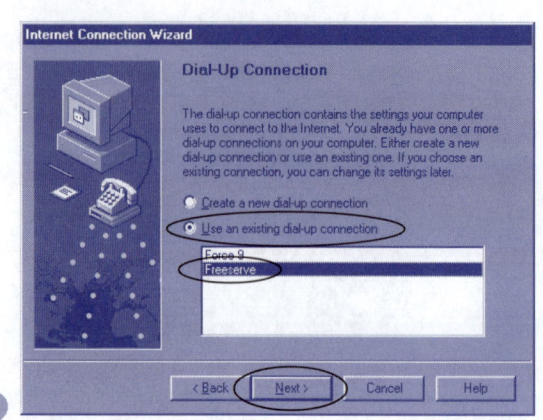

8 Choose the required connection from the list of available connections, then click on *Next*.

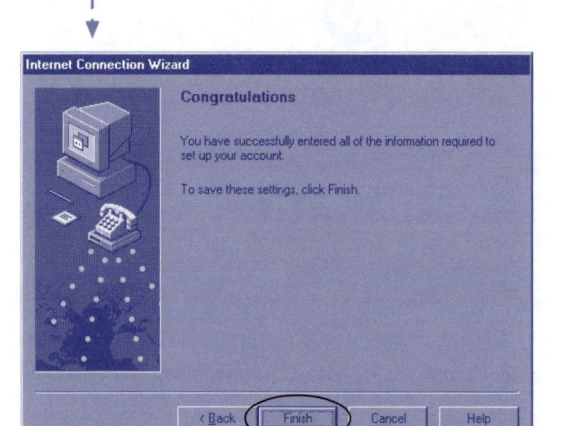

9 You've done it. Now just click on *Finish*.

Sending e-mail

Outlook Express is now ready to send and receive e-mail. To do this, start up Outlook Express by double-clicking on its icon on your desktop.

SENDING E-MAIL

WARNING: When you write an e-mail message, please do not include any information that isn't intended for public view. It is very easy for other Internet users to intercept and read your mail. You can overcome this problem by using encryption programs to encode your e-mails.

As soon as you start up Outlook Express, it will ask you if you want to open an Internet connection. If you answer 'yes' to this question, your Internet Service Provider's mail server will then send you any e-mail messages addressed to you. When writing e-mail messages, you do not necessarily need to open an Internet connection first. This means you can write your mail without being online and so keep your costs down. When you have composed your e-mail message, it is moved to the outbox. As soon as you click on *Connect*, an Internet connection will be opened and all the e-mail messages in your outbox will be sent. In the following example, however, we will open an Internet connection immediately.

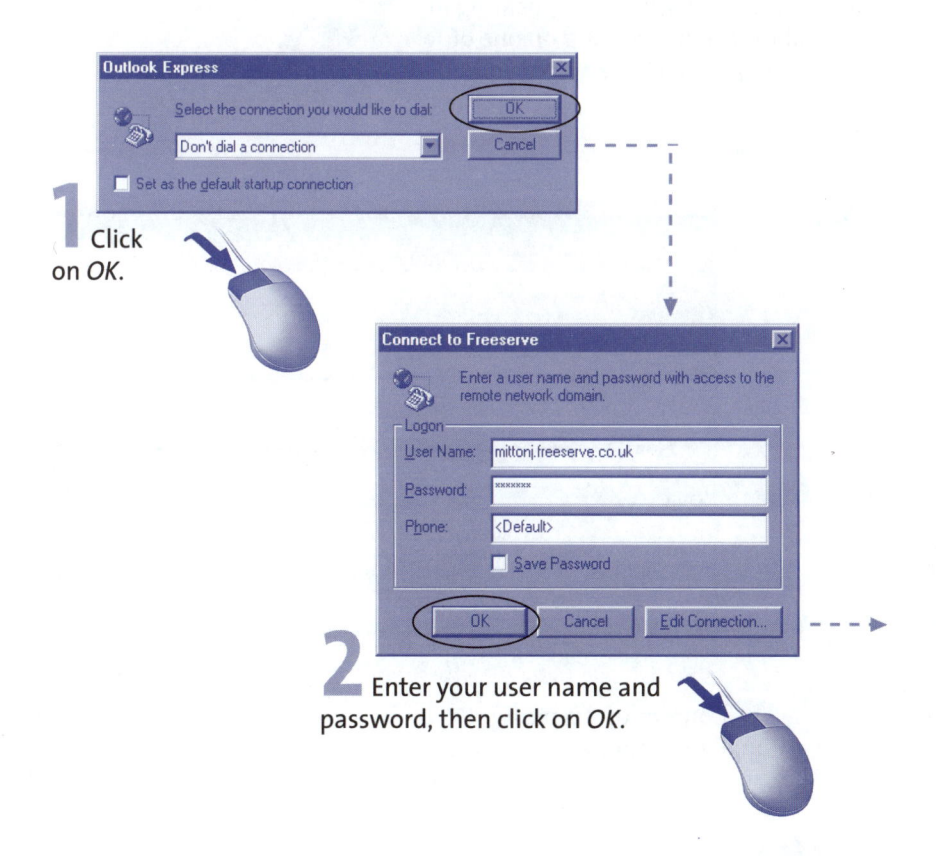

1 Click on *OK*.

2 Enter your user name and password, then click on *OK*.

305

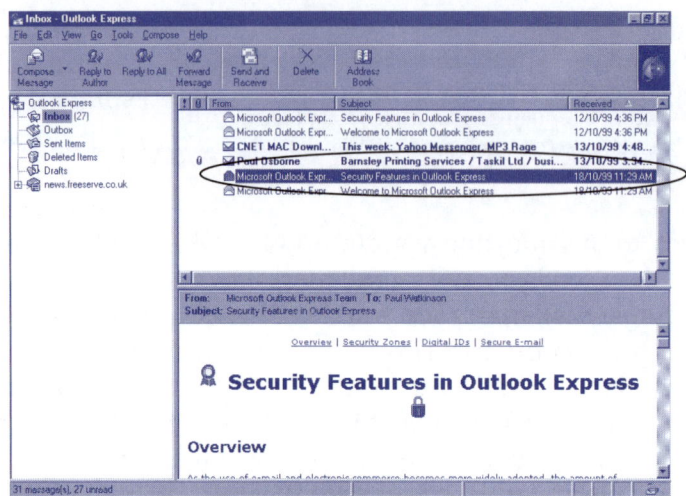

3 As soon as you are online, the first e-mail messages will start appearing in your inbox. Double-clicking on one of these messages will open it for you.

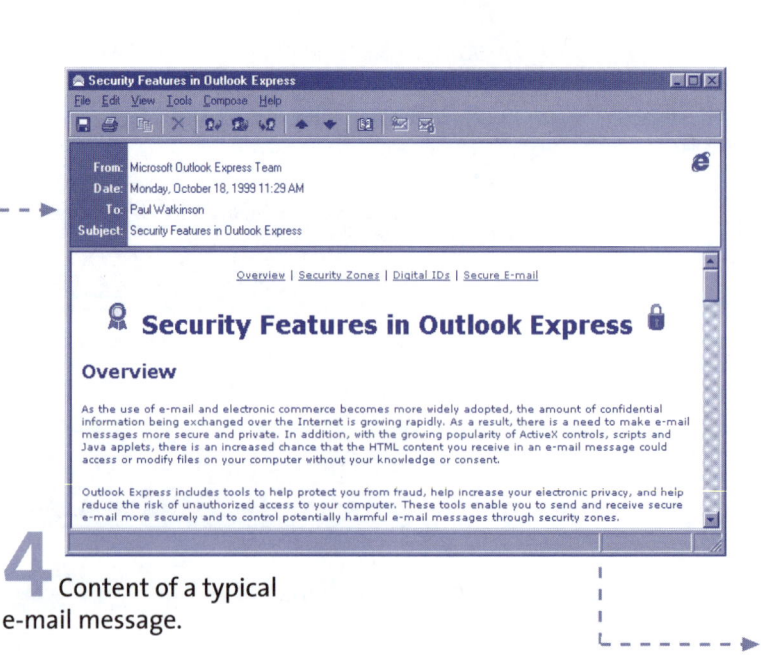

4 Content of a typical e-mail message.

SENDING E-MAIL

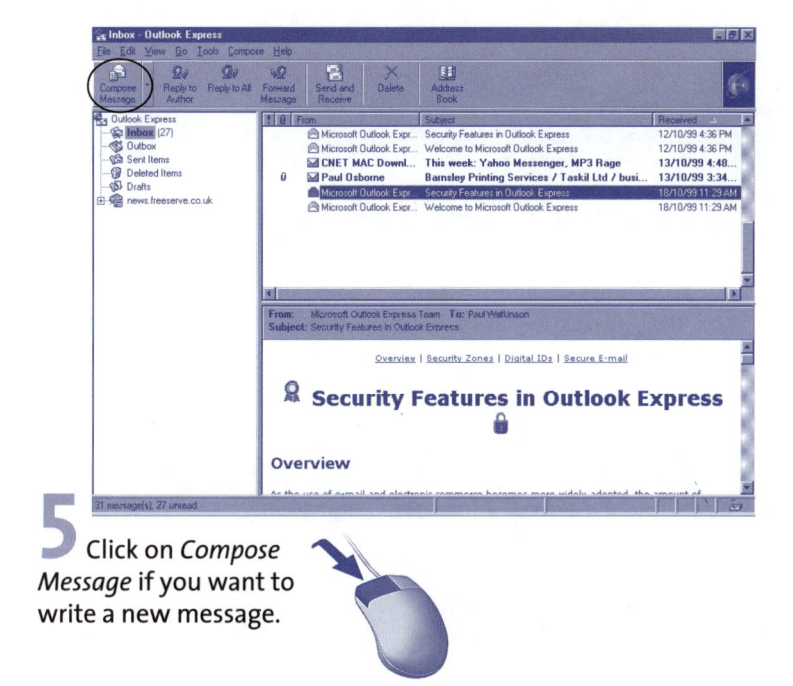

5 Click on *Compose Message* if you want to write a new message.

You must enter the **recipient's** e-mail address in the *To:* field. In the field entitled *Subject:* you can write a short description of the e-mail's content. When the recipient receives the e-mail, they will see this short description in their inbox.

If you want to attach a document or file to your e-mail, just click on the picture of a **paper clip**. All you need to do then is select the required document or file from your hard disk.

307

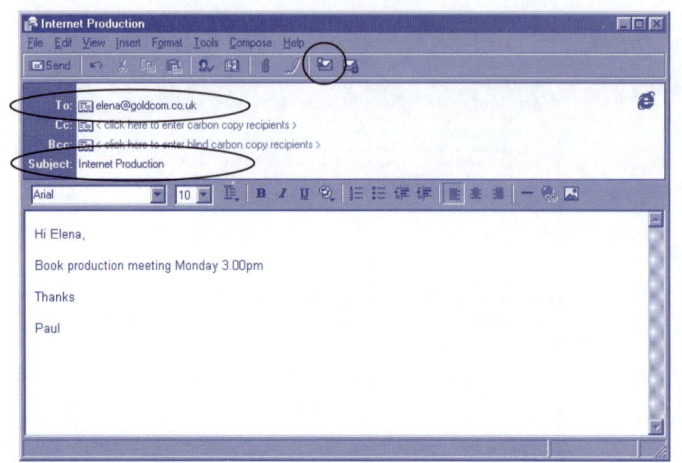

6 Enter the recipient's e-mail address, a subject, and then the main body of text. Attach a document to the e-mail that you would like to send as well. To do this, click on the picture of a paper clip in the toolbar.

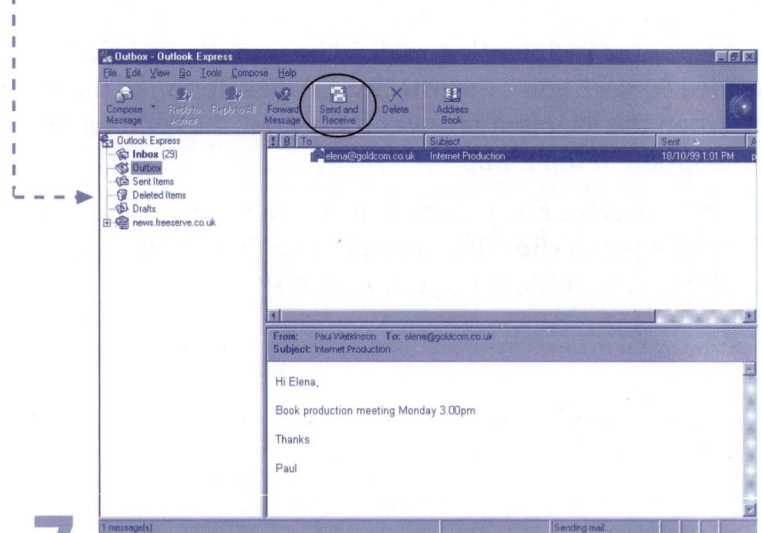

7 Your message is now moved to the outbox and, if you already have an Internet connection open, will be sent straight away or after you have clicked on *Send and Receive*.

Using IE5 and Outlook Express 5 as an e-mail program

Internet Explorer 5 came on the market in March 1999 and contains Outlook Express 5 as a standard mail program. It is not entirely necessary to move to IE5, as most of its improvements are merely cosmetic in nature. If your version of IE4 and Outlook Express are working fine, then you can confidently ignore the updated version. Despite this, we will still take a little look at Outlook Express 5.

If you have already installed IE5, you will find that Outlook Express 5 has automatically been installed as well so you do not need to think any more about this. To equip Outlook Express with the necessary default data for mail, all you will need to do is follow a few simple configuration steps.

Configuring the mail capabilities of Outlook Express 5

Start up Outlook Express by clicking either on the desktop icon or on the icon in the taskbar.

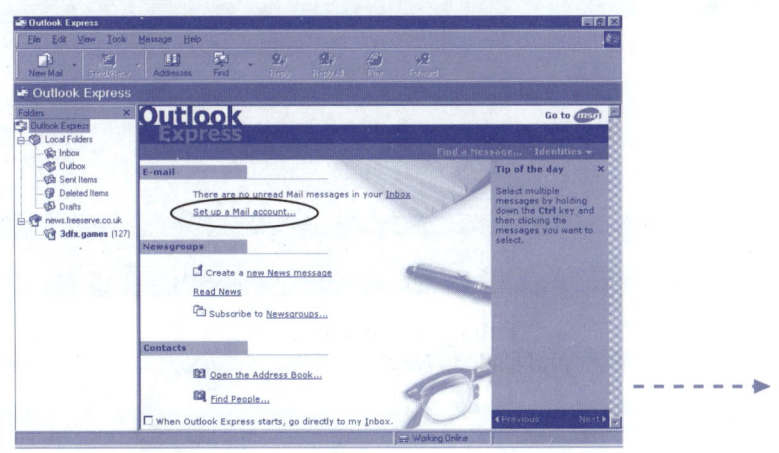

1 Click on the *Set up a mail account* hyperlink.

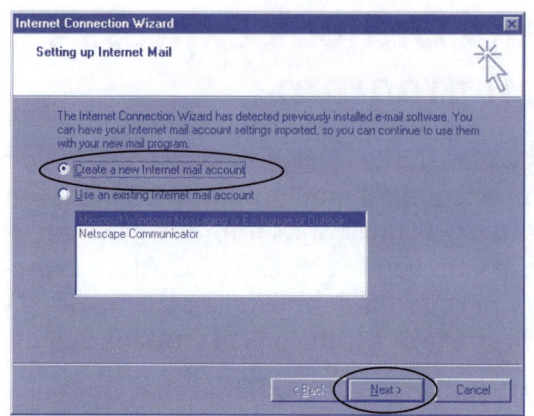

2 Click on the *Create a new Internet mail account* radio button, then click on *Next*.

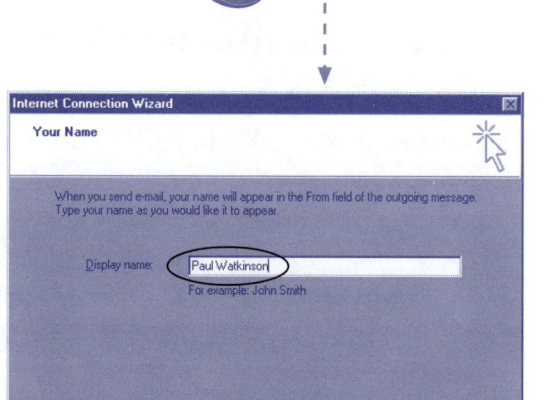

3 Enter your full name and click on *Next*.

USING IE5 AND OUTLOOK EXPRESS 5 AS AN E-MAIL PROGRAM

4 Enter your e-mail address and click on *Next*.

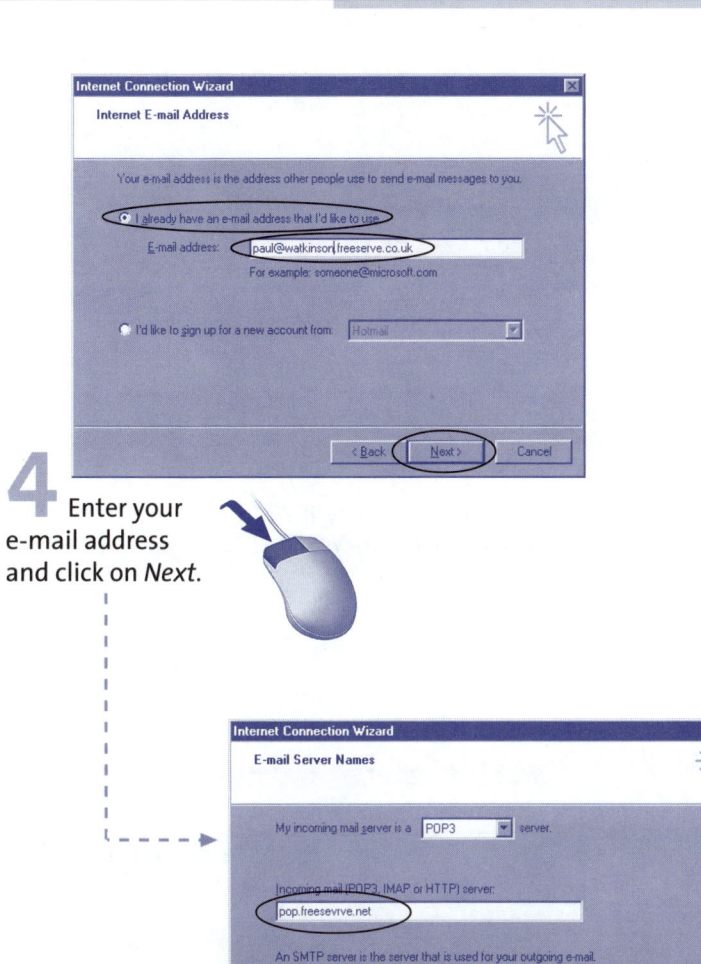

5 Now enter the names of your mail servers for incoming and outgoing mail. Then click on *Next*.

311

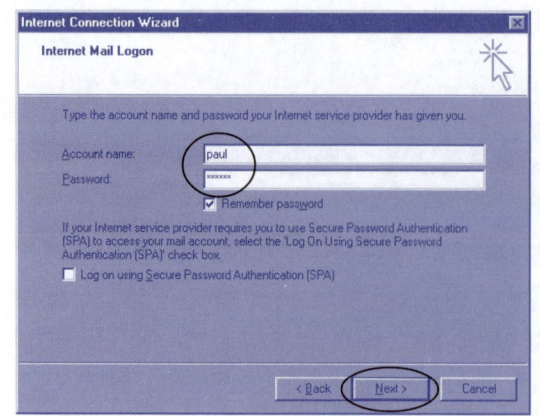

6 Enter your account name and your mail access password, then click on *Next*.

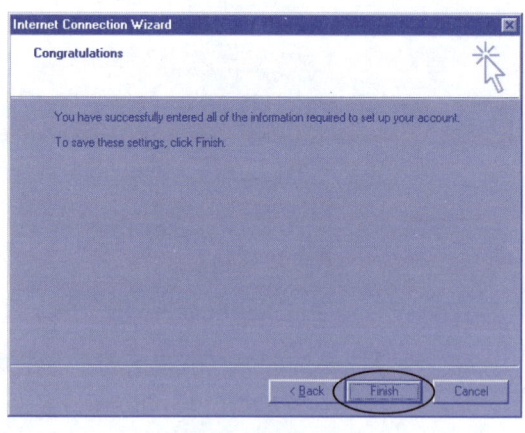

7 Finally, click on *Finish*.

Sending e-mail with Outlook Express 5

Now that Outlook Express has been configured, you will be able to send e-mail.

Open Outlook Express 5 and then do the following:

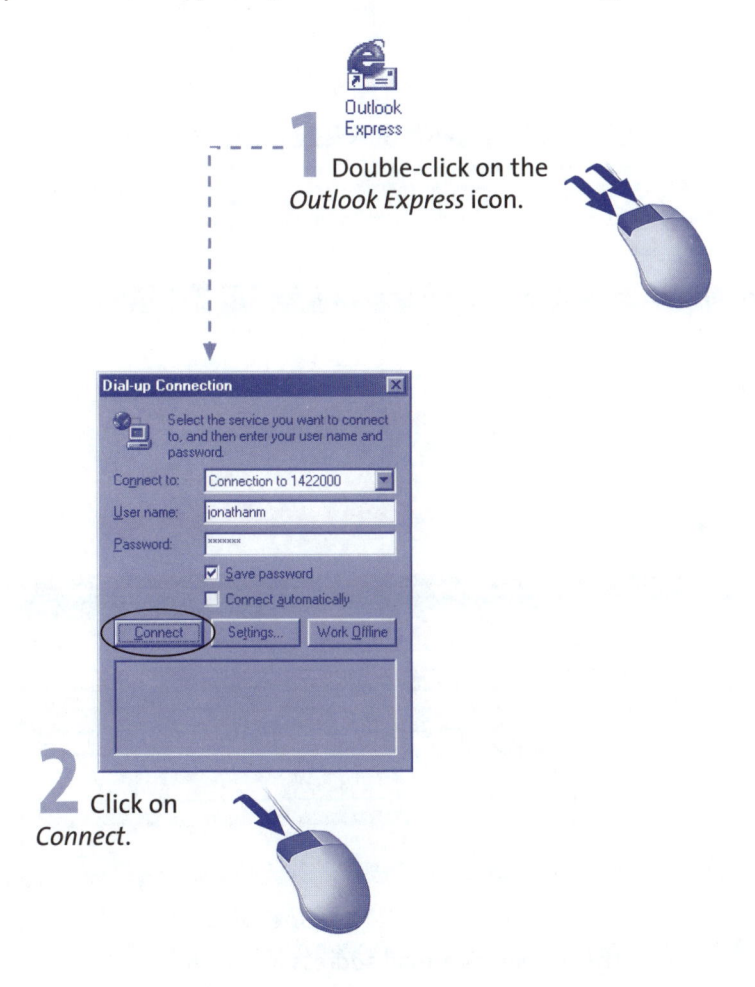

1 Double-click on the *Outlook Express* icon.

2 Click on *Connect*.

As soon as an Internet connection is established, all your newly arrived e-mail messages will automatically be sent to your computer. You do not need to click on any buttons.

3 Click on *New Mail*.

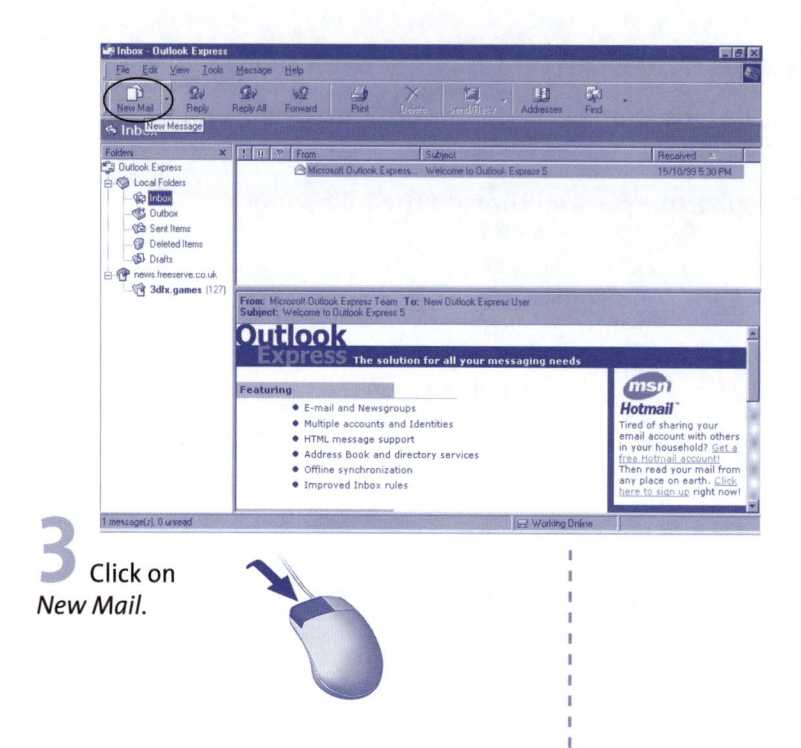

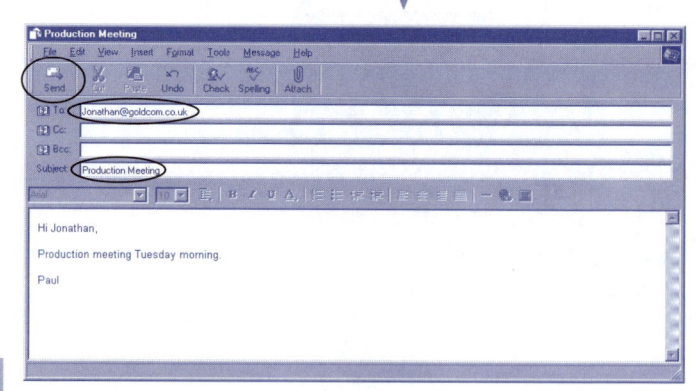

4 Enter the recipient's e-mail address in the *To:* field and then write your message in the main text box. To finish, click on *Send*.

You have to laugh – the best computer messages

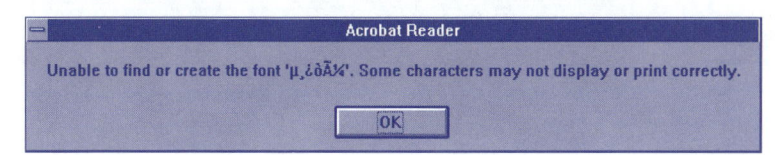

Acrobat Reader

Unable to find or create the font 'µ¸¿õĀ¾'. Some characters may not display or print correctly.

[OK]

This would not happen if the whole world wrote their messages in Windows default fonts!

13

Your own home page on the www

What's in this chapter:

Now you are familiar with all its various services, it is time for you to start actively messing around on the Internet. You will now learn how to set up a very simple Web page and, in doing so, get to know a few HTML commands. Once you have done this, you will see that there are many ways of publishing your page on the Internet. You will learn how you can publish your page via an online service, such as AOL or CompuServe.

You already know about:

Taking your first steps in the World Wide Web	67
Browsing Web pages	88
Printing Web pages	89
How a search engine works	94
Accessing the Internet with AOL	122
Accessing the Internet with BT Click	141
Configuring the Microsoft IE4 e-mail program	300
Sending e-mail	304

You are going to learn about:

A few basic notions	318
Designing your own home page	319
Publishing a home page via an online service	322

Only a few basic notions are needed

It is almost considered good form to have your own Web page these days. Some online services and many Internet Service Providers offer you the chance to rent some space on their hard disks, from where you can publish your own Web page. Are you perhaps thinking that such a service would only be of interest to computer experts? If so, you are definitely wrong. You do not need much technical knowledge to design your **home page**. If you have a little spare cash, you can then publish this page on the Internet.

Before you do this, you should get hold of all the various offers from Internet Service Providers and **online services** – it will be cheaper than you think.

> **Tip:** Avoid putting large pictures in your home page. The bigger these are, the longer it will take a user to download your Web page and the quicker he or she will give up on it.

You do not need to be an expert to design your own home page. All that is necessary is for you to surf the Internet a few times and develop an understanding of the different sorts of Web pages around.

The language used to write Web pages is called HTML, which stands for **HyperText Markup Language**. This is an Internet programming language that runs on every computer platform, and therefore delivers almost exactly the same results with every Web browser display.

You probably cannot imagine yourself as an HTML programmer just yet, but that will soon change. There are dozens of programs available on the Internet that help you to design pages in HTML. For our 'beginners page', the text editor available in Windows is more than adequate.

Your own home page

In Windows, open up the text editor as shown.

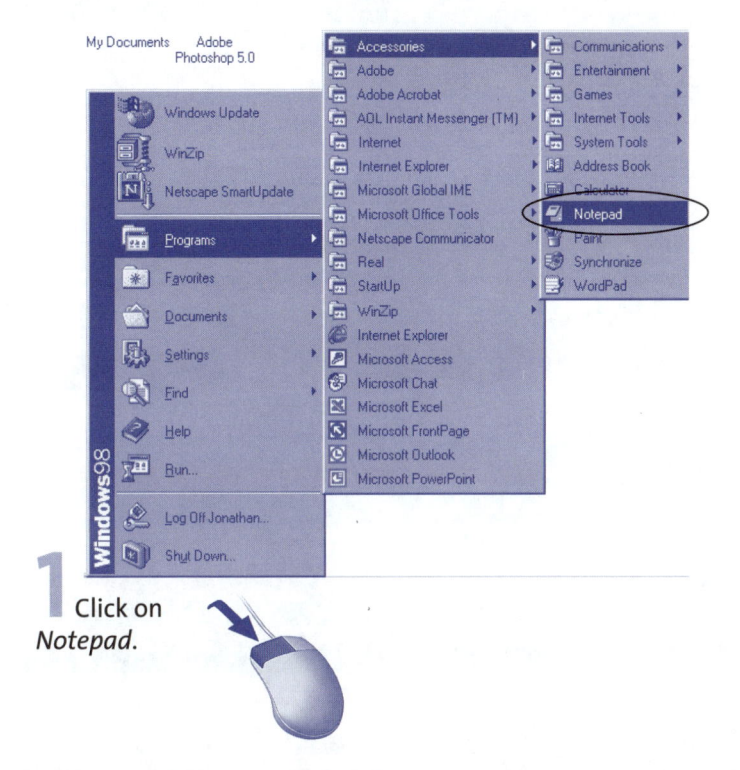

1 Click on *Notepad*.

You will now enter a short HTML program into the text editor. The commands at the start of the lines have the following meanings:

<H1>   produces a heading

<BODY> indicates normal text

<HR>   produces a horizontal line

<LI>   produces a list

<B>   indicates bold type

319

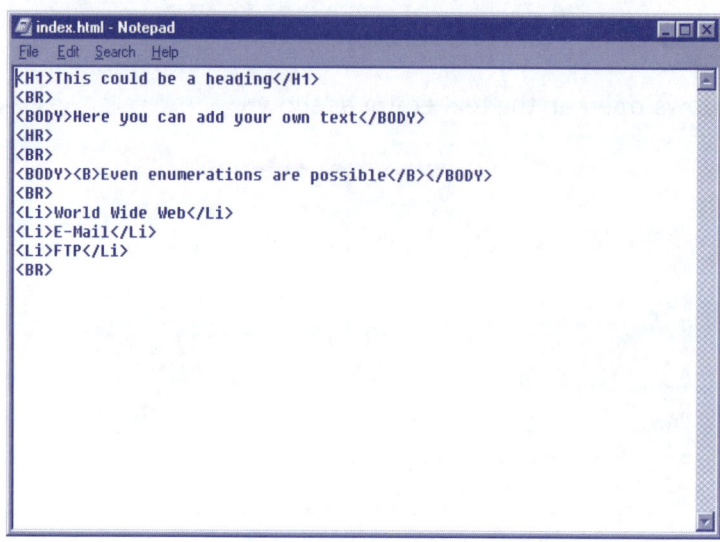

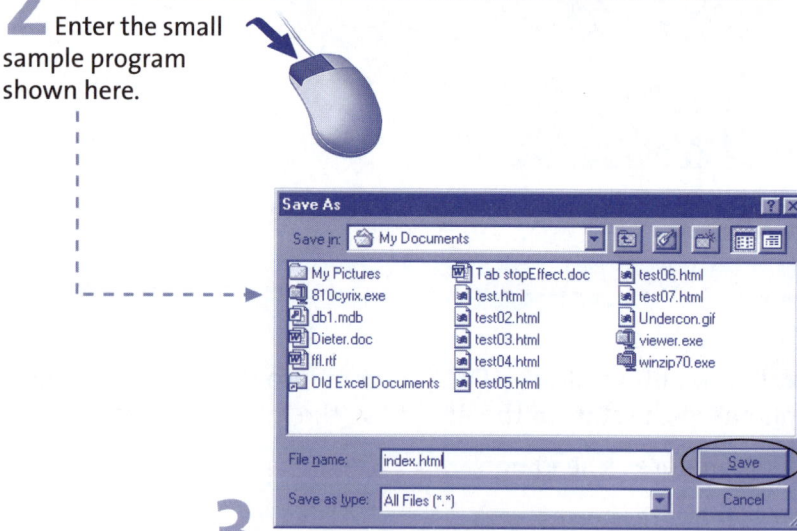

```
<H1>This could be a heading</H1>
<BR>
<BODY>Here you can add your own text</BODY>
<HR>
<BR>
<BODY><B>Even enumerations are possible</B></BODY>
<BR>
<Li>World Wide Web</Li>
<Li>E-Mail</Li>
<Li>FTP</Li>
<BR>
```

2 Enter the small sample program shown here.

3 Save the entered program under the name *index.html*.

Start up Microsoft Internet Explorer but do not open an Internet connection yet. Instead, open up your recently created Web page inside Internet Explorer.

As soon as Internet Explorer is open, go to the FILE menu and click on the OPEN menu entry.

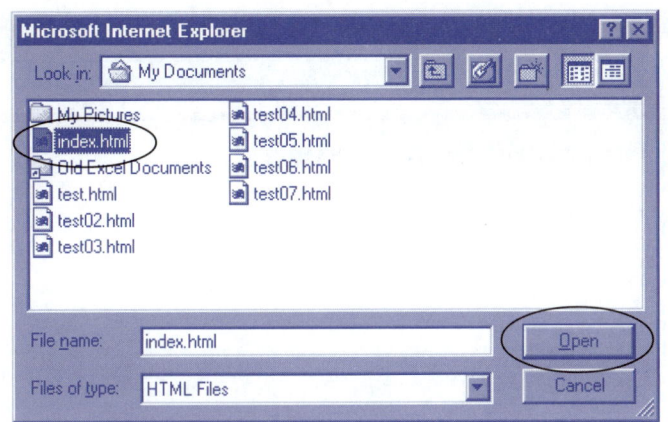

YOUR OWN HOMEPAGE

4 Open the Web page you have just created by clicking on the *Open* button.

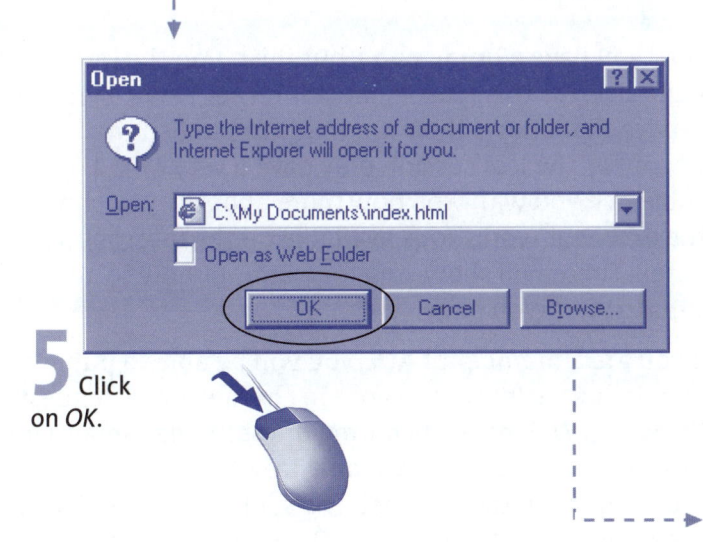

5 Click on *OK*.

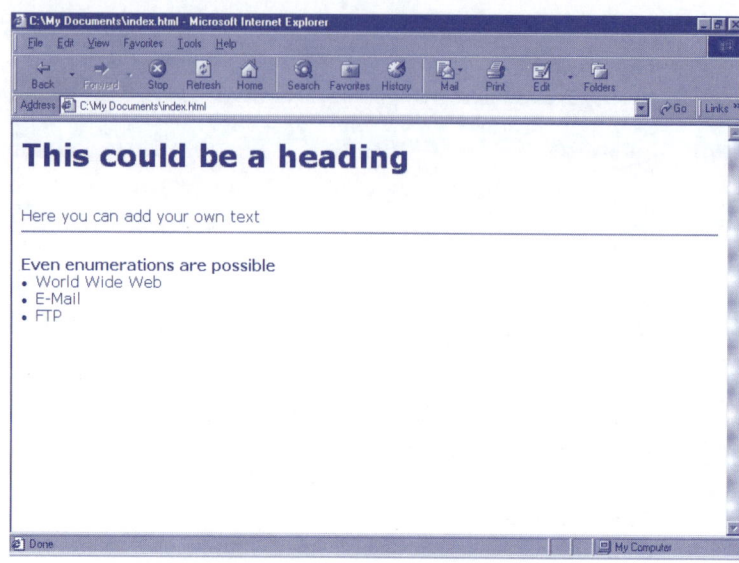

6 And there it is, the Web page you created.

Publishing a home page via an online service

Now you have a **home page**, but it isn't on the Internet, only on your hard disk. For this reason, most Internet Service Providers offer a service that allows their members to publish their own Web pages. Of course, the last session only gave a very broad overview of the subject. If you want to know more about it, you should look for one of the excellent workshops available on the Internet which go into more detail. These will show you, for example, how to add audio and video clips to your Web page.

If you are a member of **AOL**, you will be able to publish about 2 Mb of data on the Internet. Those in charge at AOL request that you send the whole Web page, including graphics, via e-mail. Once they have received all the data, it will only take them a few days to put your Web page onto the Internet. The syntax will then look like this: *http://www.aol.home.com/_AOL_Name/Index.html*.

The same process is required by **CompuServe**. Just call up the online service and send them your document.

There are also Internet Service Providers that allow non-members to publish their material on the Internet. The prices vary according to the size of the Web page and the 'data traffic' accrued. There are also some Internet Service Providers that allow their members to publish their material on the Internet for free.

You have to laugh – the best computer messages

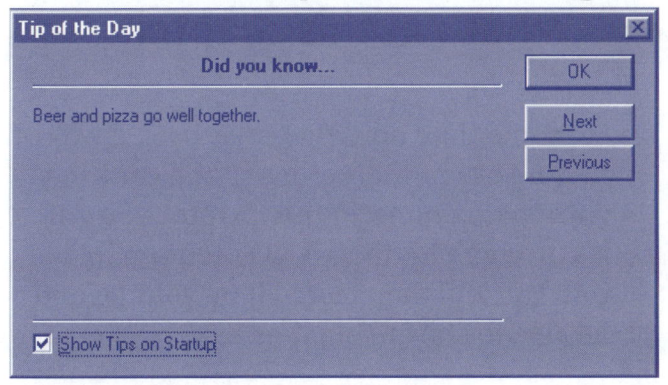

Tip of the Day	
Did you know...	OK
Beer and pizza go well together.	Next
	Previous
☑ Show Tips on Startup	

... and they always did – well before the first personal computer saw the light bulb in some genius' garage!

14

Finding Internet friends online with ICQ

What's in this chapter:

For some time now, there has been a way of finding other Internet users and chatting with them online. In this chapter, you will learn where to find an ICQ program to do this. You will then install it on your PC and be able to start using it.

You already know about:

Modems & CO.	10
Accessing the Internet with BT Click	141
Installing Netscape Communicator 4.7	166
Using FTP to download a file	258
Netiquette	293
E-mail	298
Configuring the Microsoft IE4 e-mail program	300
Designing your own home page	319
Using an online service to publish your home page	322

You are going to learn about:

Downloading an ICQ program from the Internet	326
Using the ICQ program	341

Downloading an ICQ program from the Internet

ICQ is a particularly interesting Internet tool that lets you know whenever your Internet friends are online (but only if they have ICQ as well). You can use it to talk to them, and to send and receive messages and files any time you want. The program automatically runs in the background and only requires a minimum of resources.

Every user who installs ICQ receives their own ICQ number (UIN-PIN, or ICQ#). This number, like an e-mail address, is used to contact the person. If you want to, you can release more information about yourself, so that the people you are talking to can have a rough idea of what you are like.

First of all, you need to find yourself an ICQ program on the Internet. To do this, call up your Web browser and open an Internet connection.

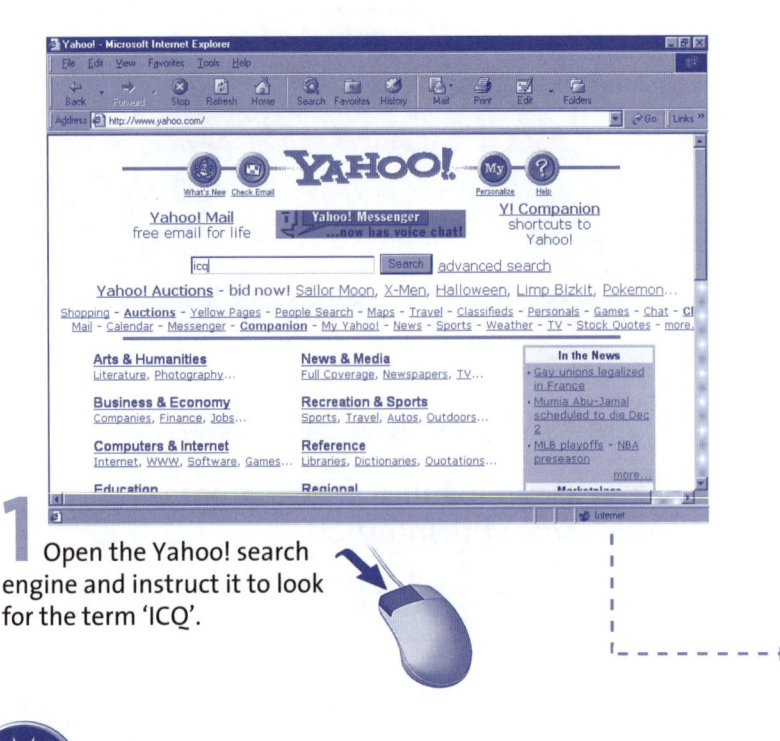

1 Open the Yahoo! search engine and instruct it to look for the term 'ICQ'.

DOWNLOADING AN ICQ PROGRAM FROM THE INTERNET

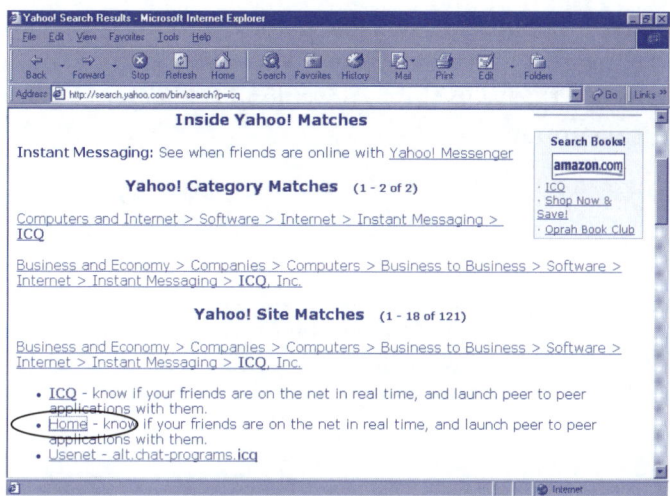

2 Click on the *Home* hyperlink.

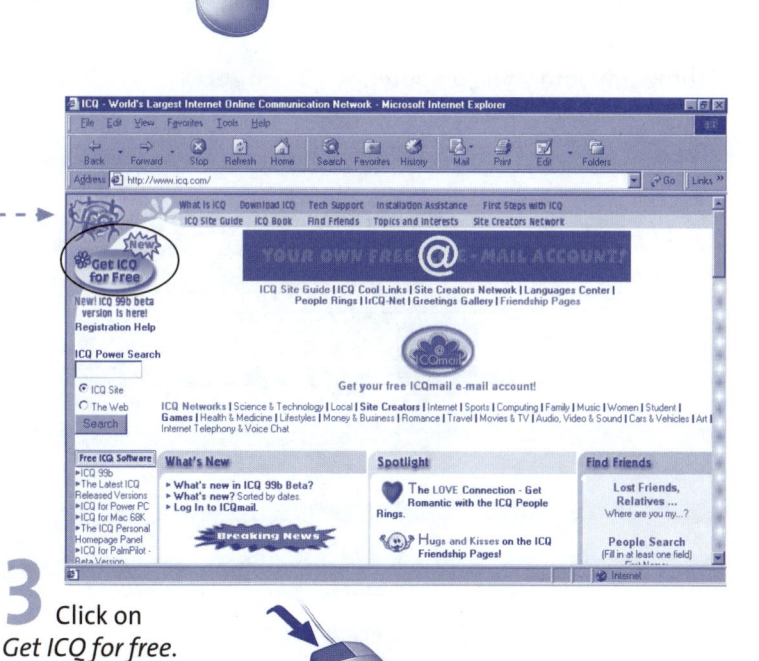

3 Click on *Get ICQ for free*.

327

On the following pages you will learn a little about the ICQ program and how to use this Internet utility. If you want to know more about ICQ, you can use this Web site to download the *ICQ User's Guide* or to call technical support.

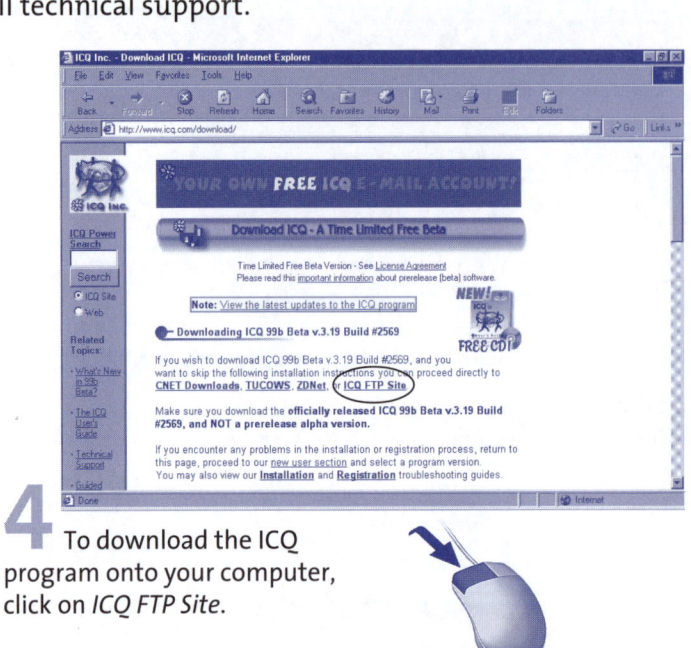

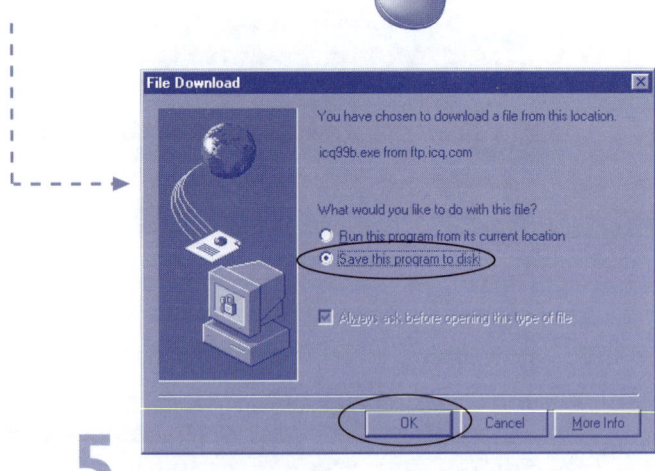

4 To download the ICQ program onto your computer, click on *ICQ FTP Site*.

5 Select the *Save this program to disk* radio button, then click on *OK*.

328

DOWNLOADING AN ICQ PROGRAM FROM THE INTERNET

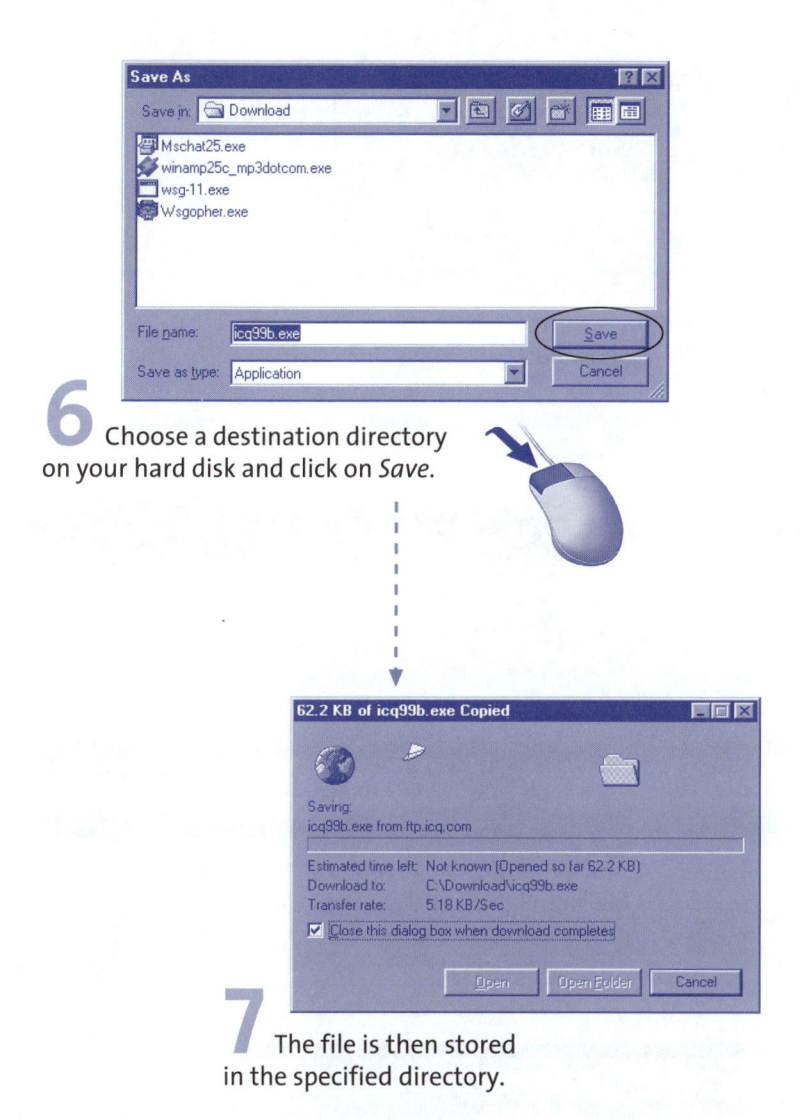

6 Choose a destination directory on your hard disk and click on *Save*.

7 The file is then stored in the specified directory.

When all the information has been downloaded, you will need to decompress the file and then start the installation process. To do this, choose the EXECUTE entry in the START menu.

329

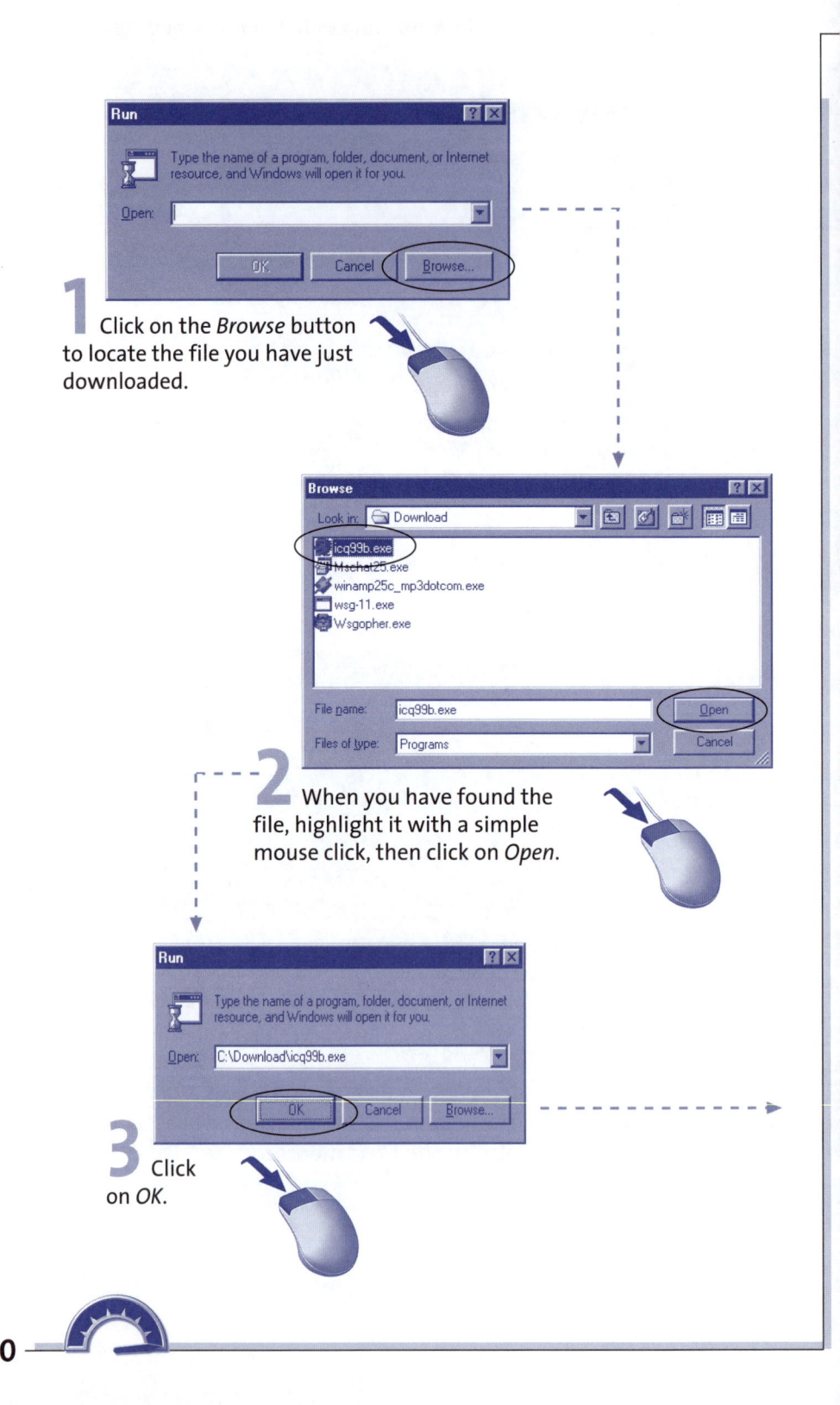

1 Click on the *Browse* button to locate the file you have just downloaded.

2 When you have found the file, highlight it with a simple mouse click, then click on *Open*.

3 Click on *OK*.

DOWNLOADING AN ICQ PROGRAM FROM THE INTERNET

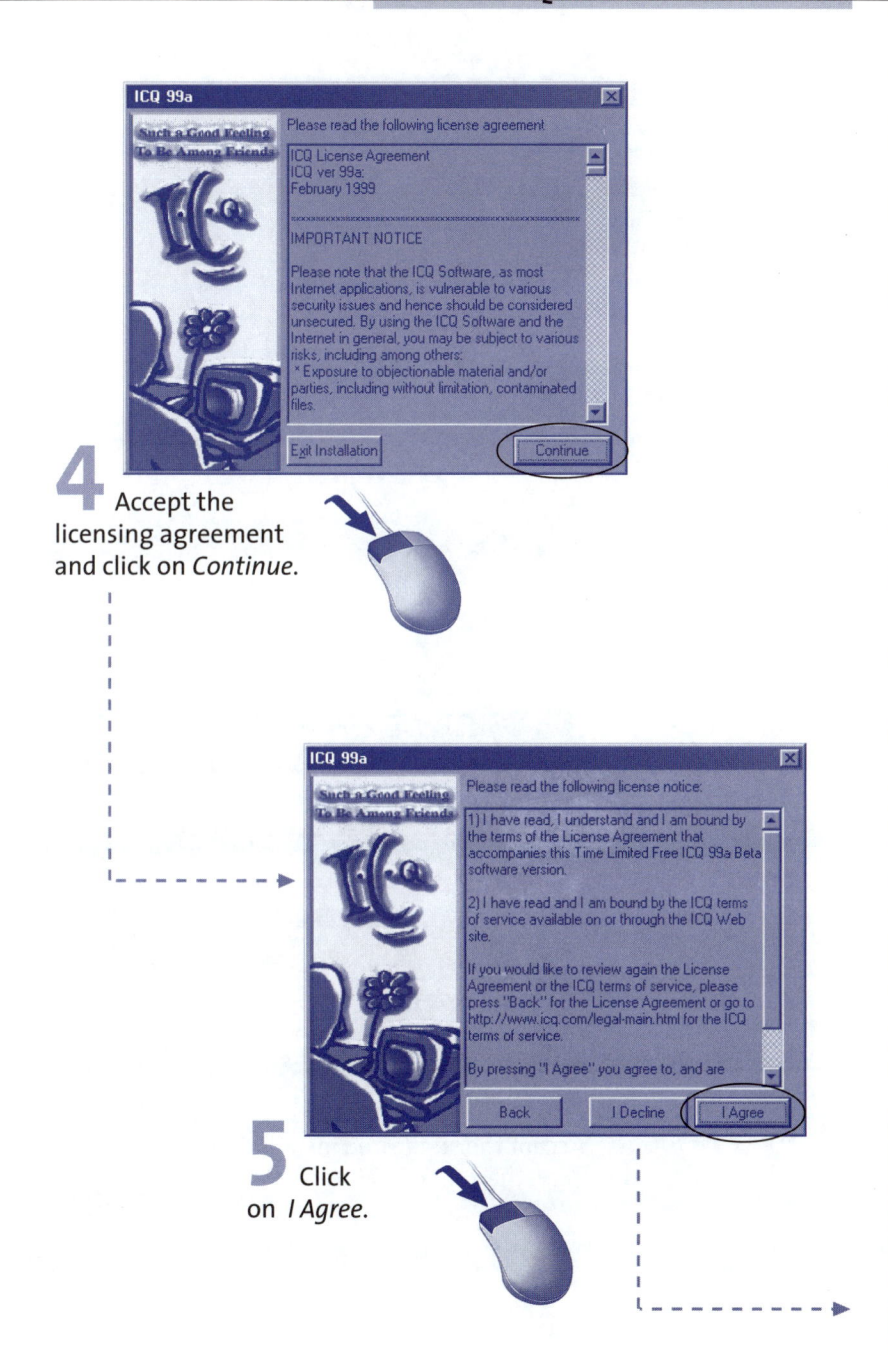

4 Accept the licensing agreement and click on *Continue*.

5 Click on *I Agree*.

6 Click on *Next*.

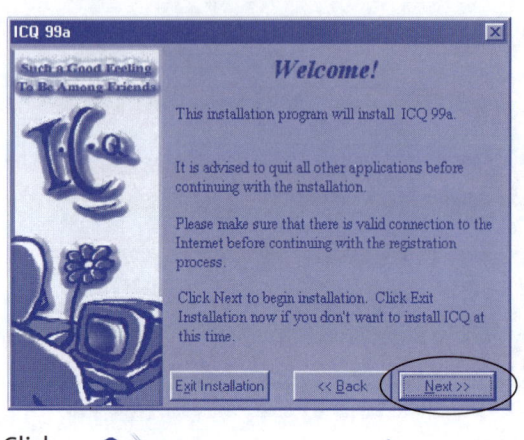

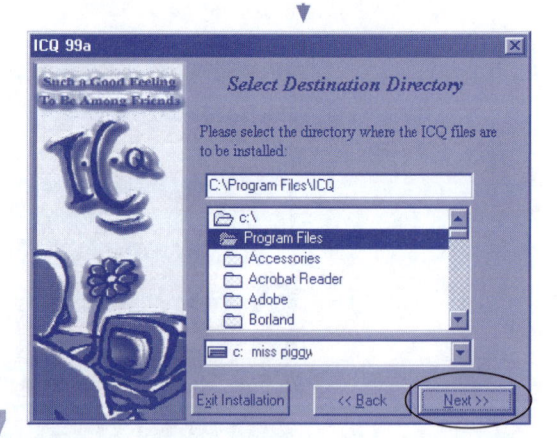

7 Accept the suggested installation directory, then click on *Next*.

332

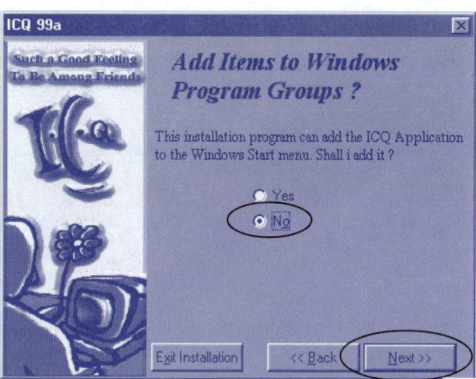

DOWNLOADING AN ICQ PROGRAM FROM THE INTERNET

8 Here you have the option of adding the ICQ entry to your Windows START menu. Make your choice, then click on *Next*.

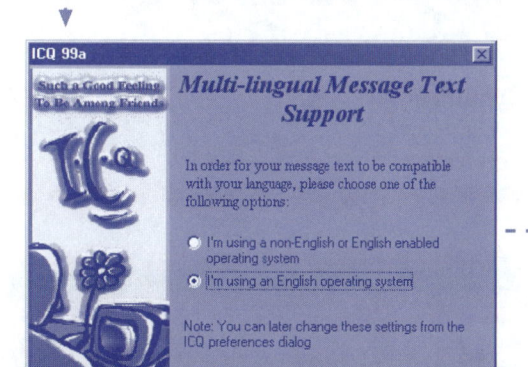

9 Select the appropriate option, then click on *Next*.

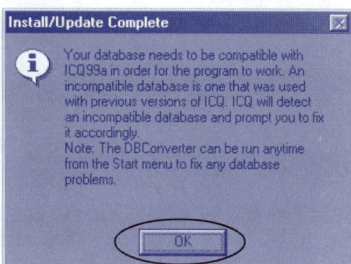

10 Installation is complete. Click on *OK*.

Now that the files on your hard disk have been decompressed and copied to the relevant directories, you can start configuring the program.

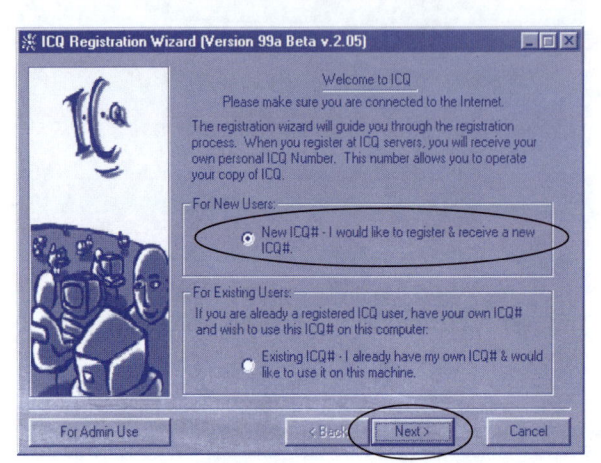

1 To receive a new ICQ number, select the *New ICQ# - I would like to ...* radio button, then click on *Next*.

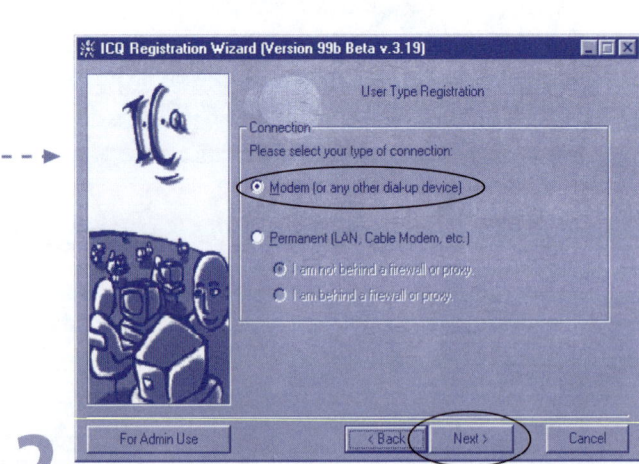

2 Select the *Modem* radio button, then click on *Next*.

334

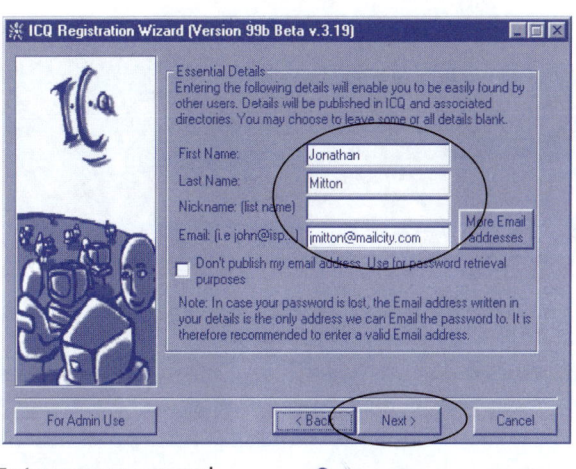

DOWNLOADING AN ICQ PROGRAM FROM THE INTERNET

3 Enter your personal information here, then click on *Next*.

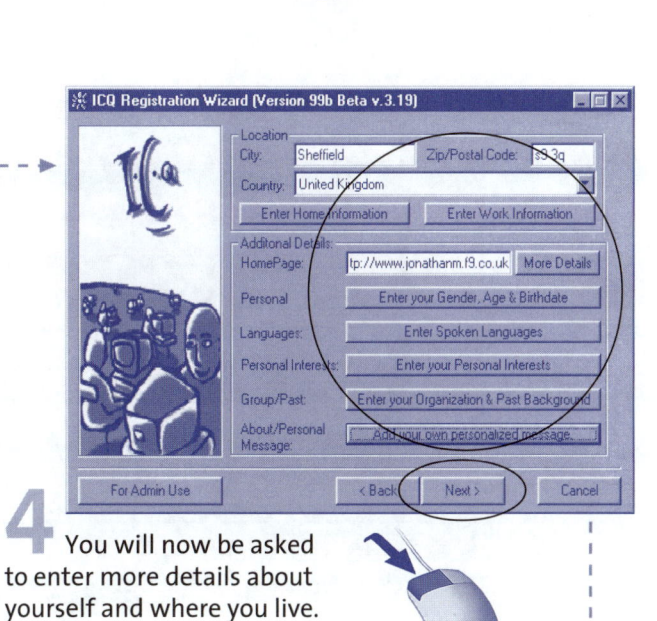

4 You will now be asked to enter more details about yourself and where you live. Then click on *Next*.

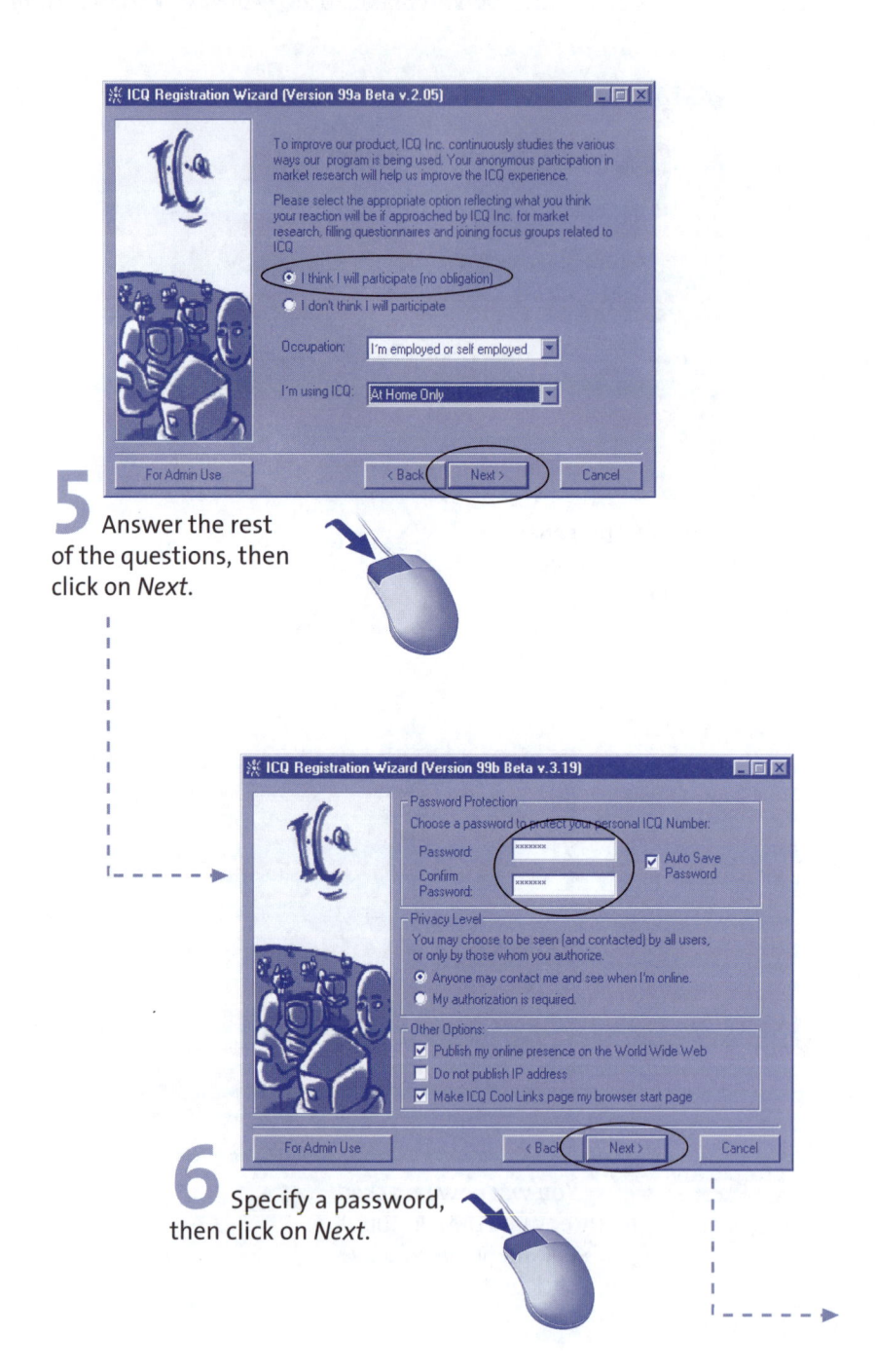

5 Answer the rest of the questions, then click on *Next*.

6 Specify a password, then click on *Next*.

Downloading an ICQ program from the Internet

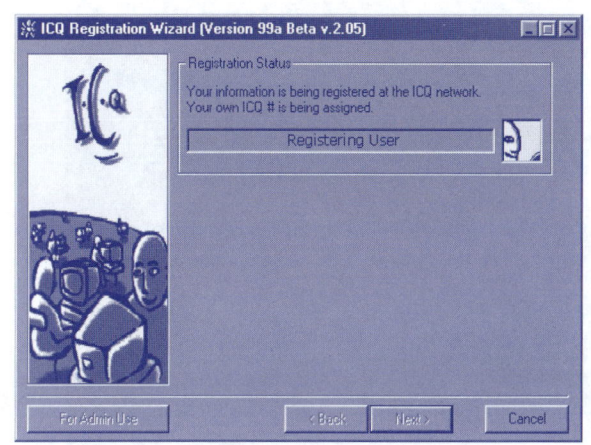

7 You are now registered and made known to your fellow users as a recognised ICQ user.

To enable the ICQ software to let other Internet users know you are an ICQ user, the configuration routine needs to connect to the Internet.

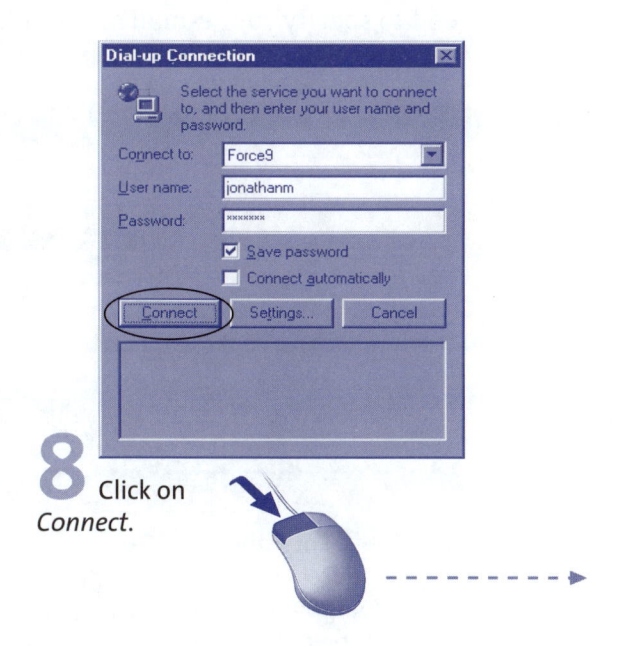

8 Click on *Connect*.

337

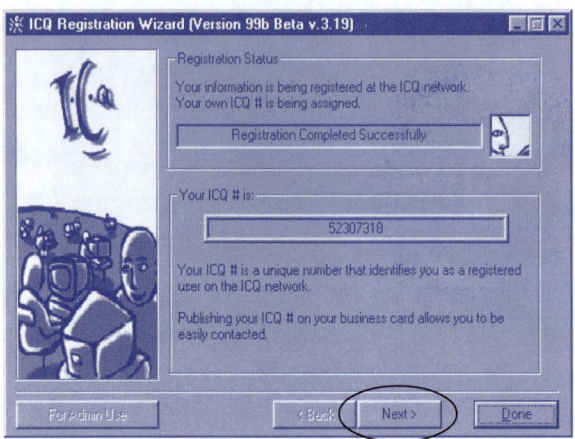

9 Your registration has been successfully completed. Click on *Next*.

The main communications component used by ICQ is the chat program. This allows you to talk to like-minded people and to send e-mails or messages over the Internet. For this reason, you will now need to specify your e-mail server address.

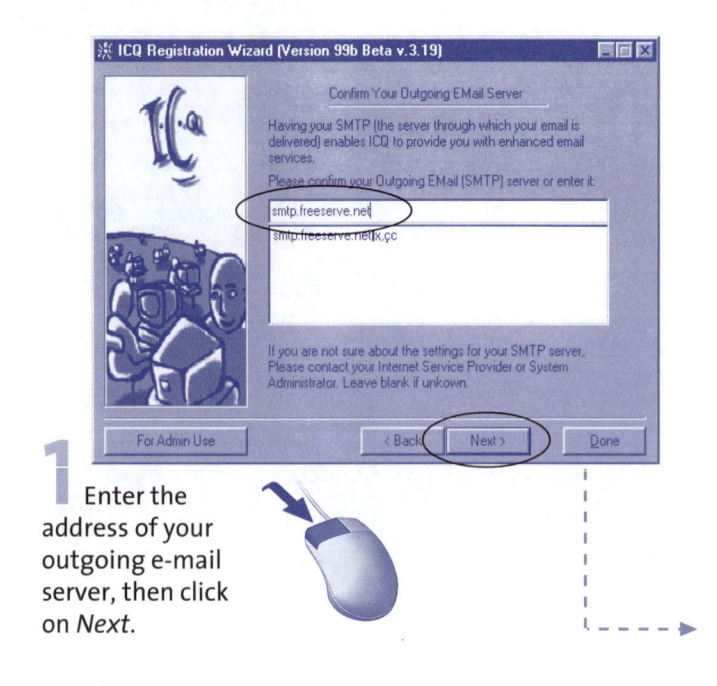

1 Enter the address of your outgoing e-mail server, then click on *Next*.

DOWNLOADING AN ICQ PROGRAM FROM THE INTERNET

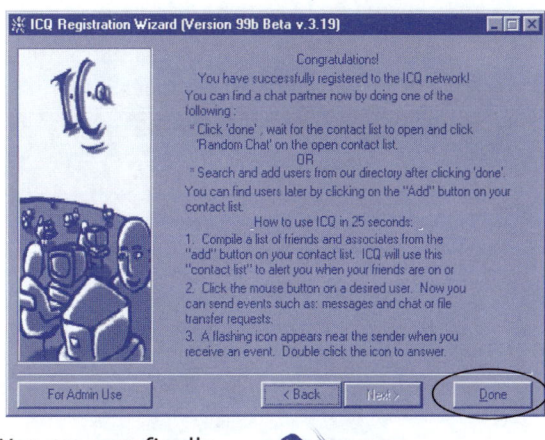

2 You are now finally registered on the ICQ network. To finish, click on *Done*.

Now, for the first time, you will be able to search the Internet for your online friends, if they are currently logged on.

3 In the field entitled *EMail*, enter either your friend's e-mail address, their nickname or, if you know it, their ICQ number. Then click on *Next*.

339

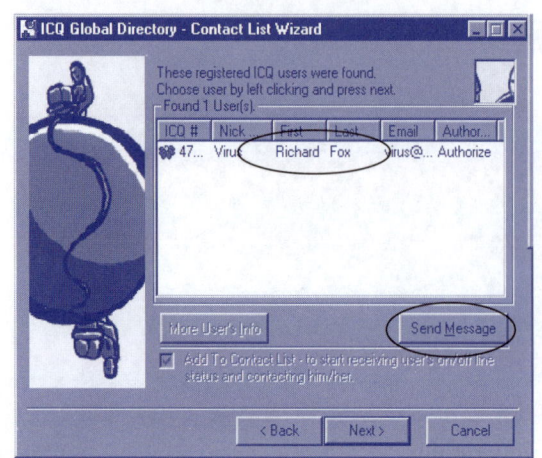

4 If the friend you are looking for is not logged on, you will be able to send him an e-mail or leave a message to try set up a new meeting. To do this, click on *Send message*.

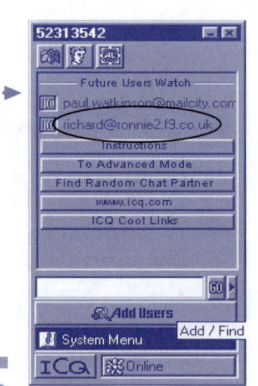

5 The program will then add the e-mail address of this person to its list of addresses to look out for, whether you managed to contact him or not. It will then be able to tell you in future if the person is online or not.

You can close the program via the *ICQ* button.

Using the ICQ program

You now have the ICQ program on your hard disk. You will also find a link to the program on your desktop. Clicking on this icon will start the ICQ application.

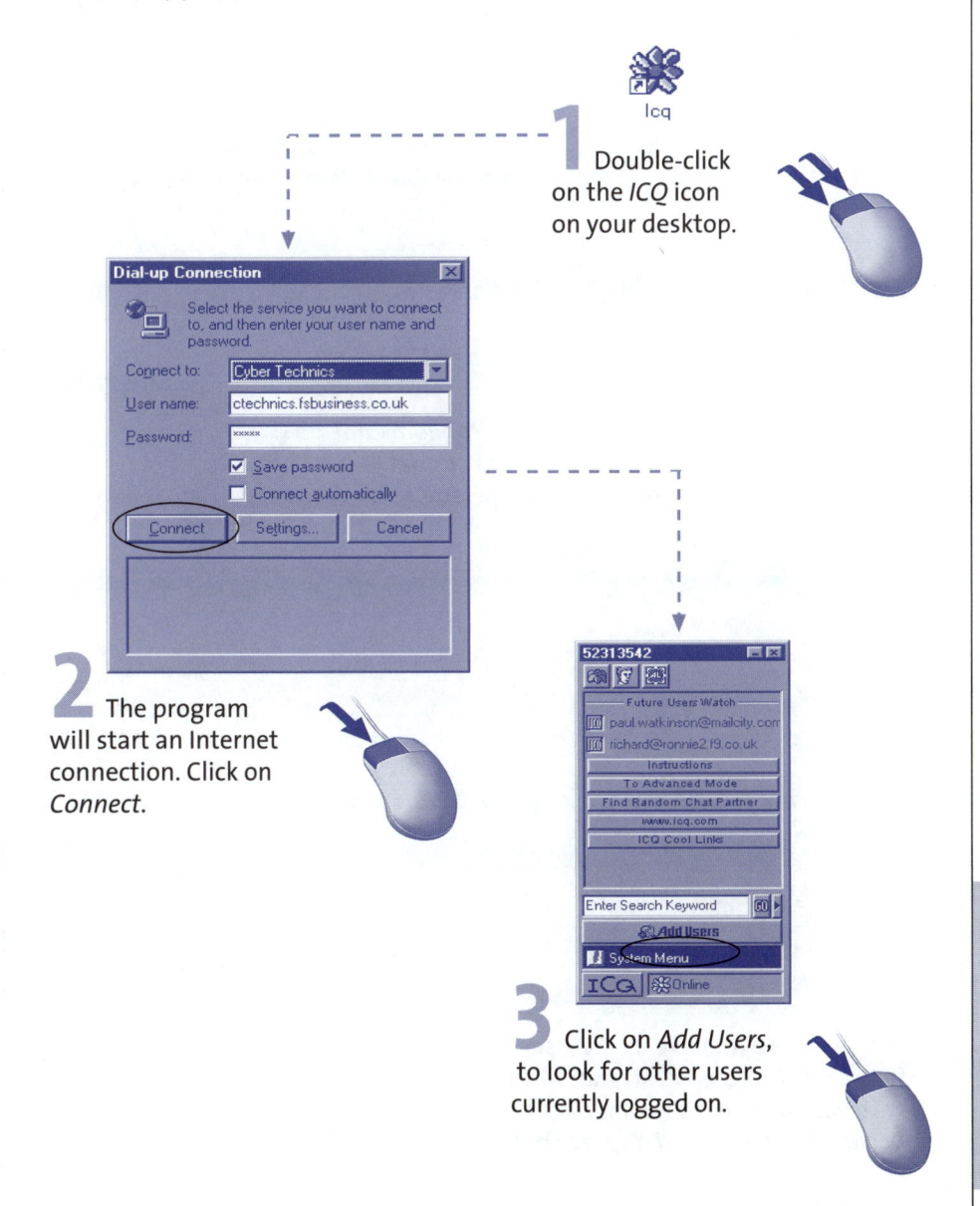

1 Double-click on the *ICQ* icon on your desktop.

2 The program will start an Internet connection. Click on *Connect*.

3 Click on *Add Users*, to look for other users currently logged on.

A window will now open which allows you to look for a particular person. You can also leave this process to chance. If you do this, the program will search randomly for anyone who happens to be online and who has an ICQ program.

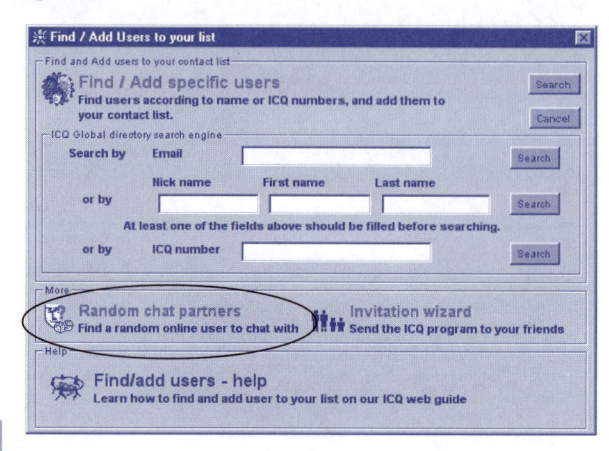

4 Click once on *Random Chat Partners* if you want to chat to a randomly chosen person.

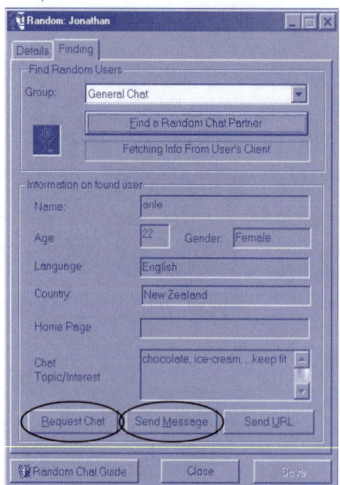

5 And here we have an ICQ user ready for a chat. You can now communicate with your partner by means of the *Request Chat* and *Send Message* buttons.

Play around with the various functions of the Mirabilis ICQ program so that you can learn what they all do. To chat to your long-distance friends, arrange to 'meet up' at a certain time, using ICQ as a low-cost means of enjoying a chat with partners across the whole world.

You have to laugh

Here is a little cartoon about Windows. You can see this one and many others on the Web page *http://www.macworks.com*. This cartoon was drawn by the well-known artist Steinfeld.

First aid for if you're having problems...

It is just like real life: very few things work straight away and stay like that.

For this reason, you will find listed here some examples of the typical problems you may come across during your 'Internet career'.

The modem won't dial

There is usually a very obvious reason for this. Sometimes people forget to switch the modem on, or perhaps the cable linking it to the computer is not properly attached, damaged or even missing. Use the cable supplied by the manufacturer whenever possible.

If still nothing happens, check that the wall plug is working properly.

Another common mistake is to install the wrong type of modem in Windows 95. Windows 95 can only work with modems that it recognises and that have actually been installed.

I can't get an Internet connection

If your modem is working fine and actually dials the number, but still cannot open an Internet connection, then it is time to check your telephone line. If you have a telephone connected to the same line as your modem, it may just be that someone is using the phone.

Make sure you have set up the correct dialling method, as you have two different setup options here: pulse or tone dialling. With pulse dialling, you will hear a clicking noise, and with tone dialling you will hear bleeps.

If your telephone is attached to a telephone exchange system, you will need to dial a particular number in order to connect to an external line, before you can dial into the Internet. This number differs from system to system.

If all the above are correct, you will then need to check the telephone number you have defined for your Internet connection. Maybe you mixed up a couple of digits, so that your modem is now dialling the wrong number.

My Internet connection breaks down

This is an especially annoying problem, particularly when you are just about to finish downloading a large file. This is usually due to an excessive amount of disturbance on your line. The only thing you can do in this situation is to redial and hope that you get a better connection.

A URL is not accepted

There can be many reasons why your Web browser cannot find a particular URL. First of all, make sure you haven't made a typing mistake.

Very often the problem will lie with disturbances on the network. It is possible that the required WWW server is under maintenance. It may also be that there are so many people using the corresponding WWW server that it can no longer cope.

A Web page cannot be found

You will often come across a message with the succinct title '404 Not Found' during your Internet career. This simply means that the page no longer exists. When Web sites are updated, individual pages can be renamed or even completely deleted. You'll just have to get used to it.

345

Glossary

America Online America Online was launched in 1985 and today accommodates several million users worldwide. This makes America Online the largest online service in the world.

Anonymous FTP Registering with an FTP server where you provide your username as your name and your e-mail address as your password.

AOL AOL is the European online service supported by America Online and Bertelsmann. It bases itself on the American example but also offers much in the way of local character in its content, for example, from Great Britain, Germany or France.

Baud Baud or baud rate means the length of signal or the number of oscillation changes per second which a modem uses. The more bauds a modem can use, the quicker it runs.

Chat Chat gives you the opportunity to communicate online with other users. These users, for example AOL members, meet up in chat rooms to discuss various topics. Particularly popular are the 'live chats', where members can put questions directly to famous people over their computer.

CompuServe Originally an American online service which now also operates as an Internet Service Provider. To gain access to the online service it is necessary to have CIM software. This can be found in different versions for the different platforms (DOSCIM for DOC, WinCIM for Windows etc.).

DNS Process whereby incomprehensible, numeric IP addresses are converted into meaningful names, which facilitates contact with, for example, a computer connected to the Internet, or a resource which can be obtained there.

DNS Server Computer at the Internet Service Provider where the conversion of IP addresses into names is saved. As well as the primary DNS server, many ISPs maintain a secondary server, which means that, in the event of a breakdown of the primary server, DNS can still be used.

Download During the downloading process, an Internet user saves a file or program from a software library or an FTP resource onto their own computer.

E-mail Electronic pieces of news which are sent in local networks, via online services or over the Internet. In order to use the e-mail service you must have an e-mail program or e-mail client which is connected to the appropriate server.

E-mail address Address under which you can be reached on a particular e-mail system.

Dial-in node Access nodes which a mailbox operator and online service or an Internet Service Provider make available for dial-in access via modem or ISDN by their members or subscribers.

Freeware Software which is free to use. It is often restricted to private use only, so that commercial users have to pay for using it.

FTP An Internet service for the transfer of files. Access to this service requires an FTP Client, which downloads files from or uploads files to an FTP server.

Gateway Carries out the conversion of information in various formats.

Home page The first Web page of a supplier on the World Wide Web.

Host A general term for a usually bigger computer which carries out a particular task.

Hyperlink Reference to another

347

resource, for example, on the Internet.

Hypertext Format of documents on the World Wide Web which is not just text, but also comprises of graphics, sound files, videos and hyperlinks.

Instant message A message which can be sent directly to an AOL member currently online.

Internet A worldwide, public network first used in the USA for military and scientific purposes. Anyone can put information on the Internet as, unlike an online service, there is no one operator to whom the Internet and all its available dial-in nodes belong. Internet Service Providers and online services such as AOL provide access to the Internet via either a modem or ISDN.

Internet Service Provider Organisations which offer Internet access to both private and commercial users. They use their own lines to establish a connection with the worldwide Internet.

IP See TCP/IP.

IP Address Unique address of a computer which is linked to a network using TCP/IP. Every computer on the Internet has a unique IP address. Worldwide controlled assignment through authorised organisations ensures that each IP address exists only once. A static IP address is always the same, while a dynamic IP is assigned to the user by the Internet Service Provider when a connection to the Internet is established. For this purpose, the Internet Service Provider has a whole range of IP addresses available.

ISDN A digital network, which is supported by BT and can be used as both a speech and file transfer service. ISDN is characterised by its high transmission speed of 64 Kb/s as well as a quick connection time to the receiver, which takes no more than 1 or 2 seconds.

Modem Artificial word made up from the words *modulator* and *demodulator*. A modem is a device that converts a computer's digital signals into analogue signals or tones for transmission over the analogue telephone system, and vice versa.

Mosaic The grandfather of all the WWW browsers. This term is also used as a synonym for this type of program.

Netiquette Rules of etiquette (a kind of online Debrett's) which govern communication via e-mail and in newsgroups.

Glossary

Network A collection of computers which are all linked together. If the computers are situated together in one location the network is known as a LAN (local area network). Other types of network include online services (private networks), and the WAN (wide area network), in which many geographically separate networks are linked together.

Newsgroups Area of the Internet where discussions on every possible (and impossible) subject take place. The communication happens offline – users leave messages which can then be read and answered by other users. To gain access to a newsgroup you will need a Newsgroup Reader, which, for example, is already part of Internet Explorer (Outlook Express) and Netscape (Messenger) software.

Online Services An operator's private network, having national or international characteristics, to which customers can connect via modem or ISDN to access data supplied by individual information providers or to provide their own data. Online services are usually accessed through dial-in nodes (points of presence) provided by the service operator.

Password Used in conjunction with a username to restrict access to its resources. It should therefore be known only to the users themselves.

PC Card Bus system which works with extension cards the size of a cheque card (formerly also known as PCMCIA card).

PCMCIA See PC card.

Pulse dial The dialling method of analogue telephone lines, whereby the receiver's telephone number is converted number by number into impulses of different lengths, which means that the dialling process takes up considerably more time than tone dialling. Today, practically all telecommunication companies worldwide provide tone dialling.

Shareware Software provided on a try-before-you-buy basis which you can use for free for a certain amount of time and then buy if you like it.

Surfing An Internet jargon expression for the process of visiting Web pages and servers, using your mouse to click on hyperlinks to jump to particular resources.

TCP/IP Network protocol used in cross-platform network

349

environments, in UNIX systems and in particular in the Internet. Often abbreviated to IP.

Telnet An Internet service (terminal emulation).

Terminal emulation Emulates a terminal on the PC in order to make contact with another computer (for example, the mainframe, the mailbox etc.), to enable input and output operations to be carried out.

Tone dial The dialling method of analogue telephones whereby the receiver's telephone number is converted number by number into tones of varying frequency (also known as multi-frequency dialling). In this way the dialling process happens considerably quicker than with pulse dialling. Today, practically all telecommunication companies worldwide provide tone dialling.

Upload Moving files from your computer into a mailbox, an online service or an FTP server.

URL Reference to a resource on the Internet.

Usenet See Newsgroups.

WWW The Internet's multimedia service which provides access to resources of various types (documents, files, videos etc.). You must have a Web browser in order to gain access to these services.

Web browser A program which the PC can use to access Web servers available on the World Wide Web and also other Internet services (FTP, Gopher etc.). Web browsers are already included in Windows 95 and 98, in the AOL software from version 2.5 onwards, and are freely available on the Internet and on various CDs distributed with most computer magazines.

World Wide Web See WWW.

Index

Symbols

<B> 319
<BODY> 319
<H1> 319
<HR> 319
<LI> 319

A

Access data 40
Active Desktop 53
Adding an entry to the Favorites menu 74
Address 83
Agent 94
America Online 346
Amiga 11
AND operation 96, 98
Anonymous FTP 250, 346
AOL 122, 299
– access 130
– all-day low rate 139
– become a member 123
– CD-ROM 130
– installation 122
– installation process 122
– modem connection 135
– program 122
– register 130
– sign off 132
AOL software
– automatic setup 127

– installation 122
Apple Macintosh 11
AT standard 14
'at' symbol 299
Attaching a document 307
Audio data 192
Audio types 192
Automatically generated index 95

B

Back 78
Baud 13, 346
Bit 13
Bookmark collection 114
Bookmarks 114, 174
BT Click 141, 300
– configuring the modem operation 158
– installation 141, 146
– software 141
BT Click access data
– configuring 150
BT Click dial-in number 159
Buffer 193

C

Cache 61, 62
Categories 116
Channel 54, 224
Chat 224, 346
Chat participant 225, 233
Chat room 225, 346
Choosing a modem 19
Coding 269
Communicator components 170
CompuServe 299, 347
Configuring Netscape Communicator 172
Connect button 71
Connecting via a local network 32
Connecting with a modem 32

Connection
– disconnect 47
– disconnecting after a period of inactivity 61
– establishing with the Internet 38
– with a modem 60
– with a proxy server 61
– with telephone and modem 39
Control Panel 17
Country code 34

D

Data packets 298
Decompressing files 51
Demodulator 12
Desktop 83
– setup options 169
Dial-in nodes 29, 347
Dialling in to AOL 126
Dial-up adapter 26, 27
Dial-up manager 157
Dial-up networking 36, 45
Differences
– Web catalogues and search engines 95
Digitalisation 192
Directory structure 103
Discussion forum 268
DNS 347
DNS Server 35, 347
Downloading 51, 347
– an ICQ program 326

E

Electronic mail 298
E-mail address 299, 347
– AOL 299
– BT Click 300
– CompuServe 299
– Talk21 300
E-mail 50, 298, 347

Index

Euro-ISDN 16
Explorer's screen 77

F

Favorites 79
Favorites menu 74
Fax machine 14
Fax modem 14
Fax programs 14
File type 85
Find next 88
Finding a random chat partner 342
Folder options 81
Forward 78
Freeware 347
FTP 248, 347
FTP address 262
FTP client 250
FTP daemon 250
FTP service 250

G

Gateway 347
Gopher 104
– bookmark entries 116
– home server 111
– server 104
– server addresses 114
– space 104

H

Hayes command set 14
Hayes compatible 14
Hayes 14
Homepage 70, 78, 347
– create a 68, 319
– your own 316
Host 347
HTML commands 319
HTML format 85

HTML pages 94
http 67
Hyperlink 83, 347
HyperText 348
HyperText Markup Language 318
HyperText Transfer Protocol 67

I

I accept the agreement 52
ICQ 326
– application 341
– chat 342
– instructions 327
– messages 326
– number 334
– user 337
ICQ# 326
Indexing 95
Indexing software 94, 97
Installation wizard 276
Installation procedure 30
Installing AOL 122
Interfaces 19
Internet 348
– address 104
– connection 46
– profile 58
– relay chat 224
– router 298
Internet access 30
–with AOL 130
Internet Connection Wizard 37
Internet discussion groups 50
Internet Explorer 4.0 50
Internet Explorer 5 37
– update 63
Internet Explorer 29
– toolbar 78
Internet gateway 141
Internet options 59, 70
Internet Service Provider 29, 34, 348
Internet setup wizard 29

353

IP 348
- address 35, 243, 348
- number 35
IRC 224
- client 224
- server 224
ISDN 15, 348
- speed 15
ISDN card
- active 15
- installation 16
- passive 15

L

Licensing agreement 146
Live chat 346
Live concerts 192
Local area code 34
Login name 34
Lycos 98

M

Mail 79
Manual set-up of Internet connection 38
Messenger 177
- newsgroups 183
Metafile 193
Microphone 243
Microsoft Chat 232
Microsoft dial-up adapter 26
Microsoft home page 78
Microsoft Plus! CD 29
Microsoft Web server 271
Modem 12, 32, 348
- wizard 17, 18
- card 18
- driver 21
- fax 14
- speed 12, 13

- type 22
- voice 15
Modifying the Chat program 236
Modulator 12
Mosaic 348
MP3 206
- decoder 206
MP3 files
- playing 215
- loading 212
MP3 player
- download 206
Multimedia extensions 50
Multimedia data 269

N

Netiquette 293, 348
NetMeeting 50
Netscape 50, 166
- installation 166, 168
Netscape Communicator 4.7 166
Netscape Communicator
- configuring 172
Netscape Messenger 177
Network 349
- card 26
- configuration 25
- protocol 25
New settings 36
New toolbar 83
News server 185
Newsgroups 50, 349
- account 285
- hierarchy 270
- reader 268
- server 172, 269
- unmoderated 268
Notebook 18

INDEX

O

Online costs   54
Online service   122, 349
Operating system   10, 16
Original layout   83
OS/2   11
Outlook Express   82
– components   271
Outlook Express 5   284, 309
– configuring   309
– configuring the news reader   284
– sending e-mail   313

P

Packets   298
Page format   91
Paper size   91
Password   29, 34, 35, 69, 179
PC card   349
PCMCIA   349
– modem card   18
PKZip   254
Print   79
Processor   10
Profile   33, 174
Proxy server   61
Pulse dialling   23, 349

Q

Quick launch   83

R

RealAudio   193
RealAudio metafile   193
RealPlayer G2   202
Receiving an e-mail   177
Registration number   130
Replying to a newsgroup enquiry   290
Request chat   342
Results list   97
Root directory   259

S

Search   78
Search engine   94
– database   94
Search term   88, 99, 101
Send message   342
Sending an e-mail   180
Setting up a modem   21
Setting up an e-mail account   41
Setting up pages   91
Shareware   349
Shortcut   257
Slash   67
Smileys   293
Software agent   94
Software updates   194
Sound card   190, 242
Sound files   192
Spiders   94
Standard installation   50, 168
Standard modem   21
Stop   78
Streaming Audio   192
Streaming Video   218
Subscribe   185
Subscription list   269
Surfing   349

T

Taskbar   82
TCP/IP   24, 27, 349
– connection   128
Telephone charges   242
Telephone number   29, 33
Telephoning over the Internet   240
Telnet   350
Temporary Internet files   62

355

Terminal emulation   350
Tone dialling   23, 350
Toolbar   78
Transfer protocol   67

U

UIN Pin   326
Uniform Resource Locator   67
University of Minnesota   104
Upload   350
Upper/lower case   89
URL   67, 350
Usenet   268, 350
– function   269
– server   268
User ID   299
User name   35

V

Video connection   243
Video live   218
Video player   219
Video quality   219
Video sequences   218
Video transfer   50
Voice modem   15
Volume   244

W

Web address   58
Web browser   350
– installing a   50
Web catalogue   95
Web crawler   94
Web Publishing Assistant   50
Web spider   94
Windows 3.x   16
Windows 95   16
Windows 98   16

Work offline   285
World Wide Web   350
Writing a newsgroup enquiry   292
Writing your own articles   187
WSGopher   105
WWW   350
– archive   89
– browser   48
– documents   85
– server   83

Y

Yahoo!   96